SAMS
Teach Yourself

Microsoft® Office
Excel 2003

in 24 Hours

Trudi Reisner

SAMS 800 East 96th Street, Indianapolis, Indiana, 46240 USA

Sams Teach Yourself Microsoft® Office Excel 2003 in 24 Hours

Copyright © 2004 by Sams Publishing

International Standard Book Number: 0-672-32551-9

Library of Congress Catalog Card Number: 2003103641

Printed in the United States of America

First Printing: September 2003

06   05   04   03   4   3   2   1

Trademarks

All terms mentioned in this book that are known to be trademarks or service marks have been appropriately capitalized. Sams Publishing cannot attest to the accuracy of this information. Use of a term in this book should not be regarded as affecting the validity of any trademark or service mark.

Warning and Disclaimer

Every effort has been made to make this book as complete and as accurate as possible, but no warranty or fitness is implied. The information provided is on an "as is" basis. The author(s) and the publisher shall have neither liability nor responsibility to any person or entity with respect to any loss or damages arising from the information contained in this book.

Bulk Sales

Sams Publishing offers excellent discounts on this book when ordered in quantity for bulk purchases or special sales. For more information, please contact

U.S. Corporate and Government Sales
1-800-382-3419
corpsales@pearsontechgroup.com

For sales outside of the U.S., please contact

International Sales
1-317-428-3341
international@pearsontechgroup.com

ASSOCIATE PUBLISHER
Greg Wiegand

ACQUISITIONS EDITOR
Michelle Newcomb

DEVELOPMENT EDITOR
Kevin Howard

MANAGING EDITOR
Charlotte Clapp

PROJECT EDITOR
Rebecca Lansberry

PRODUCTION EDITOR
Seth Kerney

INDEXER
Heather McNeill

PROOFREADER
Linda Seifert

TECHNICAL EDITOR
Jim Grey

TEAM COORDINATOR
Sharry Lee Gregory

INTERIOR DESIGNER
Gary Adair

COVER DESIGNER
Gary Adair

GRAPHICS
Tammy Graham
Tara Lipscomb

PAGE LAYOUT
Bronkella Publishing

Contents at a Glance

Contents

About the Author

TRUDI REISNER is a technical writer specializing in technical software documentation and courseware development. As both a Microsoft Office Proficient Specialist and a Microsoft Office Expert Specialist in Microsoft Excel 97, Trudi is the author of numerous books, including *Sams Teach Yourself Excel 2000 in 24 Hours*, *Easy Excel 5 for Windows*, *Easy Microsoft Office 97*, *Microsoft Excel 97 Exam Cram*, *Outlook 97 One Step at a Time*, and *Word 97 One Step at a Time*.

Dedication

To Sheryl Stone, a dear friend.

Acknowledgments

Special thanks to David Fugate, my literary agent; Michelle Newcomb, acquisitions editor; Kevin Howard, development editor; and Jim Grey, technical editor. Also, many thanks to Rebecca Lansberry and Seth Kerney at Sams for proofreading and producing the entire book.

We Want to Hear from You!

As the reader of this book, *you* are our most important critic and commentator. We value your opinion and want to know what we're doing right, what we could do better, what areas you'd like to see us publish in, and any other words of wisdom you're willing to pass our way.

As an associate publisher, I welcome your comments. You can email or write me directly to let me know what you did or didn't like about this book—as well as what we can do to make our books better.

Please note that I cannot help you with technical problems related to the topic of this book. We do have a User Services group, however, where I will forward specific technical questions related to the book.

When you write, please be sure to include this book's title and author as well as your name, email address, and phone number. I will carefully review your comments and share them with the author and editors who worked on the book.

Email: `feedback@samspublishing.com`
Mail: Greg Wiegand
Associate Publisher
800 East 96th Street
Indianapolis, IN 46240 USA

For more information about this book or another Sams Publishing title, visit our Web site at `www.samspublishing.com`. Type the ISBN (excluding hyphens) or the title of a book in the Search field to find the page you're looking for.

Introduction

Congratulations! You're using Microsoft Excel 2003, an exciting spreadsheet program. With its tie-in to the Web and other Microsoft Office programs, Excel is fun to use. Excel is the most popular spreadsheet program on the market, so you have lots of company. Excel 2003 is designed to work the way you do. After you've worked with its intuitive features and exciting graphics, Excel will probably become your favorite software program. If you're a new Excel user or have worked with previous versions of Excel or another spreadsheet program, *Sams Teach Yourself Microsoft Office Excel 2003 in 24 Hours* is the best book you can buy. The lessons avoid computer jargon, and are designed for both the home and office user. In fact, because so many Excel users work on Excel in the office, issues relating to computer networks and work groups are identified and discussed.

This book is divided into 24 segments, and each one takes roughly an hour to complete. You can work through the lessons in the space of a day (if you don't plan to eat or sleep), or you can take your time and work through the lessons an hour at a time.

At the end of each hour, you'll be able to carry out a new set of tasks. The lessons contain clear explanations of the program features and how they work. In addition, each hour includes To Do exercises that are designed as tutorials. In general, the To Do steps reinforce previously explained concepts. On occasion, however, To Do exercises introduce a new concept and enable you to work with it first hand.

Conventions Used in This Book

Features used in this book include the following:

Notes provide comments and asides about the topic at hand.

Tips offer shortcuts and hints on getting the task done.

Cautions explain roadblocks you might encounter in Excel and tell you how to avoid them.

NEW TERM   *New terms* are introduced in the text and explained below.

At the end of each hour, a question-and-answer section focuses on real-life concerns about the material covered in the hour.

PART I
Excel Basics

Hour

HOUR 1

Getting Started

The highlights of this hour include the following:

- What Excel can do for you
- How to start Excel
- How to use Excel's toolbars, menus, and dialog boxes
- Where to find online help
- The best ways to navigate Excel
- How to exit Excel

In this hour, you'll start and exit Excel, get a tour of the Excel screen, examine Excel's components such as the toolbars, menus, dialog boxes, and task panes, explore online help, and navigate a workbook and worksheet.

What Is Excel?

Microsoft Excel is a *spreadsheet program* that's designed to record and analyze numbers and data. Excel takes the place of a calculator, a ruled ledger pad, pencils and pens, and a green eyeshade. The program makes it easy for you to juggle numbers, formulas, and text. Excel's advanced publishing tools enable you to present your work in a polished, professional-looking format.

NEW TERM *Spreadsheet program*—A computer program used primarily for accounting and financial purposes. Data in spreadsheet programs is organized by rows and columns.

No job is too large or small for Excel. You can use the program to add a column of numbers or to create a complex budget or sales model for your company. You can create exciting charts. You can set up a modeling program and play "what if?" using various forecasting scenarios. You can also use Excel as a database program and create a standard form to collect and record data.

Excel's collaborative features make it a great program on which colleagues can work together. You can work with your co-workers, located across the floor or across the world, to develop and design a budget or analysis of profits. You can even save your work as a Web page and publish it to the Web for others to view. With the Web as a backdrop, people who have never worked with Excel can contribute to the design and development of a file.

Use Excel anytime you want to work with numbers. Like any other software, you need to have some idea of what you expect before you begin. Do you want to create a complex analysis or simply total a row of numbers? The data you record needs to be accurate; the old saying "garbage in, garbage out" definitely applies. For example, if you're using Excel to keep track of your checking account balance and you enter an incorrect amount for a check you've written, you'll probably soon be hearing from the bank!

Store Your Data in Workbooks

The files you create in Excel are called *workbooks*. In turn, your workbook consists of individual *worksheets*. A workbook can contain one or multiple worksheets. Worksheets can relate to other worksheets, or they can be independent entities. Within each worksheet, you can enter text and numbers, perform calculations, organize data, and more.

NEW TERM *Worksheet*—The place where you enter your data.

Figure 1.1 shows a workbook that contains three worksheets. In the example, the first worksheet contains detailed product sales information.

The terms *Excel document*, *Excel workbook*, and *Excel file* are used interchangeably in this book.

Worksheet contains detailed information

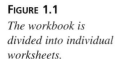

FIGURE 1.1

The workbook is divided into individual worksheets.

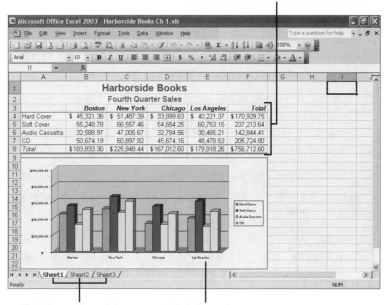

Tabs for each worksheet   3-D Column chart

Planning Strategies for Excel Worksheets

Excel is so versatile that you can use it for many different purposes. Before you begin an Excel project, take a moment to ask yourself a few simple questions, such as

- What do you want to achieve?
- Who will view the worksheet?
- Will you work alone on the worksheet or collaborate with your co-workers?
- What do you want to do with the information?

Excel is a multifeature program with lots of options. You can create a simple worksheet with a few lines or a multipage, linked file. Some examples of Excel files are available at the Microsoft Web site at http://www.microsoft.com/office/excel. In addition, if you're using Excel in the office, take a look at some of the files created by your co-workers. Chances are, a format for budgets or expense reports is already in use at your company.

As you work with Excel, remember that someone else might look at your finished product. Try not to cram all your information into one area. Organize your worksheet so that it's easy to see the flow of information. Use white space and attributes, like bold and underline, to identify important points. If the worksheet is going to be part of a presentation, consider using graphic images, charts, and maps to make your point.

If your worksheet will ultimately include the input and ideas of your co-workers, make sure that the worksheet is easy to follow. Cryptic abbreviations and notes that make sense to you might not make much sense to a colleague.

Changing the appearance of an Excel worksheet is a snap! You can also change the data contained within a worksheet. For example, you can transpose your rows with columns, and vice versa. Because Excel is part of the Office 2003 suite, you can easily integrate your Excel worksheets with the other Office programs.

After you put together the worksheet basics, experiment a little. When your work is saved, play around and add several different effects. You'll probably come up with some very special ways to present your data and have fun while you learn.

Starting Excel

You can start most Windows programs, including Excel, in several ways. The easiest way is to click the Start button on the Windows taskbar and select Programs, Microsoft Excel. The Excel window opens on your screen.

Other Ways to Launch Excel

In addition to using the Start menu to open Excel, you can start the program in the following ways:

- Click the Excel button on the Microsoft Office Shortcut bar (if you installed it).
- Click the Start button and select All Programs, Microsoft Excel.
- Open My Computer or Windows Explorer. Locate the Excel file you want to open and then double-click it to launch Excel and the file.

You can also create a shortcut icon on your desktop. Here's how:

To Do: Set an Excel Shortcut Icon

1. Click the Start button and choose Search. The Search Results window appears.
2. In the What Do You Want To Search For list, choose All Files and Folders.
3. Type **excel.exe** in the All or Part of the File Name text box, as shown in Figure 1.2, and click Search.

▼

FIGURE 1.2

Make sure that Look In indicates the drive Excel is installed on. Search for the file that starts Excel.

File name

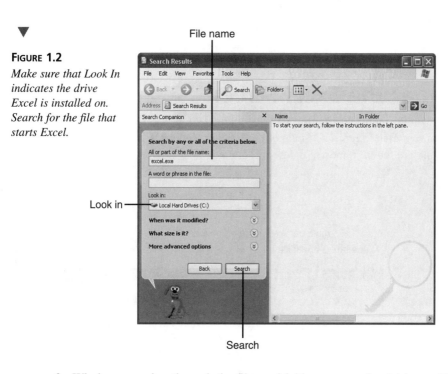

Look in

Search

3. Windows searches through the files and folders on your hard drive and locates excel.exe. Right-click excel.exe and choose Create Shortcut from the menu.

If you want to stop the search, click the Stop button at the bottom of the left Search pane at any time.

4. If you're viewing the Windows desktop, a dialog box similar to the one shown in Figure 1.3 appears, advising you that the shortcut cannot be placed on the current screen and asking whether you'd like to place it on your Windows desktop instead. Click Yes. Close the Search Results window.

FIGURE 1.3

Place the Excel shortcut icon on your desktop.

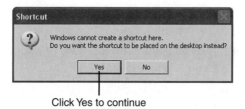

Click Yes to continue

▲   5. An icon for Excel appears on your Windows desktop. Double-click it to launch
        Excel.

Looking at the Excel Screen

Now that you've launched Excel, take a few minutes to look at the parts of the Excel
screen, as shown in Figure 1.4. Many of the screen components might look familiar
because they're found in most Windows programs.

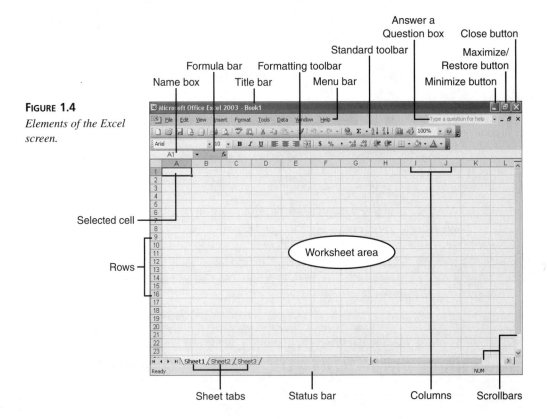

FIGURE 1.4
*Elements of the Excel
screen.*

- Title bar—The bar at the top of the Excel screen displays the program and the
  name of the file you're working on.
- Menu bar—Click any menu name to display a list of available Excel commands
  that relate to the task you're performing.
- Answer a Question box—You use this box to get help on how to perform an Excel
  task or learn more about an Excel feature.

- Toolbars—Excel contains many toolbars with buttons to help you access a program feature. Hold your mouse pointer over a button to find out what the button does. (You learn more about working with toolbars later in this chapter.)

- Name box—Displays the address of the cell or range that's currently selected.

- Formula bar—You use this area to enter Excel formulas and functions, or to edit the contents of a cell.

- Scrollbars—Both the horizontal and vertical scrollbars enable you to view different portions of the worksheet.

- Sheet tabs—Click a tab to move to another worksheet in the workbook.

- Minimize button—Click the Minimize button to shrink Excel to a button on the Windows taskbar.

- Maximize/Restore—The Maximize/Restore button enlarges Excel to a full-screen view or restores it from full-screen to its original size.

- Close button—The Close button closes Excel and any Excel documents that are open on your computer.

- Status bar—The bar at the bottom of the screen tells you what's going on in the program. For example, if you're saving a file, the status bar indicates that the file is being saved. The bar also lets you know whether the following keyboard features are turned on: Num Lock (NUM), Caps Lock (CAPS), or Scroll Lock (SCRL).

Rows and Columns Bind the Worksheet Together

Excel worksheets are laid out like grids, with horizontal rows and vertical columns. The columns in Excel are labeled with letters, and the rows with numbers. Each Excel worksheet is made up of 256 columns and 65,536 rows.

The intersection of a row and a column is called a *cell*. Cell names are made up of the column letter and the row number. For example, you might be in cell A1, or cell B16. You enter all your data in Excel into individual cells.

NEW TERM *Cell*—The primary unit of measure in Excel. Each worksheet is made up of individual cells.

With more than one million cells in a worksheet, it's easy to lose track of where you are. Fortunately, Excel provides lots of visual clues so you can pinpoint your location and not overwrite important cell entries and formulas. When you're located in a cell, its borders appear highlighted. Additionally, the row and column markers stand out. However, if you're working on a worksheet with lots of formatting or you're scrolling through the worksheet, your current location might not be apparent.

You can always track your location with the Name box, as displayed in Figure 1.5.

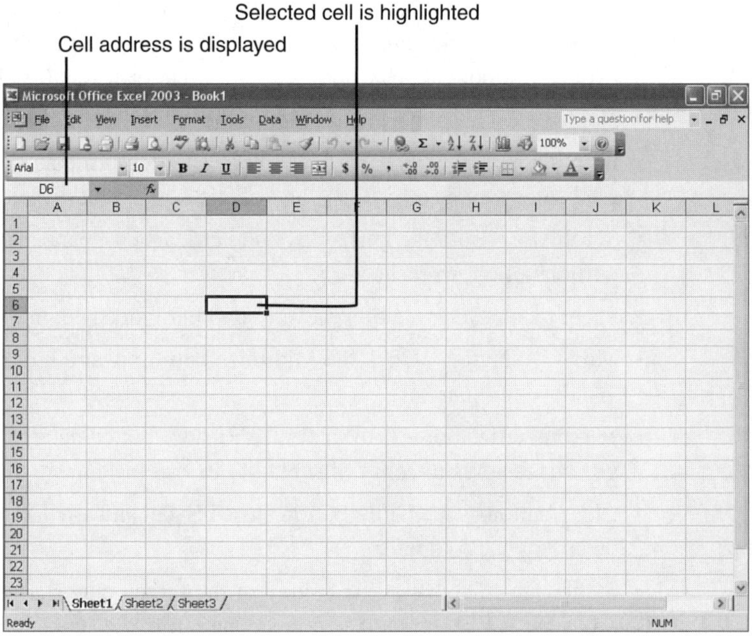

Selected cell is highlighted

Cell address is displayed

FIGURE 1.5

The Name box shows you where you are.

Working with Toolbars

Toolbars hold buttons that access shortcuts to commonly used commands. The face of each button contains a picture called an *icon* that indicates the button's function. If you're not sure what a button does, position the mouse pointer in the button and hold it still for a moment. A ScreenTip appears, displaying the function of the button.

> If a button on a toolbar appears dim, the feature is not currently available to you. Clicking a dimmed-out button does not result in any action. For example, the Redo button on the Standard toolbar is dimmed unless you've clicked Undo to reverse something you've done in the program.

Excel is chock-full of toolbars to help you get your work done. Some of Excel's toolbars are displayed by default and, unless you change them, they will be visible each time you open the program. Other toolbars are context-sensitive and appear on the screen when you're performing a specific task.

Table 1.1 lists some of the many toolbars in Excel and describes their functions.

TABLE 1.1 Some of Excel's Commonly Used Toolbars

Toolbar	What It's Used For
Standard	Includes commands for standard program functions, such as Open, Close, and Print. Many Standard toolbar buttons are included in the toolbars of other Windows programs. The Standard toolbar appears by default.
Formatting	Contains tools to format your document, including Font and Font Size; attributes such as Bold, Underline, and Italic; and buttons to change the color of cell entries and backgrounds. The Formatting toolbar appears by default.
Borders	Has buttons to help you draw border lines around cells and groups of cells anywhere on a worksheet.
Chart	Holds buttons to help you create and edit the perfect chart.
Drawing	Appears at the bottom of the worksheet when you choose to display the toolbar and holds drawing tools. Tools for drawing and editing lines, line styles, and line arrows are included.
Picture	Appears when you're working with a graphics image.
Task Pane	Displays the most recently used task pane on the right side of the Excel window.
Web	Holds links to Microsoft Internet Explorer. If you're connected to the Internet while you're working with Excel, you can use the Web toolbar to move to a Web site and view additional information you need to complete your work.

Other Excel toolbars are the Control Toolbox, External Data, Forms, Formula Auditing, List, PivotTable, Protection, Reviewing, Text to Speech, Visual Basic, Watch Window, WordArt, and XML. Some of these toolbars are covered later in this book.

Displaying Other Toolbars

When you open Excel, the Standard and Formatting toolbars are displayed. As you work with Excel, other toolbars appear and disappear. However, you can hide and display an Excel toolbar anytime.

To Do: Display Other Toolbars

1. Click the View menu and select Toolbars. A list of available toolbars is displayed, as shown in Figure 1.6.

2. Display a toolbar by clicking View, Toolbars. In this exercise, click Picture to display the Picture toolbar.

▼

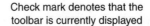

Check mark denotes that the
toolbar is currently displayed

FIGURE 1.6

*The View, Toolbars
menu holds all the
toolbars.*

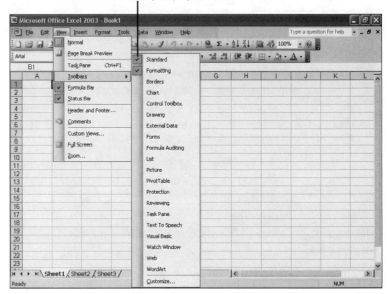

3. If a check mark appears in the box to the left of a toolbar's name, the toolbar is currently displayed. Click the check box to remove the check mark and hide the toolbar from view. In this exercise, click the check mark next to Picture. The menu closes and the Picture toolbar no longer appears.

▲ 4. (Optional) Repeat steps 2 and 3 to display and hide additional Excel toolbars.

Even though you know that you can always rely on ScreenTips to help you understand the function of a toolbar button, the buttons can look dizzyingly alike after a while. Fortunately, many of the buttons on Excel's toolbars are used in most Windows programs.

For example, most programs use a picture of a printer on the Print button, a picture of scissors on the Cut button, and a big, bold B on the Bold button.

Instead of accessing the list of Excel toolbar's from the View menu, you can right-click any Excel toolbar to quickly display the list of Excel toolbars.

Placing Toolbars Where They Work for You

Let's face it, toolbars take up valuable screen real estate. Sometimes, you don't want to waste that space; other times, you want the convenience of a toolbar, but you don't want the buttons to get in the way. Excel enables you to move or reposition toolbars so that they are in the most convenient place for you.

All toolbars float on top of your work and can be dragged around the screen. When you click the *move handle* on a toolbar, as shown in Figure 1.7, the mouse pointer takes the shape of a four-headed cross. Drag the toolbar to a new location and release the mouse button. Notice that as you drag, the toolbar changes shape. If you drag the cross to one of the edges of the Excel screen, the toolbar docks to that edge of the screen. Releasing the mouse button in the middle of the screen floats the toolbar.

FIGURE 1.7

Drag a toolbar to a new location.

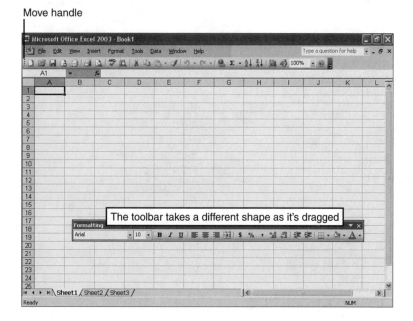

Move handle

The toolbar takes a different shape as it's dragged

NEW TERM   *Move handle*—The area on a toolbar used for dragging it or docking it. The move handle is located to the left of most toolbars and looks like a vertical bar with dashes.

You can drag a floating toolbar to another position, or you can anchor the toolbar to one of the edges of the screen. To hide a floating toolbar, click the Close button (×) in the corner of the toolbar.

If you're working with multiple worksheets, changing the way that toolbars are displayed in one file changes the view in all the other files as well.

Using Excel Menus and Dialog Boxes

Maybe you prefer using a menu instead of a button, or the command you need isn't shown on any of the toolbars displayed on the screen. In any case, you can access Excel's commands from the menu bar. To make a selection from the menu, click a menu name in the menu bar, drag the mouse down the list until the command you want is highlighted, and click (see Figure 1.8).

This command opens a dialog box

This command is available

FIGURE 1.8

A dimmed menu command means that command is not currently available.

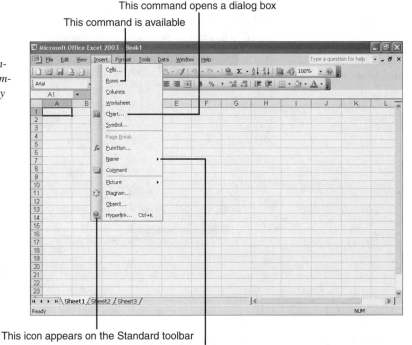

This icon appears on the Standard toolbar

This command opens submenu(s) with additional commands

What happens after you click a menu command varies with each command. If an icon appears next to the menu command, the icon appears on the Standard toolbar.

If three dots (called an ellipsis) follow a menu command, a dialog box asks you to enter more information or choose from a list of options. If an arrow follows the menu command, clicking the command opens a submenu with additional commands. Sometimes, just clicking a menu command executes it. For example, clicking File, Open accesses a dialog box, and clicking File, Save saves the file that's displayed on the screen.

Just like the buttons on toolbars, menu commands can sometimes appear dimmed. A command that's dimmed means that the command is not currently available. Clicking a dimmed menu command is a waste of time—nothing happens.

Working with Dialog Boxes

Any time you select a menu command that's followed by an ellipsis, Excel displays a dialog box. Think of a dialog box as a form that you need to complete and verify for Excel to continue. Figure 1.9 shows a dialog box and some of its standard elements.

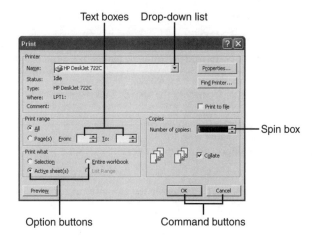

FIGURE 1.9

The Print dialog box contains typical dialog box elements.

Each dialog box contains one or more of the following elements:

- Command buttons appear in every dialog box. OK, Cancel, and Apply are commonly used in dialog boxes.

- List boxes provide two or more available choices. You select the item you want by clicking it.

- Check boxes let you turn options on or off. Click inside a check box to turn an option off if it's on (and vice versa). If multiple check boxes are displayed together, you can choose more than one option.

- Option buttons work a lot like check boxes, except that you can select only one option in a group. Clicking one option deselects the currently selected option.

- Text boxes are "fill in the blank" boxes. Click inside a text box to activate it and replace the current text, if any, with your entry.

- Spin boxes are used to change the contents of a text box. To change what's displayed, click the up or down arrow to change the setting.

- Tabs appear across the top of some dialog boxes and offer selections of related options or functions. Click a tab to see a list of options relative to the specific tab.

Examining the Task Pane

Certain Excel commands display a task pane automatically. However, when you want to display or hide a task pane, you can choose View, Task Pane.

The task pane is a small separate window that enables you to perform common Excel commands more efficiently. You can use the commands on the task pane while you are working on your files.

Types of Task Panes

Table 1.2 lists the most commonly used task panes in Excel and describes their functions.

TABLE 1.2   Some of Excel's Commonly Used Task Panes

Task Pane	What It's Used For
Home	Includes commands for opening and creating workbooks, and searching for Excel information at the Microsoft Web site.
Help	Provides a way to get help on any Excel topic.
Search Results	Lets you search for text in the current workbook or other locations.
Clip Art	Helps you search for clip art.
Clipboard	Displays copied or cut items to paste, lets you paste all items, or clear all items.
New Workbook	Gives you commands for creating a new blank workbook, creating a new workbook based on an existing workbook, and searching for templates.

Other Excel task panes are Research, Template Help, Document Actions, Shared Workspace, Document Updates, and XML Structure. Some of these task panes are covered later in this book.

Elements of a Task Pane

By default, a task pane appears on the right side of the Excel window, as shown in Figure 1.10. However, you can drag the task pane title bar to float the pane in your work area or dock it on the left or right side of the screen.

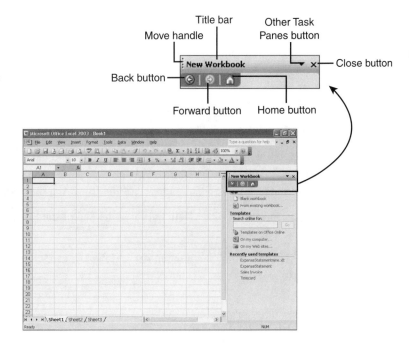

FIGURE 1.10

A task pane with common New Workbook commands.

A task bar contains the following elements:

- Move handle—Enables you to move or reposition the task pane so that it's in the most convenient place for you. Just like with toolbars, you point to the move handle and see a four-headed cross. Drag the cross to one of the edges of the Excel screen, the task pane docks to that edge of the screen. Releasing the mouse button in the middle of the screen floats the task pane.

- Title bar—Contains the move handle, the name of the task pane, and the Other Task Panes button to activate other task panes.

- Back button—Displays the previous task pane based on the order in which you viewed the set of task panes during the current session.

- Forward button—Displays the next task pane based on the order in which you viewed the set of task panes during the current session.

- Home button—Displays the Home task pane.

- Other Task Panes button—Displays a menu of task panes.

- Close button—Closes the task pane.

Getting the Most Out of Help

Besides having this book as a reference, you can get extensive onscreen help from Excel. Built directly into the program is a Help system that provides answers and support for most of your Excel questions. Before you can use online Help, you must have access to the Web from your computer.

Getting Assistance When You Need It

Microsoft has redesigned the look of Help and has changed the way Help works in Excel and all other Office 2003 products. Excel Help now provides online assistance in the Help task pane, which you invoke with one of the following methods:

- Click the Microsoft Excel Help button at the end of the Standard toolbar.
- Press F1.
- Choose Help from the main menu bar and then select Microsoft Excel Help. The Help task pane appears, as shown in Figure 1.11.

FIGURE 1.11

The Help task pane provides assistance.

To move the Help task pane, drag it by its Title bar with the mouse and drop it to the desired location. To resize the Help task pane, move the mouse pointer to any border of the pane, and a two-headed arrow appears. Click and drag the border to change the size of the pane. If the Help task pane takes up too much real estate on the screen, you can hide it by clicking the Close button in the corner of the pane.

To Do: Work with the Help Task Pane

1. When the Help task pane is visible on the screen, in the Assistance section, click in the Search box and type a topic. For this exercise, type the topic, **How do I enter data?** and click the Start Searching button (green button with right white arrow).

2. Help Assistance searches for the answer, and displays a list of related topics in the Search task pane.

3. Point to the topic or answer that most closely matches your query and click it one time. Notice that your mouse pointer takes the shape of a hand, signifying that the answer is a hyperlink. (You learn more about hyperlinks later in this book.)

4. An answer frame appears to the right of the current worksheet, as shown in Figure 1.12. Read through the information. If you want to print it, click the Print button.

5. When you're done with Help Assistance, click the Close button to close the answer frame. Then, click the Close button to close the Search task pane and return to your worksheet.

▲

Click Close to dismiss the answer frame

FIGURE 1.12

The answer frame provides the information you requested.

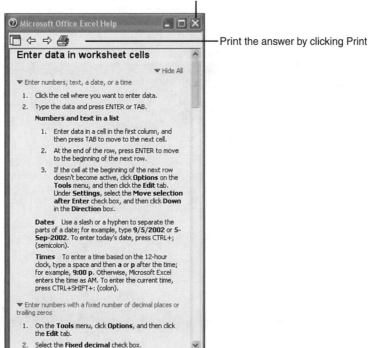

Print the answer by clicking Print

Looking Up Help with the Table of Contents

When you know the general category of a topic but not the specifics, you can look up Help in the Table of Contents. You use the Table of Contents in Excel Help as you would a table of contents at the front of a book.

On the Help task pane, beneath the Search box, click the Table of Contents link. Excel displays a list of topics. Select the topic you want, and Excel displays additional topics. Continue selecting topics until you find the information you want.

Obtaining Help with the Type a Question for Help Box

When you know the specific category of the topic in question, Help is no further away than the Type a Question for Help box. The box is located at the far right end of the menu bar. You can type a free-form question, or a keyword such as *copy*, *print*, or *save*, in the Type a Question for Help box.

To do so, click the box that contains the text `Type a question for help` (see Figure 1.13) and type your question. For example, type `How do I create a formula?` and press Enter. Excel responds by displaying the Help task pane with a list of related topics. Click a topic to obtain information on creating a formula.

Type a Question for Help box

FIGURE 1.13

The Type a Question for Help Box waits for your question or keyword.

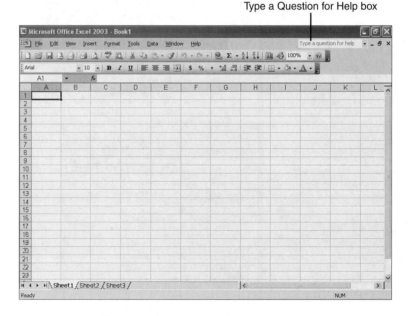

As you enter questions and keywords in the Type a Question for Help box, Excel adds them to the Type a Question for Help list. When you click the Type a Question for Help box arrow, Excel displays a list of previously asked questions and keywords.

Turning to the Web for More Answers

One of Excel 2003's most exciting features is its extensive use of Internet features. Before you can visit the Web, you must have access to the Web from your computer. If you're using Excel at the office or school, check with your network administrator to find out whether you have an established connection. If you're using Excel at home, you need a modem and an account with an Internet service provider, DSL, or a cable modem.

If you ask a question that requires a more detailed explanation than Help can provide, you can click a link in the Help task pane to find the answer on the Web. The links are located in two sections in the Help task pane: Microsoft Office Online and See Also, as shown in Figure 1.14. Click the down arrow at the bottom of the Help task pane to view all the See Also links. Of course, you must be connected to the Internet before you begin.

FIGURE 1.14
Turn to the Web for answers.

For example, click the Assistance link in the Microsoft Office Online section. Excel opens your browser and displays the Assistance Home page the browser, as shown in Figure 1.15. From here, you can click a topic in the left pane, or select a topic in the Search drop-down list and then type a keyword in the Search text box.

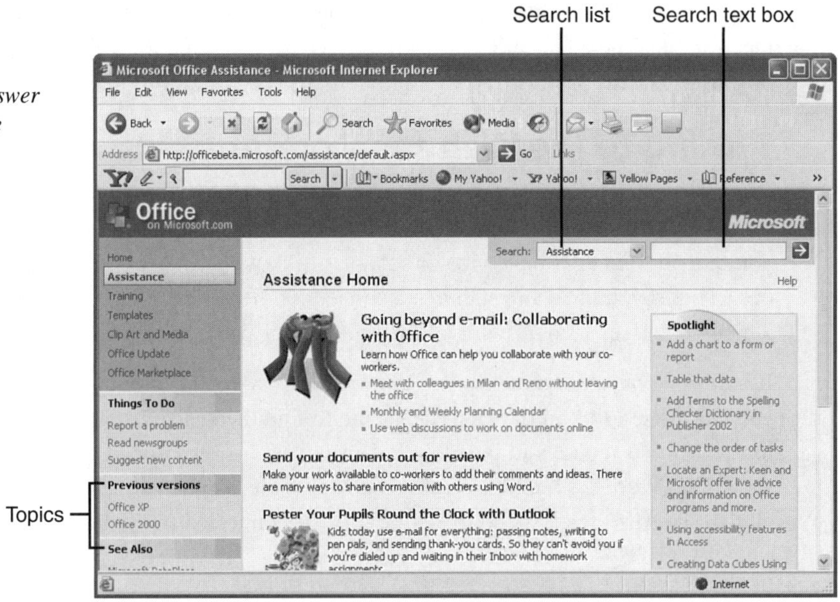

FIGURE **1.15**

*Search for an answer
on the Assistance
Home page.*

Search list   Search text box

Moving Within a Workbook

Each blank Excel workbook contains three worksheets. You can add or delete as many
worksheets as you need. Because a workbook consists of one or more worksheets, you
need to move between the worksheets. Here's how:

- Click the tab of the worksheet you want to move to. If the tab isn't visible, use the
  tab scroll buttons, shown in Figure 1.16, to bring the tab into view, and then click
  the tab.

Moving Within a Worksheet

When the worksheet you want is visible on the screen, you need to move around in it. It's
important to remember that the view on the screen might represent only a small portion
of the total worksheet. After all, a worksheet can consist of more than one million cells.
Even the biggest computer monitor can't display the entire sheet so that it is legible.

You move around your Excel worksheet with the mouse or the keyboard. To move from
cell to cell, click the cell you want to move to. Notice that a dark border, called a *selector*, surrounds a selected cell. If the cell you want to move to isn't visible, use the scrollbars to move around the sheet.

FIGURE 1.16

Choose the sheet you want to work on.

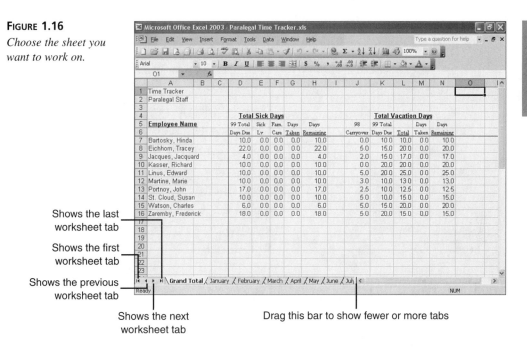

Shows the last worksheet tab

Shows the first worksheet tab

Shows the previous worksheet tab

Shows the next worksheet tab

Drag this bar to show fewer or more tabs

 If you're using an IntelliMouse, you can scroll around worksheets using the center wheel button. Hold down the wheel button and drag to quickly move through the worksheet.

Using the Keyboard

If you're entering a lot of numbers or text from the keyboard, it's easier sometimes to move around a worksheet with the keyboard. That way, you can keep your hands on the keyboard and not have to jump on and off the mouse.

Table 1.3 shows the keystrokes you use to move around in a worksheet.

TABLE 1.3 Keystrokes That Move You Through a Worksheet

Press These Keys	To Move To
Enter	One cell down or to the next cell in sequence
Shift+Tab	One cell to the left
Shift+Enter	One cell up
Up Arrow, Down Arrow, Right Arrow, Left Arrow	One cell in the direction of the arrow

TABLE 1.3   continued

Press These Keys	To Move To
Ctrl+Right Arrow or Ctrl+Left Arrow	To the right or left end of a row that contains data
Ctrl+Up Arrow or Ctrl+Down Arrow	To the top or bottom of a column that contains data
Home	To the first cell in the row
Ctrl+Home	To the first cell in the worksheet
Ctrl+End	To the lower-right cell in the worksheet
Page Up	Up one screen
Page Down	Down one screen
Alt+Page Up	Left one screen
Alt+Page Down	Right one screen
Ctrl+Page Up	To previous sheet
Ctrl+Page Down	To Next sheet
F5 or Ctrl+G	Opens the Go To dialog box

Summary

In this first hour, you learned how to launch Microsoft Excel, how to use its basic screen elements, and how to work with toolbars. You used the Help task pane and the Ask a Question box to get online help. You also learned some navigational tricks to move through workbooks and worksheets. In Hour 2, "Entering Data," you create your own worksheet.

Q&A

Q Help! My Standard toolbar is stuck on the left edge of the screen. Can I move it back to the top of the screen?

A Sure you can. Click the Move handle and drag it directly under the main menu bar. When you release the mouse button, the Standard toolbar is repositioned in its default position.

Q I typed in a question in the Answer a Question box, but the list of answers didn't match what I asked.

A Excel Help isn't perfect. If the answers provided were too general, try rephrasing your query into something more specific, or try using different keywords.

Q I inherited an Excel worksheet from someone in my office. How can I find out how many rows and columns it contains?

A The easiest and fastest way to move to the bottom right-most cell in a worksheet is to press Ctrl+End. Make a note of the cell address shown in the Name box.

Hour 2

Entering Data

This hour includes the following topics:

- How to enter text, numbers, dates, and times
- How to automate your work
- How to create a simple spreadsheet
- How to copy data
- How to make changes to the worksheet
- How to insert and delete cells
- How to work with rows and columns

The data you enter into your worksheets is the most important part of your work. Excel accepts dates and times, currency amounts, general numbers, text, and more. In fact, Excel can usually tell what type of entry you're making and adjust the appearance accordingly. Although default formatting is in place for most types of entries, you're free to change the appearance any way you'd like.

In this hour, you create a workbook and make several different types of entries. The To Do exercises walk you through the process. However, feel free to experiment with anything that's discussed during this hour.

Typing Data in a Cell

As you learned during Hour 1, "Getting Started," the intersection of a row and a column is called a *cell*. When you're working in an Excel worksheet, one cell is highlighted to display the position of your cursor. The address of the cell—described by the column letter and row number—is displayed in the *Name box*. The highlighted cell is where the data you type appears in the worksheet.

 NEW TERM   *Name box*—An area on the worksheet that displays the current location of the cursor.

When the cell in which you want to enter your data is highlighted, simply begin typing. As you type, your text appears in the cell and in the Formula bar, as shown in Figure 2.1. When you're done typing, press the Enter key or click the green check mark (called the Enter button) next to the Formula bar to place the data in the cell. If you change your mind about the entry, click the Cancel button. When you're ready to enter data in another cell, move to that cell, type your data, and press Enter.

> Make sure that you're located in the cell in which you want to enter data before you begin typing. If you're not careful, it's easy to overwrite important information.

Enter (formula) button

Cancel button   Formula bar

FIGURE 2.1

Data appears in the Formula bar and the cell as you're typing.

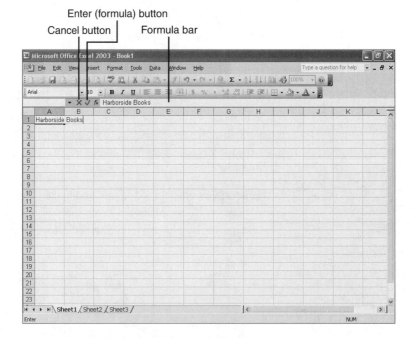

Types of Excel Data

You can make three basic types of entries into cells:

- Labels
- Values
- Formulas

Labels are text entries that contain no numeric value. Labels can consist of text or even contain numbers. For example, a cell that contains an address like 991 Northwest Ninth Street is still considered a label.

Values are numbers that you enter into cells. Because Excel is a number-crunching program, it understands how to use values when performing calculations. Numbers can be straight integers, like the number 4, or can contain decimals or fractions.

Formulas perform calculations in your worksheets. Formulas can contain numbers, cell references, and arithmetic operators. The result of a formula appears in the worksheet in the cell in which you entered the formula. For example, if cell A16 contains the formula =1+1, the number 2 will appear in the cell.

You learn more about formulas in Hour 5, "Letting Excel Do the Math."

Entering Labels

Labels are any combination of letters, numbers, and spaces. Labels have no numeric value. A label that is too long for the width of a cell floats across the cells to its right, as long as the cells don't contain any information. If the cells aren't empty, the label is truncated, or cut off. By default, labels are left-justified.

Entering text labels into the worksheet is easy. Just click into a cell to select it and start typing!

Automating Your Work

Although the design and set up of an Excel workbook can be exciting, the data entry portion—the grunt work—can be dull. Few people like to sit at their computers and type the same information again and again. Entering consecutive dates or numbers can cause your mind to wander. Fortunately, Excel has some tools to help you automate your data entry.

AutoComplete Speeds the Entry Process

As you create your worksheets, you'll probably find that you enter the same text over and over. Typing repetitive text is boring and, because you might not be paying close attention, increases your chances of making a typing mistake. Fortunately, Excel has a feature called AutoComplete to automate the entry of text you type multiple times.

AutoComplete works in two ways. In the first way, Excel completes an entry as you're typing it. (If you've typed URLs using the current versions of Internet Explorer or Netscape Navigator, you might be familiar with how AutoComplete finishes the text you type.) As you type the first few letters of an entry you made previously, AutoComplete assumes that you're typing the previous text and finishes the text for you. If the text AutoComplete fills in is not correct, just keep typing. Whatever you type overwrites the AutoComplete entry.

You can also pick from your AutoComplete entries and only insert them immediately above or below the existing entry(ies). When you need to repeat a word or phrase you used previously, right-click the cell where you want to place the duplicate text. Remember, the cell must be immediately above or below an existing AutoComplete entry. Choose Pick from Drop-down List from the shortcut menu that appears. As shown in Figure 2.2, a list of previously typed words and phrases appears underneath the cell. Click the word you want from the list. The list disappears and the word is inserted into the cell.

FIGURE 2.2

AutoComplete makes it easy to type repetitive text.

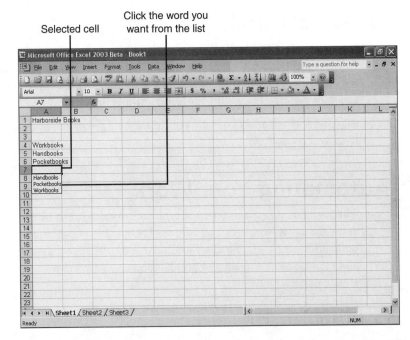

AutoFill Produces Amazing Results

With AutoComplete, you type a partial entry and Excel finishes the text for you. Excel also contains another amazing feature called AutoFill to automate your data entry. AutoFill looks at the relationship of a data series that you've already entered into your worksheet and then duplicates its results in an area you select. A *data series* can be any set of related information, such as the months of the year, the numbers of your personal checks, or incremental interest amounts. Using AutoFill is a breeze. You select a cell or cells that contain the data and then tell Excel where to fill in the rest. For example, if you have a list that contains Sunday and Monday, AutoFill can enter the remaining weekdays for you.

Fill It In with the Fill Handle

Although Excel gives you several ways to activate AutoFill, the easiest method is to use the fill handle on the bottom right-hand corner of the selected cell or cells. When you select one or more cells, the fill handle appears. Drag the handle across the adjacent cells you want to fill, as shown in Figure 2.3. As you drag, the cells appear highlighted. Release the mouse button to fill in the data series.

FIGURE 2.3

Select the first cell or two of the series and drag to continue the series.

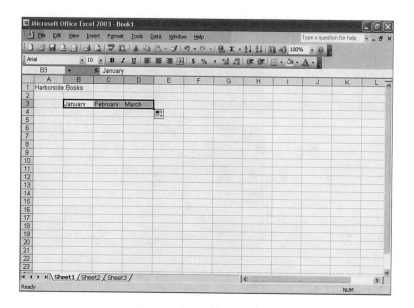

Creating a Simple Spreadsheet

Now it's time to put everything you've learned into action as you begin creating a simple worksheet. This section gives you some practice making entries into a cell and using Excel's AutoFit feature. You add to the worksheet in the other exercises contained in this hour. Before you begin, Excel should be open and visible on your computer. (If you're not sure how to open Excel, review the information in Hour 1.)

To Do: Create a Simple Spreadsheet

1. Click cell A1. A selector appears around the cell. Type **Harborside Books**. Notice that the text appears in the cell and the Formula bar. Press Enter when you're done typing.

2. Move down to cell A4 and type **Hard Cover**. Press the down-arrow key when you're done typing to enter your text and move down to the next cell.

3. Type the following text, making sure to press the down arrow key after each group of words: **Soft Cover**, **Audio Cassette**, **CD**. Be sure not to type a comma after each entry in the cell. When you're done, your screen should look like the one shown in Figure 2.4.

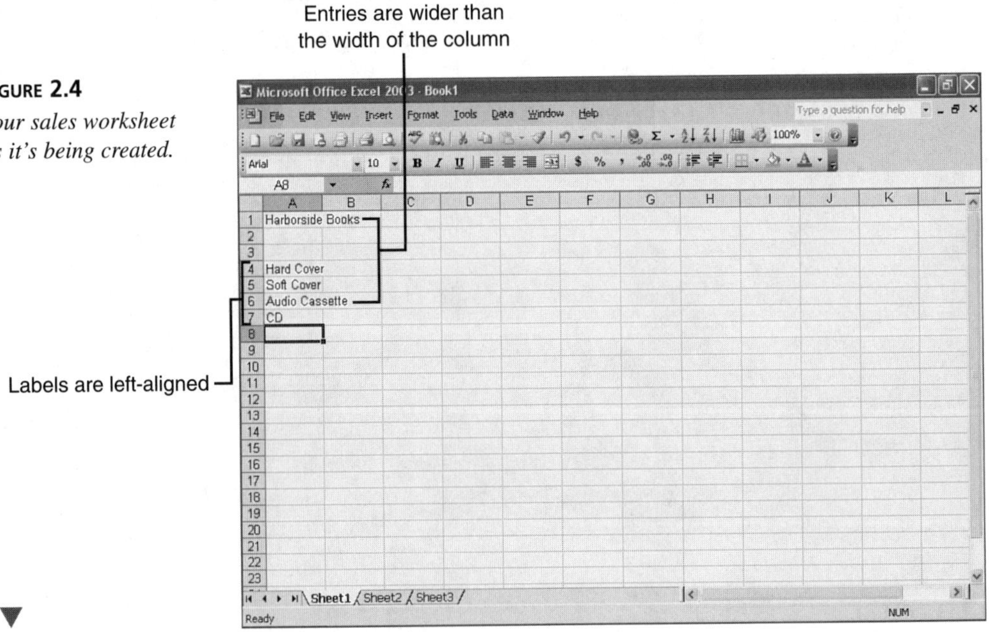

Entries are wider than
the width of the column

FIGURE 2.4

Your sales worksheet as it's being created.

Labels are left-aligned

▼ 4. Notice that some of the entries in column A are wider than the column and spill over into column B. Select column A by positioning the mouse pointer on the heading for the column (the mouse pointer assumes the shape of an open cross) and clicking one time. The entire column appears highlighted.

5. Click Format, Column and choose AutoFit Selection. The column adjusts to accommodate the longest cell entry. Deselect the column by pressing the right arrow key.

6. Click into cell B3 and type **January**. Without pressing any of the arrow keys or Enter, notice that a tiny square called a fill handle appears in the bottom-right corner of the cell.

7. Position your mouse pointer over the fill handle (the pointer assumes the shape of a small cross). Click the left mouse button and slowly drag to cell D3. As you drag, a ScreenTip displays the value of the cell that the pointer is directly over.

▲ 8. Release the mouse button. The other months are filled in and appear highlighted.

Dragging to the right or left of the portion of the worksheet visible on your computer screen can sometimes produce unwanted results. When the mouse crosses the current screen, the dragging process seems to speed up. You might need to practice your drag technique a few times before you get it right. To reverse the result of a fill that has gone too far, click the Undo button on the Standard toolbar. Then try the fill again.

Remember to always select (highlight) the cells, rows, or columns that you want to change. Any change you make from a menu or toolbar affects only the selection.

Entering Values

The procedure for entering values is identical to the procedure for entering labels. After you select the cell in which you want to enter the value, simply begin typing. As with labels, the values you type appear both in the cell and in the Formula bar.

Excel treats numbers and text differently. For one, values are aligned automatically with the right edge of the cell. Values are displayed in Excel's General number format. However, you can always change or customize the alignment, appearance, and formatting of numbers in the worksheet. If a value is too wide to fit in the current width of a cell, Excel displays a series of # characters, as shown in Figure 2.5, across the width of the cell to let you know that the number cannot be displayed. You need to adjust the width of the cell to display the number properly.

To quickly change the width of a column, select Format, Column, AutoFit. The column width is adjusted.

The number appears in the Formula bar

FIGURE 2.5

The number signs indicate that the number is wider than the column.

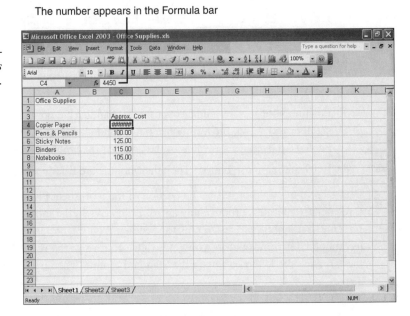

Values can begin with the following characters:

0 1 2 3 4 5 6 7 8 9 + - . (, $ %

You can also type fractions. However, if the syntax for fractions is not correct, Excel misinterprets what you're trying to enter.

To enter a fraction, type the number, a blank space, and then the fraction, such as 4 1/2. If you want to enter only the fractional portion, type a 0, a blank space, and then the fraction, similar to 0 1/2. If you just type 1/2, Excel thinks you mean January 2.

Always check your worksheet after you type in a few fractions. If a fraction is entered incorrectly, Excel might treat it as a label or a date entry, instead of the numeric value you expected.

Adding Dates and Times

Dates and times are other important values you can enter in Excel. Treating dates and times as values makes your life easier. For example, instead of counting the number of days in the current accounting cycle or determining the age of an accounts receivable account, Excel can do the work for you.

Excel keeps track of the dates you enter by assigning each date with a serial number. The first date, January 1, 1900, is assigned the number 1; January 2, 1900, the number 2; and so on. A date can be displayed in many different formats, but Excel always keep track of the date's underlying serial number. Accordingly, you can use the dates in your calculations.

When you enter a date, you can choose to enter the year in two-digit format or use the full four digits. Using four digits is safer, because Excel will always be able to identify whether the year occurs in the 19*XX* or 20*XX* range. Here's how Excel interprets the year in a two-digit year format:

- If you type **00** through **29** for the year, Excel uses the years 2000 through 2029. For example, if you type **3/18/25**, Excel assumes the date is March 18, 2025.

- If you type **30** through **99** for the year, Excel uses the years 1930 through 1999. For example, if you type **10/24/47**, Excel assumes the date is October 24, 1947.

Times are maintained in a military time format. Excel treats each time that you enter as fractional part of 24 hours. For example, Excel treats 11:30 PM as the value **23:30**. Just as with dates, you can easily use times in your calculations.

 If you are entering many dates covering a wide range, you might find it confusing to remember how the two-digit format tracks dates. Play it safe and enter the year with four digits for perfect results.

Table 2.1 shows the date formats you can use in Excel. This table also contains times because in some cases, time is incorporated into the date format.

TABLE 2.1   Date Formats in Excel

Format	Example	Comments
Month/Date/Year	12/31/99 or 12/31/1924	A two-digit year between 0 and 29 is interpreted as 20*XX*. All others are interpreted as 19*XX*.
Date-Month-Year	31-Dec-99	Same comment as the previous format. Use the full name of the month or its standard abbreviation.

TABLE 2.1   continued

Format	Example	Comments
Date-Month	31-Dec	Assumes current year.
Month-Date	Dec-31	Assumes current year.
Month-Year	Dec-98	A two-digit year between 0 and 29 is interpreted as 20*XX*. All others are interpreted as 19*XX*.
Hour:Minute	10:02AM	Use of AM is optional.
Hour:Minute	9:38PM	Enter PM if you're not using 24-hour military time.

You can quickly enter the current date or time in a cell. For the date, click into a blank cell and press Ctrl+; Enter the time by pressing Ctrl+Shift+;—this trick is useful if you or your co-workers want to keep track of when you last updated your worksheet.

If you can't enter a date in the format you want, and if you're using Excel on a network, be sure to check with your network administrator to determine whether the date entry has been set up in a special way. Excel 2003 allows network administrators to change the way dates are entered across the entire network.

The next step is to enter some sales numbers into your worksheet. Later you can update the numbers you enter for practice with your own actual amounts. The sales worksheet should be open and visible on the screen from the previous exercise.

To Do: Add Values to the Sales Worksheet

1. Click in cell B4 and type the value **600**. When you're done typing, press the down arrow key to move down to the next cell.

2. Type **278.30** and press the down arrow key. Notice that the second number to the right of the decimal point is cut off.

3. Type **160** in cell B6, the cell that displays your Audio Cassette sales in January. Press the down arrow key when you're done typing.

4. Instead of typing a number in the next cell, you're going to let Excel calculate your CD sales. To let Excel know that you're going to perform a calculation, type an **=** sign and then type **135**, the plus sign (**+**), and the number **47.82**. Your cell entry should look like the following:

    =135+47.82

▼   Take care not to enter any spaces between the numbers and the operators. Press the
      down arrow when you've checked your typing. The result of the simple calculation
      appears in the cell.

5. Move down to cell A11 and press Ctrl+; (semicolon). The current date is displayed.
   Press Enter to enter the date into the cell. Your worksheet should look similar to
▲   the one in Figure 2.6.

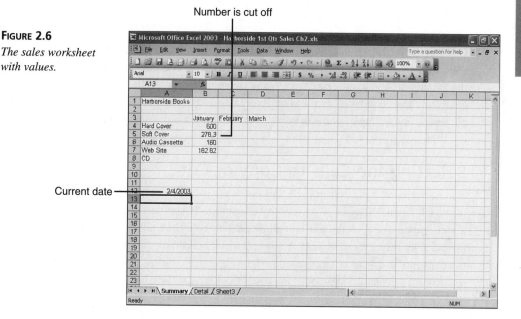

FIGURE 2.6
*The sales worksheet
with values.*

Copying from Cell to Cell

Like other Windows programs, Excel makes it easy to rearrange the data you enter in
your worksheets. You can copy data from one place to another on the same worksheet or
to other worksheets in the same workbook. You can even copy data from one workbook
to another.

In addition to copying data in Excel, you can also copy data to other pro-
grams, such as Word or Outlook. You learn how to integrate data with other
Office programs in Hour 19, "Integrating Excel with Other Office
Applications."

You can copy or cut data in Excel. If you choose to copy, a carbon-copy image of the data you copied is maintained on the Clipboard. If you cut data, the selection is actually removed from your worksheet (as if you'd cut it with scissors).

> When you copy labels or values, a carbon copy of the data is pasted. Formulas are handled somewhat differently. You have the opportunity to work with formulas in Hour 4, "Managing Your Files and Workbooks."

Copying (and cutting) data is accomplished with the aid of a handy Windows utility called the Clipboard. Whenever you use the Copy or Cut command, the data is placed on the Windows Clipboard. The Clipboard is the intermediary in the copy or cut-and-paste operation. Data can be pasted into an Excel worksheet from the Clipboard one or multiple times. For example, you can copy your company logo, a paragraph, and a graphic to the Windows Clipboard for pasting into your corporate forms.

Selecting the Cells to Copy or Cut

You need to select the cell or cells that you want to copy or cut before you can send them to the Clipboard. Select a single cell by clicking it. If you want to select multiple cells in a rectangular block, click the first cell. Press and hold the Shift key and drag the mouse pointer over the block you want to copy. A black border appears around the block, and the cells inside appear colored, as shown in Figure 2.7. When all the cells that you want to copy are selected, release both the mouse button and the Shift key.

> The first cell in a block of selected cells might not appear colored or selected. However, if a black border surrounds the block, the first, non-highlighted cell is included in the selection.

> Don't panic if you accidentally choose the Cut command instead of Copy and the cells disappear from your worksheet. Simply click the Undo button on the Standard toolbar to make the cells reappear.

In Excel, you can select multiple cells that are not located in a rectangular block. To select non-touching cells, hold down the Ctrl key as you click each cell that you want to copy. Each cell that you click appears highlighted. Release the Ctrl key when the cells you want to copy are selected.

First cell does not
appear colored

FIGURE 2.7
The cells are selected.

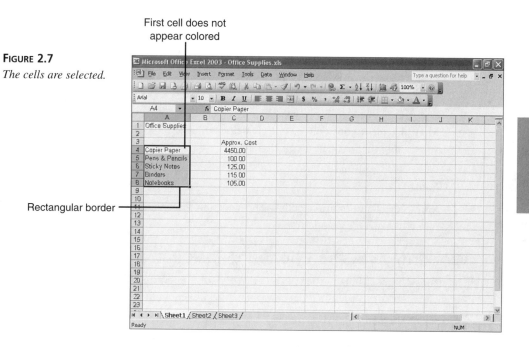

Rectangular border

Excel won't let you cut or copy many sets of non-touching cells. Cells along one row or one column seem to work best. Even then, when you paste non-contiguous cells, Excel makes them contiguous again.

Either way, click the Copy button or the Cut button on the Standard toolbar after the cells are selected. If you can't see the toolbar, or want to access the command from the menu instead, choose Edit, Copy or Edit, Cut. A marquee appears around the copied cells. If you're cutting the cells, they disappear from the worksheet.

> Press Ctrl+C to activate the Copy command from the keyboard after you've selected the cells to copy. Ctrl+X is the keyboard command to cut the cells. You paste the cells from the keyboard by pressing Ctrl+V.
>
> To get rid of the dotted marquee around the cells you copied, press the Esc key.

Pasting the Copied or Cut Cells

Pasting the cells you copied or cut is a snap. Click the first cell where you want the new cells to appear. If you're pasting a block of cells, you do not have to highlight a rectangular block; Excel assumes that you want the cells to appear in the order and shape in which they were copied. Click the Paste button on the Standard toolbar or chose Edit, Paste. The cells appear in their new location.

Excel pastes data in four ways:

- One cell to one cell—A single cell from the Clipboard is pasted to one cell.
- Multiple cells to one cell—Multiple cells are pasted into a rectangular block, of which only the first cell is selected.
- One cell to multiple cells—A single cell from the Clipboard is pasted into all high-lighted cells.
- Multiple cells to multiple cells—The selection of cells from the Clipboard is pasted into a like-sized rectangular block.

Working with the Clipboard Task Pane

The handy Clipboard task pane, as shown in Figure 2.8, holds your copied selections. Whenever you copy or cut one or more selections during your current Windows session, you can view the Clipboard task pane by choosing View, Task Pane.

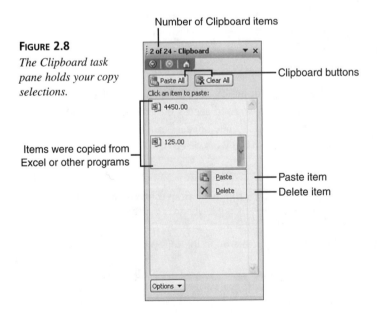

FIGURE 2.8

The Clipboard task pane holds your copy selections.

Number of Clipboard items

Clipboard buttons

Items were copied from Excel or other programs

Paste item

Delete item

The title bar on the Clipboard task pane indicates the number of items you copied or cut and the maximum number of Clipboard items you can have, which is 24. An icon that represents the Office application from which the item was copied or cut displays at the top left of the item. The Clipboard buttons for pasting and clearing all items appear beneath the task pane toolbar.

The most recent copied or cut selection appears at the top of the Clipboard gallery. When you point to an item, a border displays with an arrow on the right border. When you click the arrow, a menu appears with the Paste and Delete commands. Choose Paste to insert the item in the current cell or choose Delete to remove the item from the Clipboard.

When you want to paste all the items on the Clipboard to the worksheet, click the Paste All button. To delete all the current Clipboard items, click the Clear All button.

The Clipboard task pane provides some wonderful advantages. Instead of having to paste the last data that you copied, you can pick and choose from previously copied data. The Clipboard task pane stores up to 24 items that you copied or cut during the current Windows session. When you close Windows, the Clipboard is automatically cleared.

If you want the Clipboard task pane to display automatically when you copy items, click the Options arrow at the bottom of the Clipboard task pane. Then choose Show Office Clipboard Automatically.

Drag It and Drop It

The drag-and-drop technique is a fast, easy way to copy or move data in the visible viewing area. First, select the cells you want to move or copy. When the cells appear highlighted, move the mouse pointer over the border of the selected cells. The mouse pointer takes the shape of an arrow.

If you want to copy the selected cells, press and hold the Ctrl key. (If you're moving the cells, you don't need to hold down any key.) Now click the mouse button and drag the border. As they're being dragged, an outline of the selected cells appears. When the data is located in the spot in which you want it to appear, release the mouse button. The data appears in the new location as shown in Figure 2.9.

An outline appears as the cells are dragged

FIGURE 2.9

Drag-and-drop works best if you can see the location for the new cells.

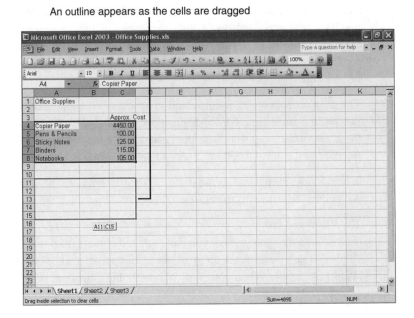

To Do: Copy Worksheet Entries with Various Copy Techniques

1. Select cell B4 by clicking it. A border appears around the cell.

2. Hold down the Ctrl key and position the mouse pointer in the border of the cell. A large plus sign appears.

3. Using the Ctrl key, move the mouse pointer to the cell directly to the right (cell C4). You've just used the drag-and-drop method to copy from one cell to another.

4. With cell C4 selected, press Ctrl+C. This copies the data in cell C4 to the Clipboard.

5. Click cell D4. The cell is highlighted, which tells Excel where you want to paste the data.

6. Press Ctrl+V. This pastes the data into the selected cell. You've just used the shortcut keys to copy and paste data from one cell to another cell.

7. Click cell B5 to select it. Point to the small square in the lower-right corner of that cell. Notice the mouse pointer changes to a small plus sign, which is called the *fill handle*.

8. Drag the fill handle to cells C5 and D5. Now you've used the fill handle method to copy data when cells are adjacent to one another.

▼   9. Select cell B6 (January's Audio Cassette amount) by clicking it and then click the
         Copy button on the Standard toolbar. A dotted marquee appears around cell B6.
         The data you selected has been copied to the Clipboard.

    10. Click into cell C6 and select cell D6 by dragging the mouse. The two cells appear
         highlighted.

    11. Click the Paste button on the Standard toolbar. The amount you copied to the
         Clipboard is copied to the cells you selected. Press Esc to remove the dotted
▲   marquee.

> Always look at the cells you've pasted from the Clipboard. It's easy to paste
> a selection to the wrong location and possibly overwrite important data. If
> you've pasted to the wrong spot, click the Undo on the Standard toolbar.

Making Changes to the Worksheet

In a perfect society, you'd never need to edit your work. However, in the real world,
you'll find yourself editing your cell entries time and time again. In addition to editing
entries, you can delete an entry you've made. In fact, you can delete an entire row or column. You can also add rows and columns. A worksheet is a work-in-progress and,
accordingly, can always be changed or improved.

Editing Cell Contents

Editing cell contents is easy. Double-click the cell that you want to edit and make your
changes. You can edit the existing cell contents or replace them. When you're done, press
the Enter key or one of the directional arrows, or click the green check mark on the
Formula bar to enter the new data into the cell. Cancel the edit by pressing Esc.

> To quickly add to the end of cell contents, select the cell and press F2. The
> insertion point appears at the end of the existing cell contents. Type the
> addition to the cell and press Enter.

Clearing Cell Contents

Instead of editing a cell, you can clear the cell's contents. Clearing the contents of a cell
is like using an eraser end of a pencil on the cell. Select the cells you want to clear and
click the right mouse button. Choose Clear Contents from the shortcut menu, as shown in

Figure 2.10. Keep in mind that the Clear Contents command does not place the cell contents on the Clipboard.

FIGURE 2.10

Use the shortcut menu to clear the contents of a cell.

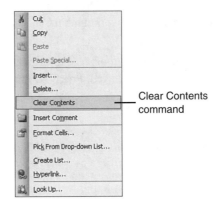

Clear Contents command

Inserting and Deleting Cells

It's no problem to insert and delete cells in your worksheet. When you insert cells, Excel moves the remaining cells in the column or row in accordance with the direction you specify. Deleting cells is the opposite of inserting cells because the remaining cells are shifted to fill in the deleted cell.

Deleting a cell and clearing a cell are two very different actions. Deleting a cell removes the physical cell from the worksheet and forces the remaining cells to fill in the hole. Clearing a cell erases the contents of the cell, but leaves the cell still in the worksheet.

Working with Rows and Columns

Working with rows and columns is very much like working with cells on a larger scale. When you insert a row, the new row spans all the columns in the worksheets. New columns and rows don't contain data and are unformatted. (You'll learn about adding formatting later in Part II: "Dress Up Your Work.")

Insert a new row or column by clicking the spot where you want the new row or column to appear. If you want to insert more than one row or column, select the number of rows and columns you want. (For example, select three rows if you want to insert three new ones.) Click the Insert menu, as shown in Figure 2.11, and choose either Rows or

Columns. Excel inserts new rows above the current row and inserts new columns to the left of the selected columns.

Insert rows

Insert cells | Insert columns

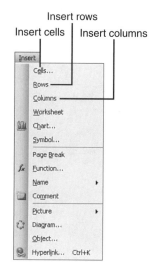

FIGURE 2.11

Add rows and columns from the Insert menu.

2

 Adding rows and columns to your worksheet does not change the maximum size of your worksheet. The worksheet cannot contain more than 65,536 rows or 256 columns.

The following exercise, in which you make some changes to the sales worksheet you started earlier, gives you a chance to put some of this knowledge to work. Don't worry if some of the changes don't make much sense; you're fine-tuning your skills right now. In later hours, you're going to turn your sales worksheet into a masterpiece!

To Do: Work with Cells, Rows, and Columns

1. Highlight cells C6 through D6 on the sales worksheet and click the right mouse button.

2. Choose Clear Contents from the shortcut menu that appears. As you see, you can clear the contents of one cell or a block of cells.

3. Let's add a row above row 7. From any column, select a cell in row 7, as shown in Figure 2.12. Because you're going to insert a row, you do not have to position the mouse pointer in a particular column.

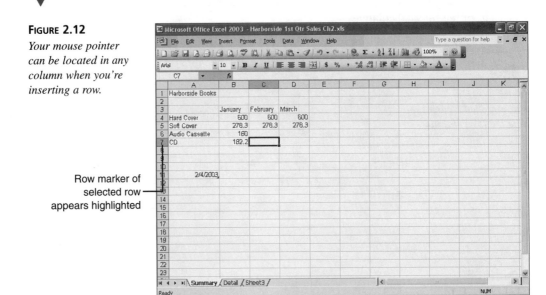

▼

FIGURE 2.12
Your mouse pointer can be located in any column when you're inserting a row.

Row marker of
selected row
appears highlighted

4. When the row is highlighted, click the Insert menu and choose Rows. A blank row is inserted above the row you selected.

5. Click in cell A7, type **Web Site**, and press the right arrow to move to cell B7. Type **300** and press Enter.

   Select cell B5, the cell that contains the Soft Cover sales amount and click Edit, Delete. The Delete dialog box, shown in Figure 2.13, appears. Make sure the option button next to Shift Cells Up is selected and click OK. Notice that the entries you'd made in the all the other categories for January were shifted upward, as shown in Figure 2.14.

FIGURE 2.13
You need to choose the behavior of the remaining cells whenever you delete a cell.

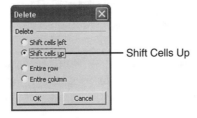

— Shift Cells Up

▼

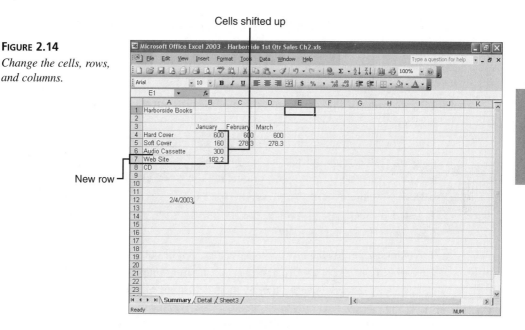

FIGURE 2.14
Change the cells, rows, and columns.

Cells shifted up

New row

7. Stop now and save the worksheet so you can work with it later. Click the Save button on the Standard toolbar or click File, Save. When the Save As dialog box appears, type **Sales 1st Qtr** in the filename box and click Save.

8. If you're planning to go right on to the next hour, click File, Close. If you need a break before you continue, close Excel now by clicking File, Exit.

Summary

Stand up and pat yourself on the back! You've covered a lot of ground during this hour. You learned about the different types of data you can enter into a worksheet and practiced working with the various data types. You learned how to edit and rearrange data in your worksheet. In Hour 3, "Organizing Your Files," you learn to organize your files and save your worksheets.

Q&A

Q Why can't I see the end of some of my labels on the worksheet? They appear correctly in the Formula bar.

A If the label appears cut off, the column isn't wide enough and there's an entry to the right. Try widening the column or using AutoFit.

Q Why do some of the buttons on the toolbar dim out when I am entering data in a cell?

A When you're typing data in a cell, you're technically in Edit mode, and most of the program features are unavailable. As soon as you enter the data (by pressing Enter, pressing a directional arrow key, or clicking the green check mark on the Formula bar), the functionality of the buttons comes back.

Q I copied several cells to the Clipboard, but I couldn't find them on the Clipboard. What happened?

A The Clipboard holds the last 24 items you copied or cut—not just from within Excel, but from the other Office programs on your computer. It's possible that the cells you copied were overwritten by more recent items you placed on the Clipboard. Delete some items or click Clear All on the Clipboard to remove all the items. Of course, when you close Windows, the contents of the Clipboard are cleared.

Q If I clear the contents of a cell, can I enter new data into it later?

A Yes—clearing the contents of a cell is like using an eraser: The cells you clear still remain in the worksheet.

HOUR 3

Organizing Your Files

This hour covers the following topics:

- How to save your work
- Understand filenames
- What you need to know about save options
- How to rearrange your files

In the previous hour, you saved the sales file you were working on. At the time, you probably were not aware that you were performing one of the most important functions of any computer program. Saving your work is a key element of working in Excel or any software. The save process only takes a few seconds and ensures that you can return to your work later. If you exit Excel without saving your worksheet, or the power cuts out, you lose all your work.

If you're using Excel in the office, or over a network, saving becomes even more important. Your worksheets might be part of a large project and need to be accessed by your co-workers. Saving your workbooks to the correct drive and folder is almost as important as the save itself. After all, you'd hate to be awakened from a sound sleep with a phone call from an irate colleague asking where you saved the amortization schedule.

In this hour, you learn the ins and outs of saving your work. During the lesson, you also refresh your knowledge of working with drives and folders within Windows. Finally, you learn how to copy files from one location to another and how to delete them altogether.

Saving Your Workbook

If you don't save your workbooks, you're playing a form of computerized Russian roulette. Your unsaved work is unprotected. If the power goes off or your system crashes, your worksheet is gone forever. Saving your work takes a few brief seconds and ensures that you or your colleagues will be able to open the workbook later. A saved workbook can be stored indefinitely.

When you save your work in Excel, you need to consider a few points:

- The location of the saved file—You can save to your computer's hard drive or to a floppy disk. If you're working on a network, you can save your files to a drive and folder on the network.

- The name of the file—The filename should be descriptive so that you or someone else can identify it. A cryptic name like SMBUD might make sense at the time you save the file, but will probably confuse you and everyone else later, especially if you need to locate that one file from a long list.

- The format of the file—If everyone in your office is using the same version of Excel, you won't have any problems. However, in many offices, multiple versions of Excel are in use. If you use a feature that isn't present in an earlier version of Excel, someone opening your file in an earlier version won't see that feature's results.

Navigating Through Files and Folders

In most cases, when you save a file, Excel automatically saves it to the My Documents folder located on your computer. However, you can place the file anywhere you like. If you're working on a network, your network administrator must have granted you access rights to save a file in a *network folder*.

NEW TERM *Network folder*—A folder that's located on one of the network drives. Network folders can be shared so that everyone on the network can access them, or they can be private, so that only you or your workgroup can access them.

Many Excel users are confused by the storage system that Windows uses for files and folders. Actually, the file system is simple to understand. Windows uses a file folder metaphor for organizing the files on your computer. Both the files you create and the software programs you used to create them are stored in folders. You work with computer folders just the way you work with the paper files in your office. You can create a filing system that contains many subfolders, or you can use a top-level folder to store your files.

The folders are stored on drives that are lettered alphabetically. A computer drive is the electronic equivalent of a filing cabinet. The hard drive on your computer is usually called the C: drive. If you're working on a newer computer with a large hard drive, your hard drive might be partitioned into more than one drive—say C, D, and E. Network users can have many drives available.

Picture your drives and folders arranged in one large file room. The order of your drives and folders is arranged hierarchically. Each filing cabinet in the room represents another drive. Within each drive is a group of folders. A folder can contain files, subfolders, or a combination of both.

If you were actually filing papers in a real file room, you'd need to put away the folders in one filing cabinet before you could open the drawers on another cabinet. Electronic filing is much the same. You need to navigate up through the folders on one drive before you can go to another drive.

3

If you're familiar with the old MS-DOS filing system, a folder is the equivalent of a directory, and a folder within a folder is analogous to a subdirectory.

Saving Your Work for the First Time

The first time you save an Excel workbook, you are asked to name your file. Excel assumes you're going to save into a default drive and folder, but gives you the option to choose a different destination. After the first time you save the file, you won't be prompted to change any information when you save the file later.

Don't wait until you've completed the workbook to save it for the first time. Because the information on the screen is stored in the temporary memory of your computer, it doesn't exist in a permanent form until you save it. Therefore, save the workbook for the first time as soon as you enter some basic information.

In Hour 2, "Entering Data," you saved a workbook using a few simple steps. In the next exercise, you perfect your saving techniques. Excel should be open and visible on the screen before you begin.

To Do: Save an Excel Workbook for the First Time

1. Click into cell A1 and type **Save Practice**. Press Enter when you're done typing.

> If you type the data in a cell and don't enter it, you won't be able to save the workbook. You enter the data by pressing Enter, pressing one of the directional arrow keys, or clicking the green check mark in the Formula bar.

2. Click the Save button on the Standard toolbar. The Save As dialog box appears, as shown in Figure 3.1.

FIGURE 3.1

The Save As dialog box provides many options for saving a file.

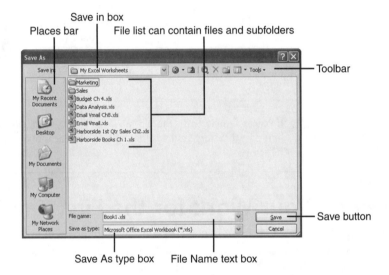

Save in box

Places bar   File list can contain files and subfolders

Toolbar

Save button

Save As type box   File Name text box

3. The default filename in the File Name text box is selected. Type **Practice Save**.

> If the default filename appears highlighted, you do not need to delete it before you type the name of the file. The new text you type overwrites any text that's selected.

4. Click the Save button. The file extension .XLS is added to the filename and the Save As dialog box closes. The filename you typed appears on the title bar.

If the file extensions do not appear in the File Name list, there is a way to show them. You need to go to My Documents or My Computer, and select the folder in which your Excel files are kept. Then select Tools, Folder Options. Click the View tab and verify that there is no check mark in the box for Hide extensions for known

▲ file types. If there is a check mark in the box, click in the box to remove the check mark, and finally click OK.

Exploring the Save As Dialog Box

The Save As dialog box, shown in Figure 3.1, contains all the tools you need to save your file for the first time. The format of the box is very similar to the File Open box that you see when you open a file that's been saved previously. Table 3.1 shows you the available options in the File Save As dialog box and provides a brief explanation of what they mean.

TABLE 3.1 Save Options

Option Name	What It Means
Toolbar	Contains buttons to help you manage your files.
Places bar	Click a location or folder icon to select a place for the file.
Save In text box	The current folder in which the workbook will be saved. If you want to change to another folder, click the drop-down arrow next to the listed folder. Excel then displays all the drives and folders available to you. If necessary, use the vertical scrollbars to navigate to the drive or folder you want. You can also click the Up One Level button on the toolbar to move up to the next highest folder.
File list	Display of files already contained in the listed folder. Change the view of the files by clicking the Views button on the toolbar.
File Name text box	The name of the file. If you don't specify a file, Excel assigns the file a name like Book1.
Save as Type text box	The type of the file. By default, Excel saves the file type as an Excel 11 workbook. If you're sharing the file with others who might not have the latest version of Excel, you can save the file in an earlier Excel format. You can also choose a format from another spreadsheet program.
Save button	After you've set all the options, click Save to make a permanent copy of the workbook.

If you want to specify a different default working folder for opening and saving Excel workbooks, choose Tools, Options, and click the General tab. In the Default file location box, type the path for the folder you want to display as the default working folder in the Open and Save As dialog boxes. For example, `c:\mywork`.

3

Saving Your Work Later

After you've done the hard work of setting a filename and determining in which folder the file is stored, saving the workbook is a breeze. Just click the Save button on the Standard toolbar or press Ctrl+S. If the toolbar isn't visible, open the File menu and choose Save.

Remember to save your work often. Keep reminding yourself that the changes made to the file on the screen exist only in temporary memory until you save them. If you exit without saving, you will lose all the changes you made since the last save.

Understanding Excel Filenames

Each workbook that you create in Excel can be saved with a unique, meaningful name. Filenames can contain up to 256 characters and include both uppercase and lowercase letters, spaces, and punctuation. However, just because you can use up to 256 characters doesn't mean that each filename should be a long, rambling sentence. Filenames that are too long are almost as frustrating as filenames that are too short! Try to use as few words as possible to name your workbooks.

> Check with your co-workers or network administrator to determine whether your company has adopted naming standards for files. For example, file-names might include a departmental name, the project title, or the year.

> If you're using Excel in the office or you're going to share your files with others, make sure that everyone is using a version of Excel (and Windows) that supports long filenames. Excel for Office 95, Excel 97, Excel 2000, Excel 2002, Excel 2003, and Excel XP all support long filenames. If you're working with an earlier version of Excel , a long filename is truncated and contains a tilde (~) character at the end, such as LEGALDE~.

File Extensions Tell a Tale

You might have noticed when you saved the practice file that Excel assigned a period character and then a three-letter suffix at the end of the filename. The software program generally assigns file extensions. Excel workbook files are assigned the extension .XLS by default.

It's not necessary to type the file extension when you're naming a file. Excel looks at the file type that's selected and adds the correct extension.

Make sure that you don't change the file extension. Although you might think that using a file extension like .BUD to identify all your budget files is a good idea, you'll have a hard time finding those files later.

The extension on a filename is a road map for Windows. When you open a file, Windows uses the file extension to determine which program that file belongs to. Table 3.2 shows the most common file extensions used by Excel and explains a bit about them.

TABLE 3.2   Excel File Extensions

File Extension	What It Means
XLS	Microsoft Excel workbook
XLT	Microsoft Excel template
HTM or HTML	Web page
XLA	Microsoft Excel add-in
XLW	Microsoft Excel workspace

Protecting Your Work with AutoRecover

Even though saving a workbook takes only a few seconds, it's easy to forget to click the Save button. When you're really busy or under the gun, you might not want to break your concentration. Unfortunately, Murphy's Law determines that it's at those crucial times that your system locks up, the electricity goes out, or some other catastrophe occurs and your work is lost.

Excel's AutoRecover feature, also present in other Microsoft Office applications, offers some protection against such disasters. AutoRecover saves your work at specified intervals without any prompting from you. If your workbook should become damaged, you can open and repair the recovered workbook file.

To Do: Set AutoRecover

1. Click the Tools menu and choose Options. Click the Save tab (see Figure 3.2).

   Make sure that the Save AutoRecover Info Every box is checked, and specify the desired number of minutes between saves in the Minutes box. To change the interval, click in the Minutes box and type the time interval you want.

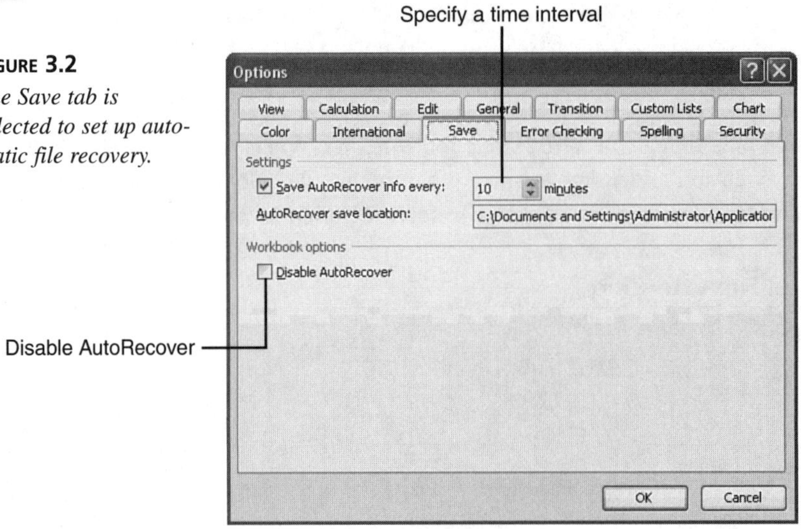

FIGURE 3.2
The Save tab is selected to set up automatic file recovery.

Specify a time interval

Disable AutoRecover

Be careful when you adjust the Minutes setting. A shorter interval decreases the risk of lost work, but increases the risk of a slow system if your file is large or your system doesn't have sufficient power.

3. Leave the default AutoRecover Save Location or specify a different folder.
4. Click OK to close the Options dialog box.
5. To deactivate the AutoRecover feature anytime you're working in Excel, click the Tools menu, choose Options, and check Disable AutoRecover.

Saving an Existing Workbook with a New Name

After you set up and save a workbook, you can save it with a different name. Saving an existing file with a different name preserves the original, pristine copy of the file. For example, in the office, you might create an expense report or budget and then save subsequent updates to different filenames. Or you might use different versions of a workbook for fore-casting or modeling. Later you can easily delete the versions of a file you don't need.

In the next To Do exercise, you save the Practice Save file with a different name. The Practice Save workbook should be open and visible on the screen from the first To Do in this hour.

To Do: Save a Workbook with a New Name

1. Click the File menu and choose Save As. The Save As dialog appears with the name of the file highlighted in the File Name box.

2. If you want to assign a completely new filename, begin typing the name you want. Your text overwrites the existing name in the box.

3. If you want to amend the existing filename, click in the File Name box and edit the name that's shown. For this exercise, edit the filename to read `Practice Save 2`.

4. (Optional) Click the drop-down arrow next to the folder name shown in the Save In box and navigate to a different drive or folder.

5. Click the Save button. The Save As dialog box closes and the new filename is dis-played on the title bar.

> You can also save your workbook to the World Wide Web. You learn all about Excel's exciting tie-in to the Web in Hour 24, "Worksheets and the Web."

Other Save Options

You can't be too careful with your data. If you operate on the premise that an ounce of prevention is worth a pound of cure, you'll always be protected against the unexpected. Most of the options discussed here take only a few seconds to set up. This small time investment will pay for itself.

What About Backups?

Backup copies of important files are essential to your peace of mind. Keeping backup copies of important files ensures that you can always retrieve workbooks that are dam-aged or lost.

Options for the Home User

If you're working with Excel on a home computer or your office computer, whether or not it's linked to a network, keeping backup files of your work is essential. Excel offers a backup option that creates a copy of your workbook every time you save the file. The backup copy of the file is saved in the same folder as the original file. If the original file is lost or damaged, you can open the backup copy.

To set the automatic backup option for the current workbook, click File, Save As to display the Save As dialog box. Click the Tools button on the Save As toolbar and select General Options. Check the box next to Always Create Backup. Click OK to close the box and return to the Save As dialog box. Now click Save to save the file. You need to set the option for each file you want to backup automatically.

One problem associated with Excel's automatic backup system is that Excel workbooks can take up a lot of hard drive space. You might not want to fill your hard drive with duplicate copies of files. In addition, automatic backups can create a false sense of security. If the hard drive of your computer crashes, the original file and backup will be gone.

Instead of setting automatic backups, consider using the CD burner to back up files. Even though you'll throw the backup CDs away eventually (and those costs can add up), with CD-Rs at a around a quarter a piece, it might be cheaper and easier to do that. For a relatively small investment, you can back up all your computer files—not only the ones you create with Excel.

Network Users Have Other Options

If you're using Excel over your company's network and saving the file to a network drive, check with your network administrator before you worry too much about backup copies. Most networks have an automatic backup system that runs every night. If you need to obtain a backup copy of your file, your administrator can furnish a recent copy of the file.

Saving Workbook Summary Information

Workbook summary information, such as the name of the person who created the file, the company name, and keywords that identify the file are helpful if you work on a lot of files. If you're working in a corporate setting, summary information tells everyone in a workgroup important details about the file.

Summary information is not completed unless you fill it in manually. To set up Excel to display the Properties dialog box every time you save a file, click Tools, Options, and select the General tab. Check the box next to Prompt for Workbook Properties, as shown in Figure 3.3, and click OK. Subsequently, the Properties dialog box appears each time you save a file for the first time. If you don't want to fill in any information, click OK.

To view the summary information about a file, click Save As. Right-click the file in the list of files (if the file isn't in the current folder, you'll need to navigate to it first). Click

Properties from the pop-up menu. The Properties dialog box for the file has five tabs across the top: General, Summary, Statistics, Contents, and Custom. Click the Summary tab to view the information that's been entered about the file, as illustrated in Figure 3.4. Typically, the author and company are filled in, the information entered when your computer was initially set up.

General tab is selected

FIGURE 3.3
Set the option to prompt for Workbook Properties each time you save a file for the first time.

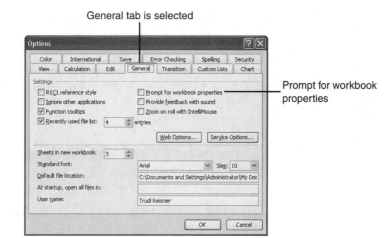

Prompt for workbook properties

3

Manager
Author

FIGURE 3.4
The summary information for the current file was entered previously.

Company

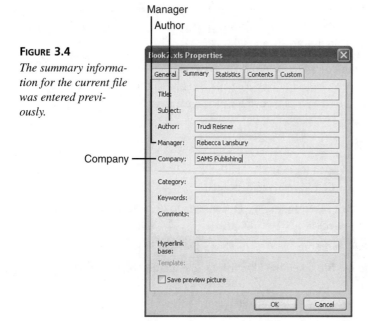

You can view or change any of the information that's displayed. Click OK to close the Properties dialog box for the file. When you return to the Save As dialog box, click Save if you made changes to the summary information. If not, click Cancel to close the Save As dialog box and return to the file on the screen.

Rearranging Your Files

While you're working in Excel, you can copy, move, and delete workbook files. You can create a new folder on the fly as you're saving a file. Excel's file management tools are fine for small, one-time jobs. If you're planning to reorganize your filing system or delete many files, My Documents and My Computer offer more powerful file-management tools.

> Remember that you need to select a file before you can do anything to it. You select a file by clicking it one time.

Deleting a File

As you learned earlier this hour, it's a good idea to save your work. There are so many ways that files can get lost or damaged. However, not every file you create needs to be saved for posterity. For example, you can discard a grocery list or some calculations that you performed in the office after you're done with it.

Files that are stored on your computer's hard drive go to the Windows Recycle Bin when you delete them. You can always go into the Recycle Bin and get them back. Files stored on network drives don't go to the local Recycle Bin. Delete a network file only if you're sure you no longer need it.

To Do: Delete a File

1. Click File, Save As to open the Save As dialog box. The Save As (and Open) dialog boxes contain Excel's file-management features.

2. A list of the Excel files saved in the My Documents folder appears. Click the Practice Save file to select it.

   Click the Delete button on the Save As toolbar, as shown in Figure 3.5.

4. Click Yes to delete the file when the Confirm Delete dialog box appears.

FIGURE 3.5
*Use the Delete button
on the Save As toolbar
to delete a file.*

File you want to delete   Delete button

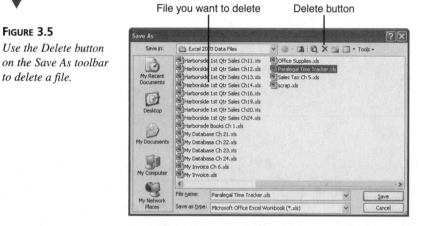

5. Because you are not deleting any other files right now, click Cancel to close the
Save As dialog box and return to the Excel screen.

> You can't delete a file that's currently open. If you get a message advising
> you that access to the file has been denied, check to see whether you or one
> of your co-workers is using the file.

Excel's Other File-Organization Tools

The Save As toolbar provides many tools to help you organize your files. Table 3.3
shows you each button and explains its function.

TABLE 3.3 Save As Toolbar Options

Button	Button Name	What It Does
	Back	Moves you to the folder you previously displayed.
	Up One Level	Moves you up to the next level of folders on your computer or network.
	Search the Web	Launches Internet Explorer. You should be connected to the Internet before you click this button.
	Delete	Deletes the selected file.
	Create New Folder	Creates a new folder beneath the current folder.

TABLE 3.3   continued

Button	Button Name	What It Does
▦	Views	Click the drop-down arrow to select a different view of the file listing in the current folder. You can even preview a selected workbook.
Tools ▾	Tools	Displays commands for printing and modifying filenames, file properties, and folders.

Summary

In this hour, you learned about saving the files you create. You also worked with some of the options Excel provides for saving your work. You also learned how to delete files you don't need any more and explored the buttons on the Save As toolbar. In Hour 4, "Managing Your Files and Workbooks," you learn how to open saved workbook files and create new ones.

Q&A

Q I accidentally closed Excel without saving my workbook. Is it gone?

A If you were working on a brand-new workbook and exited Excel without saving, the file is gone. If you were working on an existing file, only the changes you made since the last save are lost.

Q If I save a workbook file with a new name, what happens to the original file?

A Absolutely nothing! At the time you save a file with a new name, the old file closes and remains in the same folder. You can access it at any time.

Q How can I tell which one of my co-workers worked on my worksheet?

A Unless your co-worker completed the file summary information, you won't be able to determine who changed the file last. However, your network administrator might be able to tell you who saved the file last.

Q I accidentally deleted a file that I need. Can I bring the file back?

A If you did not empty the Recycle Bin after deleting the file, you should be able to restore that file. Go to your Windows Desktop, right-click on the Recycle Bin icon, and choose Open. Select the file in the list, and choose File, Restore.

Q When I attempt to delete a file, I see a message telling me that access to the file is denied.

A You're deleting a file that is currently open. Check to see whether you or one of your co-workers is using the file.

HOUR 4

Managing Your Files and Workbooks

The topics in this hour cover:

- How to create blank workbooks
- How to open workbooks
- The best ways to view your workbook
- How to work with range names
- The easiest methods for navigating workbooks and worksheets

In this hour, you learn how to create new workbooks, how to open saved files, and how to navigate through individual worksheets. At the end of this hour, you'll be able to find workbooks and open multiple files. Ready? Let's go.

Creating a Blank Workbook

When Excel opens, a blank workbook is displayed, waiting for your input. By default, the workbook contains three blank worksheets. You can enter any text or data on the worksheets that you want. The working title for the blank workbook is something like Book1. (The number following the word *Book* is based on the number of blank workbooks you've opened during the current Excel session.) When you save the file, the name you type overwrites the default name.

While you're working in Excel, you can open a new blank workbook by clicking the New button on the Standard toolbar, or by pressing Ctrl+N. Alternatively, you can click the New command on the File menu.

> You learn about using templates in Hour 6, "Using Excel Templates."

Creating Workbooks with the New Workbook Task Pane

With the New Workbook task pane (see Figure 4.1), you can create new workbooks in several other ways. The task pane is organized into three sections: New, Templates, and Recently Used Templates.

FIGURE 4.1
The New Workbook task pane for opening and creating workbooks.

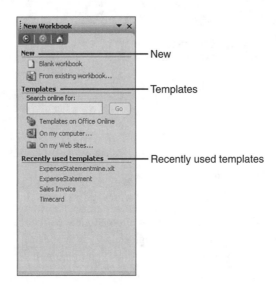

The New option features the following:

- Blank Workbook—Create a new blank workbook.
- From Existing Workbook—Creates a new workbook based on an existing workbook. Click Choose Workbook to display the New From Existing Workbook dialog box. From here, select a workbook and click the Create New button.

The Templates on Microsoft Office Online option presents the following choices:

- Search—If you already know the type or name of the template you want to use, type the template name or keyword in the Search box: **calendar**, for example. Excel will display a list of templates related to the keyword you entered. Click the template you want and Excel creates a new workbook based on that template.

- Templates Home Page—If you don't know the name of a template, click Templates Home Page to find a template at Microsoft Office Online. On the Templates home page, the templates are organized by category. Click the links to find the template you want to use, and click Edit in Excel to download the template into a new workbook. The template link will appear at the top of the list in the Other templates section in the New Workbook task pane for your convenience.

The choices available with the Other Templates option are as follows:

- On My Computer—Click On My Computer and Excel displays the general templates on your computer in the Templates dialog box. Select a template and click OK. Excel creates a new workbook based on the selected template.

- On My Web Sites—Click On My Web Sites and Excel displays your favorite Web sites, or templates from the Microsoft Web site.

Opening an Existing Workbook

Excel provides many ways for you to open workbook files. If the file you want is one that you've worked with recently, you can launch Excel and open the file at the same time. Click the Windows Start button, choose My Recent Documents from the Start menu, and then click the file you want from the list of the most recent documents you opened.

If Excel is already open, or you aren't sure of the exact name or location of the file, your best bet is to use Excel's Open command. Click the Open button on the Standard toolbar, or choose File, Open, to display the Open dialog box. You'll feel comfortable with the Open dialog box (see Figure 4.2) because it looks and acts very much like the Save As dialog box you worked with in the last hour.

> The last four files you opened are listed at the bottom of the File menu. If you've recently opened and closed a file, click the File menu and then click the file you want from the list.

File list can contain
files and subfolders

Look in box

FIGURE 4.2

*The Open dialog box
looks similar to the
Save As box.*

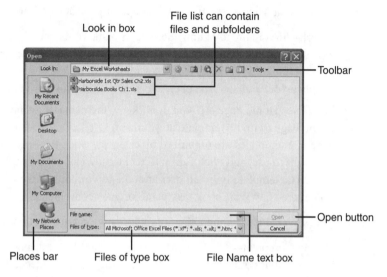

Toolbar

Open button

Places bar   Files of type box   File Name text box

Click the file you want to open from the File list and then click Open. The Open dialog box closes, and the workbook you selected appears on the Excel screen. If the file you want isn't shown on the File list for the current folder, click the drop-down arrow next to Look In and navigate to the correct folder.

When you get really busy and you're working with many different files, you might forget that you've already opened a workbook. If you try to open a file that's already open on your computer, Excel does not open the file again. Instead, it displays the already-open file message on your computer screen.

Different Open Options

Excel offers five options for opening a file. After you've selected the file you want to open, choose one of the options by clicking the drop-down arrow to the right of the Open button (see Figure 4.3). If you don't select an option, Excel assumes you want to open the file with the Open option, granting you full rights.

- Open—You have full rights to view, modify, or save the workbook.
- Open Read-Only—The file can be viewed or modified, but you'll have to save it with another name.

FIGURE 4.3

Options for opening a file.

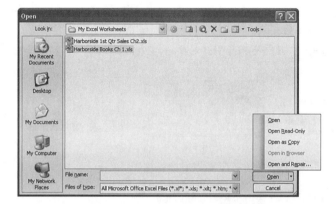

- Open as Copy—When you open a workbook as a copy, a new copy of the workbook is created in the folder that contains the original workbook. You might choose this option if you're working on a group project where you're assigned a specific duty.

- Open in Browser—Opens the workbook in your default browser.

- Open and Repair—Opens and repairs a workbook that you were having trouble opening.

> If you attempt to open an Excel workbook that one of your co-workers has already opened, Excel tells you that the file is in use. In this case, you can open the file in Read-Only format, but you must save any changes you make to a new filename. Don't do it! Multiple copies of the same file with slightly different data are hard to manage and track.

Making Use of the Getting Started Task Pane

Another way to open and create Excel workbooks is with the Getting Started task pane, as shown in Figure 4.4. The Getting Started task pane is organized into two sections: Microsoft Office Online and Open.

The Microsoft Office Online choices are as follows:

- Connect to Microsoft Office Online—Connect to the Microsoft Office Web page.

- Get the latest news about using Excel—Connects you to the latest information on Excel at Microsoft Office Online.

- Get online training for Excel—Connects you to online Excel courses at Microsoft Office Online.
- Search—Get online Help on any Excel topic.

FIGURE 4.4
The Getting Started task pane for opening and creating work-books.

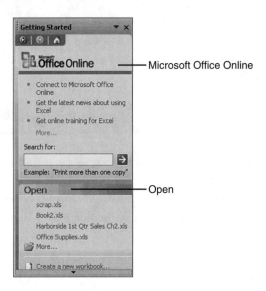

With the Open options, here's what you can do:

- Workbook name—Excel displays up to four workbook files you recently opened.
- More—If the workbook does not appear in the list, click the More link to open a workbook from the Open dialog box.
- Create new workbook—If you want to create a new blank workbook, click the Create a New Workbook link.

If you cannot see all the information at the bottom of the task pane, move the mouse pointer to the down arrow at the bottom border of the task pane. The information scrolls up so that you can view the rest of the information. To scroll up, move the mouse pointer to the up arrow at the top border of the task pane, beneath the task pane toolbar. Now you can see the information at the top of the task pane.

Searching for the Right File

It happens to everyone at one time or another—you navigate to what you think is the correct folder, but you can't find a particular file. Or you know that you saved a file, but just can't remember the exact name. If you can't locate a file, don't fret. Excel can help you find what you're looking for.

The File Search feature helps you search for files saved on your local hard drive or a network drive. You can search for a file by the filename or type, or by data within the file or the file properties.

Using File Search to locate files requires a little preparation. Table 4.1 shows you search tips that help you locate the files you need.

TABLE 4.1   Search Tips

If You're Looking For	Type	Example
A phrase	" "	"Awards for the First Quarter"
One character	?	Thomas Ega?
Multiple characters	*	Sales Fig*
One or another word	,	Sales, Awards
One word with another word	&	Sales & Awards
Does not contain	-	Awards – Premiums

In the next To Do exercise, you search for the Budget file you created during Hour 2, "Entering Data." If Excel isn't already open and visible on your computer screen, open the program before you begin the exercise.

To Do: Find a File with the Basic Search Task Pane

1. Close the Sales 1st Qtr file.

2. Choose File, File Search. The Basic File Search task pane appears on the right side of the workbook window (see Figure 4.5).

3. In the Search Text box, type **Sales 1st Qtr**.

   In the Other Search Options area, you can specify a location and a file type.

4. Click Search. Excel looks through the drives and folders on My Computer, by default. In a moment, the results of the search are displayed in the Search Results task pane.

   To stop the search, click Stop at the bottom of the task pane. To modify your search criteria, click Modify.

FIGURE 4.5

The Basic File Search task pane for finding an existing file.

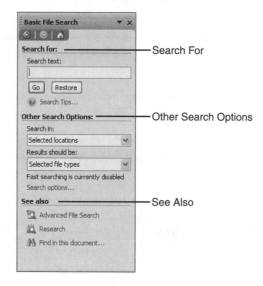

5. Point to the Sales 1st Qtr file and click. The Sales 1st Qtr file you worked on previously appears on your screen.

6. (Optional) To create a new workbook based on a file in the Search Results list, point to the file in the list, click the down arrow, and choose New From This File. On the menu, you can also copy a link to the Clipboard and view the properties of the file.

> At the bottom of the Basic File Search task pane, you can click Find In This Document to display the Find and Replace dialog box and search for text in the current workbook.

Working with Workbooks and Worksheets

An Excel workbook is made up of individual worksheets. By default, three worksheets are set up with each workbook file. You can add or delete as many worksheets as you want. Each worksheet is an individual portion of the workbook and does not need to link to the other worksheets.

Getting a View of the Workbook

A workbook is a pretty big place. No matter how large your computer monitor, you will never be able to see all the rows and columns of all the individual worksheets at the same time. Sometimes it helps to remind yourself that even though you might not be able to see all of the data, it's still there.

The vertical and horizontal scrollbars on each worksheet provide some navigational aids. Each scrollbar has directional arrows on either side of the bar. Click the directional arrow that points in the direction you want to go.

Another way to jump from cell to cell in a worksheet is by typing the address of the cell you want to move to in the Name box. (The Name box is located above the column labels at the left side of the screen.)

To move from worksheet to worksheet, click the tab of the worksheet you want to bring to the front.

Using Ranges

If you know the cell address of the data you need to locate, you'll have no trouble moving to the spot. But unless you have a photographic memory, you probably won't remember the cell locations of all your important data. Even if you can spout cell locations, the cell addresses of your data change as you add and delete cells, rows, and columns.

Ranges provide a better way to organize and describe your data. A *range* is a rectangular block of cells that can be named with a descriptive name. Instead of trying to remember where the Utilities budget is located, you can specify the range name that holds the information to have Excel whisk to the first cell of the range. You can also use ranges for formatting and printing, and you can use range names in formulas.

A range can consist of one cell (after all, one cell is a rectangular block), or it can comprise the entire worksheet. Each range has two anchor points: the top-left and bottom-right cells. You can add or delete cells, rows, or columns within the body of the range, but you cannot make changes at either anchor point of the range.

Assigning Range Names

Instead of calling a range by its coordinates, it makes much more sense to assign it a descriptive name. Follow the rules shown here when you assign names to your ranges:

- Begin each range name with an underscore character or a letter.
- Keep your range names short, descriptive, and to the point.

- You can't use spaces or hyphens in range names, so separate words with the underscore character; for example, [Jan_Sales].

- You can use upper- and lowercase letters.

In the next To Do exercise, you set up and name some ranges in your Sales 1st Qtr workbook. The workbook should be open and visible on the screen before you begin.

To Do: Set Range Names

1. Select cells A4 through A8 on the Sales 1st Qtr workbook. These cells make up the sales categories.

2. When the cells appear highlighted, click the Insert menu, choose Name, and then choose Define. The Define Name dialog box appears, as shown in Figure 4.6. Excel has assigned the range name to the text shown in the first cell.

FIGURE 4.6

The name Excel assigns to the range is selected so you can change the range.

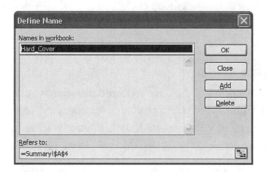

3. Because the default name is already highlighted, you don't need to delete it to type a new name. For this example, type **Categories** and click OK. The box closes, and the range name is added to the workbook.

4. Excel provides an alternative way of assigning range names. Highlight the cells that hold the labels January through March (B3:D3). Click inside the Name box and type **Months**. When you're through, your screen should look like the example in Figure 4.7.

5. Deselect the highlighted cells by pressing the right arrow key.

6. Move to the first range you defined by typing **Categories** in the Name box and pressing Enter. The mouse pointer moves to the first cell in the range, and the cells in the range appear highlighted.

7. Use a keystroke shortcut to view all the range names in the workbook. Press Ctrl+G to open the Go To dialog box.

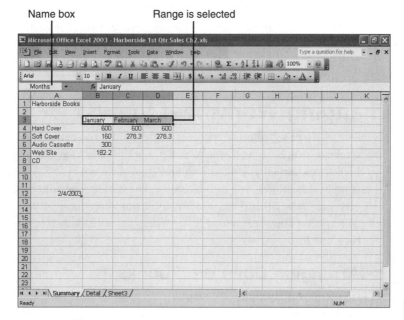

FIGURE 4.7

The Name box holds the range name.

Name box   Range is selected

8. The Go To dialog box contains a listing of all the named ranges within the worksheet, both by coordinates and assigned names. Click Months and click OK.

9. The Months range is selected. Deselect the cells by pressing the right arrow key.

Editing Range Names

You're never locked into the ranges you create. You can edit the range coordinates and rename or delete the range. Click the Insert menu, choose Name, and then choose Define to open the Define Name dialog box. When you click a range, the name appears in the Names In Workbook text box. To rename a range, type a new name in the Names In Workbook box. Then you can delete the old range name by selecting the name in the Names In Workbook box, and clicking the Delete button.

The range coordinates appear in the Refers To text box and are represented by the worksheet and anchor cells of the range. A range name might look something like =Sheet1!$A$4:$A$12. Although it might seem somewhat cryptic, each character has a distinct meaning. The column and row indicators appear after each $ character. If you want to change the range coordinates, replace only the column letters and row letters with the new coordinates for the range. Take care not to delete or change any other characters.

The dollar signs in the range name indicate absolute cell references. You'll learn about absolute cell references during Hour 5, "Letting Excel Do the Math."

Changing Worksheet Views

One of Excel's greatest strengths is its flexibility. You can change the look of the Excel screen to match the work you're doing. For example, if you've opened several workbooks, you can set your screen so that all of them are visible. If you're working on a complicated project, you can maximize the program and adjust the screen view to magnify your data. Other times you can zoom out to see more of the worksheet. You can even split a large worksheet into separate windows, called *panes*, to keep you from scrolling back and forth.

Arranging Open Workbooks

If you're working with more than one Excel workbook, jumping back and forth between them becomes tedious very quickly. Instead of viewing one file at a time, you can set Excel to display all the open files on the screen.

To Do: Arrange Open Workbooks

1. When you've opened more than one Excel workbook, click the Window menu and choose Arrange. The Arrange Windows dialog box, shown in Figure 4.8, appears.

FIGURE 4.8

The Arrange Windows dialog box enables you to set your screen to view more than one workbook.

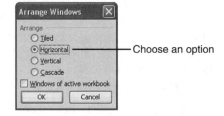

Choose an option

2. Click the option button next to the option you want. The following options are available:

   Tiled—The open workbooks are arranged in individual tiles; the more open files, the smaller the individual tiles.

   Horizontal—The workbooks are displayed in horizontal strips.

   Vertical—The workbooks appear in vertical strips.

▼ Cascade—The workbooks are reduced in size and displayed diagonally. The top
workbook is the active one. If you chose this option, you'll need to click in one of
the inactive workbooks to bring it to the top.

3. Click OK to close the Arrange Windows dialog box. The workbooks are arranged
on your screen in the view you selected. Figure 4.9 shows a vertical arrangement of
▲ three windows.

FIGURE 4.9

Arrange windows in vertical strips.

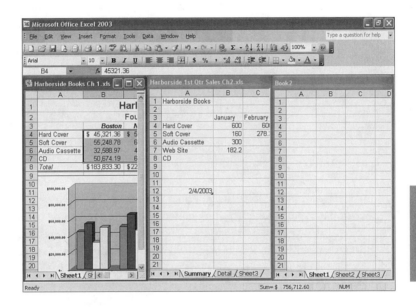

 Each time you open a workbook file, an icon for that file appears on the
Windows taskbar. Position your mouse pointer in the taskbar icon to see the
full name of the file. Even if you don't arrange the workbooks on your computer screen, you can easily see how many workbook files are open by looking at the taskbar.

Comparing Workbooks Side by Side

Comparing data in two open workbooks and bouncing from one to the other to view the
data can be a painstaking task. Instead of examining one file at a time, you can set Excel
to display both open files side by side on the screen.

With the two workbooks open, choose Window, Compare Side by Side. Excel displays
one workbook in the top half and the other in the bottom half of the Excel window. You
also see the Compare Side by Side toolbar, as illustrated in Figure 4.10.

FIGURE 4.10

Compare Side by Side lets you compare data in two workbooks at once.

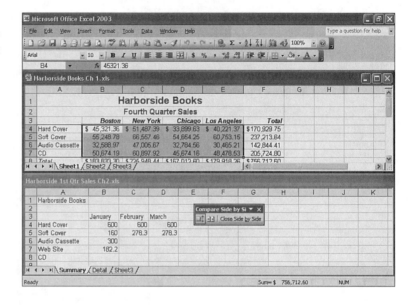

You can scroll simultaneously in both workbooks, but if you want to turn off this feature, click the Synchronous Scrolling button on the Compare Side by Side toolbar. If you want to reset the window position in a workbook, move to the new location in one of the workbooks, and click the Resets Window Position button on the Compare Side by Side toolbar. To return to viewing individual workbooks, click the Break Side by Side button on the Compare Side by Side toolbar.

Zooming In and Out

Change the view of your worksheet by zooming in and out. To change the zoom percentage, click the Zoom button on the Standard toolbar. Choose the size at which you want to view the screen.

The lower the percentage, the more you see of the screen. However, at a low percentage, like 25%, you probably won't be able to read the text. Use the low percentages to examine the look of the screen. If you choose a high percentage, you see less of the total screen, but each cell appears larger.

Another way to adjust the change the zoom percentage is to click the View menu and choose Zoom. The Zoom dialog box, as shown in Figure 4.11, enables you to choose from a variety of magnification levels. The Custom selection allows you to specify a level as low as 10% or as high as 400%.

FIGURE 4.11

The Zoom dialog box lets you control the view of the screen.

Figure 4.12 shows data on a worksheet at a magnification level of 200%.

FIGURE 4.12

Zooming in to get a closer look at your data.

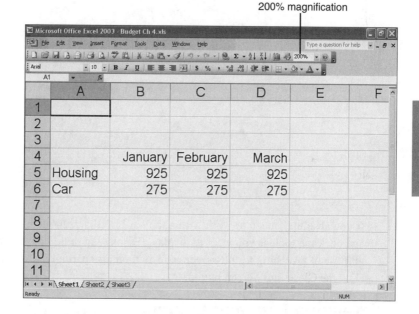

200% magnification

4

Additionally, you can highlight a block of cells and choose Fit Selection to magnify the block so that its cells all fit in the window. After you adjust the Zoom magnification, you can change it back or switch to a new percentage at any time.

Changing to Full-Screen View

Most times, when you're working in Excel, it's helpful to be able to see the toolbar buttons, the title bar, and other screen elements. However, these elements take up valuable screen real estate and reduce your viewing area. Excel makes it easy to switch to a full-screen view, in which the worksheet, sheet tabs, and menu bar are displayed. You can toggle between full-screen and normal view at any time.

To display the worksheet in full-screen view, click the View menu and choose Full Screen. Your screen should look similar to the one in Figure 4.13.

Click this button to return to Normal view

FIGURE 4.13

Full-screen view shows more of the worksheet.

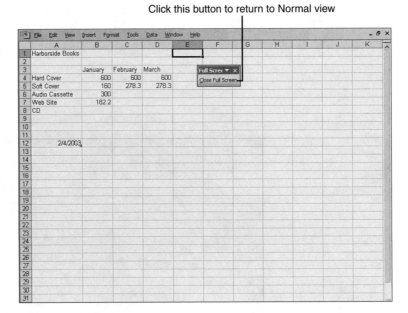

If you absolutely need to work with a toolbar in full-screen view, open the View menu and click the toolbar you want to display. (Displaying more than one toolbar defeats the purpose of switching to full-screen, so add toolbars sparingly.) To return to normal view, click the Close Full Screen button.

Keeping Row and Column Headings Visible

Many large worksheets contain row and column headings that identify the data. However, as you scroll the worksheet, the headings become obscured. Instead of trying to guess which row or column heading matches the current cell, you can freeze the headings into panes. Here's how:

- Freeze the top horizontal pane by clicking the row *below* where you want the split to appear.
- Freeze the left vertical pane by clicking the column to the right of where you want the split to appear.

- Freeze both the upper and left panes by clicking the cell below and to the right of where you want the split to appear.

NEW TERM *Pane*—An individual section of a window.

Next, click the Window menu and choose Freeze Panes. Figure 4.14 displays a worksheet window that has been split into panes. The row and column headings remain on the screen as you scroll through the worksheet, enabling you to always know where you are. You can unfreeze the window any time by clicking Window, Unfreeze Panes.

FIGURE 4.14

The row and column headings remain constant.

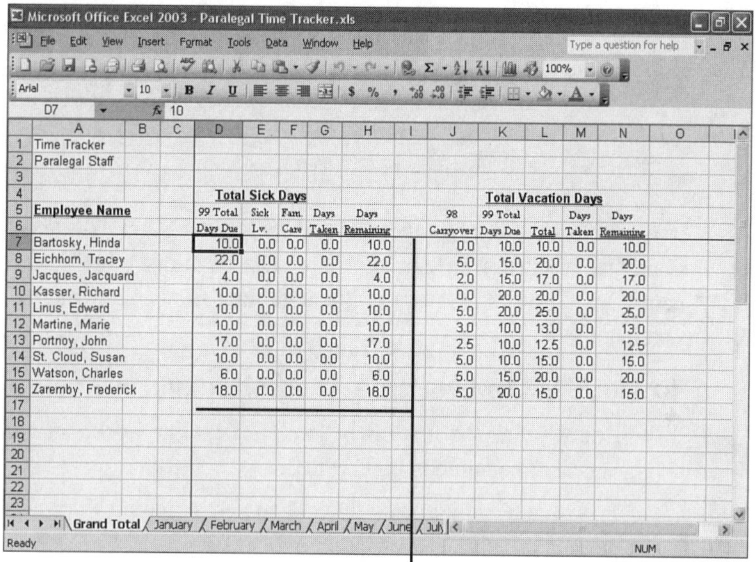

The gridlines indicate where the panes are frozen

Workbook and Worksheet Navigation Tools

In a large workbook, you might create many different worksheets. Why not? Individual worksheets make good sense. They allow you to organize your data on separate sheets. The workbook in Figure 4.14 is a good example for separate sheets; the first worksheet holds the total vacation days and total sick days for each employee, and each monthly worksheet tracks the time by days and hours.

You can add or delete as many worksheets to a workbook file as you want. By default, Excel names the sheets with a number. The name is displayed on the worksheet's tab. Most times, the names Sheet1, Sheet2, and so on aren't descriptive of the sheet's purpose; you can easily change the sheet names to be more descriptive.

Moving around a large workbook requires a few simple navigational skills. Clicking a worksheet's tab brings that worksheet to the front of the screen and makes it active. If your workbook contains many sheets, or if the sheet names are long, it's hard to see all the tabs.

Each workbook file is set up with worksheet scroll arrow buttons, located at the far end of the horizontal scrollbar. The arrow buttons always appear, no matter which worksheet you're working in. Use the arrow buttons to scroll through the individual sheet names. When the sheet name you want appears, click its tab to make the sheet active.

Scrolling through the worksheet tabs provides only a view of the names of other worksheets in the workbook. You must click a worksheet name to make it active and view its contents.

In the next exercise, you add worksheets to your Sales 1st Qtr workbook. You learn how to rename a worksheet. You also copy data from one worksheet to another, using a range name. Make sure the Sales 1st Qtr workbook file is open and visible on the screen before you begin.

To Do: Set Up Multiple Worksheets

1. Double-click the first tab of the Sales 1st Qtr workbook that currently reads Sheet1. The name is highlighted.

2. Type **Summary** and press Enter. The new name now appears on the worksheet tab.

Although worksheet names can contain up to 256 characters, keep the names descriptive, short, and simple. Short names are easier to read as you scroll through the worksheets. Additionally, formulas that reference a cell in a worksheet are easier to construct and edit if the name is short.

You can rename a worksheet from a shortcut menu. Right-click the tab you want to rename and choose Rename from the shortcut menu. Type the new name and press Enter.

3. Add a new worksheet by clicking the worksheet tab that's before the position in which you want to insert the new sheet. In this case, click the tab that reads Sheet3.

You can change the default number of worksheets in a new workbook from three to any number you want. Choose Tools, Options and click the General tab. In the Sheets In A New workbook box, enter the number of sheets you want added when you create a new workbook.

4. Click the Insert menu and choose Worksheet. Excel inserts a new tab with a default name. Double-click the tab of the new worksheet and type **Detail**.

You can color code your worksheet tab, making it easier to depict one sheet from another. To do so, select the sheet you want to color. Choose Format, Sheet, Tab Color. Click the color you want and click OK.

5. The second worksheet is not needed in the current workbook. Right-click the tab that reads Sheet2 and choose Delete.

FIGURE 4.15

Set up two worksheets.

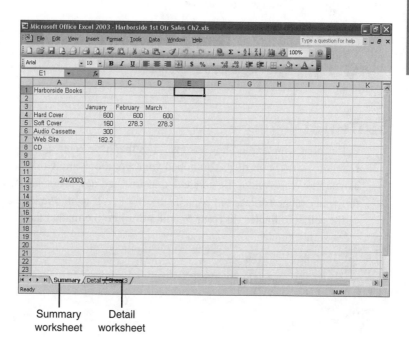

Summary worksheet   Detail worksheet

4

> Delete worksheets with care. When you delete a worksheet, all the data it contains is erased forever.

6. Click the Summary tab to make that worksheet active. When the Summary worksheet appears on the screen, click in the Name box and type **Months**. Excel selects the names of the months (cells B3 through D3).

7. Click the Copy button on the Standard toolbar.

8. Click the Details tab and click cell B3 in the Details worksheet.

9. Click the Paste button on the Standard toolbar. The month labels now appear on both the Details worksheet and the Summary Sheet.

10. Save the Sales 1st Qtr worksheet by clicking the Save button on the Standard toolbar.

11. If you're planning to practice your file- and workbook-management skills, or you want to move into the next hour, leave Excel open. Otherwise, close Excel by opening the File menu and choosing Exit.

> The Sales 1st Qtr worksheet is a work-in-progress. You continue working with it during the next hour.

Summary

In this hour, you learned how to open files that have been saved previously and how to search for workbook files. You honed your workbook and worksheet navigational skills as you moved around a file and added and named new worksheets. You also learned how to specify range names, and copied a block of cells using the block's range name instead of the cell coordinates. In Hour 5, you move into the mathematical arena, as you learn to work with formulas.

Q&A

Q Several of my co-workers and I opened the same workbook file at the same time. Why couldn't we see each other's changes?

A When more than one person opens the same file, the file is opened in read-only format by all but the first person who opened it. In effect, the read-only files are copies of the file. Changes made to the read-only copies cannot be saved to the same filename as the original file.

Q I created an Excel file in the office. The filename appeared on the list of the last four files I opened, but Excel couldn't open it when I took my laptop home. Why?

A If you save a file on a network drive, you must be logged in or connected to the network to open it. To work at home, you need to save a copy of the file to a floppy disk. You can copy the file to your local hard drive from the disk. Then you can open the file locally.

Q I deleted a worksheet that I thought was meaningless, and now some of the other worksheets are showing up with funny characters. What's wrong?

A You have a big problem! The cells in the worksheet you deleted were referenced in other worksheets. Unfortunately, when you delete a worksheet, it's gone for good. If you're working on a network, ask your network administrator whether you can retrieve an older copy of the file from the network backup.

4

Hour 5

Letting Excel Do the Math

This hour covers the following topics:

- What a formula can do for you
- How to create a simple formula
- How to use AutoSum
- How to use range names in formulas
- When to use relative and absolute addressing
- How to copy formulas
- How to troubleshoot formula errors

Unless you were born with a mathematical mind, numbers probably scare you. Creating a meaningful spreadsheet usually involves lots of numbers—enough to bring all but the bravest souls to their knees.

Relax! In this hour, you learn how to let Excel do the math for you. Now you learn how to add some power to the sales worksheet by adding formulas to it. Formulas take most of the hard work out of the arithmetic portion of your worksheets. When you use Excel, you can put away your calculator, scratch pads, and pencils.

Why Use Formulas?

Formulas are Excel's most powerful aid for getting your work done. Excel formulas handle the mathematical chores in your worksheet. In its simplest form, a formula is a quick calculation, similar to one you'd make on a calculator or adding machine. However, you can also use a formula to make predictions, figure out a car payment, or perform some other complex task.

 Formulas—The way Excel performs calculations in your worksheets. Another way to describe Excel formulas is to call them "equations."

Formulas speed up the creation of your worksheets. You don't need to worry about whether a calculation is correct, because Excel doesn't make mistakes. Best of all, you can change any value contained in a formula, and Excel will update the results automatically.

How Formulas Work

A formula is a cell entry that calculates values to return a result. Each Excel formula must have three key elements: the equal sign (=) that signifies that the entry is a formula, the values or cell references to be calculated, and the mathematical operators, such as a plus sign (+) for addition or a minus sign (-) for subtraction.

All Excel formulas must begin with the equal sign. The equal sign tells Excel that the entry is a formula. If your formula begins without an equal sign, Excel treats it as a regular cell entry and doesn't perform the calculation.

> If you begin a formula with a plus sign (+), Excel converts it to an equal sign (=). That's because Lotus 1-2-3, another spreadsheet program, uses the plus sign as its opening formula-entry character. Excel makes it easy for Lotus users to switch to Excel.

Mathematical Operators

When you create a formula in Excel, you need to include an operator. All formulas must contain mathematical operators so that Excel knows what calculation to perform. Table 5.1 lists the arithmetic operators used in Excel.

TABLE 5.1 Excel Formula Operators

Operator	What It Does
+	Addition
-	Subtraction
*	Multiplication
/	Division
=	Equal to
<	Less than
<=	Less than or equal to
>	Greater than
>=	Greater than or equal to
<>	Not equal to
%	Percentage
^	Exponentiation

Figure 5.1 shows a very simple formula. The intent is pretty clear—the formula asks Excel to add 20,000 to 1,000.

Plus sign (+) indicates addition operator

FIGURE 5.1

The formula in cell D4 contains a mathematical operator.

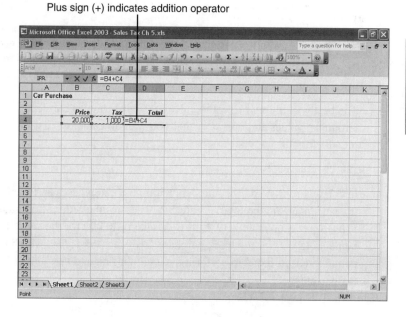

5

Order of Operations

In a simple formula, such as the one shown in Figure 5.1, Excel is asked to perform only one calculation. However, formulas can often contain instructions to perform multiple calculations. If you were to talk out a more complicated formula, you might say something like this: "Add together the price of a car that costs $20,000 and a truck that costs $18,000 and then multiply the combined price by 5% sales tax to determine the sales tax due on the combined cost of the vehicles."

You might think that you'd enter the value for the formula this way:

```
=20,000+18,000*.050
```

However, if you typed that formula in a cell, the formula would be incorrect. The reason is that Excel uses something called operator precedence to perform calculations. *Operator precedence* determines the order in which calculations are performed. Calculations are performed from left to right in the following order:

1. All operations enclosed in parentheses
2. All exponential operations
3. All multiplication and division operations
4. All addition and subtraction operations

> Many old-style math teachers explain the mathematical order of operations with the phrase *My Dear Aunt Sally*. The first letter of each word stands for its mathematical equivalent: multiply, divide, add, and then subtract.

The best way to force Excel to calculate your formulas correctly is to use parentheses. Group the values and operators that you want to calculate first in parentheses. For example, the formula

```
(20,000+18,000)*.050
```

tells Excel to first add the numbers within the parentheses and then to calculate the sales tax percentage on the total. Figure 5.2 illustrates the order of operations with the formula =(B4+B7)*.0.05 in cell B9. Cell B4 contains 20,000 for the car purchase and cell B7 contains 18,000 for the truck purchase. The sales tax is 5%, which is .050. The parentheses tell Excel to perform the addition first and then multiply the sum by the tax percentage.

Excel performs the
multiplication second

FIGURE 5.2

*The formula in cell B9
groups the values and
mathematical operator.*

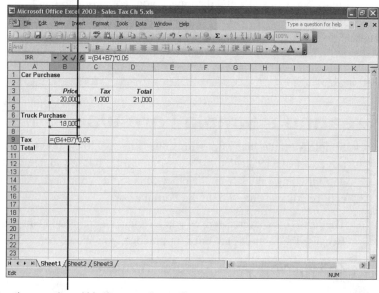

Excel calculates the equation within the parentheses first

You can even nest parentheses within parentheses to further break down how you want
Excel to calculate your formula. Just remember that each opening parenthesis must have a
closing parenthesis. If your formula does not contain the required number of parentheses,
Excel displays an error message similar to the one in Figure 5.3. Excel even attempts to
place the missing parenthesis. If your formula doesn't contain the proper number of parentheses, Excel displays each parentheses set in a different color, to help you track your error.

5

FIGURE 5.3

*Excel tells you when a
formula has not been
entered correctly.*

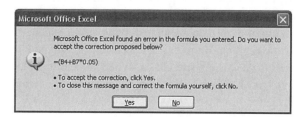

When Excel detects a formula error because of too many or too few parentheses, it attempts to place the missing characters. If you let Excel correct
your formula, check it over carefully. After all, Excel doesn't know what your
calculation should accomplish.

Your best choice is to make the correction yourself. When you click No, Excel displays a
message that provides further information on how to make the correction, as shown in
Figure 5.4. Click OK and then make your correction to the formula.

FIGURE 5.4

Excel tells you the for-
mula is missing a
parenthesis.

Creating a Simple Formula

Simple formulas that work with values are easy to create. In essence, simple formulas
use Excel like a calculator. These simple formulas are somewhat limiting because they
don't use any values from the other cells in the worksheet. You can enter a formula into a
cell, or you can enter it into the Formula bar.

The next To Do exercise gives you a chance to create and edit some simple formulas.
Because the formulas are only for practice, you should be working on a blank worksheet.

To Do: Work with Simple Formulas

1. The first formula adds a series of numbers together. Click into a blank cell on the
   worksheet and type =35+35+35. When you're done typing, press the Enter key.
   Notice that the result of the calculation, 105, appears in the cell. The formula is
   displayed in the Formula bar when the cell is selected.

2. Amend the formula by clicking it and then pressing F2. The formula is displayed
   in the cell with the cursor flashing at the end of the formula. Type *15 and press
   Enter.

3. Now edit the formula to add some parentheses. Double-click the cell that contains
   the formula. The formula appears. Notice that because you're in Edit mode, many
   toolbar buttons are unavailable. Use the left arrow keys to move to the first character to the right of the equal sign and then type an opening parenthesis. Use the
   right arrow key to move to the last character before the multiplication operator (*)
   and then type a closing parenthesis. When your formula looks like the one in
   Figure 5.5, press Enter. Notice how the order of calculations changes the result of
   the calculation.

The keystrokes that move you to the beginning and end of a file also work
while you're editing a formula. Press Ctrl+Home to quickly move the cursor
to the beginning of the formula. Press Ctrl+End to move to the end.

Excel calculates the equation
within the parentheses first

FIGURE 5.5

The parentheses change the order of operation in the formula.

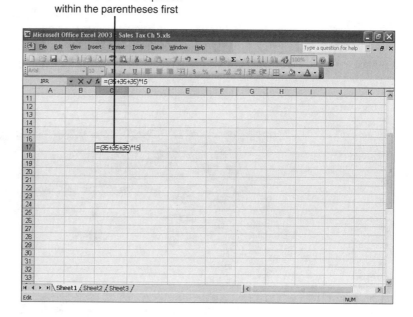

Referencing Cells

In addition to typing values into your worksheets, you can enter references to cells. Using cell references is often more effective than typing actual values when you want to build formulas. If a value in a referenced cell changes, the formula that points to the reference is updated automatically. Best of all, one cell can be referenced in an unlimited number of formulas. A cell reference does not need to contain an operator unless you want to use it to perform a calculation.

For example, if you're calculating the amount of sales tax due on a car purchase, you can reference the cell that contains the current sales tax percentage in each formula. If the sales tax percentage changes or you enter it incorrectly, updating the percentage amount also updates the car purchase formula, as shown in Figure 5.6.

Each time you reference a cell while you're building a formula, you need to type an operator. Otherwise, Excel won't store the cell reference, and your formula will be incomplete.

5

Don't press the Enter key while you're still constructing a formula by pointing to cells. Pressing Enter is equivalent to clicking the green check mark
and tells Excel that the formula is complete.

Sales tax is referenced cell in formula
Sales tax

FIGURE 5.6

*Referencing the sales
tax percentage in a
formula.*

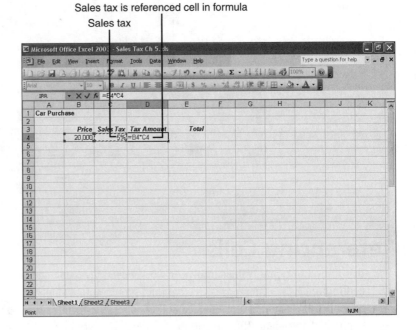

If you need to edit a formula, press F2 and make your changes. You can type the values
and cell references, or you can point to them with the mouse. Click the Enter button
when the formula is complete.

Excel uses color coding to assist you when you're editing a cell, as illustrated in Figure
5.7. Each cell reference and the cell it refers to in the worksheet are displayed in the same
color. You can use the color coding to identify which references in the formula match
which cells in the worksheet.

First cell reference

Formula in Formula bar

FIGURE 5.7
Press F2 to edit a formula.

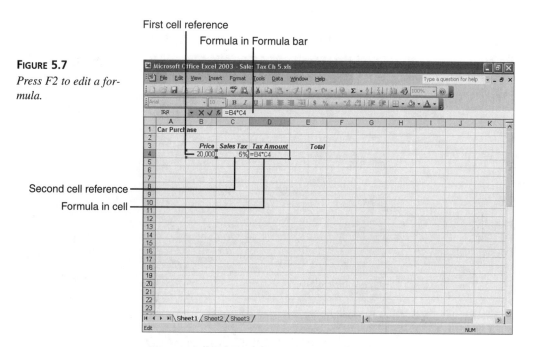

Second cell reference ―

Formula in cell ―

Using AutoSum

The AutoSum button on the Standard toolbar is one of the most useful tools in Excel. AutoSum automatically totals a range of values. Click into the cell where you want the total to appear and click the AutoSum button. The SUM formula appears in the cell and a marquee surrounds the range of values in the column. Click the AutoSum button again. A total of the range in the column directly appears in the last cell.

AutoSum can total cells in a row, as well as a column. Click the first empty cell in a row that contains values and click AutoSum, as illustrated in Figure 5.8. The SUM formula appears in the cell and a marquee surrounds the range of values in the row. Click the AutoSum button again. The total of the preceding cells appears in the last cell.

AutoSum adds ranges that contain values. If an empty cell appears in the column or row, AutoSum does not add cells that appear before the blank one.

5

Range of values
Sum formula   AutoSum button

FIGURE 5.8

Using AutoSum to total cells in a row.

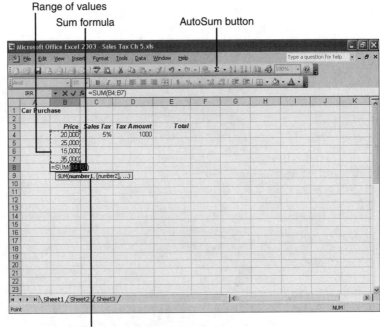

Screen Tip shows you how to build a SUM formula

Using Range Names in Formulas

Using range names can sometimes help you create and troubleshoot formulas. The use of range names is especially important if more than one person is going to be working on the file, because names are easier to understand than cell references. For example, a cell named SALES_TAX would make a sales tax calculation easy to understand.

 Review the information in Hour 4, "Managing Your Files and Workbooks," if you need help naming a range.

You must name a range before you can use it in a formula. If you remember the range name, you can type it into the formula in place of a cell reference. Remember, though, that you must type the range name perfectly, or Excel won't accept it. If you don't remember the exact name of a range, let Excel provide the name for you.

When you come to the place in the formula where you want to insert a range name, click the Insert menu and choose Name and then Paste. The Paste Name dialog box, as displayed in Figure 5.9, appears. Select the range name you want to include in the formula and click OK. The box closes, and the range name is included in the formula.

FIGURE 5.9

Choose a range name to include in your formula.

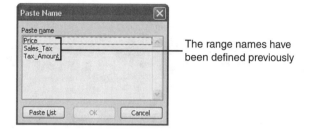

The range names have been defined previously

> You can select the cells to name and then type a name in the Name Box that appears above the Column A heading. For example, if you select A1:A9 and label it Salaries, you can enter `=SUM(Salaries)` in some other cell.

Using Relative and Absolute Addressing

When you enter a formula that contains cell references into a cell, Excel keeps track of it in two ways. The first is to record the value of that cell and use the value in the calculation. The second way is to keep track of the relative position of the cells in the formula to one another.

Here's how relative addressing works if you enter the formula `=a1+a2` in cell A3.

If the formula could talk, it would say, "Take the cell two rows above me and add the value of that cell to the cell one row above me and display the results in my cell." (Talking formulas would be great, wouldn't they!) If you copied the formula in A3 to C3, the new formula would read `=C1+C2`. Why? Because the new formula would be looking at the cells one and two rows above it.

Relative cell referencing is great if you're adding a number of like columns. Imagine how tedious it would be to have to create a formula in the total column for each day. With relative cell referencing, you create the formula in the first total column for January and then copy it to all the other months.

What if your calculation isn't so straightforward? Suppose you want to calculate the projected payroll for the next six months. You would multiply the percentage amount of increase by the current payroll amount. For example, The formula in cell B9 would be `=B18*B6`, as shown in Figure 5.10. When you copy the formula to cells in other columns, Excel adjusts the cell references for each column automatically.

After you copy the formula in cell B9 to C9, the February payroll projection in cell C9 would be `=C18*C6`. Although the cell reference C6 (February revenue) is correct, the cell reference C18 references an empty cell. The formula for cell C9 should be `=B18*C6` rather than `=C18*C6`. In this case, you need to keep a cell reference in a formula the same when you copy the formula.

5

FIGURE 5.10

*The relative cell reference formula is =B18*B6.*

Relative cell reference B18   Relative cell reference B6

Revenue in cell B6

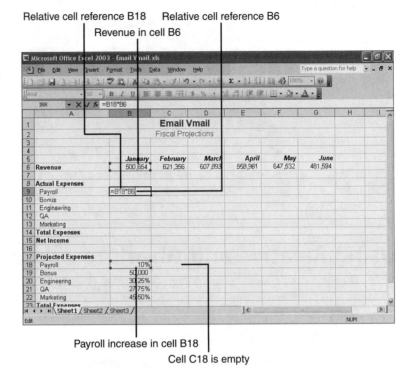

Payroll increase in cell B18

Cell C18 is empty

To keep a cell reference constant when you copy a formula or function, Excel uses *absolute referencing*. The concept of absolute cell referencing is somewhat difficult to understand. To make it easier to understand, keep in mind that the paste function is the only one affected by an absolute cell reference. An absolute cell reference tells the paste function to keep the same cell reference as it copies a formula from one cell to another.

When you're entering a cell reference into a cell, you can type the dollar signs to make the reference absolute. Or, if you're using the mouse to point to the cells you want to use in the formula, click the cell and press F4. The dollar sign character appears before both the column and row indicators, meaning the cell reference is absolute.

To make only the column or row portion of a cell address absolute, press F4 again. Each time you press the F4 key, the $ moves to a different coordinate of the cell address. For example, $A$1 becomes A$1, $A1, and so on each time you press the F4 key.

For example, $B$18 is an absolute reference, whereas B18 is a relative reference. Both reference the same cell. The difference is when they are pasted into other cells. A formula using the absolute reference $B$18 tells Excel to keep the cell reference B18 constant (absolute) as you paste the formula into a new location. A formula using the relative cell reference B18 tells Excel to adjust the cell reference as it pastes.

Cell B9 contains the payroll formula =$B$18*B6, as shown in Figure 5.11. To enter this formula, click cell B9, type = (equal sign), and then click cell B18. Press F4 to change B18 to an absolute cell reference in the formula. Type * (asterisk) and then click cell B6.

FIGURE 5.11

The absolute formula displays in cell B9 and in the Formula bar.

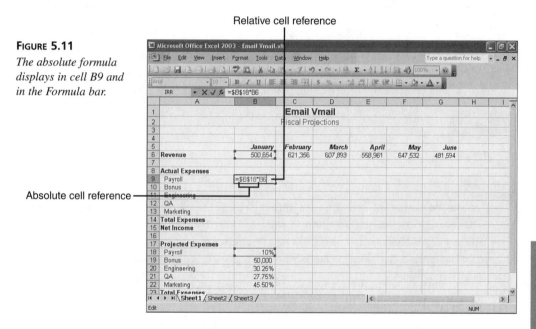

Working with Simple Functions

Excel contains a range of *functions* designed to help you enter formulas easily. Excel functions run the gamut of simple calculations to complex, multitiered equations. You can use an Excel function to total a range of numbers or calculate a car payment. Excel contains more than 100 functions for your use.

NEW TERM   *Functions*—Built-in calculations available in Excel.

In Hour 15, "Using Functions," you explore functions in greater detail. This section examines a few of Excel's simpler functions. Table 5.2 shows some simple, commonly used functions.

TABLE 5.2   Common Excel Functions

Function	What It Does
SUM	Adds a range
AVERAGE	Determines the average of a range
NOW	Inserts the date based on the system clock; updates the date whenever the worksheet is opened or saved
PMT	Computes a monthly loan payment
HYPERLINK	Sets a hyperlink

Excel functions are handled like formulas. Each function begins with an =. Next enter the function name, which is usually a one-word description of what the function does. Following the function name is an opening parenthesis, and arguments follow that. The function is concluded with a closing parenthesis.

 Arguments—The information provided to a function so that an answer can be computed.

The function

`=SUM(A1:A5)`

returns the sum of the cells from A1 through A5. (The colon character indicates *through*.) The function could also be written as =SUM(A1+A2+A3+A4+A5). Although writing it with all the cells is technically correct, it makes more sense (and conserves space) to use range coordinates. If a function has more than one argument, commas separate the arguments.

A few functions don't use arguments. For example, =NOW() enters the serial number for the current date in the cell.

Copying Formulas

Instead of creating a formula each time you need one, Excel allows you to copy existing formulas from cell to cell. The rules for copying (discussed in Hour 3, "Organizing Your Files") are in effect when you copy a formula. Just like text and values, formulas that you copy are sent to the Windows Clipboard. You can paste the formula to one cell or to many.

When you copy a formula, relative addressing will change the cells that are referenced by the formula. If you need any of the cells to remain constant, make sure that absolute addressing has been added to the original formula before you copy it.

> Formulas can be moved as well as copied. Instead of selecting the Copy command, choose Cut to move a formula.

In the final exercise in this hour, you work with a few simple functions and copy some formulas. The My Budget workbook should be open and visible on the screen before you begin.

To Do: Work with Functions

1. Click the Summary tab on the Sales 1st Qtr workbook to make the Summary sheet active. Click into cell B8, type 500, and press Enter to enter sales for CDs.

2. Click into cell B9. A border appears around the cell. In this cell, you're going to use the AutoSum function to create a formula that totals all the sales listed in the column.

3. Click the AutoSum button on the Standard toolbar. The SUM formula appears in the cell and a marquee surrounds the range of values in the columns. Figure 5.12 shows the suggested range of cells to be added.

4. Click the AutoSum button again. The total of the preceding cells appears in the last cell.

5. The completed formula can be copied to the total columns for the other two months. Click the fill handle located at the bottom-right corner of the cell and drag it across the row to cell D9. When you release the mouse button, the totals appear in the monthly columns.

6. Click cell A12 and press Delete to remove the date you had entered when you created the worksheet in Hour 2.

7. Click into the Formula bar and type =TODAY(). Press Enter when you're done. The current date appears inside the cell. Now whenever you open or save the Sales 1st Qtr file, the correct date appears.

8. Save the file by clicking the Save button on the Standard toolbar. Unless you're planning to make additional changes, close the file by clicking the Close button or by opening the File menu and choosing Close.

5

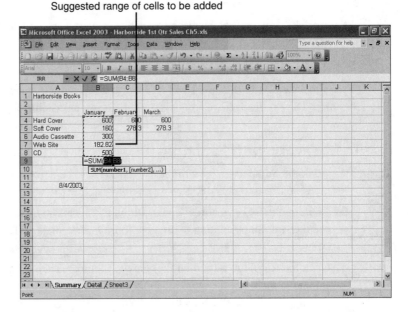

FIGURE 5.12

*The SUM function does
the hard work for you.*

Suggested range of cells to be added

Troubleshooting Formula Errors

When you enter a formula incorrectly into a cell, Excel displays an error message. Formulas can be entered incorrectly for a variety of reasons. Typing mistakes are usually the biggest cause of formula errors. If you mistype an operator or function name, Excel returns an error instead of the desired result.

The next biggest reason that formulas return error values is improper syntax. Syntax is everything when you're entering formulas; your formula must conform exactly to Excel's format. For example, if your formula contains a blank space, the formula errors out.

Excel often provides information about the errors it finds in formulas. With Excel's help, you can usually fix the problem. If the formula looks okay but still isn't producing the results you expect, check it over. If you inadvertently reference the wrong cell or use the wrong function, such as SUM instead of AVERAGE, your answer will not be correct.

 Garbage in, garbage out! If the data you're using for your calculations is bad, the results of the formulas will be wrong as well. Make sure that you're using current data to perform your calculation. Computing a foreign currency rate on last month's rate is probably a waste of time.

Table 5.3 shows some common formula errors with explanations.

TABLE 5.3 Common Formula Errors

Error	Description
####	The column is not wide enough to accommodate the data. Widen the column to see the entire cell contents by clicking on the column border and dragging it to increase the size of the column width. You can also double-click the column border to automatically size the column to exactly fit the data. The error disappears.
#DIV/0!	The formula is trying to divide a number by 0 or an empty cell.
#NAME?	The formula contains incorrectly spelled cell or function names.
#VALUE!	The formula contains non-numeric data, or cell or function names that cannot be used in the formula.
#REF!	The formula contains a reference to a cell that is invalid. Often, this means you deleted a referenced cell.
Circular reference	Results when one of the cells you are referencing in the formula is the cell in which you want the formula to appear. All the other items in this table show up as codes in the cells, while the circular reference error shows up as an error message.

Summary

In this hour, you advanced by leaps and bounds as you moved into the world of working with numbers. Mathematics is the heart and soul of Excel, and you did a great job with constructing formulas and copying them. In Hour 6, "Using Excel Templates," you'll have fun working with Excel templates.

Q&A

Q When I enter a formula, I get a #NAME? error. What does it mean?

A The most likely cause for this error is that you're entering the range name incorrectly. Try using the Insert, Name, Paste command to ensure the range name in your formula is correct.

Q I created a formula that referenced a workbook file that was created by one of my co-workers. Today Excel says it can't find the file my colleague created. What do I do?

5

A Check to see whether your co-worker deleted, moved, or renamed the file. The formula won't work if the file is gone or moved. If the file has a new name or a new location, update your formula accordingly.

Q I work on a laptop connected to a network that I take home at night. Why do formulas that work in the office produce errors at home?

A If your formulas reference files on the network, Excel won't be able to see them if you're not connected.

Q How do I know whether Excel is computing my formulas correctly?

A Excel doesn't make mathematical errors, so you don't need to worry about calculation mistakes. However, you still need to make sure your worksheet has been set up correctly. If your worksheet contains incorrect numbers or percentages, the calculations based on them will be wrong as well.

Q Why does my worksheet display the word `Circular with a cell address` beneath the sheet tabs on the status bar?

A A circular reference means that a formula you entered into a cell references itself. Excel displays the word `Circular` with the cell address that contains the incorrect formula. For example, if the formula in cell G31 reads `=SUM(G15:G31)`, the formula contains a circular reference. The word `Circular` and cell G31 appear beneath the sheet tabs on the status bar. Formulas should never reference the cell in which they're located.

HOUR 6

Using Excel Templates

The highlights of this hour are as follows:

- What a template can do for you
- How to open an Excel template
- How to change an Excel template
- How to create your own template
- How to save a worksheet as a template

Excel offers a collection of templates to use in creating a workbook. Templates enable you to create a workbook based on the special text and formatting elements the templates provide. You could create these elements yourself, but the job would take some time.

Some examples of what you can use a template for include an invoice, purchase order, balance sheet, expense statement, time card, or loan amortization spreadsheet.

During this hour, you discover that creating a workbook using an Excel built-in template is easier than you think. Using a ready-made design gives you a running start on creating a professional-looking workbook. You also learn how to change the template, create your own template, and save an existing worksheet as a template.

What Is a Template?

Templates provide a pattern and tools for creating a variety of workbooks. A template can help you create workbooks that are consistent, and can help you customize your workbooks to suit a particular need. If you create a weekly expense report and you don't want to re-create the entire report each week, you can save one of your reports as a customized template and then insert new numbers in the basic format each week.

NEW TERM *Template*—Generic, model workbook that might consist of basic formatting, styles, text, numbers, and graphics.

Each newly created workbook must be based on a template. When you create a new workbook, Excel bases it on the default template called WORKBOOK.XLT.

Exploring Excel Templates

An Excel built-in template can contain boilerplate text, graphics, styles, macros, and custom toolbars. Several templates can assist you in planning your finances and running your business: Balance Sheet, Expense Statement, Loan Amortization, Sales Invoice, and Timecard. You can use or modify the general purpose templates supplied by Excel.

You can access additional Microsoft Excel templates on the World Wide Web. These templates are designed for planning your personal finances. To obtain the templates, click File, New, and then in the Templates on Microsoft.com area, search for one by keyword or click the Templates home page link.

Opening a Template

When you open a template in Excel, you should see boilerplate text, which is standard text that you can keep or change.

Figure 6.1 shows the Sales Invoice template that contains a placeholder for your company logo, placeholder text for invoice information, and columns where you can enter your invoice data. The template also contains a Template toolbar for working with various elements in the Invoice template.

Insert company name, address, phone and
fax number here as your boilerplate text

FIGURE 6.1

*The Sales Invoice tem-
plate.*

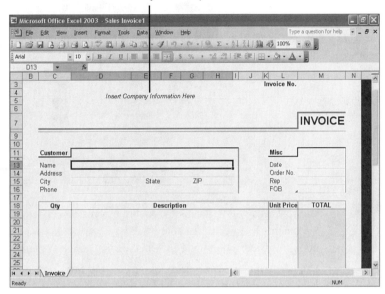

In the upcoming exercise, you open a predefined Excel template called Sales Invoice.

To Do: Open the Sales Invoice Template

1. To open the Sales Invoice template, click the File menu and then click New. The
   New Workbook task pane appears.

2. On the New Workbook task pane, in the Other Templates section, click On My
   Computer. The Templates dialog box appears. You should see two tabs: General
   and Spreadsheet Solutions.

3. Click the Spreadsheet Solutions tab. This tab contains several templates, as shown
   in Figure 6.2.

> If you don't see all the template icons on the Spreadsheet Solutions tab in
> the New dialog box, you need to install the templates using your Microsoft
> Office 2003 or Microsoft Excel 2003 software CD-ROM.

4. Click the Sales Invoice template icon. Notice how a portion of the Sales Invoice
   template pops up in the Preview area on the right side of the dialog box. Click OK.

6

Templates

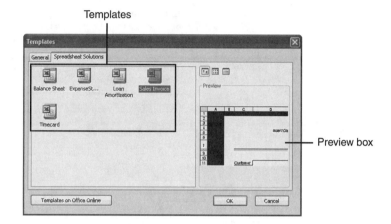

FIGURE 6.2
The Spreadsheet Solutions tab in the Templates dialog box.

Preview box

5. If Excel asks you to disable or enable macros associated with the template, enable the macros by clicking Enable Macros. Excel copies the template into a new workbook, ready for you to add information or change the template.

6. Save the template in a workbook named My Invoice. Click the File menu and then click Save As. The Save As dialog box appears.

7. In the Filename text box, type **My Invoice** to name the workbook.

8. Click Save. Excel saves the workbook. You should see the name My Invoice in the title bar. Figure 6.3 shows the Sales Invoice template in the workbook called My Invoice. You should see the Sales Invoice template name at the top of the Other Templates list in the New Workbook task pane.

▲

Changing the Template

After you open a template, you can use it right away by entering data, but most likely you'll want to customize the template to meet your needs. You can change a template at any time. Some of the things you can do include adding a comment to a cell, hiding the comments, changing the template options, or adding your company information to the template.

You can add comments to a cell to further explain the data that can be entered in that cell. A red triangle in the upper-right corner of a cell indicates that the cell contains a comment. When you move the mouse pointer over a red triangle on the template, Excel displays a box containing a helpful comment. You can opt to either display or hide comments entered in cells.

My Invoice workbook

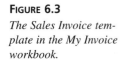

FIGURE 6.3

The Sales Invoice template in the My Invoice workbook.

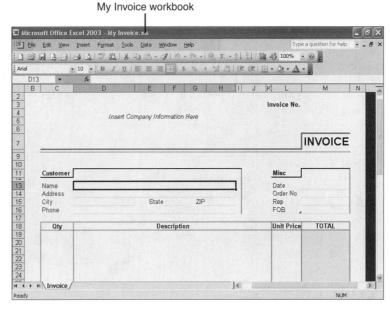

The next exercise demonstrates how to make some changes to the Sales Invoice template. The My Invoice workbook that contains the Sales Invoice template should already be open.

To Do: Change the Sales Invoice Template

▲ TO DO

1. You can use your company's information to customize the invoice. In the Company Name box, type your company's name. Enter the address, city, state, and Zip Code in the appropriate boxes. In the Phone Number box, type your company's phone number. See the sample data in Figure 6.4.

2. Click to the right of the word Payment and a comment appears asking you to select a payment type. Click the Payment down arrow and select Cash.

3. To save the changes you made to your template, choose File, Save As.

4. Name the template using your company's name. In the File Name text box, type the name followed by the word `Invoice`. In the Save As Type list, select Template (*.xlt) and then click Save. Excel saves the customized version of the template in the Templates folder. You should see the customized version of the template on your screen.

5. You're finished using the template. Click the Close Window (×) button to close the workbook.

▼

6

▼

FIGURE 6.4

Sample data in the invoice template.

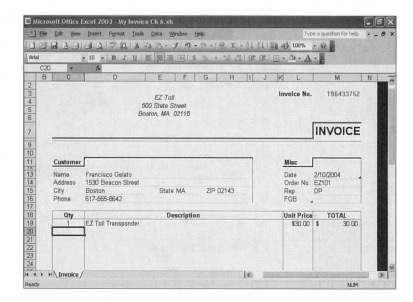

▲

Creating Your Own Template

You can save yourself lots of time by saving your favorite workbook as a template. Simply take an existing Excel workbook, get it to look the way you want for a template form, and then create a template from it.

For example, suppose you have a sales report that you update monthly. You can delete all the numbers that change in the worksheet, leaving the column and row headings intact. Then save the sales worksheet as a template. The next time you want to use the sales worksheet, open the sales template worksheet and just fill in the numbers. It's as easy as pie!

In the next exercise, you prepare the Summary worksheet in the Sales 1st Qtr workbook (the workbook you last used in Hour 5, "Letting Excel Do the Math") for a template form. You need to delete the numbers and keep the column and row headings.

To Do: Create a Template

1. To open the Sales 1st Qtr workbook, which contains the Summary worksheet, click the Open button on the Standard toolbar. The Open dialog box appears.

2. To select the file, double-click on Sales 1st Qtr.xls. The sales workbook appears in the Excel window. Notice that the worksheet contains column and row headings and data.

▼   3. Select the range that contains the data you want to delete; in this case, select the range B4:D8.

4. Press Delete. Now press the right arrow key to deselect the range. The data disappears. You want to keep the title, column headings, row headings, and date (see Figure 6.5). Now the worksheet is ready to be saved as a template (as explained in the next section).

▲

FIGURE 6.5

The worksheet without numbers, with the title, column headings, and row headings, ready for the template form.

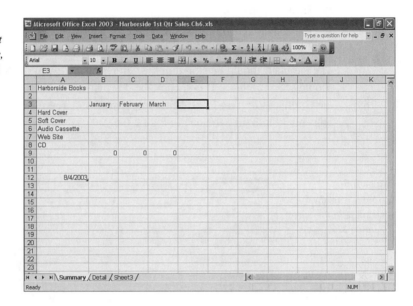

Saving a Worksheet as a Template

After you prepare your worksheet for the template form, the next step is to save the worksheet as a template file. A template file has the file type .XLT. You need to use the Save As command to save the workbook file and change it into a template file format.

You can save your template file into three locations:

- The Templates folder, or a subfolder of the Templates folder in the Microsoft Office or Microsoft Excel folder.

- The XLStart folder in the Microsoft Excel folder.

- The location you specified as an alternate startup file location: Click the Tools menu, choose Options, click the General tab, and enter the location (folder) in the At Startup Open All Files In text box.

The practice exercise shows you how to save the Sales 1st Qtr workbook as a template with the name Sales Form.

6

To Do: Save a Worksheet as a Template

1. To save the Sales 1st Qtr workbook as a template, click the File menu and click Save As. The Save As dialog box opens.

2. Tell Excel the file type that you want to save the file as. Click the Save As Type drop-down arrow. You should see a list of file types. The Template (*.xlt) type is the one you want, so click on it. Now Template (Sales 1st Qtr.xlt) appears in the Save As Type box.

3. In the File Name text box, highlight the default filename, and type **Sales Form** over the existing name.

4. The template should be stored in the Templates folder. In the Save In box, you should see Templates. If not, click the down arrow in the Save In box and choose the C: drive, Program Files, Microsoft Office, and Templates. Your Save As dialog box should look like the one in Figure 6.6.

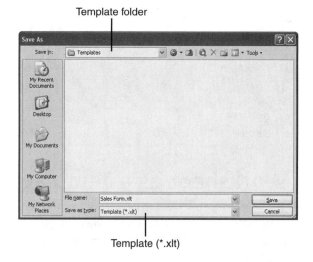

FIGURE 6.6

Saving a worksheet as a template in the Save As dialog box.

Template folder

Template (*.xlt)

5. Click Save. Excel creates and saves the template. In the Title bar, you should see the name Sales Form.xlt. When you want to use this template, you can find it on the General tab in the New dialog box or the New Workbook task pane.

6. You're done using this workbook, so click the Close Window button to close the workbook.

7. To try out that new template, click File in the menu bar and choose New. On the New Workbook task pane, you should see the Sales Form link, as shown in Figure 6.7. Click on it.

FIGURE 6.7

Your template icon on the General tab in the New dialog box.

8. There it is—the Sales Form template, ready and waiting for your data.

9. Now that you've seen your template masterpiece, you can close the workbook. Click the Close Window button.

Summary

Templates are valuable timesavers in Excel, and in this hour you did a nice job with opening, changing, and creating them. In the next hour, you have the pleasure of learning how to print your workbooks.

Q&A

Q Why is a built-in template missing in my version of Microsoft Excel?

A Evidently that built-in template was not installed on your computer. You need to install the template using your Microsoft Office 2003 or Microsoft Excel 2003 software CD-ROM.

Q I saved a file as a template with the .xlt file type, but why can't I use it as a template?

A If you typed the .xlt file type following the filename in the File Name text box, Excel doesn't save the file in template format. You need to use the Save As command and select Template (*.xlt) in the Save As Type list.

6

Q Why doesn't my template appear in the New dialog box?

A You need to save your template in one of these four locations: the Templates folder or a subfolder of the Templates folder in the Microsoft Office or Microsoft Excel folder, the XLStart folder in the Microsoft Excel folder, or the location you specified as a startup file location in the Options dialog box. When you do, the template shows up in the New dialog box.

Q In addition to the templates that come with Excel 2003, are any other Excel templates available?

A You can access additional Microsoft Excel templates at Microsoft Office Online. These plates are designed for planning your personal finances. To obtain the templates when you're in Excel, click Help, Microsoft Office Online.

HOUR 7

Printing Your Workbook

The highlights of this hour are as follows:

- The value of hard copy
- How to check your spelling
- The best ways to set up your page
- How to add headers and footers
- How to choose what to print
- How to control where pages break
- How to print what you want

This hour introduces the basics of printing worksheets. You learn how to check your spelling before you print, set up your page, print what you have, choose what to print, and print in different ways. In Excel, you can print your worksheets using a basic printing procedure, or you can enhance the printout using several page setup options. Plus, you can enhance the printout for special needs by adding page numbers, headers, footers, and more. Keep in mind that printing a worksheet in Excel is a fairly simple process.

The Value of Hard Copy

Eventually, when you've built a worksheet that's a masterpiece, you'll want other people to see it. Even if it isn't a masterpiece, you probably have no choice, because most worksheets are created for the sole purpose of distribution.

You have some choices about the way your publication is printed, and in this hour you check out the options available to you. With a little experimentation and practice, you can to create some very interesting printed results.

Checking Your Spelling Before You Print

What's more embarrassing than having spelling errors in your worksheets? The answer: Nothing. Excel's important proofing tool, the spelling checker, is just what you need to save yourself a lot of embarrassment. This tool helps you correct spelling errors.

Excel's spelling checker works similarly to spelling checkers in word processors. If it finds a word in your worksheet that isn't in its dictionary, it alerts you. If a similar word is in the dictionary, Excel's spelling checker suggests that you might want to use that word instead.

The spelling checker also alerts you if it finds repeated words (for example, the the), uncommon capitalization (tHe), or words that should be capitalized but aren't (boston). If the word in question is similar to words in the spelling checker's dictionary, the spelling checker offers alternative spellings that you may use for the correction. You can also add new words to the dictionary so that Excel's spelling checker won't flag them again.

Although the spelling checker is not a substitute for careful proofreading, it can often catch errors that the human eye might inadvertently overlook. Keep in mind, however, that a spelling checker cannot catch a word that is out of place in a sentence, grammatically incorrect, or misspelled in a way that makes a different valid word. For example, the spelling checker will not find the error in the phrase "and then their was light." The word *their* is a correctly spelled pronoun in English, even though it is used incorrectly in this context. (The word *there* is the correct choice.)

Excel's spelling checker leaves the actual decision to you. Only you can decide whether you want to make specific changes in your data. However, this tool can help you see possible weak points in your writing and offer various options to make your worksheet look professional and letter-perfect.

The following are three ways to check spelling:

- Click the Spelling button on the Standard toolbar.
- Click the Tools menu and click Spelling.
- Press F7.

All three methods display the Spelling dialog box only when there's a potential spelling error. When the spell check comes back clean, you see a dialog box that says so. A nice spelling checker feature is the Undo Last button in the dialog box, which lets you undo the most recent spelling correction.

You'll start the next exercise by introducing an intentional typo and other spelling errors so that Excel has some errors to find. You'll then run the spelling checker and correct the misspelled words. Once again, you are working with the My Budget workbook. If the file isn't open right now, open it before you begin the exercise.

To Do: Check Spelling

▼ To Do

1. Click the Detail sheet tab. In cell A4, type **Hard Covar** and then press Enter.

2. In cell A5, type **quinn Soft Cover** and then press Enter.

3. In cell A6 , type **Audio Audio Cassette** and then press Enter.

4. Start the spelling checker at the top of the worksheet. Press Ctrl+Home. The active cell is now cell A1, the worksheet's beginning.

> When you begin the spell check, Excel checks from the active cell forward. If you start the spell check when the active cell is in the middle of the worksheet, Excel checks from that location to the end of the worksheet, and then asks whether you want to continue checking at the beginning of the sheet. Click Yes to agree, or click No to cancel spell-checking.

5. Click the Spelling button on the Standard toolbar. The Spelling dialog box opens, as shown in Figure 7.1.

> You can also use the spelling checker to check a selected word. Click in the cell that contains the word you want to check. Then click the Spelling button on the Standard toolbar.

6. Excel shows you the first misspelled word in the upper-left corner of the dialog box with the reason why it was flagged. The word is Covar, and it is not in the dictionary. Suggested spellings appear in the Suggestions list. The first suggestion, Cover, is the correct spelling of the misspelled word. The word Cover is already highlighted in the Suggestions list. Click the Change button. Excel changes the word in the cell.

7. The spelling checker finds the next possible misspelled word and displays the word, quinn, and the reason for its flagging, which is Capitalization. Click Change. Excel corrects the capitalization of the word.

▼

7

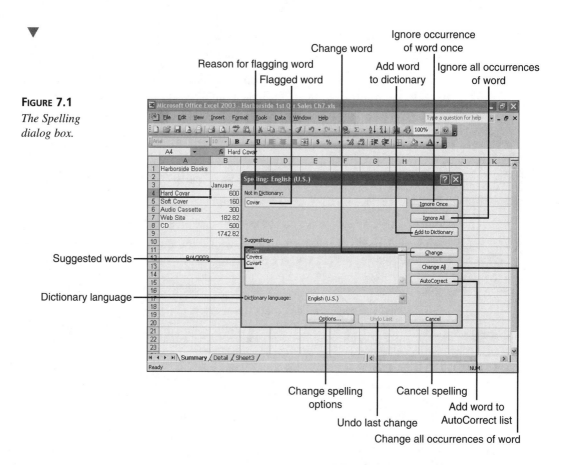

FIGURE 7.1
The Spelling dialog box.

Ignore occurrence of word once

Change word

Reason for flagging word   Add word   Ignore all occurrences
                                to dictionary   of word

Flagged word

Suggested words

Dictionary language

Change spelling options   Cancel spelling

                                Add word to
Undo last change   AutoCorrect list

Change all occurrences of word

8. A repeated word Audio is flagged next. Click Delete. This step deletes the second occurrence of the word.

If you frequently use a word that the spelling checker keeps flagging, you might want to add that word to the dictionary. Simply click the Add to Dictionary button in the Spelling dialog box. Excel then accepts the word as the correctly spelled word in all future Excel sessions.

9. The spelling checker doesn't find any more misspelled words and displays the message: The spelling check is complete for the entire sheet. Click OK. The message disappears.

> If you mistakenly select the wrong Spell option, you can click the Undo Last button in the Spelling dialog box to undo the last option you chose, or you can correct the mistake after you exit the spelling checker.

Working with AutoCorrect

By default, Excel's AutoCorrect feature automatically corrects common typing errors as you type. For instance, if you type two capital letters at the beginning of a word, AutoCorrect changes the second capital letter to a lowercase letter. If you type a lowercase letter at the beginning of a sentence, Excel capitalizes the first letter of the first word in the sentence. If you type a lowercase letter at the beginning of the name of a day, Excel capitalizes the first letter for you. Finally, if the Caps Lock key is accidentally turned on, in the case of words that should be capitalized, Excel reverses the case of those letters and then turns off the Caps Lock key for you.

You can change the AutoCorrect settings at any time. To do so, select Tools, AutoCorrect Options. The AutoCorrect dialog box appears with the AutoCorrect tab, as shown in Figure 7.2.

All the AutoCorrect options are turned on, but you can turn any of them off. At the bottom of the dialog box is the Replace Text As You Type list. This list contains commonly misspelled words and their correct replacement words. For example, if you always type chnage instead of change, Excel corrects the word automatically because it is in the Replace Text As You Type list. You can add words to or delete words from the list. When you're finished with the AutoCorrect settings, click OK.

You can use AutoCorrect to make things easier, such as typing an acronym or abbreviated term to expand to the longer version of the word. For example, if you work for Boston City Developmental Center, something onerous to type frequently, you can set bcdc in AutoCorrect to expand to the full company name.

7

AutoCorrect options

FIGURE 7.2
*The AutoCorrect
dialog box.*

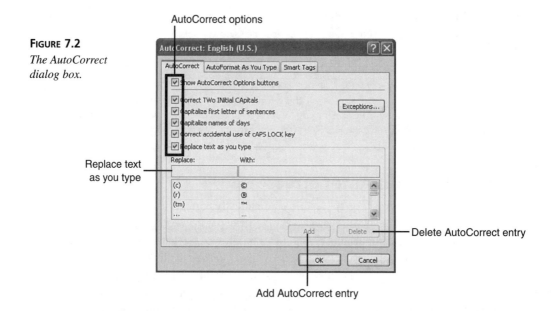

Replace text
as you type

Delete AutoCorrect entry

Add AutoCorrect entry

Setting Up Your Page

In Excel, you can print your worksheets just the way they look after you enter the data, or you can enhance the printout using several page layout options. When you select Excel's Page Setup command, the Page Setup dialog box offers four tabs: Page, Margins, Header/Footer, and Sheet. In this section, you learn how to change the orientation and paper size on the Page tab; change the page margins on the Margins tab; work with headers and footers using the Header/Footer tab; and use the Gridlines option on the Sheet tab.

Changing the Orientation and Paper Size

The Page tab in the Page Setup dialog box is where you can change the page orientation and paper size. The two choices for page orientation are Portrait (vertical), which is the default, or Landscape (horizontal).

As for the paper size options, the default paper size is Letter (8.5×11), but you can choose Legal (8.5×14); Executive (7.25×10.5); A4, A5, and B5 (European sizes); envelopes; index cards; or a customized paper size.

In the next exercise, you experiment with changing the orientation and paper size. You should be working with the My Budget workbook.

To Do: Select the Orientation and Paper Size

1. Click the File menu and choose Page Setup. The Page Setup dialog box opens. You should see four tabs: Page, Margins, Header/Footer, and Sheet (see Figure 7.3).

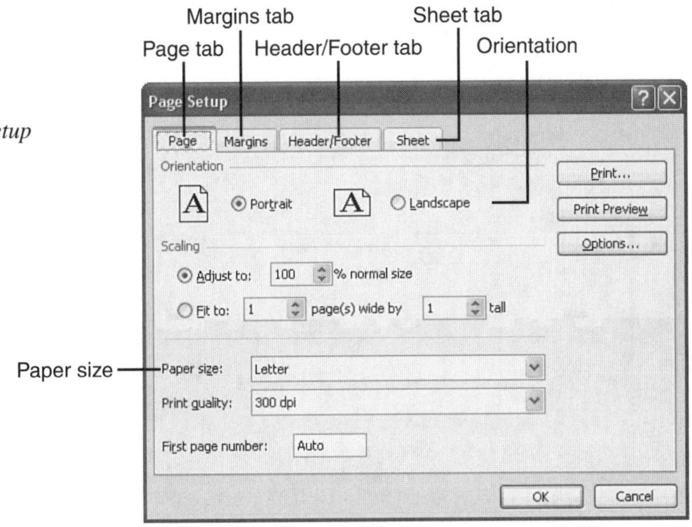

FIGURE 7.3

The Page Setup dialog box.

Margins tab   Sheet tab
Page tab | Header/Footer tab   Orientation

Paper size — Paper size: Letter

2. On the Page tab, change the orientation to landscape. In the Orientation area, click the Landscape option button.

3. Print the worksheet from the Page Setup dialog box. Click the Print button. The Print dialog box appears.

4. In the Print dialog box, click OK to print the worksheet. You should get a printout in landscape orientation on your 8.5×11-inch paper.

Changing the Page Margins

Margins are the empty spaces around the four edges of a page. Setting margins in Excel is very easy to do on the Margins tab in the Page Setup dialog box. You can change the margins before, during, or after you enter data in a worksheet.

Excel presets the top and bottom margins at 1" and the left and right margins at 0.75." You can adjust the margins for the top, bottom, left, and right sides of a page, as well as set the header and footer margins.

7

To Do: Change the Page Margins

1. Click the File menu and choose Page Setup. The Page Setup dialog box opens.

2. Click the Margins tab. Excel shows you a sample page with the margin settings surrounding the page, as shown in Figure 7.4.

FIGURE 7.4

The Margins tab.

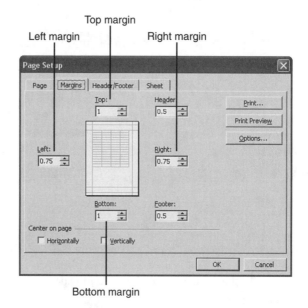

3. Change the left margin setting to 1". In the Left box, click the up arrow once. The number 1 should appear in the box. This setting tells Excel to print the worksheet with a 1" left margin.

4. Change the right margin setting to 1". In the Right box, click the up arrow once. The number 1 should appear in the box. Now Excel knows to print the worksheet with a 1" right margin.

5. Print the worksheet from the Page Setup dialog box. Click the Print button. The Print dialog box appears.

6. In the Print dialog box, click OK to print the worksheet. Your worksheet should print with 1" left and right margins.

Printing Gridlines

By default, Excel worksheets print without gridlines, which separate the cells. Your worksheets often look cleaner without the grids. However, you can change the overall appearance of your worksheet by printing the gridlines.

You get to try out printing the gridlines in the Summary sheet by completing the next exercise.

To Do: Print Gridlines

1. Click the File menu and choose Page Setup. The Page Setup dialog box opens.

2. Click the Sheet tab. In the middle section of the Sheet tab, you should see the Print section with several options.

3. You want the Gridlines option in the Print section. Click the Gridlines check box to put a check mark in the box. This setting tells Excel to print the gridlines on the worksheet.

4. Print the worksheet from the Page Setup dialog box. Click the Print button. The Print dialog box appears.

5. In the Print dialog box, click OK to print the worksheet. Your worksheet should print with gridlines.

Adding Headers and Footers

Headers and footers are lines of text that you can print at the top and bottom of every page in a print job—headers at the top, footers at the bottom. You can include any text, the current date and time, or the filename, and you can even format the information in a header and footer. Excel also gives you a variety of preset headers and footers to choose from in case you don't want to create your own.

Using Excel's Preset Headers and Footers

Because a workbook can contain multiple worksheets, you might need to reference a cell in another worksheet, or even another workbook file. No problem! As long as you follow the proper syntax, you can type a formula that contains a reference to any file.

Figure 7.5 shows you what a preset Excel header looks like on a page in a worksheet.

The next To Do exercise gives you some hands-on practice in using an Excel preset header and footer.

7

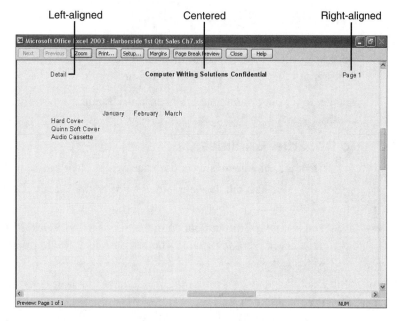

FIGURE 7.5
An Excel preset header at the top of a page.

To Do: Add an Excel Preset Header and Footer

1. Click File, Page Setup. In the Page Setup dialog box, click the Header/Footer tab. You should see the header and footer options, as shown in Figure 7.6. The default header is (none).

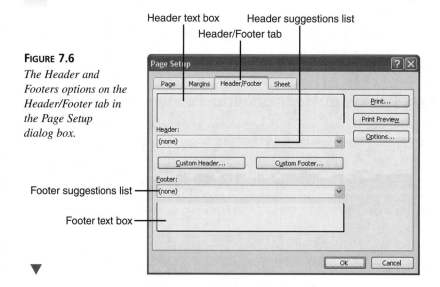

FIGURE 7.6
The Header and Footers options on the Header/Footer tab in the Page Setup dialog box.

▼   2. Click the Header down arrow, and a list of suggested header information appears. Scroll through the list to Detail, Page 1, and then click it. The sample header appears centered at the top of the Header box.

3. By default, the footer (none) appears in the Footer text box. Click the Footer down arrow, and a list of suggested footer information appears. Scroll through the list to Sales 1st Qtr.xls and then click it. The sample footer appears centered at the bottom of the Footer box.

4. Click OK to confirm your choices.

5. To see the header and footer, click the Print Preview button on the Header/Footer tab of the Page Setup dialog box. Print Preview displays page 1 with the header Detail and Page 1 at the top, and the footer Sales 1st Qtr.xls at the bottom.

6. Click on the header to zoom in. Now you can see how Excel will print your header in the worksheet.

7. Click anywhere on the page to zoom out.

8. Click on the footer to zoom in. Now you can see how Excel will print your footer in the worksheet.

9. Click anywhere on the page to zoom out.

10. Keep clicking the Next button to view each page with its header and footer information.

▲   11. Click the Close button on the PrintIn Preview toolbar to close Print Preview.

Creating Your Own Headers and Footers

You might want to customize a header or footer to enter your own information and format the text the way you want. The next To Do exercise gives you practice in creating your own header and footer. And again, you are working with the My Budget workbook. If the file isn't open right now, open it before you begin the exercise.

To Do: Create a Header and Footer

1. Click File, Page Setup. In the Page Setup dialog box, click the Header/Footer tab if necessary.

2. Click the Header down arrow, scroll to the top of the list to None and then click it. The Header text box should now be empty.

3. Click the Custom Header button. The Header dialog box opens, as shown in Figure 7.7. A Header toolbar contains buttons for formatting the header text. Three boxes are visible: Left Section, Center Section, and Right Section.

7

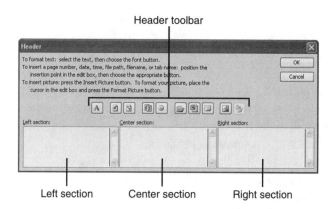

FIGURE 7.7
*The Header
dialog box.*

4. Starting in the Left Section box, type your name. Press Tab. In the Center Section box, click the page number button (a page with a number sign [#] on the Header toolbar) and press Tab. The page number code &[Page] appears in the Center Section box. In the Right Section box, type **Detail**. The worksheet name is now in the Right Section box.

5. Click OK to confirm your header information.

6. Click the Footer down arrow, scroll to the top of the list to None and then click it. The Footer text box should now be empty.

7. Click the Custom Footer button. The Footer dialog box opens. A Footer toolbar contains buttons for formatting the footer text. Three boxes are visible: Left Section, Center Section, and Right Section.

8. Click in the Center Section box and click the Filename button (a page with a green X) on the Footer toolbar. The filename code &[File] appears in the Center Section box.

9. Click OK to confirm your footer information.

10. To see the header and footer, click the Print Preview button on the Header/Footer tab of the Page Setup dialog box. Print Preview displays page 1 with the header information at the top, and the footer information at the bottom.

11. Click on the header to zoom in. You can see how Excel will print your header in the worksheet.

12. Click anywhere on the page to zoom out.

13. Click on the footer to zoom in. You can see how Excel will print your footer in the worksheet.

14. Click anywhere on the page to zoom out.

▼ 15. Keep clicking the Next button to view each page with its header and footer information.

▲ 16. Click the Close button on the Print Preview toolbar to close Print Preview.

 If something unexpected prints at the top or bottom of your worksheet, check the Header or Footer text box. If you don't want a header or footer, choose None in the Header or Footer suggestions list.

Choosing What to Print

In some cases, you might want to choose what to print—perhaps only a portion of the worksheet, and not the whole worksheet or workbook. Excel's Print Area feature lets you single out an area on the worksheet that you want to print. The Print Titles feature lets you repeat the title, subtitle, column headings, and row headings on every page.

Excel's Fit To option lets you shrink the pages to fit any number of pages you want by shrinking a worksheet down so small that you can't read the text. If you shrink it to some suitable multiple-page setting, such as 1 page wide by 3 pages high, you could read the text comfortably.

Selecting a Print Area

To print specific portions of a worksheet, such as a range of cells, you can single out an area as a separate page and then print that page.

Before you select a print area, you need to think about which area you want to single out, excluding any column and row headings that are going to print at the top edge and left side of every page. To select the print area, highlight the cells that contain the data. Don't highlight the column and row headings.

 Too many selections can spoil the print area. Do not include the title, subtitle, or column and row titles (headings) in the print area. If you include these titles in the print area, Excel prints the titles twice.

Next click File, Print Area, Set Print Area. Excel inserts automatic page breaks to the left and right and the top and bottom of the range you selected. You should see a dashed line border around the print area.

7

To remove the print area, click File, Print Area, and Clear Print Area. The automatic page breaks should disappear in the worksheet.

Printing the Column and Row Headings

You can select titles that are located on the top edge (column headings) and left side (row headings) of your worksheet and print them on every page of the printout.

The upcoming exercise shows you how to print the title, column headings, and row headings.

To Do: Print Column and Row Headings

1. Click File, Page Setup and click the Sheet tab. You see the Sheet options. Notice the Print area contains the range B4:G12. For a moment, focus on the Rows To Repeat At Top and Columns To Repeat At Left boxes that appear in the Print Titles section.

2. Click in the Rows To Repeat At Top text box, or press Tab twice to move the insertion point there.

> Drag the dialog box out of the way if it's covering the area you want to select.

3. Click on any cell in row 1 and drag down to include the title, subtitle, and column headings.

4. Click in the Columns to Repeat at Left text box or press Tab to move the insertion point there.

5. Click on any cell in column A to include the row headings.

6. Click OK to confirm your choices. All data above and to the left of the dashed-line border (print area) repeat on every page.

> To remove the row and columns headings you want to repeat, delete the cell coordinates in the Rows to Repeat at Top and Columns to Repeat at Left boxes on the Sheet tab in the Page Setup dialog box.

Fitting Your Worksheet to a Number of Pages

If you have a large worksheet divided into several pages, you can shrink the pages to fit on one page by using the Fit To option. For instance, if the worksheet is two pages wide by three pages tall, you can reduce the worksheet to fit on one page by selecting the Fit To option. Because the default setting for this option is one page wide by one page tall, Excel prints your worksheet on one page. You can compare the Fit To option to the reduction feature on a copier machine.

The Fit To option works this way: Click the File menu and choose Page Setup. When the Page Setup dialog box opens, click the Page tab. In the Scaling section, choose the Fit To option. Specify the number of pages wide by the number of pages tall.

Controlling Where Pages Break

If your worksheet is too large to fit on one page, Excel splits the work over two or more pages. Excel makes the split based on your current page dimensions, margins, and cell widths and heights. Excel always splits the worksheet at the beginning of a column (vertically) and/or row (horizontally), so the information in a cell is never split between two pages.

An automatic page break appears as a dashed line with short dashes in your worksheet. These dashed lines run down the right edge of a column.

If the automatic page breaks are not right for your worksheet, one of the many ways to make adjustments is to override Excel's defaults. The worksheet still prints on two or more pages, but you can control where each new page begins.

Setting a Manual Page Break

As long as each page fits into the prescribed page size and margin setting, you can set a manual page break anywhere on the worksheet. Manual page breaks remain active until you remove them. Establishing new page breaks does not alter existing breaks; it simply adds to them.

To set a page break, click in any cell, row, or column where you want the break to appear. Click the Insert menu and choose Page Break. Excel inserts a manual page break, which is indicated by a dashed line. Onscreen, manual page breaks have longer, thicker dashed lines than automatic page breaks (see Figure 7.8).

If you're using the Fit To page setup option, the manual page break does not appear.

To remove a manual page break, just select the cell, row, or column that was used to create the break and choose Insert, Remove Page Break.

7

FIGURE 7.8

Inserting a manual page break.

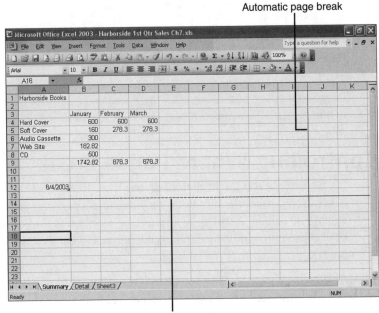

Automatic page break

Manual page break

The Remove Page Break option appears in the Insert menu only when the cell pointer is in the correct cell, row, or column. Be sure to click in the right place to remove the page break.

Printing What You Want

Excel gives you several ways to print a worksheet:

- Select File, Print.
- Press Ctrl+P.
- Click the Print button on the Standard toolbar.

When you select File, Print or press Ctrl+P, Excel displays the Print dialog box. This dialog box enables you to print some or all the pages within a worksheet, selected data, the active worksheet, or the entire workbook. You can also specify the number of copies of the printout, and you can collate pages when you print multiple copies of a multipage worksheet. You can even print a worksheet to another file.

If your printer options are already set up for printing the document, you can simply click the Print button on the Standard toolbar. Excel doesn't display the Print dialog box and prints the worksheet immediately. This printing method is useful for quick printing, but you can't change any options.

It's a good idea to save your workbooks before printing—just in case a printer error or other problem occurs. That way, you won't lose the work.

Checking Your Printer

Before you use your printer with Excel, it's advisable to check the Printer Setup options. You often need to provide more details about your printer so Excel can use the options and capabilities that are available with your particular printer.

For most printers, the Printer Setup options let you select the paper size and paper type. You can choose the paper feed type: cut-sheet (single sheets of paper) or banner (continuous form paper). You can also select from three types of print quality:

- Best—Highest quality, slower printing than Normal mode; uses more ink.
- Normal—Letter quality; normal printing speed.
- EconoFast—Draft quality, lighter output, faster printing than Normal mode. Uses less ink than other modes and reduces the frequency of replacing your print cartridges; available only when you select Plain Paper as the paper type.

You can try your hand at checking the printer setup options in the next exercise.

To Do: Check the Printer Setup Options

1. Click File, Print. The Print dialog box appears. In the Printer section, you should see the printer name, status, type, where it's connected on your computer, and any comments.

Your computer might be set up to run on different printers, depending on your output needs. For example, you might want to use a laser printer when you need a high-quality printout; at other times, the output from your inkjet printer might be sufficient.

7

2. Make sure the correct printer is selected. To select a different printer, click the Name down arrow and choose a printer from the list.

▼   3. Click the Properties button next to the printer name. The dialog box with your printer's name appears. The first two tabs are usually Setup and Features. Any other tabs that appear, depend on the printer you have.

4. Click the Setup tab, if necessary. The Setup options include paper options and print quality.

5. Change any printer setup options you want and click the Close button to close the dialog box.

▲   6. Close the Print dialog box by clicking Cancel.

Printing Your Worksheets

If you want to print one worksheet just the way it is without changing any print options, simply click the Print button on the Standard toolbar. But suppose you want to print more than one worksheet. No problem—you just need to tell Excel which worksheets you want to print. You can print contiguous or noncontiguous worksheets.

NEW TERM   *Contiguous* worksheets—Worksheets that are next to each other in the workbook, without any worksheet that you don't want in between them.

NEW TERM   *Noncontiguous* worksheets—Worksheets that are separated by several worksheets that you do not want.

To select worksheets, you click on the worksheet tabs. An active worksheet's tab is white, whereas the tab of an inactive worksheet is gray.

You learn how to print contiguous and noncontiguous worksheets in the upcoming exercise.

To Do: Print Worksheets

1. First you select and print contiguous worksheets. Select the sheet tab that contains the first worksheet you want to print. If necessary, click the Summary sheet tab.

2. Select the sheet tab that contains the last worksheet you want to print. Hold down the Shift key and click the Sheet3 tab. This step selects all the worksheets you're going to print. The selected sheet tabs are white.

3. Click the Print button on the Standard toolbar to print the selected worksheets.

4. Next you select and print noncontiguous worksheets. Hold down the Ctrl key and click on the Detail sheet tab and the Sheet3 sheet tab. This step deselects the sheets, and the tabs should be gray.

5. Select the sheet tab that contains the first worksheet you want to print. Click the Summary sheet tab, if necessary.

6. Select the sheet tab that contains the next worksheet you want to print. Hold down the Ctrl key and click the Sheet3 tab. This step selects the worksheets you're going to print. The selected sheet tabs are white.

7. Click the Print button on the Standard toolbar to print the selected worksheets.

8. Hold down the Ctrl key and click the Sheet3 sheet tab. This step deselects the sheet, and the tab should be gray.

Printing a Range

You can choose which pages you want to print in the Print Range area in the Print dialog box. You have two choices: All or Pages. Printing all the pages in your active sheet is the default print range setting. However, you can print specific pages by choosing the Page(s) option and entering the page numbers in the From and To boxes. For example, if you type **1** in the From box and **3** in the To box, Excel prints pages 1 through 3.

The next exercise demonstrates how to print only page 2.

To Do: Print Ranges

1. Press Ctrl+P to show the Print dialog box. In the Print Range area, the All option is already selected.

2. Click the Page(s) option button. This step tells Excel that you want to select specific pages.

3. In the From box, type **2**. Press the Tab key and type **2** in the To box. This step tells Excel that you want to print page 2.

4. Click OK to print the specified page.

Printing a Selection

What if you want to print a portion of the worksheet? You can do just that by selecting the cells, rows, and/or columns you want to print. Then click File, Print. In the Print dialog box, in the Print What section, choose Selection. This option prints only the portion of the worksheet you selected.

Printing the Entire Workbook

You can print the entire workbook with all its worksheets in one fell swoop. To do so, click File, Print. In the Print dialog box, in the Print What section, choose Entire Workbook. This option prints the whole workbook.

7

If you want to save your print settings, you can store them in a custom view. To create a custom view, first get the print settings the way you want them. Then choose View, Custom Views. The Custom Views dialog box opens. Click the Add button, type a name for the view in the Name text box. Leave the Print settings check box checked. Click OK. You have now saved your print settings, so you can print the worksheet with those settings at any time. To display the custom view, choose View, Custom Views. In the Custom Views dialog box, click on the view name in the Views list and click the Show button. The view appears onscreen, and then you can print the worksheet with its print settings.

Faxing a Workbook

You can fax a workbook if you have fax software and hardware installed and set up on your computer. To send a workbook as a fax, choose File, Print. In the Name drop-down list, select the fax service that appears in the list. Select the fax options you want and click OK.

Canceling Printing

You can cancel a print job either before it prints or while it prints. Canceling a print job does not work for workbooks such as the one in the exercises in this hour, unless you are on a network or have other workbooks lined up to print. Excel prints a small worksheet faster than you can cancel it.

While a worksheet is printing, Windows displays a Printer icon at the right end of the Windows taskbar. To stop a worksheet from printing, double-click the printer icon to display the Print Queue dialog box (see Figure 7.9). Click the document name and select Document, Cancel from the menu bar in the dialog box to cancel the print job. Click the Close button to close the dialog box.

FIGURE **7.9**

Canceling printing in the Print Queue dialog box.

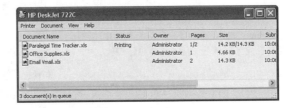

Summary

Hour 7 has given you all the tools you need to print your documents in a myriad of ways. Now you should be able to print your worksheets and workbooks with ease, and if you ever need any help, just refer to this hour at any time.

Hour 8 examines how to format your text by changing fonts, font styles, font sizes, rotating text, copying formatting, adding comments, and much more.

Q&A

Q Why didn't the spelling checker flag a spelling error at the top of my worksheet?

A You probably started spell checking in the middle of your worksheet. Excel checks from the location where you start to the end of the worksheet. You should see a message box asking whether you want to continue spell checking at the beginning of the worksheet. Click Yes. Always start spell checking at the worksheet's beginning by pressing Ctrl+Home.

Q How can I move the Spelling dialog box that covers up the change in the worksheet?

A Drag the Spelling dialog box by its title bar out of the way so you can see the changes as they occur.

Q I selected the wrong Spell option. How can I correct this mistake?

A Click the Undo Last button in the Spelling dialog box to undo the last option, or you can correct the mistake after you exit the spell checker.

Q My worksheet doesn't print on my printer. What next?

A If you have difficulty printing, the incorrect printer might be selected in the Print dialog box.

Q I usually print my worksheets in a portrait (vertical) orientation, but how can I print a worksheet in a landscape (horizontal) orientation?

A In the Page Setup dialog box, choose the Page tab; in the Orientation section, choose Landscape.

Q I created my own header and footer information and didn't get the results I wanted when I printed the worksheet. How can I fix this?

7

A If something unexpected prints in your header and footer, choose None in the Header and Footer suggestions lists. Now you can start all over and create your own custom header and footer. Also, click the Print Preview button to see what the header and footer information looks like before you print it.

Q Why don't my manual page breaks show on the screen?

A Manual page breaks do not show in your worksheet on the screen when you use the Fit To page setup option.

PART II

Dress Up Your Work

Hour

HOUR 8

Changing the Appearance of Text

The highlights of this hour are the following:

- What formatting does for data
- How to use fonts
- How to change cell alignment
- How to control the flow of text
- How to copy formatting with the Format Painter
- How to adjust column width
- How to alter row height
- How to work with comments

This hour introduces the subject of formatting, which enables you to change the appearance of text in your worksheets. You learn how to apply various formatting features to your text to give your worksheet a more professional look. In this hour, you practice changing the font, font style (bold, italic, underline), font size, and text alignment. You also learn how to rotate text, center a heading, control the flow of text, copy formatting with the Format Painter, and work with comments. You'll find many uses for these features in your worksheets.

By the end of this hour, you will be using Excel's formatting tools to make your worksheets more attractive and readable.

Formatting Your Text

You've added data to a worksheet, and it's well planned out. Good for you! But you're not finished. You have to make sure that your nicely thought out arrangement of data gets noticed. Bold and italic characters, underlined numbers, and special fonts can make your worksheet shine.

The best way to produce a good-looking worksheet is to worry about the text first and the formatting second. Type in your text and then make the changes in the appearance. Bold, italic, and other formatting changes are easy to accomplish from the Formatting toolbar.

All the buttons on the Formatting toolbar are shortcuts to items that appear in the Format menu. The menu, however, offers a great many formatting options in addition to those on the toolbar. You can use the dialog boxes available through the menu items to fine-tune some of the special formatting effects.

Treating Numbers Like Text

Excel evaluates each of your entries and determines whether the entry is a value or label. A mixed cell entry that contains both values and text is automatically treated like a label. For example, an address like 1750 Clint Moore Road is treated like a label.

> A mixed cell entry that contains numbers and text cannot be used as part of a calculation.

You can also enter numbers in a cell and have Excel treat the entry as a label. You might want to consider telephone numbers, ZIP Codes, and invoice numbers as labels instead of values. Whenever you want Excel to treat a numeric cell entry as a text, preface the entry with a single quotation mark ('). The quotation mark is not visible in the cell, although you can see it on the Formula bar, as shown in Figure 8.1.

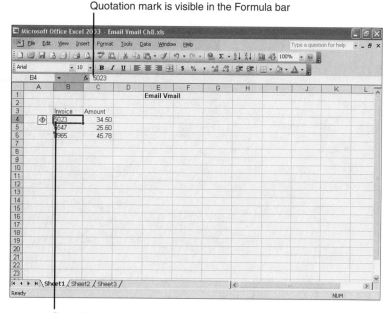

Quotation mark is visible in the Formula bar

FIGURE 8.1

The single quotation mark tells Excel to treat the entry as a label.

Quotation mark treats numbers as text

Using Fonts

You might be asking yourself what a font is. Simply put, a *font* is a style of type that is a particular typeface and size. Excel comes with many different fonts ready for you to use, and you can switch between them at any time. In the Normal template, which is the one applied when you create a new workbook, the default font is Arial and the font size is 10 points.

NEW TERM *Font*—A typeface and size set for letters, numbers, and special characters.

Excel displays various fonts on the Formatting toolbar and provides a fast way to change the font. You can select a font from the Font box on the Formatting toolbar.

The Formatting toolbar contains tools for changing the appearance of your text. Figure 8.2 shows you the formatting tools you need for changing the font, font size, and font style.

FIGURE 8.2

The Formatting toolbar.

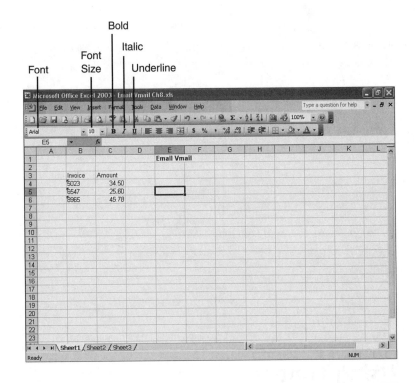

Bold
Italic
Font
Size
Underline
Font

Use a contrast of font sizes on the same worksheet to enhance or emphasize the text and numbers. You can also use bold type, italic, outline borders, and shading so that your finished product is both pleasing to look at and emphasizes the correct information. To create outline borders and add shading to a range of cells, use the Border tab and Patterns tab in the Format Cells command, as described in Hour 10, "Adding Borders, Colors, and Fills."

Changing the Font Style

Sometimes you need to emphasize certain text to make sure it's read or to make sure the readers understand how important the text is. Bold works best for titles, subtitles, column headings, and row headings. Other times, italic type is necessary to make your text stand out. You can even combine bold and italic to draw attention to your text in the worksheet.

Because boldface and italic print are so common, Excel offers a quick and easy way to apply these styles to your worksheet data. Simply click the Bold (its tool is a boldface capital letter B) or Italic button (its tool is an italicized capital letter I) on the Formatting toolbar. The highlighted cells are immediately formatted with bold and/or italic.

Another font style you can apply to text is the underline. Just click the Underline button (its tool is an underlined capital letter U) on the Formatting toolbar to underline characters.

8

Boldface can increase the width of the characters and might change the length of the text entry in a cell. The text might spill over into the next cell. In this case, you should widen the column with the long entry to accommodate the boldface text. Adjusting column width is explained later in this hour.

You can use keyboard shortcuts for changing the font style: Ctrl+B for bold, Ctrl+I for italic, and Ctrl+U for underline.

Changing the Font Size

In the Normal template, which is the one applied when you create a new workbook, the default font size is 10 points. Font size is measured in points.

NEW TERM *Point*—A standard measurement of type size; it equals 1/72 of an inch. For example, characters in a 10-point font size are 10/72 of an inch tall. Typically, worksheets use either a 10- or 12-point setting for text. The higher the point size, the bigger the text.

Excel lets you adjust font size in two ways:

- The Font tab in the Format Cells dialog box
- The Font Size box on the Formatting toolbar

No matter which method you choose to change font size, you can change the size of the font to whatever suits your needs.

In the next exercise, you change the font, font style, and font size for the title. You also change the font style for the column headings. You'll be working with the Sales 1st Qtr workbook once again. If the file isn't open right now, open it before you begin the exercise.

To Do: Change the Font, Font Style, and Font Size

1. Select cell A1.
2. Click the Font down arrow on the Formatting toolbar.
3. Scroll down the list until you see Courier New and then click it.

A rule of thumb for professional spreadsheet designers is to limit the number of fonts on a page to just a few. Otherwise, the page gets too busy.

4. Click the Font Size down arrow on the Formatting toolbar.

5. Scroll down the list until you see 16. Click it.

6. Click the Bold button on the Formatting toolbar.

You can activate the text attributes you want before you type text. For example, if you want a title in bold, 12-point Arial, select the cell that will contain the title. Before you start typing, choose Arial from the Font box, 12 from the Font Size box, and click the Bold button on the Formatting toolbar. When you type the text, Excel applies the bold, 12-point Arial text attributes.

7. Select cells B3:D3.

8. Click the Bold button on the Formatting toolbar.

9. Click the Italic button on the Formatting toolbar.

10. Click any cell to deselect the range. Figure 8.3 shows what your formatted text should look like.

FIGURE 8.3

Font, font size, and font style changes.

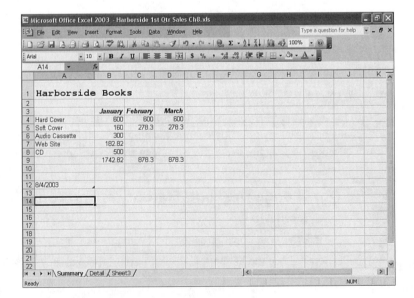

Changing Cell Alignment

8

The default alignment for data is General. When you enter data into a cell, numbers, dates, and times automatically align with the right side of the cell. Text aligns with the left side of the cell. You can change the alignment of information at any time. For instance, you might want to fine-tune the appearance of column headings across columns, or you can right-align column headings across the columns to line up with the numbers that are right-aligned.

 NEW TERM *General alignment*—The default alignment for data, which means that numbers are right-aligned and text is left-aligned.

In the To Do exercise, you right-align the column headings in the My Budget workbook.

 ## To Do: Align Data

1. Select cells B3:D3.

2. Choose Format, Cells. Excel opens the Format Cells dialog box.

3. Click the Alignment tab.

 A fast way to change the alignment of text is to use the Align Left, Center, and Align Right buttons on the Formatting toolbar. Just select the cell or range of cells you want to align and then click one of the alignment buttons.

4. Click the Horizontal down arrow and choose Right (Indent), as shown in Figure 8.4.

FIGURE 8.4

The Alignment tab in the Format Cells dialog box.

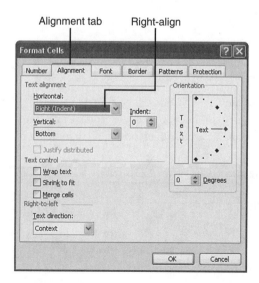

5. Click OK to confirm your choice.

6. Click any cell to deselect the range. Excel adjusts the text according to the alignment option you have chosen. In this case, the column headings are aligned right, as shown in Figure 8.5.

FIGURE 8.5
Column headings aligned right.

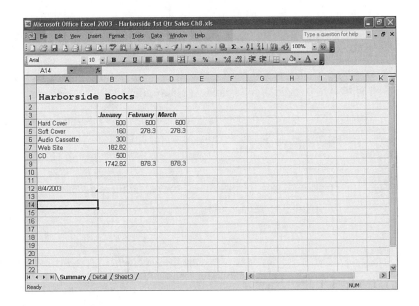

> To repeat the alignment format command in another cell, use the Repeat Format Cells command from the Edit menu or press the F4 (Repeat) key. Actually, you can repeat any format command in another cell by using the F4 key.

Types of Alignments

The Alignment tab in the Format Cells dialog box makes several types of alignments available. The Horizontal alignment options let you specify left/right alignment in the cell(s). Table 8.1 lists and describes the Horizontal alignment options.

TABLE 8.1 Excel Horizontal Alignment Options

Alignment	What It Does
General	Aligns numbers and dates with the right side of the cell and text with the left side.
Left (Indent)	Aligns selected data with the left side of the cell.

TABLE 8.1   continued

Alignment	What It Does
Center	Centers data within the cell.
Right (Indent)	Aligns selected data with the right side of the cell.
Fill	Repeats the data to fill the entire width of the cell.
Justify	Aligns text with the right and left side of the cell. Use with the Wrap Text option in the Text Control section on the Alignment tab.
Center Across Selection	Centers a title or other text inside a range of cells, such as over columns.
Distributed (Indent)	Aligns text with the right and left side or top and bottom of the cell. Use with the Wrap Text option in the Text Control section on the Alignment tab.

The Vertical alignment options let you specify how you want the text aligned in relation to the top and bottom of the cell(s).

Text orientation, located on the right side of the Alignment tab, is explained in the next section. The Text control options are discussed later in this hour.

Rotating Cell Entries

One of Excel's most exciting alignment features lets you change the orientation of text in the cell. You can rotate the text vertically, arranging the text so that you can read it from top to bottom within the cell. Flipping the text sideways lets you print it from top to bottom rather than left to right.

If you don't want to flip the text horizontally or vertically, you can angle the text by specifying the number of degrees of an angle you want to rotate. Rotated text appears slanted and looks fancier than ordinary text.

The next To Do exercise shows you how to rotate text at an angle.

To Do: Rotate Text

1. Select the range that contains the text you want to rotate; in this case, select cell A12.

2. Choose Format, Cells. The Format Cells dialog box appears.

3. Click the Alignment tab if necessary.

4. In the Orientation section, type **45** in the Degrees box. This entry specifies the number of degrees you want the text to rotate.

▼ 5. Click OK.

6. Click any cell to deselect the range. The text you selected should appear slanted.
▲ See Figure 8.6.

FIGURE 8.6

Rotated text.

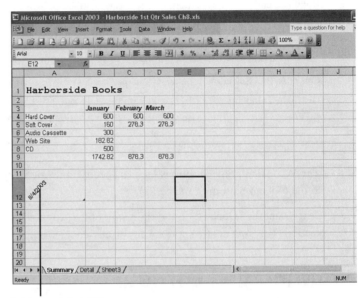

Current date is rotated 45°

Centering a Heading

In Excel, you can use another type of alignment command called Merge and Center. The Merge and Center button (its icon has a page with the letter *a* and two arrows) on the Formatting toolbar lets you quickly center text in the left-most cell across the entire range of cells you select. This feature is good for centering a title and subtitle at the top of a worksheet. Figure 8.7 shows a title centered across the table in cell F1.

You can undo a set of merged and centered cells by splitting the merged cells. To do so, select the merged cells and click the Merge and Center button on the Formatting toolbar.

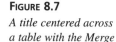

FIGURE 8.7

A title centered across a table with the Merge and Center button.

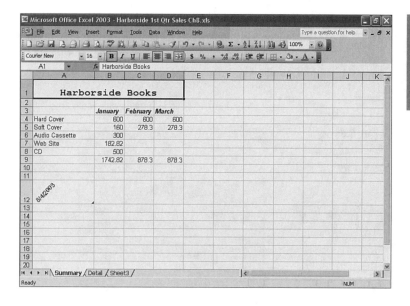

Controlling the Flow of Text

Excel offers several ways to control the flow of text within cells. Here are two of the most common text control features:

- Indent text from the left border of the cell
- Wrap text to break the text into multiple lines

Using Indents

You might want to indent your text to make it stand out in a column of text or numbers. Using the Detail worksheet in the My Budget workbook as an example, you can indent the Rent, Mortgage, Parking, Condo/Fees, and Misc row headings beneath the row heading Housing. That way, the items under housing stand out and are easier to depict in the column.

In the To Do exercise, you indent data using the Format Cells dialog box and the Increase Indent button on the Formatting toolbar.

To Do: Indent Data

1. Click the Detail sheet tab. Select cells A4:A6.

2. Choose Format, Cells. Excel opens the Format Cells dialog box.

3. Click the Alignment tab. You should see Text Alignment options at the top of the tab.

▼   4. Click the Horizontal down arrow and choose Left (Indent).

5. In the Indent box, click the up arrow once. The Indent number changes from 0 to 1, indicating the indentation will be one character width. Figure 8.8 shows the Indent option on the Alignment tab.

Left (indent)   Indent (character width amount)

FIGURE 8.8

The Indent options on the Alignment tab in the Format Cells dialog box.

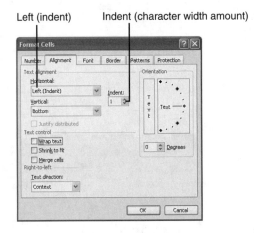

6. Click OK. Excel adjusts the text according to the Indent option you chose.

For faster indenting, based on the default of one character width of the standard font (10-point Arial), you can use the Indent tools on the Formatting toolbar. Just click the Increase Indent button to indent a cell entry to the next character width. Click the Decrease Indent button on the Formatting toolbar to move the indented text to the previous character width.

7. Click any cell in row 4 and insert a new row. Click in cell A4, type **Boston**, and press Enter.

8. Click in cell A7, type **Web Site**, and press Enter. Click in cell A8, type **CD**, and press Enter.

9. Select cells A17 through A8.

10. Click the Increase Indent button on the Formatting toolbar.

▲   11. Click any cell to deselect the range. Figure 8.9 shows the indented text in column A.

FIGURE 8.9

Indented text in a column.

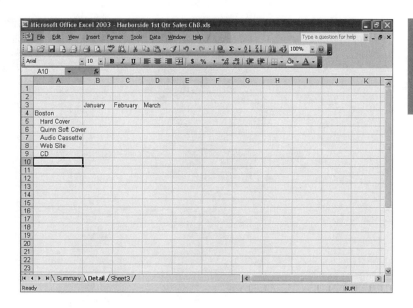

Breaking Text into Multiple Lines

Normally, Excel displays all text in a cell on one line. However, you can tell Excel to wrap long lines of text within a cell without changing the width of the cell.

The next To Do exercise lets you try your hand at breaking text into multiple lines.

To Do: Break Text into Multiple Lines

1. Click cell A30.

2. Type **This detail sales report shows the sales for the first quarter for Boston**.

3. Press Enter.

4. Click cell A30 to select the cell that you want to break into multiple lines.

5. Choose Format, Cells. Excel opens the Format Cells dialog box.

6. Click the Alignment tab. You should see Text Control options at the bottom left on the tab.

7. Click the Wrap Text check box.

8. Click OK.

9. Click any cell to deselect the range. Excel wraps the text from one line to the next within the cell, as shown in Figure 8.10.

FIGURE 8.10

Wrapping text on multiple lines.

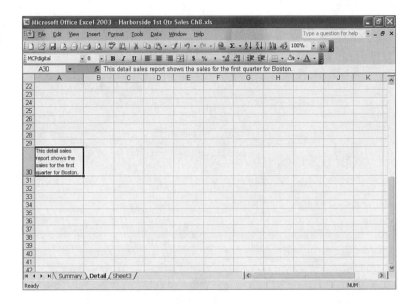

Copying Formatting with the Format Painter

The Format Painter is like a mini-formatting copier that is available on the Standard toolbar (its tool looks like a paintbrush). To use the Format Painter, select the text you want to use as a model, click the Format Painter tool, and then click the target cell or range of cells to "paint" it with the same formatting. The mouse pointer changes to a paintbrush during this process.

The next To Do exercise demonstrates how to use the Format Painter tool to copy formats in the My Budget workbook.

To Do: Copy Formats with the Format Painter Tool

1. Click the Summary sheet tab. Select cell B3.

2. Click the Format Painter button on the Standard toolbar. You should see a copy marquee surrounding cell B3. The mouse pointer should change to a white cross with a paintbrush. The cross and paintbrush indicate that you are copying formats, as shown in Figure 8.11.

3. Click and drag the mouse pointer down through cells A4 to A8.

4. Release the mouse button. The copied formatting should be applied to the selected cells. The row headings are right-aligned with bold and italicized text. You want to left-align the headings.

▼ To Do

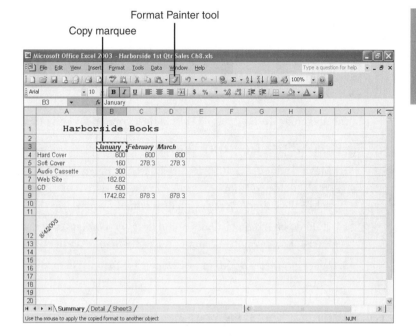

FIGURE 8.11
*Copying formats with
the Format Painter.*

5. Click the Left Align button on the Formatting toolbar.

6. Click any cell to deselect the range. Now the row headings look much better.

Removing Formatting

To turn off bold, italic, or underline, select the cells that contain the font style you want to remove and click the buttons (Bold, Italic, Underline) again on the Formatting toolbar.

You can remove the alignment you've added to a cell or range of cells by changing it back to the General alignment setting. To do so, select the cells that have the alignment you want to change, choose Format Cells, click the Alignment tab, and choose General in the Horizontal drop-down list.

Another way to remove the alignment you've attached to a cell or range is to use the Edit, Clear command and choose the Formats option from the Clear menu. Be sure to first select the cells that contain the formatting you want to clear. Then click the Format menu, choose Clear, and choose Formats. This action clears not only the alignment but also the fonts and other formatting you added to cells.

Adjusting Column Width

Adjusting column width makes the best use of the worksheet space. You can set the column width manually or let Excel make the adjustments for you with its AutoFit feature. By default, column width is set to 8.43 characters, based on the default font and font size, 10-point Arial.

In the upcoming To Do exercise, you adjust column width with a mouse.

To Do: Adjust Column Width

1. Move the mouse pointer to the right column header border at the top of column A. You should see a double-headed arrow, as shown in Figure 8.12. Use the right border of the column header to adjust column width.

2. Hold down the mouse button and drag the border. As you are dragging the border, Excel shows you the column width in a ScreenTip (a buff-color box).

3. When you see a width of 18.00, release the mouse button. The column width is adjusted.

The column width ScreenTip

FIGURE 8.12

Dragging the right border of a column changes its width.

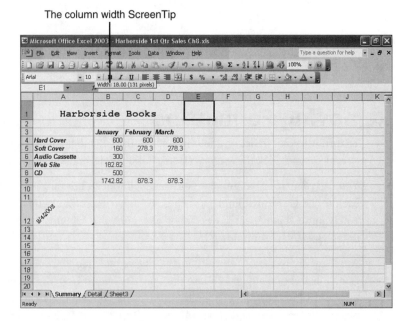

To change the column width for two or more columns, click and drag over the column headers with the mouse pointer. Then release the mouse button. Move the mouse pointer to one of the column header borders. Use the right border of the column header to adjust the column width. Hold down the mouse button and drag the border. Release the mouse button, and the column width is adjusted for all the columns you selected.

You can make use of Excel's AutoFit feature to quickly make a column as wide as its widest entry. Just double-click the right border of the column header. To change more than one column at a time, click and drag over the desired column headers and then double-click the right-most column header border.

Altering Row Height

Altering row height makes the best use of the worksheet space, just like adjusting column width does. You can set the row height manually or let Excel make the adjustments for you with its AutoFit feature.

By default, Excel makes a row a bit taller than the tallest text in the row. For instance, if the tallest text is 10 points tall, Excel makes the row 13.5 points tall. The default row height is set to 13.5 points, based on the default font size, 10 points.

In the upcoming To Do exercise, you alter row height with a mouse.

To Do: Alter Row Height

1. Move the mouse pointer to the bottom row header borders, row 1. You should see a double-headed arrow. Use the bottom border of the row header to adjust row height.

2. Hold down the mouse button and drag the border. As you are dragging the border, Excel shows you the row height in a ScreenTip (a buff-color box).

3. When you see a height of 30.00 in the ScreenTip, release the mouse button. Excel makes the row taller.

To change the row height for two or more rows, click and drag over the row headers with the mouse pointer. Then release the mouse button. Move the mouse pointer to one of the row header borders. Use the bottom border of the row header to alter row height. Hold down the mouse button and drag the border. Release the mouse button, and the row height is adjusted for all the rows you selected.

Excel's AutoFit feature lets you quickly make a row as tall as its tallest entry. Simply double-click the bottom border of the row header. To change more than one row at a time, click and drag over the desired row headers and then double-click the bottom row header border.

Finding Data

With Excel's Find command, you can locate specific data, text, characters, formatting, and special characters. For example, what if you want to find the row that contains sales data for any category with the word *cover* in it. You can search for data in three ways:

- Find the first occurrences of the data
- Find other occurrences of that data
- Find all occurrences of that data

In the next To Do exercise, you search for the first instance of the word *cover*.

To Do: Find Data

1. Choose Edit, Find. Excel opens the Find and Replace dialog box.
2. Click the Find tab, if necessary.

> You can use the keyboard shortcut Ctrl+F to display the Find and Replace dialog box with the Find tab selected.

3. In the Find What text box, type **cover**.
4. Click the Find Next button. Excel finds the first occurrence of the information and makes it the active cell.
5. If you want to continue searching for other instances of the data, click the Find Next button.

> If you want to specify how to search for the data, click the Options button. You can search by rows or columns, select a worksheet element such as Formulas, Values, or Comments, distinguish to match upper- and lowercase, and find only cells with the exact characters in Find What text box.

To find all instances of the data, click the Find All button. At the bottom of the Find dialog box, Excel displays a list of the cells found, as shown in Figure 8.13. You should see six columns in the list: Book, Sheet, Name, Cell, Value, and Formula. The Book, Sheet, and Cell columns indicate the location of the cell. If there is a name or formula associated with the cell, you will see them in the Name and Formula columns. The data you entered in the Find What box should match the data in the Value column.

FIGURE 8.13
The Find and Replace dialog box with a list of all cells found.

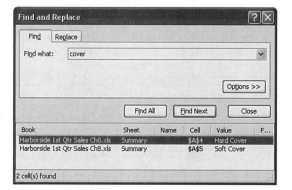

Replacing Data

The Edit Replace command lets you quickly locate and replace numbers, text, data formats, and special characters. Suppose you have text that you entered incorrectly or that has changed throughout a large worksheet. You can use the Edit Replace command to have Excel search for and replace all occurrences of the incorrect information with the correct information. You can find and replace data in three ways:

- Replace the first occurrence of the data
- Replace specific occurrences of the data
- Replace all occurrences of the data

In the next To Do exercise, you search for the first instance of the word *cover* and replace it with the word *volume*.

To Do: Replace Data

1. Choose Edit, Replace. Excel opens the Find and Replace dialog box.
2. Click the Replace tab.

> You can use the keyboard shortcut Ctrl+H to display the Find and Replace dialog box with the Replace tab selected.

3. In the Find What text box, type **Cover**, if necessary.
4. In the Replace With text box, type **Volume**.

You can specify the format of the data you are searching and replacing. To do so, click the Format button next to the Find What or Replace With text box and select the format options you want.

5. Click the Find Next button. Excel finds the first occurrence of the information and makes it the active cell.

6. Click Replace. Excel replaces the word. The word Volume appears after the word Hard in the cell.

7. If you want to continue replacing specific instances of the data, click the Find Next button and click the Replace button.

8. To replace all occurrences of the data, click the Replace All button.

If you want to specify how to find the data, click the Options button. You can search within a sheet or workbook, search by rows or columns, select a worksheet element such as Formulas, distinguish to match upper- and lowercase, and find only cells with the exact characters in Find What text box. Figure 8.14 shows the search options for finding data you want to replace.

FIGURE 8.14

The Find and Replace dialog box with the Find options on the Replace tab.

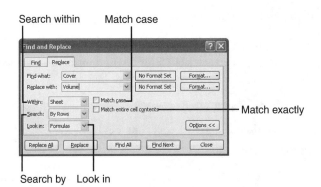

Working with Comments

The Insert Comment command enables you to add comments to your worksheets. Adding comments is useful if you are going to share your work with others. Some explanation might be necessary to clarify certain portions of a worksheet or workbook. Adding comments is also helpful for tracking your work or tracing your footsteps if you are using complex formulas and references. Comments enable you to remind yourself of how a portion of a worksheet operates and to insert questions or comments for others to read.

Adding a Comment

In the next To Do exercise, you add a comment to explain the data in a cell.

8

To Do: Add a Comment

1. Select the cell for which you want to enter a comment; in this case, select cell B4.

2. Choose Insert, Comment. You should see a box with an insertion point in it next to cell B4.

3. In the Comment box, type **See the Detail sheet for a breakdown of hard volume sales**. Your name appears in the comment, followed by the text you entered.

> If you want to enter a comment for multiple cells, select the range of cells and then add the comment. Excel places the comment in the first cell you select in the range.

4. Click another cell to close the comment. A red triangle appears in the upper-right corner of the cell that contains the comment.

> You cannot close a comment by pressing Enter—that just adds a blank line. To close a comment, click another cell.

Displaying a Comment

To display a comment, point to the cell that contains the comments. The comment should pop up, as shown in Figure 8.15.

Editing a Comment

To edit a comment, choose View, Comments. Excel displays the Reviewing toolbar and the comments you added to the worksheet, as shown in Figure 8.16. To move from comment to comment, click the Next Comment and Previous Comment buttons on the Reviewing toolbar.

A red triangle indicates that the cell contains a comment

FIGURE 8.15
Displaying a comment.

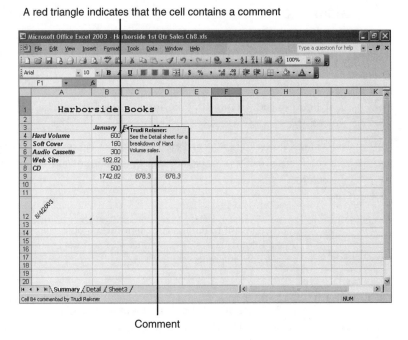

Comment

Previous Comment
Next Comment
Hide All Comments

FIGURE 8.16
The Reviewing toolbar.

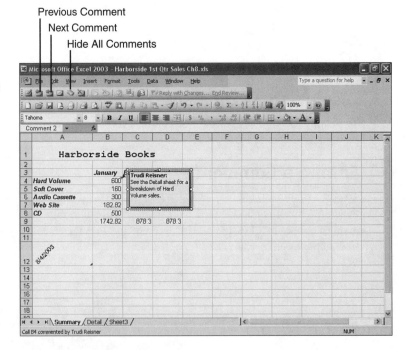

8

When you find the comment you want to change, click it and use the Editing function (discussed in Hour 2, "Entering Data") to make your changes.

To hide all the comments, click the Hide All Comments button on the Reviewing toolbar. You no longer see any comments on the worksheet.

When you're finished using the Reviewing toolbar, close the toolbar by right-clicking anywhere in the toolbar area, and choose Reviewing on the Toolbars menu.

Deleting a Comment

When you're ready to delete a comment, choose View, Comments and click the Comment box. You should see selection handles (white squares) and a diagonal-line border surrounding the box. Click the comment's border. The selection handles remain, and the border is shaded with dots. The dots mean that the comment is selected. Press the Delete key to delete the comment.

Summary

In this hour, you learned about formatting text in Excel. Good job! In the next hour, you find out how to apply formatting to numbers.

Q&A

Q How can I change the default font when I start a worksheet?

A Before you enter any data, choose a new font in the Font box on the Formatting toolbar.

Q When I applied a font to text, why did I get a lot of little pictures?

A Some fonts, such as Wingdings, are made up of symbols, not of letters and numbers. Select another font.

Q When I changed the size of the font for the title, and added bold to text in Column A, why does the text now spill over into the next column?

A Larger font sizes and boldface can increase the width of the characters and can change the length of the text entry in a cell. Therefore, the text spilled over into the next cell. In the column that contains the title, double-click the column border to widen the column. Widen column A by double-clicking on its column border. Excel will automatically widen the column to fit the long entries.

Q **After I copied some formatting with the Format Painter tool, I didn't like the results in the new location. What can I do to fix it?**

A Click the Undo button on the Standard toolbar immediately after you finish painting the format.

Q **When I pressed Enter in a Comment box to close it, why did Excel add a blank line to my comment text and not close the box?**

A You cannot close a comment by pressing Enter—that just inserts a blank line. Click another cell to close the Comment box.

Hour 9

Changing the Look of Values

The topics covered in this hour include the following:

- What formats are available
- How to choose a number style
- How to work with decimal places
- How to design custom numeric formats
- How to format conditionally
- How to hide zeros
- How to work with dates

During this hour you get all the information you need on how to format numbers—from finding out what number formats are available in Excel to choosing number styles, working with decimal places, designing your own number formats, using conditional formatting, hiding zeros, and working with dates.

At the end of this hour, you'll be a pro at formatting numbers with Excel's formatting tools, making your numbers clearer to read and understand.

What Formats Are Available?

Numeric values are usually more than just numbers. They often represent dollar values, dates, percentages, or some other value. You can select the
format type that appears as a real value in the Format Cells dialog box. To narrow the list of formats, first select a category in the Category list, then specify the number of decimal places. The default number of decimal places is two.

Excel lets you display numeric values in many ways. Formatting a number means changing the way it is displayed. You can format the number 500 to look like currency, in which case it's displayed as *$500.00*. You can even specify as many decimal places as you want to display.

You can choose from four currency styles:

- Currency with negative numbers preceded by a minus sign
- Currency with red negative numbers
- Currency with negative numbers enclosed in parentheses
- Currency with red negative numbers enclosed in parentheses

Excel's preformatted number formats are listed in Table 9.1.

TABLE 9.1   Excel Number Formats

Number Format	Sample Number	What It Does
General	4500	Default number format. Has no specific number format. With General format, you can type a number with a decimal point, dollar sign, comma, percent sign, date, time, or fraction in a cell. Excel automatically displays the value with the format you entered.
Number	4,500.50	Used for general display of numbers. The default Number format is two decimal places and negative numbers are black preceded by a minus sign. You can display the number of decimal places, whether you want a comma for a thousand separator, and negative numbers in red or black, preceded by a minus sign or enclosed in parentheses.
Currency	$4,500.50	Used for general monetary values. The default Currency format is two decimal places, with a dollar sign, and negative numbers are black preceded by a minus sign. You can display the number of decimal places, whether you want a dollar sign, and negative numbers in red or black, preceded by a minus sign or enclosed in parentheses.

TABLE 9.1   continued

Number Format	Sample Number	What It Does
Accounting	$4,500.00	Used for aligning dollar signs and decimal points in a column. The default Accounting format is two decimal places and a dollar sign. You specify the number of decimal places and whether you want a dollar sign.
Percentage	85.6%	The default Percentage format is two decimal places and a percent sign. Multiplies the value in a cell by 100 and displays the result with a percent sign.
Fraction	1/4	The default Fraction format is up to one digit on either side of the slash. Used to display the number of digits you want on either side of the slash and the fraction type such as halves, quarters, eighths, and so on.
Scientific	4.50E+03	The default Scientific format is two decimal places. Used to display numbers in scientific notation.
Text	278MC99	Used to display both text and numbers in a cell as text. Excel displays the entry exactly as typed.

Choosing a Number Style

After you decide on a suitable number format, you can choose a number style using either of two methods:

- Click the number style buttons on the Formatting toolbar.
- Choose Format, Cells and select a number style from the Format Cells dialog box.

Using the Toolbar to Change Number Formats

The Formatting toolbar offers several tools for changing number formats. Figure 9.1 shows the Formatting toolbar and the number style tools you use in this hour.

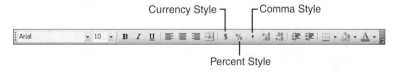

FIGURE 9.1
Number style tools on the Formatting toolbar.

The following To Do exercise shows you how to use the Formatting toolbar to change number formats in the Sales workbook, Summary sheet. Your job is to format the numbers. If the workbook isn't open now, open it before you start the exercise.

To Do: Change Number Formats Using the Formatting Toolbar

1. Select the cells in which you want to display commas; in this case, select cells B4:B8.

2. Click the Comma Style button on the Formatting toolbar. Excel applies the Comma Style, displaying no commas, and two decimal places.

3. Select cell B9.

4. Click the Currency Style button on the Formatting toolbar. You should see the dollar sign, a comma, and two decimal places in the selected cell.

> If any cells display number signs, you can widen the column to display the numbers. Double-click the column border to the right of the column letter for the column you want to adjust.

Using the Format Cells Dialog Box

Instead of using the number style tools on the Formatting toolbar, you can select a value's format type in the Format Cells dialog box. That way, you can get a number format to look exactly the way you want it.

The next To Do exercise steps you through changing the number format for a range of cells using the Format Cells dialog box. You start by entering a column of numbers, so that you can format them in the Sales workbook.

To Do: Use the Format Cells Dialog Box to Change Number Formats

1. Click cell C6, type **275**, and press Enter. In cell C7, type **195.50**, and in cell C8, type **1000**.

2. Select the cells in which you want to display commas; in this case, select cells C4:C8.

3. Click the Format menu and choose Cells. The Format Cells dialog box opens.

> To quickly display the Format Cells dialog box, press Ctrl+1.

4. Click the Number tab. On the left is a list of number format categories. On the top right is a Sample box, where Excel shows you what a sample number would look

▼   like formatted with that type. Also, you should see a description of the selected
            number category at the bottom of the dialog box.

> You can also change the number format of a cell by using the shortcut
> menu; select the cell, click the right mouse button on the cell to display the
> shortcut menu, and then choose Format Cells.

9

5. Click Number in the Category list. On the right, you see a number in the Sample
   box, the Decimal Places box, the Use 1000 Separator (,) check box, and a list of
   negative number formats. You need a 1000 separator, which is the comma.

6. Click the Use 1000 Separator (,) check box. A check mark appears in the box,
   indicating you want to format your numbers with commas (see Figure 9.2).

FIGURE 9.2

*Number format
options in the Format
Cells dialog box.*

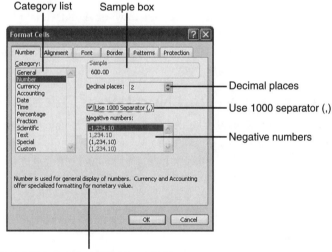

7. Click OK. You should see commas and two decimal places in the selected cells.

8. Select the cell in which you want to display a dollar sign; in this case, select cell C9.

9. Press Ctrl+1 to open the Format Cells dialog box.

10. On the Number tab, click Currency in the Category list. On the right, you see a
    number in the Sample box, the Decimal Places box, a Symbol drop-down list, and
    a list of negative number formats. The default Currency options is suited to what
▼   you want.

▼

If you select zero decimal places, Excel rounds the value to fit this format. For example, if you enter 5.5 in a cell, Excel rounds this number to 6 when formatting to zero decimal places.

11. Click OK. You should see dollar signs, commas, and two decimal places in the selected cell. Click any cell to deselect the range.

▲

If you want to format a number with the Euro, choose Currency, click the Symbol drop-down arrow, and select Euro (≠123) or Euro (123≠).

Working with Decimal Places

All of Excel's number formats use either two or zero decimal places. The exception is General format, which uses as many places as needed for a value. You can establish a fixed number of decimal places or let Excel automatically round numbers for you. The following sections examine both ways to work with decimal places.

Establishing a Fixed Number of Decimal Places

To establish a fixed number of decimal places, use a numeric format other than General format. Two tools on the Formatting toolbar enable you to change the number of decimal places for numbers. The tools are Increase Decimal (its icon contains .0 and .00 with a left arrow) and Decrease Decimal (its icon contains .0 and .00 with a right arrow). Here's how these tools work:

- Click the Increase Decimal button each time you want to move the decimal point one place to the left.
- Click the Decrease Decimal button each time you want to move the decimal point one place to the right.

In the To Do exercise, you change the number of decimal places from two to zero for numbers in the Sales workbook.

To Do: Specify Decimal Places

1. Select the cells in which you want to decrease decimal places for numbers with commas; in this case, select cells B4:C8.

2. Click the Decrease Decimal button on the Formatting toolbar. Excel moves the decimal point one place to the right. Notice that the number of decimal places for numbers in the selected cells has changed from two to one.

▼

▼   3. Click the Decrease Decimal button on the Formatting toolbar again and click any cell to deselect the range. The number of decimal places for the numbers is now zero, showing whole numbers.

4. Select cells B9:C9.

5. Click the Decrease Decimal button on the Formatting toolbar twice. Excel moves the decimal point two places to the right. Notice that the number of decimal places for numbers in the selected cells has changed from two to zero, displaying whole numbers.

▲   6. Click any cell to deselect the range.

> To repeat the number format change in another cell, select the Repeat Format Cells option from the Edit menu or press the F4 (Repeat) key. By the way, you can repeat any format command in another cell by using the F4 key.

Rounding Numbers

Excel can store up to 15 decimal places for a value. Many of Excel's preformatted format settings round numbers to two decimal places. For instance, if you enter the value $50.768 into a cell, Excel displays $50.77. Excel uses a dollar format to display the value with two decimal places and a dollar sign.

Remember that the value in the cell has not been changed. The value is merely displayed to look like it has been changed. The cell's actual value is still 50.768, and any references to this cell's value receive the value 50.768. Therefore, formatted values are not rounded at all; they only appear to be rounded.

To round numbers, use the Increase Decimal and Decrease Decimal tools on the Formatting toolbar.

Designing Custom Numeric Formats

In addition to using Excel's preformatted number format settings, you can create your own formats. Here's how it goes: Choose the Custom category on the Number tab in the Format Cells dialog box. You'll see format codes in the Type list on the right. Choose one of the codes as a starting point for the custom format you want to design. Then make your changes to the existing code you selected.

The next To Do exercise gives you a chance to create a custom numeric format. Using the Summary sheet in the Sales workbook, create a custom format that displays a dollar sign followed by one space with commas and zero decimal places.

To Do: Create Your Own Numeric Format

1. Select the cell that contains the number you want to format; in this case, select cell B9.

2. Choose Format, Cells. The Format Cells dialog box appears.

3. Click the Number tab.

4. In the Category list, click Custom.

5. In the Type list box, choose `#,##0`. The code displays in the Type text box. This entry is a starting point for designing your custom format.

6. In the Type text box, click before the first #, and type $ followed by a space. Excel shows you a formatted sample number in the Sample box, as shown in Figure 9.3. This custom number format displays a dollar sign followed by a space with commas and zero decimal places. This custom format is stored at the bottom of the Type list.

FIGURE 9.3

A custom format in the Format Cells dialog box.

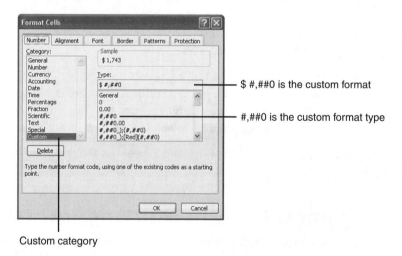

$ #,##0 is the custom format

#,##0 is the custom format type

Custom category

You can reuse all modified custom number formats within a worksheet without retyping them. Excel stores all customized formats at the bottom of the Type list. That way, you can select them over and over. However, if you create a custom format for one workbook, you have to re-create the format for other workbooks.

▼ 7. Click OK. Excel applies the custom format to the number you selected.

▲ 8. Click any cell to deselect the range.

Formatting Conditionally

You probably are asking yourself, "What is formatting conditionally?" Formatting conditionally lets you apply special formatting settings that take effect when the contents of a cell meet specified conditions. For instance, if the values fall below a specific number, you can show those values in bold pink, and if the values are greater than a specific number, you can display those values in bold blue. Excel's Conditional Formatting command helps you easily format your values based on specific conditions.

In the upcoming To Do exercise, you step through the process of setting up conditional formatting for values on the Summary sheet in the Sales workbook.

To Do: Format Values Conditionally

▼ To Do

1. Select the cells that contain the values you want to format conditionally; in this case, select cells B4:B8.

2. Choose Format, Conditional Formatting. The Conditional Formatting dialog box pops open, as shown in Figure 9.4. You should see boxes for setting up Condition 1 and the Format button for specifying the format for the values.

Condition 1

FIGURE 9.4
The Conditional Formatting dialog box.

Format

3. In the Condition 1 area, leave the Cell Value Is option. In the next box, choose Less Than, and type **500** in the last box.

4. Click the Format button. The Format Cells dialog box appears.

5. In the Font Style list, choose Bold, and select the pink color patch in the Color palette.

▼ 6. Click OK.

9

▼   7. Click the Add button.

         8. In the Condition 2 area, leave the Cell Value Is option. In the next box, choose
            Greater Than, and type **500** in the last box.

         9. Click the Format button. The Format Cells dialog box appears.

        10. In the Font Style list, choose Bold, and select the blue color patch in the Color
            palette.

        11. Click OK to close the Format Cells dialog box. Click OK again to confirm your
            conditional formatting choices. Click any cell outside of the selected range. Excel
            displays numbers less than 500 in bold pink and numbers greater than 500 in bold
▲   blue.

Hiding Zeros

Worksheets are often cluttered with zeros as a result of calculations or information that
hasn't been entered. Formulas frequently display a zero when referenced cells are blank.
These zeros can make a worksheet confusing.

If you enter the sum formula in row 10 on the Detail sheet in the Sales workbook, the
formulas produce unwanted values of zero (see Figure 9.5). This worksheet shows several columns where data has not been entered. Therefore, the cells with the formulas that
total the empty columns produce zeros. In this case, you might want to suppress the
zeros.

There are a couple of ways to hide zeros in a worksheet:

- Use the Tools, Options command to hide all values of zero in the worksheet. In the
  Options dialog box, click the View tab (see Figure 9.6). In the Window Options
  section, click the Zero Values check box to remove the check mark, which hides all
  zeros on the worksheet.

- Create a custom number format in the Format Cells dialog box to hide zeros in a
  range of cells.

The To Do exercise coming up walks you through hiding zeros in a range of cells on the
worksheet. Use the Summary Sheet of the Sales workbook to see how it works.

FIGURE **9.5**

Formulas that produce unwanted values of zero.

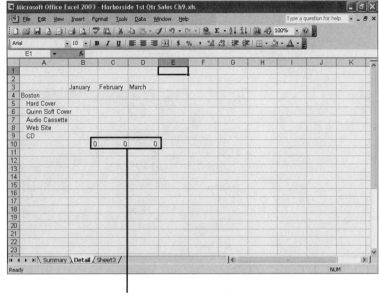

Unwanted zeros

View tab

FIGURE **9.6**

Zero Values option in the Options dialog box.

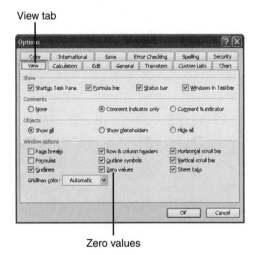

Zero values

To Do: Hide Zeros in a Range of Cells

1. Select the range that contains the zeros you want to hide; in this case, select cells B10:D10.

2. Choose Format, Cells. The Format Cells dialog box appears.

3. Click the Number tab.

▼   4. In the Category list, click Custom.

5. In the Type text box, the General category appears, which is the type you want. Click after the l in General and type a semicolon (;) followed by General and another semicolon (;) See Figure 9.7.

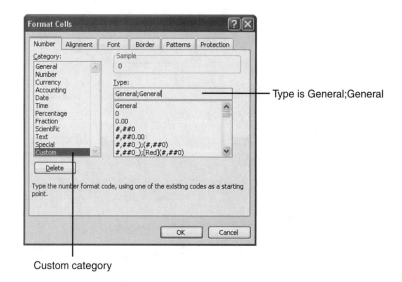

Type is General;General

Custom category

6. Click OK.

▲   7. Click any cell to deselect the range. The zeros are hidden in the selected range.

Working with Dates

Dates and times are actually numeric values that have been formatted to appear as dates and time. You can change the way Excel displays the date and time if you want.

The Date and Time categories are in the Category list on the Number tab in the Format Cells dialog box. You can use the Date format to display date and time serial numbers as date values with slashes or hyphens. The default Date format is the month and day separated by a slash; for example, 7/2. To display only the time portion, use the Time format.

The Time format lets you display date and time serial numbers as time values with hours, minutes, seconds, AM, or PM. The default Time format is the hour and minutes separated by a colon; for example, 11:00. You can perform calculations on the time values. To display only the date portion, use the Date format.

Understanding Date and Time Formats

Excel offers a wide variety of date and time formats, which are listed in Table 9.2.

TABLE 9.2   Excel's Date and Time Formats

Date/Time Format	Sample Date/Time
m/d	7/2
m/d/yy	7/2/98
mm/dd/yy	07/02/98
d-mmm	2-Jul
d-mmm-yy	2-Jul-98
dd-mmm-yy	02-Jul-98
mmm-yy	Jul-98
mmmm-yy	July-98
mmmm d,yyyy	July 2, 1998
m/d/yy h:mm	7/2/98 7:30
m/d/yy hh:mm	7/2/98 19:30
hh:mm	13:35
h:mm AM/PM	1:35 PM
h:mm:ss AM/PM	1:35:50 AM

Changing Date Formats

After you figure out which date and time format you want to use, you can change the dates using the Format Cells dialog box.

In the To Do exercise, you need to format the date on the Summary sheet in the Sales workbook.

To Do: Change a Date Format

1. Click the Summary sheet tab. Select the cell that contains the date you want to format; in this case, select cell A12.

2. Click the Format menu and choose Cells. The Format Cells dialog box opens.

3. Click the Number tab.

4. Click the Date category in the Category list. On the right, you see a date in the Sample box and a list of date types (see Figure 9.8).

FIGURE 9.8
Date format options in the Format Cells dialog box.

Date category   Date types

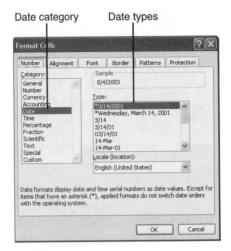

5. In the Type list, click the seventh date format (Mar-01) in the list. In the Sample box, Excel shows you what a sample date would look like formatted with that type.

6. Click OK. You should see the formatted date in the selected cell.

Creating Custom Date Formats

If Excel doesn't have a preformatted date format that suits your needs, you can create your own date format. To do so, choose the Custom category on the Number tab in the Format Cells dialog box. Excel displays format codes in the Type list on the right. Choose one of the date format codes as a starting point for your custom date format. Then make your changes to the format you selected.

You can reuse all modified custom date formats within a worksheet without retyping them. Excel stores all customized date formats at the bottom of the Type list. That way, you can select them again and again. However, if you create a custom date format for one workbook, you have to re-create the format for other workbooks.

Summary

Congratulations! You've done a nice job of working through all the formatting exercises in this hour. Now that you have text formatting (refer to Hour 8, "Changing the Appearance of Text") and numeric formatting under your belt, you're probably ready for adding pizzazz to your worksheets with borders, colors, and fills, which is explained in the next hour.

Q&A

Q When I selected two decimal places, why did the numbers display with # signs?

A If any cell displays number signs (#), you can widen the column to display the numbers. Double-click the column border to the right of the column letter for the column you want to adjust.

Q Does Excel have a fast way to display the Format Cells dialog box?

A Absolutely. Press Ctrl+1.

Q I like using a shortcut menu for making changes to my worksheet. Can I format numbers with a shortcut menu?

A Yes. You're in luck! Select the cells you want to format and then click the right mouse button in one of the selected cells. Your shortcut menu should appear. Then choose Format Cells.

Q Does Excel have a shortcut for applying the same number format in various places throughout a large worksheet?

A Certainly. You can repeat a number format change in another cell by selecting Repeat Format Cells from the Edit menu or by pressing the F4 (Repeat) key. Either way, you save time and keystrokes.

Q After I created a custom numeric format in one workbook, why couldn't I use it in another workbook?

A You can reuse all modified custom numeric formats within a worksheet without retyping them. Excel stores all customized formats at the bottom of the Type list. That way, you can select them over and over. However, if you create a custom format for one workbook, you have to re-create the format for other workbooks.

Adding Borders, Colors, and Fills

The highlights of this hour include the following:

- How to change the color of cell entries
- How to add borders to cells and ranges
- How to work with fills, shading, and color
- How to format with AutoFormat

This hour covers adding borders, colors, and fills to your worksheets. Excel offers many types of borders that can be applied in different thicknesses and colors to add pizzazz and style. You learn how to change the font color, add shading to cells, and use color fills to put some spice into the background of your worksheet. In addition, you use the AutoFormat command to apply pre-fab formats to your worksheets in one shot so that you don't have to apply each type of format individually.

When this hour ends, you'll know how to add all kinds of borders, colors, and fills to make important data stand out and grab your readers' attention.

Have It Your Way

You can embellish your worksheets with borders, shading, and colors that are cool, elegant, or professional. Your choice of formatting depends on your mood and the data inside the border. Sometimes a worksheet needs to be decorated to grab the reader's attention.

Always keep your audience in mind when you design a worksheet. If you're giving the worksheet to the comptroller of your company, you might want to make it more reserved and subtle. You could add thick line borders to point out the bottom-line figures at a glance. Or you could add gray shading to the important numbers on the worksheet. Keep it simple, and you can't go wrong.

If you're going to make the worksheets into slides for a presentation, you need to add bright colors and spiffy shading. Add borders, several colors, and a couple of patterns that do justice to your worksheet, but don't overwhelm it. Experiment with Excel's pre-fab AutoFormat table formats until you find the one that flatters your worksheet.

Changing the Color of Cell Entries

You already know how to change the font, font style, and font size. This section shows you how to change the font color. By default, the font color is Automatic, which is black. The Font Color command lets you change font color in two ways:

- Choose a color on the Font tab in the Format Cells dialog box.
- Click a color in the Font Color palette on the Formatting toolbar.

A good example of when you would want to change font color is when you add dark cell shading that causes the text to disappear. Consider using the Font Color command to select a light color for the text. Another example is when you are using one font color for one set of numbers such as the first-quarter figures and want to use a different font color for numbers in the second quarter.

If you have a color printer, you can get some beautiful and professional-looking results by changing the font colors to draw attention to important data.

In the upcoming To Do exercise, you change the font color for the title and date on the Summary sheet in the Sales workbook. Open the Sales 1st Qtr workbook if it isn't open already.

To Do: Change Font Color

1. Select cell A1. This step selects the title you want to format.
2. Click the Format menu and choose Cells. The Format Cells dialog box opens.

A fast way to change the font color is to click the Font Color down arrow on the Formatting toolbar and choose any color you want from the Font Color palette.

3. Click the Font tab. The Font options move to the front.

You can change the font color by using the shortcut menu; select the cell, click the right mouse button on the cell to display the shortcut menu, and then choose Format Cells.

10

4. Click the Color down arrow. You should see a palette of colors, as shown in Figure 10.1.

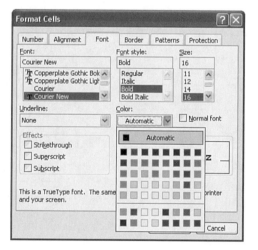

FIGURE 10.1

Font color options in the Format Cells dialog box.

5. Click the Blue color patch.

6. Click OK. Excel applies the color to your selected text.

7. Click any cell to deselect the range.

If the font color isn't what you expected, you can either pick a new color or return to the default Automatic (black) color. Select the cells that contain the font color and click the Font Color down arrow on the Formatting toolbar. On the Font Color palette, choose a new color or Automatic.

The toolbar makes it a snap to change the color of cell entries. The Font Color button tool on the Formatting toolbar provides a medley of color choices.

To change the color of text, select the text you want to change. Then click the Font Color button on the Formatting toolbar. A palette of many colors appears, as shown in Figure 10.2. Next click any color patch you want. Excel applies the color to the selected text.

FIGURE 10.2

Font color palette on the Formatting toolbar.

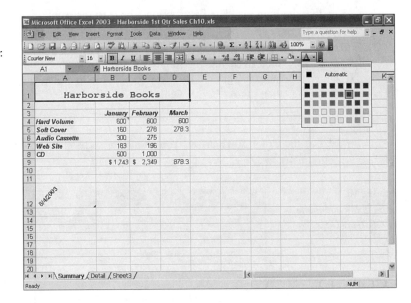

Adding Borders to Cells and Ranges

One way to improve the appearance of a worksheet is to add borders to the data on the worksheet. You can add boxes around cells and ranges, add emphasis lines anywhere on the worksheet, and change the thickness and color of the border lines.

As you work with your worksheet onscreen, each cell is identified by a gridline that surrounds the cell. In print, these gridlines might appear washed out. To have better defined lines appear on the printout, you can add borders to selected cells or cell ranges.

You can frame selected cells with a border to make your data stand out. Highlight parts of a table to emphasize the content by placing a thick border around the specific cells you want to attract attention to. Select the cells you want to use and then apply the border.

Adding a border to a title, title and subtitle, total row, and total column are just some ways you can use borders. More specifically, you can have a single, thick, outline border that creates a box around a title for the worksheet. Or, you can add a double underline on the bottom of cells to call attention to the totals.

Applying a Border

The Borders feature lets you manipulate the placement of the borders, the thickness of the lines, and color for any border lines. You can make borders a little more interesting by changing the thickness and color of specific border lines. You can have a different thickness and a different color for each border, or any combination of thickness and color.

By combining border options, you get various results. Try combining border options with row-height and column-width options to get different effects. Experiment on your worksheets for best results.

Applying a border is a cinch; it's making the decisions about the elements of the border that's difficult. The standard borders that Excel offers work just fine, but if you want to get creative, just click away on the Borders tab in the Format Cells dialog box until you get the border you want.

In the next exercise, you add a single-line top border and double-line bottom border to the totals in row 9 in the Summary sheet in the Sales 1st Qtr workbook.

To Do: Add a Border

1. Select the cells that will be surrounded by a border; in this case, select B9:D9.
2. Click the Format menu and choose Cells. The Format Cells dialog box opens.
3. Click the Border tab. The Border options jump up front, as shown in Figure 10.3.

A fast way to add a border is to click the Borders button on the Formatting toolbar and choose the type of border you want from the Borders palette.

You can add borders to your worksheet by using the shortcut menu; select the cell, click the right mouse button on the cell to display the shortcut menu, and then choose Format Cells.

4. Click the top of the Border preview diagram to add a top single-line border.
5. Click the double-underline line style.
6. Click the bottom of the Border preview diagram to add a bottom double-line border.
7. Click OK. Excel should apply a single-line top border and double-line bottom border to the selected cells.

FIGURE 10.3

Border options in the Format Cells dialog box.

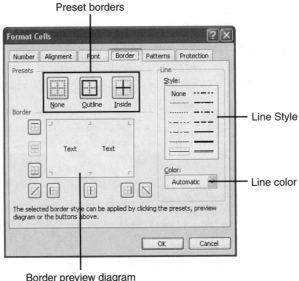

Preset borders

Line Style

Line color

Border preview diagram

The outline border still can be hard to see because the gridlines are displayed onscreen. If you want to turn off the gridlines, choose Tools, Options and then click the View tab. In the Window Options section, choose Gridlines and click OK.

8. Click any cell to deselect the range. Figure 10.4 shows the border on the Summary sheet.

9. Using Figure 10.4 as a guide, enter the rest of the numbers in column D. Format the numbers in column D to match the number formats in columns B and C.

▲ 10. Move the date in cell A12 to cell E1. Make row 1 taller, if necessary.

To remove a border, select the cells that contain the border, click the Borders down arrow on the Formatting toolbar, and choose No Border.

FIGURE 10.4

A border applied to a range of cells.

Single top border   Date in cell E1

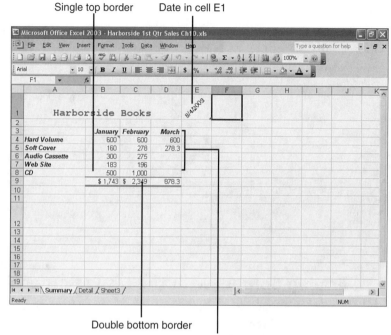

Double bottom border
Rest of formatted entries in Column D

Using the Toolbar to Apply a Border

When you're in a hurry to add borders, you can use the Borders button on the Formatting toolbar to apply a border. First, select the cells around which you want the border to appear. Then click the down arrow to the right of the Borders button on the Formatting toolbar. A palette of border choices appears, as illustrated in Figure 10.5. Click the desired border.

If you click the Borders button itself (rather than on the arrow), Excel automatically adds a bottom border or the border you last chose to the selected cells.

Figure 10.5
Borders palette.

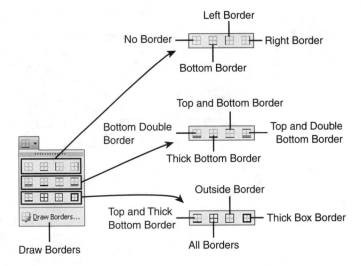

Draw Borders

Adding Borders with the Draw Border Tools

You can draw borders exactly where you want them with the Draw Border feature. This feature enables you to draw a border using the mouse. The Draw Border tools are on a separate toolbar, called the Borders toolbar. To display the Borders toolbar, click the down arrow to the right of the Borders button on the Formatting toolbar. Then click Draw Borders. The Borders toolbar appears, as shown in Figure 10.6.

Figure 10.6
The Borders toolbar.

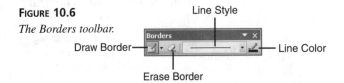

To draw a border on any side of a cell, click the down arrow to the right of the Draw Border button on the Borders toolbar. Choose Draw Border. The mouse pointer looks like a pencil. You can create borders by clicking the left mouse button and dragging the pen along any side of any cell.

> If you want to change the line style, click the Line Style down arrow on the Borders toolbar and select a line style. If you want to change the line color, click the Line Color button on the Borders toolbar and select a color from the palette.

To draw border grids anywhere on the worksheet, click the down arrow to the right of the Draw Border button on the Borders toolbar. Choose Draw Border Grid. The mouse pointer looks like a pencil with a grid next to it. You can create border grids by clicking in any cell and dragging it across the cells where you want a border grid to appear.

> To erase a border, click the Erase Border button on the Borders toolbar. The mouse pointer looks like a rubber eraser. Drag the eraser over the cells that contain borders you want to remove. Excel removes the borders.

Working with Fills, Shading, and Color

For a simple but dramatic effect, try adding fills, shading, and color to the cells in your worksheets. Add some zest to the appearance of your worksheets by using splashes of color to illuminate some of your data. Excel provides a way to fill cells with colors and color patterns.

Adding Background Patterns and Colors with the Format Cells Dialog Box

One way to add background colors and patterns is via the Format Cells dialog box. Color adds plain color and overall shading to cells.

A pattern is a black-and-white or colored pattern that lies on top of the overall shading. Patterns put texture into color, creating a more interesting eye-catcher than a plain color. Keep in mind that a pattern is busier than a plain color, so you don't want to use a pattern on a busy worksheet.

This To Do exercise walks you through adding background colors and patterns to selected cells in the Summary sheet.

To Do: Add Background Patterns and Colors

1. Select the cells you want to shade; in this case, select cells A4:A8.
2. Click the Format menu and choose Cells. The Format Cells dialog box opens.
3. Click the Patterns tab. The shading options jump to the front, as shown in Figure 10.7. The Color options let you choose a color for the overall shading. The Pattern options let you select a black-and-white or colored pattern that lies on top of the overall shading. The Sample box displays a preview of the result.

10

A fast way to add shading is to click the Fill Color down arrow on the
Formatting toolbar and choose any color desired from the Fill Color palette.

FIGURE 10.7
*Shading options in
the Format Cells
dialog box.*

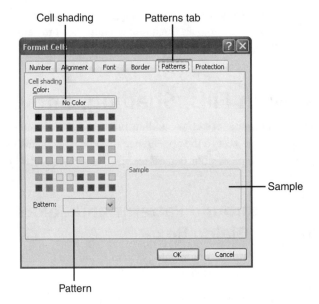

You can add shading to your worksheet by using the shortcut menu; select
the cell, click the right mouse button on the cell to display the shortcut
menu, and then choose Format Cells.

4. In the top Color palette, in the last row, sixth column, click the pale blue color
   patch.

5. Click the down arrow next to Pattern. You should see a grid that contains all the
   colors from the color palette, as well as patterns. Figure 10.8 shows the Pattern
   palette.

6. In the first row, last column, click the 6.25% gray pattern. This subtle pattern suits
   the data on the worksheet.

7. Click OK. You should see shading with a pattern in the selected cells.

8. Click any cell to deselect the range.

FIGURE 10.8

Pattern palette on the Patterns tab.

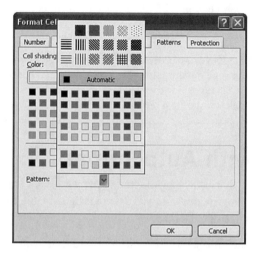

10

Selecting a Fill Color from the Toolbar

If you want to speed up the process of adding a fill color to your worksheet, use the Formatting toolbar. First, select the cells that you want to shade. Then click the Fill Color down arrow on the Formatting toolbar. Excel displays a palette of color choices, as shown in Figure 10.9.

Shaded pattern in a range of cells

Fill Color button

FIGURE 10.9

Fill Color palette.

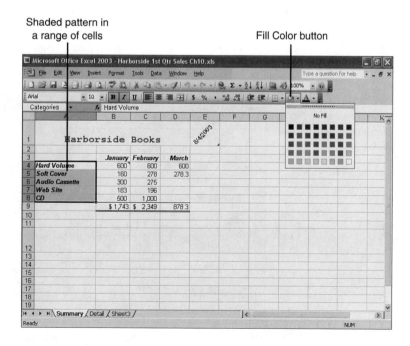

Pick a color, any color. Excel adds the color to the selected cells. Click any cell to dese-lect the range so you can get a good look at those colorful cells.

> If the shading doesn't tickle your fancy, you can either pick a new shade or clear the shading altogether. Select the cells that contain the shading and click the Fill Color down-arrow button on the Formatting toolbar. On the Fill Color palette, choose a new shade or No Fill.

Formatting with AutoFormat

Excel's AutoFormat feature takes away some of the hard work involved in formatting a worksheet. AutoFormat provides you with 16 predesigned table formats that you can apply to a selected range of cells on a worksheet.

Instead of applying each format to your data, one at a time, you can apply a group of for-mats in one shot with one of Excel's predesigned formats. The AutoFormat command lets you select a format and transform your table with a couple of mouse clicks.

In this To Do exercise, you get to try out a predesigned format using the AutoFormat command.

To Do: Apply an AutoFormat

1. Select the cells that contain the data you want to format; in this case, select cells A3:D9.
2. Choose Format, AutoFormat. The AutoFormat dialog box pops open, as shown in Figure 10.10. You see a palette of predesigned table format samples, each with a name.

FIGURE 10.10

Predesigned table for-mats in the AutoFormat dialog box.

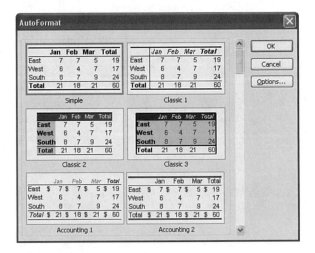

▼   3. Scroll through the table format samples. Stop at the List 2 sample.

4. Click the List 2 sample table format.

> To view the elements that make up the selected table format, click the Options button. You can turn off any Format option to customize the look of the table format.

5. Click OK. Excel formats your table to make it look like the one in the sample you selected. It looks great!

6. Click any cell to deselect the range. Figure 10.11 shows the table formatted with the
▲   List 2 AutoFormat. The green bars make the worksheet more attractive and readable.

10

FIGURE **10.11**

The worksheet format-
ted with the List 2
AutoFormat.

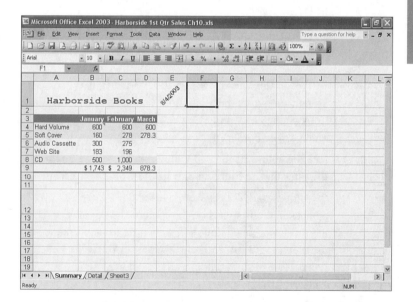

> What if you don't like what AutoFormat did to your worksheet? No problem. To remove a prefab format, press Ctrl+Z to undo the format.

Summary

In this hour, you learned about formatting your Excel data with each individual type of format (borders, shading, colors, and patterns), as well as formatting in one fell swoop with AutoFormat. In the next hour, you learn how to draw shapes and insert ready-made art objects to spice up your worksheets.

Q&A

Q I changed the font color several times and didn't care for the results. Is there an easy way to return to the original black text?

A Sure. Select the cells, click the Font Color down-arrow button on the Formatting toolbar, and choose Automatic.

Q When I shaded my cells with black, why couldn't I see my text?

A Use the Font Color command to select white or a light color for the text.

Q After I added an outline border to my worksheet, why is the border so hard to see?

A Outline borders can be hard to see because the gridlines are displayed onscreen. To turn off the gridlines, choose Tools, Options and click the View tab. In the Window Options section, choose Gridlines and click OK.

Q How do I remove two of the borders in a box?

A To remove two borders in a box, you need to use the Border tab in the Format Cells dialog box. In the Border preview diagram, click each border you want to remove. The border in the diagram disappears. Click OK to confirm your changes.

Q Are the colors in the Fill Color palette on the Formatting toolbar the same as the ones on the Patterns tab in the Color section?

A Good question! The answer is yes and no. Here's the yes answer: The 40 color patches in the first grid on the Patterns tab and the 40 color patches in the grid on the Fill Color palette on the Formatting toolbar are the same. The no answer is that the second grid (beneath the 40-color grid) on the Patterns tab contains 16 additional color patches that are mixed colors. You get more color choices on the Patterns tab.

Q I filled some cells with color, and now I've changed my mind. How do I remove the color from the cells?

A Don't sweat the small stuff. It's easy to remove the color. Select the cells, click the Fill Color down-arrow button on the Formatting toolbar, and choose No Fill.

Q I applied an AutoFormat table format to my table, and it's not what I want. How do I remove the AutoFormat?

A To remove a prefab format, select the table and choose Format, AutoFormat. Scroll to the bottom of the format sample palette and choose None to remove the AutoFormat.

PART III

Interactive Data Makes Your Worksheet Come Alive

Hour

HOUR 11

Working with Graphics Objects

The topics in this hour include the following:

- What a graphic object is
- Why use graphics
- How to use the Drawing toolbar
- How to add clip art
- How to add special effects with WordArt
- How to combine multiple objects
- How to manipulate graphic objects
- How to delete graphic objects

During this hour, you are introduced to Excel's drawing tools, pictures in worksheets, and the WordArt feature that lets you create logos and fancy-looking words in your worksheets.

When this hour ends, you should know how to add graphics objects to your worksheets and produce some pretty interesting artwork.

What Is a Graphics Object?

Clip art, word art, pictures, photographs, or any shape you draw is called a *graphics object*. After you add a graphics object to your worksheet, you can select it and perform actions such as copying, moving, sizing, and applying attributes. The possibilities are endless.

With Excel's powerful drawing tools, you can create a simple illustration with rectangles, squares, ovals, circles, straight lines, curved lines, and freeform lines; and then you can embellish your drawing with the editing tools on the Drawing toolbar.

Why Use Graphics?

As they say, a picture is worth a thousand words. And how! When you add graphics to your worksheets, you're adding emphasis, visual impact, excitement, and visual interest with a sprinkling of artwork.

Despite the huge variety of wonderful clip art that's available, you still might not be able to find that perfect image. Or perhaps you'd just prefer to create your own art. In either case, you don't have to be a talented artist to create vibrant, eye-catching graphics.

Excel gives you such a wealth of artwork and effects to add to your worksheets that you might not know where to begin. But, nevertheless, graphics can make your worksheets explode with life and energy.

Using the Drawing Toolbar

Like drawing on paper, using Excel's Draw feature takes patience and practice. The Drawing toolbar offers many drawing tools for drawing and modifying lines and shapes, including 3D shapes. The drawing tools also come in handy for annotating your worksheet data and charts.

To display the Drawing toolbar, you click the Drawing button on the Standard toolbar. Figure 11.1 depicts the tools on the Drawing toolbar. To hide the Drawing toolbar, click the Drawing button on the Standard toolbar again.

Table 11.1 lists the drawing tools on the Drawing toolbar and describes what they do.

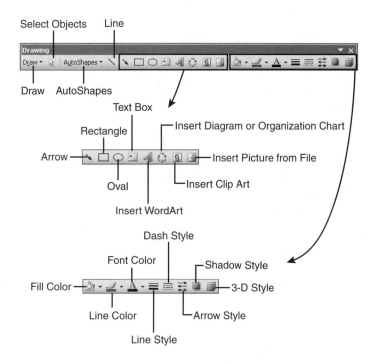

FIGURE 11.1

The tools on the Drawing toolbar.

TABLE 11.1   Excel's Drawing Tools

Tool	What It Does
Draw	Displays a Draw menu that contains commands for rotating, flipping, nudging, and positioning objects.
Select Objects	Selects drawing objects so that you can move or edit them.
AutoShapes	Adds predesigned shapes to your drawing.
Line	Adds solid, dotted, and dashed lines to your drawing.
Arrow	Adds arrows to your drawing.
Rectangle	Adds a rectangle or square to your drawing.
Oval	Adds an oval or a circle to your drawing.
Text Box	Adds a box into which you can type text.
Insert WordArt	Lets you insert WordArt into your worksheet.
Insert Diagram or Organization Chart	Lets you insert a diagram or organization chart into your worksheet.
Insert Clip Art	Lets you insert clip art into your worksheet.
Insert Picture from File	Lets you insert a picture file into your worksheet.

11

TABLE 11.1   continued

Tool	What It Does
Fill Color	Adds, removes, and changes the fill color in an object.
Line Color	Adds and removes lines and changes the line color in an object.
Font Color	Changes the color of the font.
Line Style	Changes the line style for lines in objects. Choose any line style from thick to thin from the Line Style palette.
Dash Style	Changes the line style from dots to dashes.
Arrow Style	Changes the arrowhead type for a line, an arc, or a polygon.
Shadow Style	Adds and removes a drop shadow from the border of selected objects.
3-D Style	Adds and formats 3D objects.

After you draw an object, small squares, called *selection handles*, surround the object's border. The selection handles indicate the object is selected and let you modify the object. Before you can move, resize, or edit an object, you must select it. To select an object, just click anywhere on it. When the selection handles appear, you can then use the handles to move and resize the object.

Other alterations you can make to an object you have created include changing the color, border, and fill. Filling an object places a pattern or color inside the object to make the shape more interesting. You can also delete objects when you no longer need them.

Drawing a Shape

With Excel's drawing tools, you can create an almost endless variety of shapes. You can start with a simple drawing and then build on it. When you want to draw a shape, you click a shape tool on the Drawing toolbar, drag the crosshair pointer straight in a particular direction or diagonally to draw the shape you want, and then release the mouse button. A nice feature about drawing shapes in an Excel worksheet is that you have the gridlines on the worksheet to use as guides for starting and ending an object.

Are you ready to draw some shapes? You don't have to be a talented artist to create vibrant, eye-catching graphics. Try out the Line and Rectangle tools to draw a line and a rectangle in the next To Do exercise. Again, you need to use the Sales workbook, so be sure to have it open before you begin the exercise. You'll be drawing shapes in the Sheet3 sheet.

To Do: Draw a Shape

1. Click the Sheet3 tab. This sheet is where you'll draw your shapes.

2. Click the Drawing button on the Standard toolbar. The Drawing toolbar appears at the bottom of the Excel window.

3. Click the Line button on the Drawing toolbar. The mouse pointer changes to a crosshair when you move it over the worksheet.

4. Move the crosshair over cell B4. This cell is where you want the object to begin.

5. Click and drag your crosshair from the left edge of cell B4 to the right edge of C4. This cell is where the object ends. Release the mouse button. Figure 11.2 shows the line object and the Drawing toolbar. Notice the selection handle on each end of the object. These handles indicate the object is selected. You can drag the handles to resize the line object.

FIGURE 11.2

A line object and the Drawing toolbar.

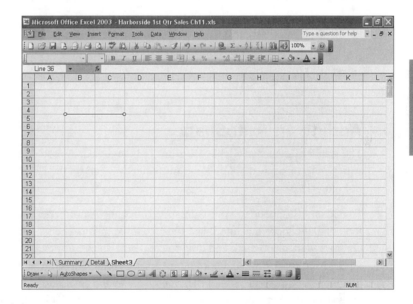

11

6. Click outside of the line object to make the selection handles disappear.

7. To draw a rectangle, click the Rectangle button on the Drawing toolbar. The crosshair pointer appears on the worksheet.

▼

If you want to draw a perfect square, click the Rectangle button, and hold down the Shift key when you drag the crosshair pointer diagonally to draw the square. If you want to draw a perfect circle, click the Oval button, and hold down the Shift key when you drag the crosshair pointer diagonally to draw the circle.

8. Move the crosshair over cell D3. This cell is where you want the rectangle to begin.

9. Click and drag diagonally from the top-left corner of cell D3 to the bottom-right corner of cell E5. This cell is where the object ends. Release the mouse button. Now you should see a rectangle on your worksheet.

10. Click outside of the rectangle object to make the selection handles disappear.

If the shape didn't turn out the way you want it to, click the shape to select it and press the Delete key. Or click the Undo button on the Standard toolbar.

Adding an AutoShape

The standard shapes available are a line, rectangle, square, oval, and circle. For a greater variety, use those available via the AutoShapes menu on the Drawing toolbar, as shown in Figure 11.3.

To add an AutoShape to your worksheet, click the AutoShapes button on the Drawing toolbar and choose an AutoShape type from the menu. Then click the shape that you like. On your worksheet, click and drag to create the shape. For example, if you click Callouts on the AutoShapes menu, choose the Cloud Callout, and hold down the Shift key while dragging the crosshair pointer diagonally across the cells, Excel inserts the cloud shape on your worksheet. An insertion point appears inside the cloud, ready for you to type text. Type My Artwork and click any cell in the worksheet. Figure 11.4 shows the cloud callout pointing to the shapes you drew earlier.

If you want to draw a perfect AutoShape shape, hold down the Shift key when you drag the crosshair pointer diagonally to draw the shape.

FIGURE 11.3

The AutoShapes menu on the Drawing toolbar.

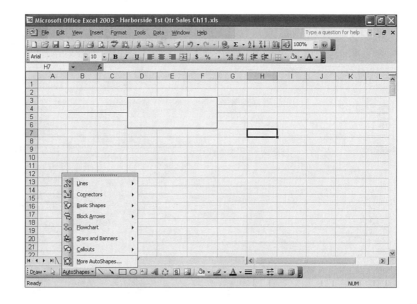

The Draw menu on the Drawing toolbar contains a command intended for use with AutoShapes. The Change AutoShape command is a special command for converting one AutoShape to another.

11

FIGURE 11.4

The cloud callout AutoShape.

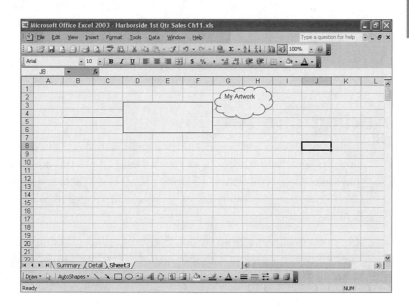

To change an AutoShape, click the Draw button on the Drawing toolbar and choose
Change AutoShape. You should see a menu of shape types. Click a shape type, and a
palette of shapes appears, as shown in Figure 11.5. Click any AutoShape you like. Excel
inserts the shape into your worksheet.

FIGURE 11.5

Change AutoShape
command on the Draw
menu.

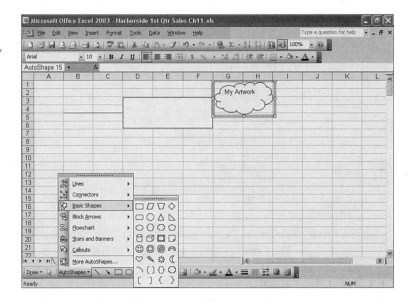

Rather than change the AutoShape, you can delete the AutoShape and start over. Be sure
to select the AutoShape you want to remove and then press the Delete key. Repeat the
steps mentioned earlier to insert a different AutoShape.

Adding Clip Art

Instead of drawing your own pictures in your worksheet, you can use ready-made clip art
and photographs to spruce up your data. Plenty of pictures come with Excel, so all you
have to do is insert a picture wherever you want it to appear in a worksheet. Excel's clip
art collection contains a myriad of professionally prepared pictures that can enhance a
wide range of topics.

Microsoft organizes clip art by descriptive keywords including almost any popular art—
from academic to zoo. In addition to art, you can insert sound effects, music, videos, and
other media clips into your worksheets to add auditory and visual interest.

You can get clip art from the following places:

- Microsoft's clip organizer
- Clip art on the Web
- Clip art software packages

Getting Clip Art from the Clip Art Task Pane

NEW 2003 The Microsoft Clip Organizer lets you store collections of your favorite clip art, photos, and sounds. Excel automatically adds any clips you select from the Web to the Clip Organizer.

To organize your clips, click Organize Clips at the bottom of the Clip Art task pane, and the Microsoft Clip Organizer appears. Click a folder in the Collection List in the left pane, and click Search or Clips Online to find and select the clips you want to store in the folder. For example, click the + next to Downloaded Clips, click the Academic folder, and then click Search or Clips Online to find and download your favorite academic clips.

After you download clips into the Microsoft Clip Organizer, you can copy and paste any clip you want. Simply point to a clip, click the down arrow on the right side of the clip, and choose Copy. Right-click in a cell on the worksheet where you want the clip to appear and choose Paste.

In addition to copying and pasting clips from the Microsoft Clip Organizer, you use clips that come with Excel. You can insert clip art pictures in your worksheet with the Insert, Picture, Clip Art command. For example, you could insert a graphic in a sales report to spice it up. In the next exercise, you insert clip art in Sheet3.

To Do: Insert Clip Art

1. Select cell B8. This cell is where you want to insert the clip art.
2. Click the Insert menu and choose Picture, Clip Art. The Clip Art task pane opens.
3. In the Search For text box, type **sunshine**, as shown in Figure 11.6.

> You can also insert clip art from the Drawing toolbar. Just click the Insert Clip Art button on the Drawing toolbar to display the Clip Art task pane.

4. Scroll down through the thumbnails of sunshine clips until you see the thumbnail that shows the sun and a pair of sunglasses. If you don't see this clip, select any clip that shows the sun. When you point to the thumbnail, Excel displays a ScreenTip that contains the clip's categories, dimensions (width and height), size

(KB), and file type. For example, one of the sunshine clips belongs to the categories Household, Seasons, Summer; its dimensions are 239 (width) by 259 (height) pixels; its size is 11KB; and it has the file type WMF.

FIGURE 11.6

The Clip Art task pane.

To widen the palette of thumbnails, click the button with a pane and left arrow at the top of the task pane beneath Results. To narrow the palette of thumbnails, click the button with a pane and right arrow at the top of the task pane beneath Results.

5. Point to the sunshine clip and click the down arrow on the right side of the clip. A menu appears, which contains commands for working with the clip, as shown in Figure 11.7.

6. Choose Insert on the shortcut menu. Excel inserts the clip into your worksheet.

If the clip file was not installed or had been deleted, you need to install the clip art from the Microsoft Office or Microsoft Excel CD-ROM software. After you insert the CD, click OK to install the clip art.

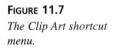

FIGURE 11.7
The Clip Art shortcut menu.

7. Click the Close button in the upper-right corner of the Clip Art task pane to close the pane. You should see the cartoon on your worksheet along with the Picture toolbar, which you don't need now. Selection handles (white squares) surround the picture.

8. Click the Close button on the Picture toolbar to close the toolbar.

9. Click outside the picture to deselect it. Notice that the picture overlaps the rectangle, but there's no need to worry. We will fix that later by moving objects on the worksheet.

> To remove a piece of clip art, click it to select it and press the Delete key. Excel removes the clip art from the worksheet.

Visiting the Web

The Web offers thousands of pieces of clip art and photographs that you can insert in your worksheets. You just need to tell Excel and your Web browser where to find the clip art and photographs you want, and Excel will get them for you.

To insert clip art from the Web, first make sure you're connected and online if necessary. Then choose Insert, Picture, Clip Art. The Clip Art task pane opens. At the bottom of the task pane, click Clip Art on Office Online. This link lets you access the Clip Art and Media Web site for more pictures.

Other Sources for Clip Art

There are other sources for clip art besides Excel and the Web. Images galore! They're out there, ready for you to use. You can buy packages of clip art (in black and white or color) from software stores and mail-order catalogs. These clip art "libraries" are packaged by topics such as animals, business, holidays, music, and people. Clip art is also sold on CDs. If you want more professional artwork, look for photo collections, which are usually sold on CDs.

Adding Special Effects with WordArt

You can use Excel's WordArt to create special text effects and insert the text into your worksheet. Perhaps you want to create logos, display type, or other interesting and eye-catching text for your Excel worksheets using WordArt. You can bend, twist, turn, and angle WordArt text; change the font size, and font style; and add formatting features to the text using one or more colors or textures. You can even add a drop shadow to the text.

Creating a WordArt Object

When you create a WordArt object, you can take creative license to make up any kind of logo, fancy text, or piece of text artwork to embellish your worksheet. WordArt styles range from funky to serious and somber.

The next exercise walks you through creating fancy text with WordArt on the Sheet3 sheet.

To Do: Insert WordArt

1. Click the Insert menu and choose Picture, WordArt. The WordArt Gallery dialog box opens. Thirty WordArt styles are available, as shown in Figure 11.8.

2. Click the WordArt style in the first row, fourth column to select the WordArt style for the fancy text you're going to create.

> You can also insert WordArt from the Drawing toolbar. Simply click the Insert WordArt button on the Drawing toolbar to display the WordArt Gallery dialog box.

3. Click OK to confirm your style selection. The Edit WordArt Text dialog box appears (see Figure 11.9). This dialog box is where you type your text for the WordArt object. You can also change the font, font size, and font style here.

FIGURE 11.8

The WordArt Gallery dialog box, displaying WordArt styles.

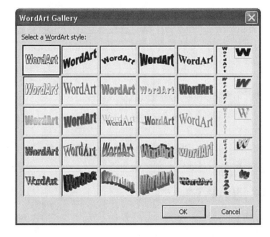

> To delete a WordArt object, click it to select it and press the Delete key. Excel removes the WordArt text from the worksheet.

11

4. Type **Email Vmail**, which is the text for your WordArt creation.

5. Click OK. The WordArt object and WordArt toolbar should appear in your worksheet. The white squares (selection handles) indicate that the object is selected.

6. Click outside of the WordArt logo to deselect the object and hide the WordArt toolbar.

FIGURE 11.9

The Edit WordArt Text dialog box.

Modifying a WordArt Object

After you insert a WordArt object, you can format the art to make it as plain or fancy as you want. When you insert a WordArt object into a worksheet, Excel displays the WordArt toolbar (see Figure 11.10). This toolbar contains tools for making changes to WordArt objects.

FIGURE 11.10
WordArt toolbar.

In the To Do exercise, you learn how to modify the WordArt logo you created. You change the font, font size, and color for the logo.

To Do: Modify WordArt

1. Click the WordArt logo to select it. Selection handles appear around the artwork, and the WordArt toolbar shows up.

2. Click the Edit Text button on the WordArt toolbar. The Edit WordArt Text dialog box appears. Here's where you can change the font, font size, and font style.

3. Click the Font down arrow and choose Book Antiqua (or any other font you want).

4. Click the Font Size down arrow and choose 28.

5. Click OK.

6. Click the Format WordArt button on the WordArt toolbar. The Format WordArt dialog box opens, as shown in Figure 11.11. This dialog box has options for colors, lines, size, protection, properties, and the Web.

FIGURE 11.11
Format WordArt dialog box.

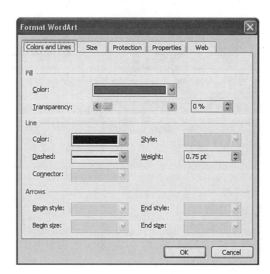

▼   7. Click the Colors and Lines tab if necessary. This tab offers fill, line, and arrow options. You want to change the color of the WordArt text.

      8. Click Color down arrow in the Fill section. Choose Red.

      9. Click OK.

▲   10. Click outside the object to make the selection handles and WordArt toolbar disappear.

Manipulating Graphics Objects

It's never too late to make changes to the object you've created. You can refer to Table 11.1 earlier in this hour for a list of the editing tools on the Drawing toolbar and explanations on how to use them. Remember, you must select an object before you can edit it.

You can move an object wherever you want in the worksheet. First you need to select the object, and then you can use the mouse to move the object to a new location. The images you place in the worksheet might need to be moved to a better position. Some images might be overlapping each other or hiding data in the worksheet. In these cases, you would want to move the objects to a different place on the worksheet.

In addition to the editing tools on the Drawing toolbar, commands on the Draw menu on the toolbar let you work with your drawing objects or with clip art images that have been inserted with the Insert, Picture, Clip Art or Insert, Picture, From File commands. These Flip commands let you flip an object left, right, up, or down. The Rotate commands enable you to rotate objects at an angle, so they appear slanted on the worksheet.

Excel lets you enlarge or reduce the size of an object. After you select an object, you can use its selection handles (circles) and the mouse to resize the object. When the pictures in your worksheet are in place, you can do one more improvement to make them picture-perfect—you can resize them.

Moving Objects

Moving an object in Excel is easy. But before you can move an object, you must select the object. Just click anywhere on the object to select it. Then point to the object and drag it to the new location.

In the upcoming To Do exercise, you move the objects you drew on Sheet3 earlier in this hour. You also move the WordArt object to a new location on the worksheet.

11

To Do: Move an Object

1. Click the rectangle shape to select it. You should see selection handles surrounding the rectangle, as shown in Figure 11.12. The mouse pointer changes to a four-headed arrow.

2. Drag the rectangle to cell I10. You have now moved an object.

3. Click the WordArt text to select it. The selection handles should appear on all sides of the piece of art. When you point to the WordArt text and a four-headed arrow appears, you're ready to move the object.

4. Drag the WordArt object so that it's below the cloud and to the left of the rectangle. You have now moved another object.

5. Click any cell to deselect the WordArt object.

If you moved the object to the wrong location, click it and drag it to another part of the worksheet.

FIGURE 11.12

Selecting an object to move it.

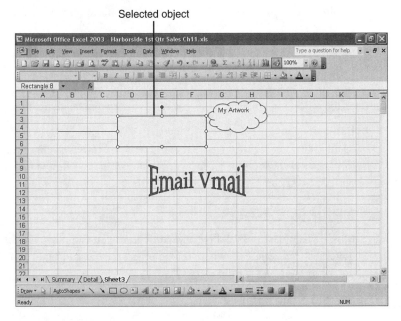

Resizing Objects

After you insert an object and place it where you want in the worksheet, you can stretch or shrink the object to improve its appearance. Making an object shorter, taller, wider, or narrower can make a difference in how the object looks in proportion to other objects and your data on the worksheet.

You resize an object by pointing to a selection handle. When you see a double arrow, drag the handle until the object is the size you want.

In the upcoming To Do exercise, you're going to resize an object you drew earlier in this hour on the Sheet3 sheet.

To Do: Resize an Object

▼ To Do

1. Click the rectangle to select it. The selection handles on the rectangle's border pop out.

2. Point to the right-middle handle until you see a double arrow, as shown in Figure 11.13. The double arrow means that you can drag the handle in either direction to resize the object. In this case, you can drag the object to the right to enlarge it or drag to the left to shrink it.

FIGURE 11.13

You can resize an object by dragging the double-arrow mouse pointer.

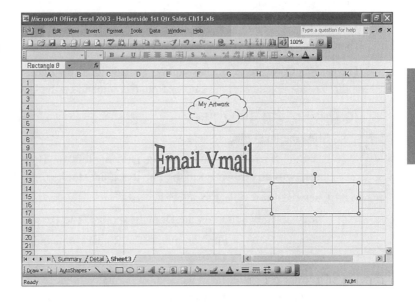

11

3. Click and drag the right-middle handle one column to the right to make the rectangle wider.

4. Click and drag the bottom-middle handle two rows down to make the rectangle taller.

5. Click and drag the lower-right corner handle two rows down and one column to the right to make the rectangle taller and wider at the same time.

▼ 6. Click outside of the rectangle object to deselect it.

If you resized the object and didn't get the right results, just click the object and size the object again. To size an object proportionally, hold down Shift as you drag a corner handle.

Rotating Objects

The fastest and easiest way to rotate an object is to drag the green rotation handle that appears at the top of a selected clip left or right.

Another way to rotate an object is to use Excel's Free Rotate tool on the Drawing toolbar. To rotate an object, click the Free Rotate tool and drag the round handles in the direction in which you want to rotate the object. Click anywhere in the worksheet to turn off the rotate option.

Another way to rotate an object is to use the Flip or Rotate command on the Draw menu. Then you can pick the type of rotation you want from the Rotate menu.

The next To Do exercise teaches you how to add an arrow to the end of the line object and rotate the object with the Flip or Rotate command on the Draw menu.

To Do: Rotate an Object

1. Click the line object to select it.
2. Click the Arrow Style button on the Drawing toolbar. Then select Arrow Style 5. Excel adds an arrowhead to the line that points to the right.
3. Click the arrow object to select it.
4. Click the Draw button on the Drawing toolbar. The Draw menu pops up.
5. Click the Rotate or Flip command. The Rotate commands appear on the menu, as shown in Figure 11.14.
6. Choose Rotate Right 90°. The object is rotated 90 degrees, and now it points down. The top portion of the arrow is hidden.
7. Drag the arrowhead down a few cells so that the entire arrow shows.
8. Click outside of the object to make the selection handles disappear.

If the shape is rotated too much or too little, click it to select it and then choose a different Rotate option. Or click the Free Rotate tool on the Drawing toolbar to rotate the object an exact amount. Or click the Undo button on the Standard toolbar.

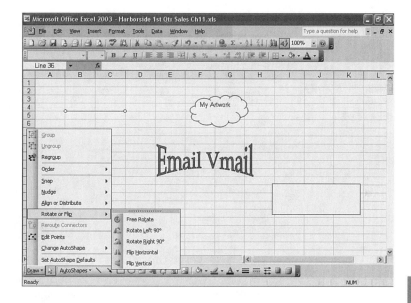

FIGURE 11.14

The Rotate options on the Rotate or Flip menu.

Flipping Objects

The Draw menu on the Drawing toolbar has the Rotate or Flip command that you use only with Drawing objects. This special command controls the orientation of the selected object and can be used to create mirror images.

Working with the Sheet3 worksheet, the To Do exercise shows you how to use the AutoShapes command to create a block arrow that points left. Then you flip the arrow so that it points right.

To Do: Flip an Object

1. Click the AutoShapes button on the Drawing toolbar. Choose Block Arrows and click the Left Arrow shape. The mouse pointer changes to a crosshair when you move it over the worksheet.

2. Move the crosshair over cell D14. This cell is where you want the object to begin.

3. Click and drag your crosshair from the left edge of cell D14 to the right edge of F17. This cell is where the object ends. Release the mouse button. Now you've drawn an arrow object that is horizontal on the worksheet and pointing left. The arrowhead is in cell D14. Now flip the arrow to point right.

4. With the arrow object selected, click the Draw button on the Drawing toolbar. The Draw menu pops up.

5. Click the Rotate or Flip command. A menu of rotate and flip choices appear, as shown in Figure 11.15.

FIGURE **11.15**

The Rotate or Flip command on the Draw menu can help you position items on your worksheets.

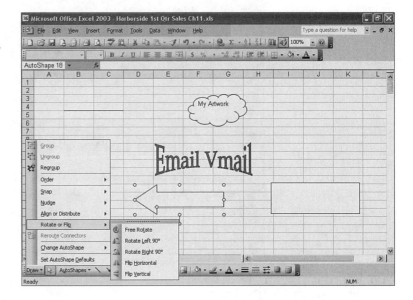

6. Choose Flip Horizontal. The arrowhead points right now.

7. Click outside of the line object to make the selection handles disappear.

Combining Multiple Objects

Objects can overlap each other. When you draw an object in the same general location as an existing object, the new object covers up the previously drawn object. You can use this feature to strategically create special effects, but you might need to change the overlapping order of objects if you don't happen to draw them in the correct sequence. Excel's Bring to Front, Send to Back, Send Forward, and Send Backward commands let you position the objects where you want them on the worksheet.

You can also group objects so that they respond as a single object. This procedure is similar to selecting several cells at the same time, but grouping objects keeps them together as a single object until you ungroup them.

Once you group objects together, you can modify the grouped object by using any of the formatting commands you use for a single object.

Positioning the Objects

Each object that is placed on the worksheet exists on its own layer. Therefore, some objects (those that are closer to the top of the pile) can appear to cover up parts of other objects (those toward the bottom of the pile). Figure 11.16 shows a set of objects arranged in different orders from front (the top of the pile) to back (the bottom of the pile).

FIGURE 11.16

Objects toward the front can hide parts of other objects.

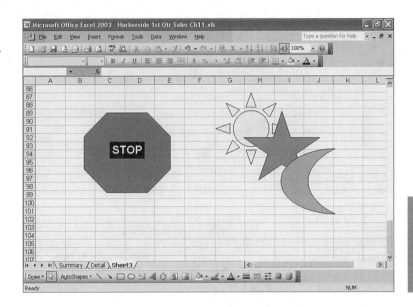

New objects are drawn at the very front of the slide (on the top of the pile). Because objects toward the front of the slide can cover those toward the back, it is often necessary to change the order of the objects. Fortunately, commands on the Draw menu are available for just that purpose.

If you want an object to appear behind all of the other objects (so that those objects can hide part of the object in the back), select the object and then select the Send to Back command on the Draw menu. On the other hand, if you want an object to appear at the very front of the worksheet (so that all of it is visible and it covers up parts of the objects behind it), select the object and then select Bring to Front on the Draw menu.

In general, text should appear at the very front of the drawing. You exercise even greater control over the order of the objects on the slide by using the Send Backward and Bring Forward command on the Draw menu.

In this To Do exercise, you position a circle and a rectangle on the Sheet3 worksheet. First, you draw a circle so that you can position it in front of and behind the square.

11

To Do: Position Objects

1. To draw a circle, click the Oval button on the Drawing toolbar. The crosshair pointer appears on the worksheet.

2. Move the crosshair over cell I2. This cell is where you want the circle to begin.

3. Hold down the Shift key and click and drag diagonally from the top-left corner of cell I2 to the bottom-right corner of cell J7. This cell is where the object ends. Release the mouse button. Now you should see a circle on your worksheet.

4. Drag the circle so that it appears on top of the rectangle.

5. With the circle object selected, click the Draw button on the Drawing toolbar. The Draw menu appears.

6. Choose Order. Figure 11.17 shows the positioning commands available on the Order menu.

7. Choose Send to Back. The circle object is now behind the rectangle. Only the top of the circle shows; the bottom is hidden by the rectangle.

▲   8. Click any cell to deselect the object.

FIGURE 11.17

Positioning commands on the Order menu.

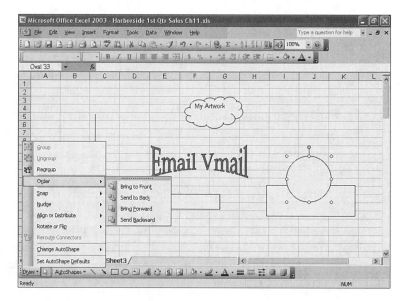

Grouping Objects

After you've drawn and carefully placed several objects, group them to prevent accidentally messing up your placements. By creating a group, you can use a single command to change all the objects at once; for example, when you want to perform an action, such as adding a fill color, to more than one object at a time. Figure 11.18 shows a grouped object.

Select the first object and then hold down the Shift key while selecting additional objects. Next choose Group from the Draw menu. The objects are now grouped together into one object. Only one set of selection handles surround all the objects in the group.

If you change your mind and no longer want to group the objects, select the object and choose Ungroup from the Draw menu. The objects are independent again.

> You might find it quicker to ungroup objects by right-clicking the object and choosing Ungroup from the shortcut menu.

FIGURE 11.18

Grouped objects.

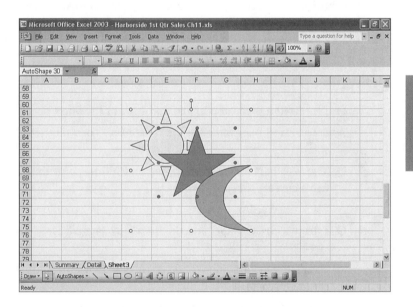

After you ungroup the objects, you don't have to reselect them with the Shift+click method to group them again. Just select one of the objects and choose Regroup from the Draw menu. To work with an individual object, make sure that you select one of the objects before you do anything else. This step ensures that the group is no longer selected.

Modifying a Grouped Object

You can modify a grouped object the same way you would an individual object. Make sure the grouped object is selected and then use any of the tools on the Drawing toolbar to modify the grouped object.

Deleting Graphics Objects

Deleting a graphics object is easier than inserting or creating it. Just click the object to select it and then press the Delete key. Excel removes the graphics object from the worksheet. You can delete grouped objects this way, too.

If you want to bring the object back, it's never too late. Just click the Undo button on the Standard toolbar. Excel displays the graphics object on your worksheet.

Summary

This hour gave you lots of practice with creating and modifying graphics objects. Good job! Now you can feel more comfortable with using pictures in your worksheets. The next hour discusses adding all kinds of charts to your worksheet, giving you the information you need to transform numeric data into pie, column, line, and other various and sundry Excel charts.

Q&A

Q I inserted a piece of clip art, and it's not the one I need. What can I do?

A Select the clip art and press the Delete key. Then start over to insert the clip art you want.

Q The WordArt text is overlapping and hiding some data on the worksheet. How can I correct this problem?

A Click the WordArt object and drag it to a better position.

Q I drew a circle shape, and the lines look jagged. How can I draw a perfect circle?

A To create an exact circle (or an oval), hold down the Shift key while dragging the crosshair pointer.

Q I wanted to insert a piece of clip art in my worksheet, but the clip is not available when I select Insert on the Clip Art shortcut menu. Where can I find the pictures?

A If the images are not available in the Clip Art task pane, they probably were not installed or have been deleted. No problem—just install the clip art through the Add/Remove Programs panel in the Windows Control Panel using the Microsoft Office or Microsoft Excel CD-ROM software.

Q I want to ungroup a grouped object. What is the fastest way to do so?

A You might find it quick to ungroup objects by right-clicking the object and choosing Ungroup from the shortcut menu.

HOUR 12

Adding a Chart

The highlights of this hour are as follows:

- Reasons for using a chart
- The chart elements
- The chart types
- How to create charts with the Chart Wizard
- How to work with charts
- How to format charts
- How to pull a pie slice from a chart

This hour provides complete instructions for creating Excel charts. First, you get a brief overview of the charting process. After this, you get an explanation of some basic charting terminology used throughout the rest of the hour and in Excel's commands and options. Details about creating charts follow.

At the end of this hour, you'll realize that Excel's charting capabilities give you a lot of control in how you can present data.

Why Use a Chart?

Rather than using only a worksheet to represent data, you can create a chart to represent the same data. For example, you might want to create a chart and print the chart and worksheet together for a presentation. That way, your audience can easily see trends in a series of values.

If you change any data in the specified chart range, Excel will update the chart accordingly, to reflect the new data in the worksheet. Perhaps you want to track the sales trends of several products with a line chart. Make as many "what if?" projections as you want in the worksheet by increasing and decreasing the values. As you change the values in the worksheet, Excel updates the chart instantly. Excel's charts let you view the sales trends in a picture representation onscreen and the numbers in the worksheet simultaneously, making your sales forecasting more efficient.

Charting is really simple to do. Don't let all the charting commands and options make you think otherwise.

Chart Elements

Before you begin to create charts, you need to be familiar with the chart elements shown in Figure 12.1. Take a few moments to look over the elements of a chart. Figure 12.1 shows a basic column chart with various elements identified.

Table 12.1 lists the chart terms and provides an explanation of each chart element that you need to keep in mind when you're working with charts.

TABLE 12.1   Excel's Chart Elements

Element	What It Is
Data series	The bars, pie wedges, or other elements that represent plotted values in a chart. Often, the data series corresponds to rows of data in your worksheet.
X-axis	The number of elements in a series. For most two-dimensional charts, categories are plotted along the Category (X) axis, which is usually horizontal. Categories generally correspond to the columns that you have in your chart data, with the category labels coming from the column headings.
Y-axis	For most two-dimensional charts, data values are plotted along the Value (Y) axis, which is usually vertical. The y-axis reflects the values of the bars, lines, or plot points. In a two-dimensional bar chart, the axes are reversed, with the values being plotted on the x-axis and the categories on the y-axis. In a 3D chart, the z-axis represents the vertical plane, and the x-axis (distance) and y-axis (width) represent the two sides on the floor of the chart.
Legend	The element that designates the separate categories of a chart. For example, the legend for a column chart shows what each column of the chart represents.
Gridlines	The lines that depict the x-axis and y-axis scale of the data series. For example, major gridlines for the y-axis help you follow a point from the x- or y-axis to identify a data point's exact value.

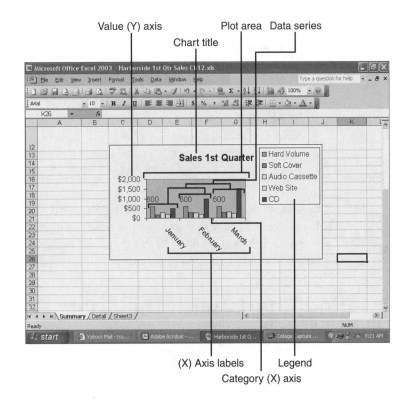

Chart elements.

Types of Charts

The most common chart types include pie, bar, column (default), line, and area. Table 12.2 lists these chart types, their descriptions, and how you would use them.

TABLE 12.2   Excel's Chart Types

Chart Type	Description/How to Use It
Pie	Plots only one category of data, but each wedge of the pie represents a different data series. Use this chart to show the relationship among parts of a whole.
Bar	Horizontal representations of column charts, often called histograms. Use this chart to compare values at a given point in time, emphasizing the performance of a group of items. Often, different patterns are not required for bar chart data series.
Column	Similar to a bar chart; use this chart to emphasize the difference between items over a period of time. Columns make it easy to compare the values of items in each category. Column charts are best for comparing two or more items.

TABLE 12.2   continued

Chart Type	Description/How to Use It
Line	Use this chart to emphasize trends and the change of values over time, showing how one or more items have changed over time. Lines emphasize the change, not the comparison of one item to another. Also useful for plotting numerous categories of data for multiple data series.
Area	Similar to the line chart and stacked column chart in that an area chart shows how items combine to form a total. Use this chart to emphasize the amount of change in values, providing a more dramatic representation of the change in values over time.

Most of these basic chart types also come in 3D. A standard, flat chart is professional looking, but a 3D chart can help your audience distinguish between different sets of data. When you choose a chart type and a chart subtype, you can display, in a professional manner, interesting and meaningful results based on your worksheet data.

Creating Charts with the Chart Wizard

One of the terrific features in Excel is the Chart Wizard. The easiest way to create a chart in Excel is to use the Chart Wizard. The Chart Wizard leads you step by step through the task of creating a chart. Excel plots the data and creates the chart where you specify on the worksheet.

Creating charts with the Chart Wizard is a snap because you get help every step of the way. You are guided through four dialog boxes from which you create your chart: Chart Type, Chart Source, Chart Options, and Chart Location. You can preview the sample chart in all the steps and make changes to the chart at any time.

You can select data before you create a chart, or if you don't select anything and your worksheet is relatively simple, Excel grabs the data automatically. You begin with Excel's default (or automatic) chart and then modify it to your liking. With so many chart types and options, you have carte blanche for creating a chart that best suits your needs.

All charts start out basically the same. You have to create a basic chart with Excel's automatic settings before you can create more customized charts. If desired, you can modify the basic chart, using various tools. The first task is to select the data you want to chart. The second task is to bring up the basic chart.

Selecting the Chart Type and Subtype

You can choose a chart type from the Chart Type list and then choose a chart subtype from the Chart Subtype gallery in a Chart Wizard dialog box. A description of the chart type appears in the lower-right side of the Chart Wizard dialog box when you click a chart subtype.

Choosing the Data Range and Series

To control the orientation of your chart, you choose the data range and then plot a series in rows or columns. Sometimes when Excel produces a chart from a highlighted range, the chart is backward. The data series appears where categories should be and vice versa. How does Excel know which orientation to use? Well, Excel makes a guess based on your selected data. If you have more columns than rows, the columns become the categories on the x-axis. If you have more rows than columns, the rows become categories along the x-axis.

You can always change Excel's orientation for a chart if Excel guesses wrong. Here's how you can change the orientation. Choose to plot your data in rows if you want the rows to be translated into data series and columns into categories. The rows option is best used when the selected data range contains more columns than rows. In the Chart Wizard—Step 2 of 4—Chart Source Data dialog box, you select the Rows option.

In some instances, you can create a chart by plotting your data in columns, which turns your columns into data series and rows into categories. This situation would occur when you have more rows than columns.

The chart's appearance depends on your choice, so make sure you choose a setup that fits your needs best.

When you select a range for the chart, be sure to include the labels such as the months of the year and the categories at the beginning of each. However, do not select the totals in rows or columns.

Setting Chart Options

All kinds of chart options are available for your chart, including titles, axes, gridlines, legend, data labels, and data table. These are the tabs in the Chart Wizard—Step 3 of 4—Chart Options dialog box. Here's where you can add descriptive text to the chart if you like. For example, you can add labels to the Category (X) axis along the bottom of the chart and Value (Y) axis labels along the left side of the chart.

12

Choosing a Location for the Chart

In the final Chart Wizard dialog box, you can specify where you want to place the chart. You have two choices: As New Sheet and As Object In. The As New Sheet option lets you insert the chart on a separate chart sheet. A chart sheet is a separate element from the worksheet and is stored in the current workbook.

The As Object In option enables you to insert the chart as an object in the worksheet that contains the data you're charting. A chart object on a worksheet is useful for showing the actual data and its graphic representation side by side.

The first To Do in this hour helps you create a default chart (clustered column chart) using the Chart Wizard. The chart will be an embedded chart because Excel draws the chart on the same worksheet as the data. In the case where you are charting the totals, select only the totals in the row or column and not data that create them.

To Do: Create a Chart with the Chart Wizard

1. Select cells A3:D8 on the Summary sheet of the Sales 1st Qtr workbook to identify the range you want to chart.

2. Click the Chart Wizard button on the Standard toolbar. The Chart Wizard—Step 1 of 4—Chart Type dialog box opens, displaying the chart types. The Clustered Column chart is the default chart type. You want to use this chart type.

> When you create a chart, make sure the range you select includes the labels, but not the totals in rows or columns.

3. Click the Next button to accept the Clustered Column chart type, and the Chart Wizard—Step 2 of 4—Chart Source Data dialog box should appear with a sample chart.

4. If you leave the Columns option selected, each column or data series represents the values for each product category by month. Hard Volume, Soft Cover, Audio Cassette, Web Site, and CD are the Category (X) axis labels. The month category names appear in the legend for the data series. The clustered column chart in Figure 12.2 shows the data series plotted by columns, which compares each product category by month. The chart is backward because you have more columns than rows. As a result, the columns become the categories on the x-axis. The Columns option is not a good choice. Instead, you want to compare each month by product categories. To do this, you need to plot the data series by rows rather than columns.

FIGURE **12.2**
*The Chart Wizard—
Step 2 of 4—Chart
Source Data dialog
box, plotting data in
columns.*

Compares each product category by month
Months selected in the worksheet
Months appear in the legend

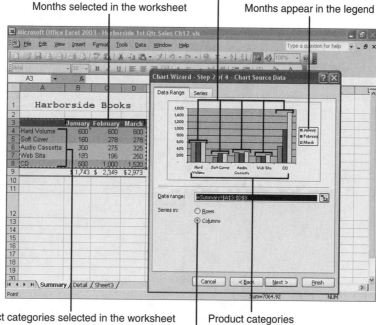

Product categories selected in the worksheet
Product categories
Series in Columns option

5. Select the Rows option (as shown in Figure 12.3). Each column or data series represents the values for each month by product category. January, February, and March are the Category (X) axis labels. The product category names Hard Volume, Soft Cover, Audio Cassette, Web Site, and CD appear in the legend for the data series.

6. Click the Next button. Excel displays the Chart Wizard—Step 3 of 4—Chart Options dialog box. The dialog box contains a sample chart and options for adding titles, changing the legend, and formatting other elements in the chart.

12

To return to a previous Chart Wizard dialog box while using the Chart Wizard, click the Back button. To go to the next Chart Wizard dialog box, click the Next button. You can stop the process of creating a chart by clicking the Cancel button in any Chart Wizard dialog box.

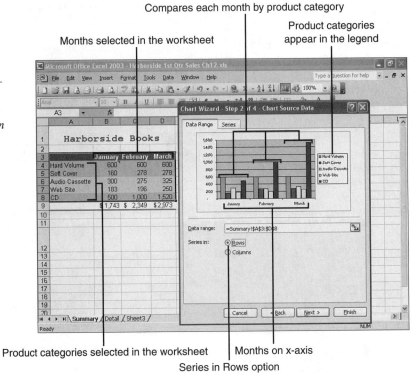

FIGURE 12.3

The Chart Wizard—Step 2 of 4—Chart Source Data dialog box, plotting data in rows.

Compares each month by product category

Product categories appear in the legend

Months selected in the worksheet

Product categories selected in the worksheet

Months on x-axis

Series in Rows option

7. On the Titles tab, click the Chart Title text box and type `Sales 1st Quarter`. Excel bolds the chart title text.

8. Click the Next button. You should see the Chart Wizard—Step 4 of 4—Chart Location dialog box. You can place the chart on a separate chart sheet or as an object in an existing worksheet. A chart sheet is a separate element from the worksheet and is stored in the current workbook. Keep the As Object In option and Summary sheet selected.

9. Click the Finish button. The chart appears near the top of the worksheet. The chart has a plot area with data series columns, and a legend on the right. Selection handles surround the border of the chart. You also should see the Chart toolbar. Sometimes the Chart toolbar does not always automatically appear when the chart is displayed. Figure 12.4 shows the clustered column chart and the Chart toolbar.

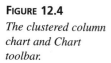

FIGURE 12.4

The clustered column chart and Chart toolbar.

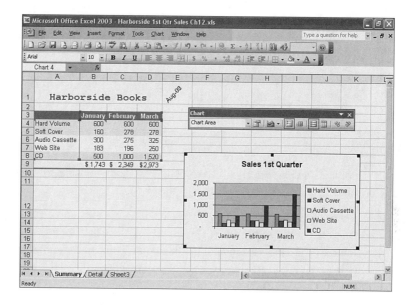

A chart is handled as an object in an Excel worksheet, and so you can move and resize the chart, just as you would any object in Excel.

To move a chart on a worksheet, click anywhere in the chart to select it and then hold down the left mouse button. When the mouse pointer changes to a four-headed arrow, drag the chart to a new place.

To change the size of a chart, select the chart and then drag one of its handles (the black squares that border the chart). Drag a corner handle to change the height and width or drag a side handle to change only the width.

When you save the worksheet, Excel saves the chart along with it. Unless you remove it, this chart appears on the worksheet. You can remove a chart by clicking it and then pressing the Delete key.

Working with Charts

Now that you know how to create a chart in Excel, you're ready to discover how you can customize and modify your charts. Excel lets you control most of the chart's elements, including the axes, chart text, and series patterns and colors.

The Chart toolbar is very useful for making changes to charts. When working with charts, you frequently add data labels to a chart to further describe the data in each data

12

series. You decide on the elements of your chart, such as whether to show or hide a legend and gridlines, select a different chart type to fit your needs, and re-order a chart's data series.

Before you can change anything on a chart, you must select the chart. Click anywhere on the chart. You should see selection handles (black squares) surrounding the chart, which indicate that the chart is selected.

In addition, Excel's chart commands require that you select the element on the chart that you want to change before making any changes. An element can be the entire chart, the plot area, a data series, or an axis. The command you select then applies to only the selected elements on the chart.

You can select an element by simply clicking the element in the chart or by choosing a chart element from the Chart Objects list on the Chart toolbar. Excel then displays selection boxes around the element. At this point, you can customize the chart with the chart tools on the Chart toolbar or with the commands in the menu bar.

Working with the Chart Toolbar

After you create a chart, you can use various chart tools to edit and format the chart. You can use the Chart toolbar to change legends, gridlines, the x-axis, the y-axis, background, colors, fonts, titles, labels, and much more. Figure 12.5 shows the tools on the Chart toolbar.

Figure 12.5
The Chart toolbar.

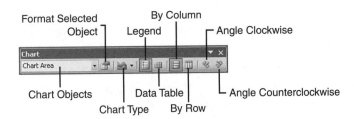

Table 12.3 lists the tools on the Chart toolbar and describes what they do.

Table 12.3   Chart Toolbar Tools

Chart Tool	What It Does
Chart Objects	Lets you select a chart object that you want to change.
Format Selected Object	Lets you format the selected object.
Chart Type	Changes the chart type.
Legend	Adds or removes a legend.

TABLE 12.3 continued

Chart Tool	What It Does
Data Table	Inserts a data table on the chart.
By Row	Plots the data by rows.
By Column	Plots the data by columns.
Angle Clockwise	Changes the text so that it slants downward.
Angle Counterclockwise	Changes the text so that it slants upward.

 If you don't see the Chart toolbar, select View, Toolbars, Chart. If the Chart toolbar is docked next to the Standard or Formatting toolbar, point to the Chart toolbar (not on a button) and drag it into the worksheet area so that it's near the chart.

Labeling Data Elements in the Chart

You can add data labels above data series and data points on your chart. To do so, simply select the data series on the chart or in the Chart Objects list on the Chart toolbar. For example, you would choose Series "Hard Volume" in the Chart Objects list.

Next click the Format Data Series button on the Chart toolbar. Excel opens the Format Data Series dialog box. Click the Data Labels tab, as shown in Figure 12.6. This tab offers data label options that include Series Name, Category Name and Value. The options that are grayed out are not available for this chart type.

12

FIGURE 12.6

The Data Labels tab in the Format Data Series dialog box.

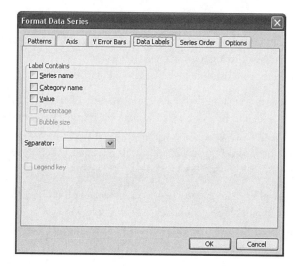

Choose the Data Label type Value, and then click OK. Excel adds the data labels to your chart. Each data series bar for "Hard Volume" should show a value above it, as shown in Figure 12.7.

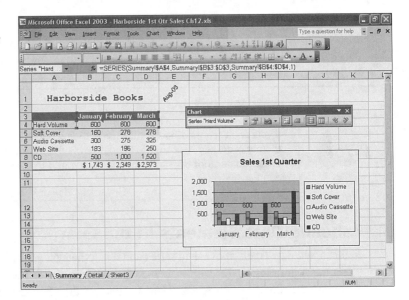

Deciding on the Elements of Your Chart

A chart legend describes the data series and data points; it provides a "key" to the chart. By default, Excel adds a legend to the chart, and it already knows which chart labels make up the legend (the data series labels in the first column of the chart range). Keep in mind that a pie chart does not need a legend, but by default Excel inserts one, anyway.

You can hide the legend, if you so desire. To do so, click the Legend button on the Chart toolbar. Excel makes the legend disappear from the chart. To display the legend, simply click the Legend button on the Chart toolbar again.

The default location for a legend is on the right side of the chart. But you can change the placement of the legend by clicking on it and dragging it. Among the standard locations for the legend are the bottom, corner, top, right, and left side of the chart. Experiment to get the results you want. Figure 12.8 shows the legend in the upper-right corner of the chart.

Gridlines are another chart element. A grid appears in the plot area of the chart and is useful for emphasizing the vertical scale of the data series. You can remove the gridlines by clicking on a gridline on the chart and then pressing the Delete key. Excel removes the gridlines from the chart. You can display them again by clicking the Undo button on the Standard toolbar. Figure 12.9 shows a chart without gridlines.

FIGURE 12.8

A legend in the upper-right corner of the chart.

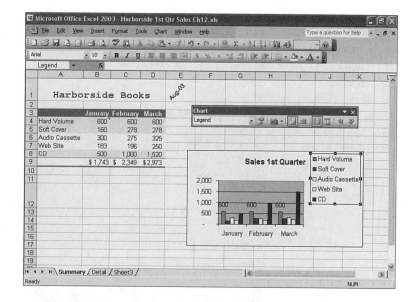

FIGURE 12.9

A chart without grid-lines.

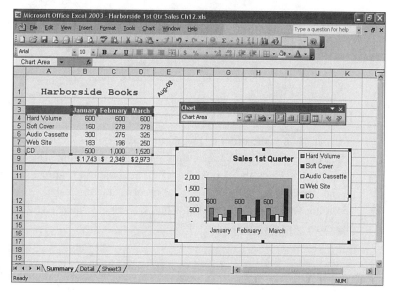

12

Selecting a Different Chart Type

Excel offers a myriad of chart types for presenting your data. You'll find that certain chart types are best for certain situations. To change to a different chart type, select your chart and click the Chart Type down arrow on the Chart toolbar. A palette of chart types appears, as shown in Figure 12.10. Click any chart type. Excel transforms your chart into that chart type. Experiment with chart types until you get the chart that best suits your needs.

FIGURE 12.10

The Chart Type palette on the Chart toolbar.

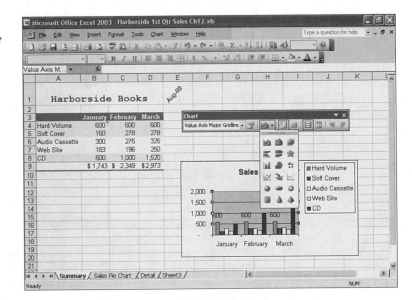

Re-ordering Chart Series

You can change the order of the chart series. To do so, click a data series on the chart. Click the Format Data Series button on the Chart toolbar. The Format Data Series dialog box appears. Click the Series Order tab, as shown in Figure 12.11. Choose the data series in the Series order list that you want to move and click the Move Up or Move Down button to move the series in the list. Click OK. Excel places the data series on the chart in the order you specified.

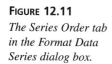

FIGURE 12.11

*The Series Order tab
in the Format Data
Series dialog box.*

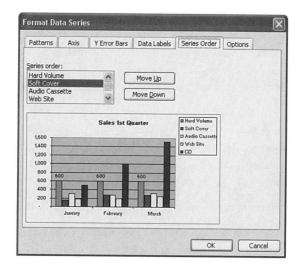

Chart Formatting Techniques

Many people like to change the chart colors, lines, patterns, and styles of the data series
for special effects. Although Excel's default colors and patterns help to distinguish one
data series from another, you might find some colors and patterns more attractive than
others. For example, you might want to remove all patterns and use only color.

The vertical axis in a chart is referred to as the Value axis. Excel automatically scales the
value axis for your charts to best fit the minimum and maximum values being charted.
The values along the vertical (Y) or horizontal (X) axis are set with minimum and maximum values, as well as a number of intermediate points along the axis. These intermediate points are called major units and minor units. You can choose from a number of axis
and tick-mark formats to change the appearance of an axis.

You can change the view of a 3D chart by using the Chart, 3-D View command. The
view options let you adjust the elevation and rotation of the chart.

Excel places category labels next to the horizontal axis along the bottom of the chart. If
you're not satisfied with the category labels that go with your chart, you can change
them. You can angle the text upward or downward.

Changing Chart Colors, Lines, Patterns, and Styles

Most of the color, line, pattern, and style options in the Format Axis dialog box are self-
explanatory. But here are some highlights if you want the real lowdown on the options.

12

If you have a color printer, keep in mind that the patterns have two parts: the foreground and the background. Each part can be a different color. The foreground is the pattern itself, and the background is the color on which the pattern is drawn. Experiment with the foreground and background colors to see how these work. Note that the solid pattern (the first pattern in the list) provides the solid version of whichever foreground color you choose.

The Patterns tab is divided into two groups for data series—Border options and Area options—which might require some explanation. The Border options affect the perimeter of the selected element, including the style, color, and thickness of the border line. The Area options control the inside of the element, such as its color and pattern.

The Automatic option tells Excel to take care of choosing the colors and patterns.

Perform the steps in the next To Do to change chart colors, lines, patterns, and styles for the Category (X) axis so that you can spice up your chart.

To Do: Change the Chart Colors, Lines, Patterns, and Styles

1. Select the chart by clicking anywhere on it. You should see the Chart toolbar.

2. Click the Chart Objects down arrow on the Chart toolbar. A list of chart objects appears.

3. Choose Series Soft Cover.

4. Click the Format Data Series button on the Chart toolbar. The Format Data Series dialog box appears.

5. Click the Patterns tab, as shown in Figure 12.12. You can use the Border and Area options to change the color, patterns, lines, and styles for the border and area of your data series. The Sample box shows the current color of the data series. You want to change it.

> If you want to remove all patterns from the chart and use only colors for the data series, select the solid pattern for each data series.

6. In the Area color palette, click the Bright Pink color patch, in the fourth row, first column.

7. Click OK to apply the new color to the Soft Cover data series. You should see bright pink bars on your chart.

FIGURE 12.12

The Patterns tab in the Format Data Series dialog box.

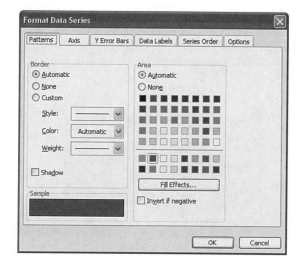

Formatting an Axis

The Axis options include the style, color, and weight of the axis line. The Tick Mark Type options involve styles for the major and minor tick marks on an axis. The Tick Labels options control the appearance of the scale numbers that appear along the Value (Y) axis.

The next exercise demonstrates how to format the Value (Y) axis scale by adding dollar signs to the numbers.

To Do: Format a Chart Axis

1. Select the chart by clicking anywhere on it. You should see the Chart toolbar.

2. Click the Chart Objects down arrow on the Chart toolbar. A list of chart objects appears.

3. Choose Value Axis.

4. Click the Format Axis button on the Chart toolbar. The Format Axis dialog box appears. Here's where you can change the patterns, scale, font, numbers, and alignment for an axis.

5. Click the Number tab. This tab contains options for changing the number formats for the vertical axis.

6. Choose Currency in the Category list.

12

▼ To Do

▼ 7. Change the number of decimal places to 0 by clicking the down arrow twice in the Decimal places box. In the Symbol list, select the dollar sign ($), as shown in Figure 12.13.

8. Click OK. Excel applies the format to the vertical axis, which changes to reflect the values you set. You should see dollar signs next to the numbers.

▲ 9. To move the chart, click it and drag it so that it starts in row 11.

FIGURE 12.13

The Number tab in the Format Axis dialog box.

Changing Chart Views

If you have a 3D chart, you can change the way you view it by using Excel's 3-D View command. To change the view of a 3D chart, select the chart and choose Chart, 3-D View. The 3-D View dialog box opens, as shown in Figure 12.14.

FIGURE 12.14

The 3-D View dialog box.

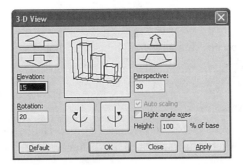

Click the large up or down arrow to change the elevation of the chart. Click the large rotation buttons to rotate the chart. Then click OK. Excel changes the view of your 3D chart. If you don't care for the results, repeat the steps to change the elevation and rotation until you get the view you want.

Using Rotated Text on a Chart

If you want to rotate the category text labels along the bottom of the chart, you can angle them upward or downward. By default, Excel angles Category axis labels upward.

To rotate text for category text labels, in the Chart Objects list on the Chart toolbar choose Category Axis. Click the Angle Clockwise or Angle Counterclockwise button on the Chart toolbar. Excel slants the text along the x-axis in the direction you chose. Figure 12.15 shows category text labels angled downward.

FIGURE 12.15

Category text labels angled downward.

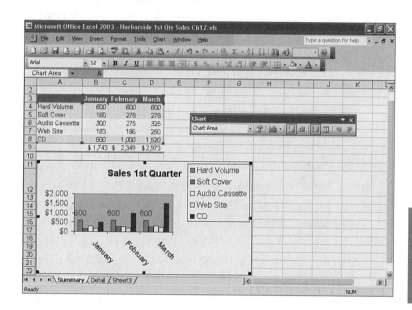

Creating a Pie Chart

You can use a pie chart to show the relationship or proportion of parts to a whole. Each slice of the pie shows what percent that slice contributes to the total, which is 100%. A good example of a pie chart is comparing the January sales to the other months in the Sales 1st Qtr workbook.

The next exercise shows you how to create a pie chart on a separate sheet using the Chart Wizard. The pie chart will show the relationship between the total sales amounts for each month on the Summary sheet in the Sales 1st Qtr workbook.

To Do: Create a Pie Chart

1. Select cells B3:D3 on the Summary sheet of the Sales 1st Qtr workbook to identify the month names you want to chart. Hold down Ctrl and select cells B9:D9 to identify the range of data that determines the size of the slices in the pie.

> The month names will identify the slices and are called *category names*. The three months will create three pie slices and are called the *data series*.

2. Click the Chart Wizard button on the Standard toolbar. The Chart Wizard—Step 1 of 4—Chart Type dialog box opens, displaying the chart types. Click Pie in the Chart type list. The Pie chart subtype is the one you want.

3. Click the Next button to display the Chart Wizard—Step 2 of 4—Chart Source Data dialog box. You should see a sample of the pie chart and the chart data range. A marquee surrounds the ranges you selected on the Summary sheet.

4. Leave the Rows option selected. Each cell in the row or data series represents the values for each month. January, February, and March are the x-axis category names that appear in the legend for the data series.

5. Click the Next button. Excel displays the Chart Wizard—Step 3 of 4—Chart Options dialog box. The dialog box contains a sample pie chart and chart options.

6. On the Titles tab, click the Chart Title text box and type `Three-Month Net Income`. Excel automatically bolds the chart title.

7. Click the Legend tab and then click Show Legend to remove the check mark from the check box. Excel displays the pie chart without a legend.

8. Click the Data Labels tab. In the Label Contains section, check the Category name and Percentage check boxes. Excel redraws the pie chart with data labels and percentages.

9. Click the Next button. You should see the Chart Wizard—Step 4 of 4—Chart Location dialog box. To place the chart on a separate chart sheet, click the As New Sheet option. In the text box, type `Sales Pie Chart` to name the sheet tab in the workbook.

10. Click the Finish button. Click the Close button on the Chart toolbar to hide the toolbar. The pie chart appears on a separate chart sheet in the Sales 1st Qtr workbook, as illustrated in Figure 12.16.

FIGURE 12.16
The pie chart.

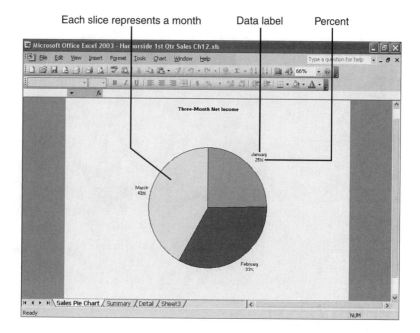

Making the Pie Chart 3-D Style

To enhance a pie chart with a 3-D visual effect, right-click anywhere on the pie chart, and choose Chart Type. Excel displays the Chart Type dialog box. In the Chart subtype palette, row 1, column 2, select the pie chart called Pie Chart with a 3-D visual effect. Then click OK. The pie slices with a 3-D visual effect should now pop out more on the chart sheet (see Figure 12.17).

Pulling a Pie Slice from a Chart

To emphasize a data series in a pie chart, you can pull a pie slice away from the pie chart. To do so, click the desired pie slice. Then hold down the left mouse button and pull out the selected slice. Figure 12.17 shows the pie slice pulled from the pie chart.

Let's move the Sales Pie Chart sheet tab so that it appears after the Summary sheet tab. To do so, click and drag the Sales Pie Chart sheet tab to the right of the Summary sheet tab.

12

FIGURE 12.17

A pie slice pulled from a pie chart.

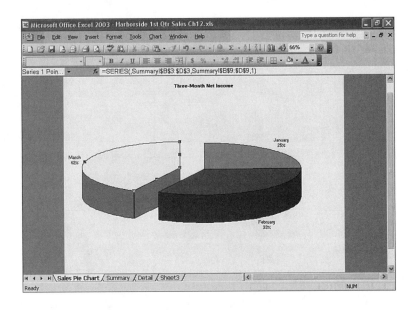

Summary

This hour gave you a complete education on Excel's powerful charting capabilities. You did a fine job going through all the exercises and grasping the chart skills you need to create professional-looking charts in your worksheets.

In the next hour, you are shown how to make other types of charts in Excel, such as organization charts, picture charts, and geographical data maps.

Q&A

Q When I created a chart, I selected the totals row and didn't get the results I wanted. How can I fix this?

A When you create a chart, make sure the range you select includes the labels, but not the totals. If you are charting the totals, be sure to select only the total rows, and not the data that created them.

Q My chart is plotted in rows and looks different from what I expected. What should I do next?

A Sometimes when Excel produces a chart from a highlighted range, the chart is backward. The data series appears where categories should be, and vice versa. Excel makes a guess based on your selected data. If you have more columns than rows, the columns become the categories on the x-axis. If you have more rows than columns, the rows become categories along the x-axis. To change the chart so that it is plotted in columns, select the chart and click the By Column button on the Chart toolbar.

Q How can I make the plot area larger so that I can easily see the data series in the chart?

A Simply click the chart to select it, point to a corner selection handle, and drag the chart's corner border diagonally until you see the plot area better.

Q The Chart toolbar doesn't display with my chart. What should I do?

A If you don't see the Chart toolbar, select View, Toolbars, Chart. If the Chart toolbar is docked next to the Standard or Formatting toolbar, point to the Chart toolbar (not on a button) and drag it into the worksheet area so that it's near the chart.

Q Do I need a legend for my pie chart?

A No. A pie chart does not need a legend, but by default Excel inserts one anyway. A legend describes the data series and data points; it provides a "key" to the chart (bar chart, column chart, line chart, and so on). To remove the legend, click the Legend button on the Chart toolbar.

Q Is there a way to change a chart on a chart sheet to an object so that it's next to my worksheet data?

A Certainly. Click the chart sheet tab, and click the Chart Wizard button on the Standard toolbar. In the final Chart Wizard dialog box, choose As Object In. This option enables you to insert the chart as an object in the worksheet that contains the data you're charting. Click the Finish button. Excel removes the chart sheet and displays the chart object on the worksheet.

12

Hour 13

Other Types of Charts

The subjects covered in this hour include the following:

- How to create other chart types
- How to create an org chart
- How to create a picture chart
- How to create a diagram

In this hour you learn how to create organization (or *org*) charts, pictures, and geographical data maps.

By the end of this hour, you'll have the knowledge to create some other types of magnificent and useful charts in Excel.

Creating Other Chart Types

A few other chart types that you can create in Excel are organization charts and picture charts.

Excel's organization chart program lets you illustrate the structure of authority and responsibility (chain of command) in an organization. You don't have to draw boxes and lines with the program because it automatically inserts the boxes and lines for you. After you build the organization chart, you can change the font, font size, and font color for the text in the boxes; the box style; the line style; and the background color for the chart.

A picture chart contains pictures in each data series instead of a solid color or pattern.

Creating an Org Chart

The Organization Chart feature enables you to build an organization chart in an Excel worksheet from scratch. You can access this program with Excel's Insert Picture Organization Chart command. When you create an organization chart, Excel treats it as an object in a worksheet.

You can show the levels of hierarchy and various members of departments within your company in a chart with boxes and lines.

In the following To Do exercise, you create an organization chart and examine how it works. First you insert a new sheet in the Sales 1st Qtr Workbook so that you can place the org chart on a sheet by itself.

To Do: Create an Org Chart

1. Click the Sheet3 sheet tab. Choose Insert, Worksheet. Excel inserts a new sheet between the Detail and Sheet3 sheets, named Sheet1.

2. To rename the sheet, double-click the Sheet1 tab, type **Org Chart**, and press Enter. This sheet is where you create the org chart.

3. Choose Insert, Picture, Organization Chart. An organization chart object and the Organization toolbar appear, as shown in Figure 13.1. You should see placeholder text in boxes and lines connecting the boxes. You click in the Click to add text placeholder text in a box and then type a name in the empty box.

FIGURE 13.1

An organization chart object.

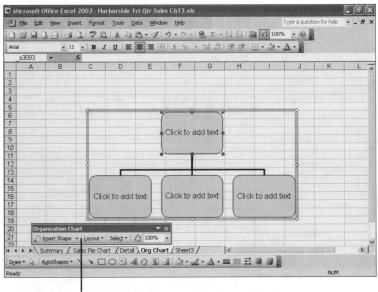

Organization Chart toolbar

▼   4. Click in the top box, type a name and press Enter.

5. Then type a title for an individual who should be included in this box.

6. For the rest of the boxes, click the placeholder text and type names and titles for the individuals you want to include in the boxes.

7. Click in any cell to deselect the org chart. Your org chart should look similar to the
▲   one in Figure 13.2.

FIGURE 13.2
An organization chart.

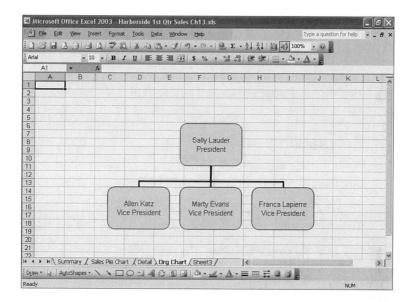

Modifying an Org Chart

You can add more boxes to your org chart if you want. Several types of boxes are available: a subordinate box, a co-worker box, a manager's box, and an assistant box. The Organization Chart toolbar, accessed by double-clicking on the chart, supplies a set of tools for modifying an org chart, as shown in Figure 13.3.

13

FIGURE 13.3
Organization Chart toolbar.

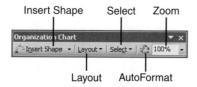

To add boxes, click the button on the Organization Chart toolbar that matches the relationship to an existing box that you want to create. For example, to add a subordinate to a box that is already on the chart, click the Subordinate button and then click the box to which you want to attach it. A box with placeholder text appears in the chart. Then you can fill in the name and title in the box.

To delete a box, select it and then press the Delete key. You should no longer see the box on the org chart.

Because an organization chart is handled as an object in an Excel worksheet, you can move and resize the organization chart, just as you would any object in Excel.

To move the organization chart, point to the chart in the worksheet and, when you see a four-headed arrow, drag the org chart to the new location.

If you want to resize the org chart in the worksheet, move the mouse pointer to a side border or corner until you see a double-headed arrow. Then drag the border to stretch or shrink the chart.

Formatting an Org Chart

After you add and remove boxes in your org chart, you can format it with the AutoFormat command on the Organization Chart toolbar.

In the next To Do exercise, we add color, a shadow to the boxes, and change the line style and color of the connecting lines.

To Do: Format an Org Chart

1. Click the AutoFormat button on the Organization Chart toolbar. The Organization Chart Style Gallery dialog box opens, as shown in Figure 13.4.

FIGURE 13.4

Choices in the Organization Chart Style Gallery.

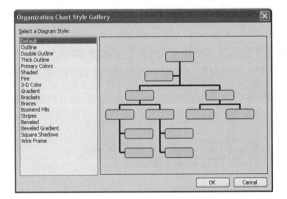

▼ 2. Click on different styles in the Diagram Style list to see which format you like best. When you find the one you like, click on the style and click Apply. The diagram style in Figure 13.5 is Double Outline.

FIGURE 13.5

An organization chart formatted with Primary Colors AutoFormat.

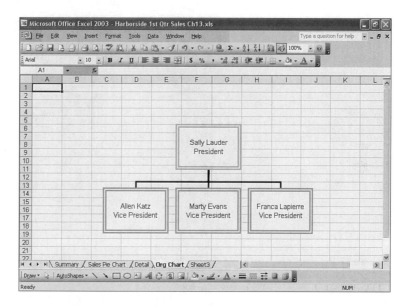

3. Click in any cell to deselect the org chart. Notice that the connecting lines in the org chart have a new line style.

Creating a Picture Chart

To create a picture chart, which is a chart that has pictures representing each data series, first create a chart using the Chart Wizard. Then select a data series in the Chart Objects list on the Chart toolbar. Click the Format Data Series button on the Chart toolbar. Next click the Patterns tab. Click the Fill Effects button at the bottom of the Area section, and the Fill Effects dialog box appears. Click the Picture tab.

Click the Select Picture button and change to the drive and folder that contain pictures. Pictures are stored either in the My Pictures subfolder under the My Documents folder, in a subfolder under the Program Files folder, or on a CD-ROM. Select a picture file and click OK. The picture appears in the Picture box on the Picture tab, as shown in Figure 13.6. Click OK to return to the Picture tab displaying a sample of the selected picture. Click OK to insert the picture in the data series. Figure 13.7 shows a picture chart.

13

FIGURE 13.6

The Picture tab in the Fill Effects dialog box.

FIGURE 13.7

A picture chart with stacked columns.

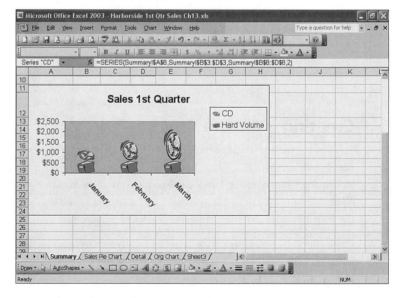

Creating an Excel Diagram

NEW 2003 The Excel Diagram feature enables you to create professional-looking diagrams with predefined shapes and diagramming tools on the Drawing toolbar. With the Diagram feature, you don't need to know how to draw. There are several types of diagrams you can create that include the following:

- Cycle—Shows a process that has a continuous cycle, such as a life cycle or water cycle diagram.

- Organization—Shows hierarchical relationships, such as the structure of an organization.

- Pyramid—Shows foundation-based relationships, such as the food guide pyramid.

- Radial—Shows relationships of elements to a core element, such as the relationship of workstations to a network.

- Target—Shows steps toward a goal, such as the steps necessary in training for a marathon.

- Venn—Uses circles or other shapes to represent sets, with the position and overlap of the circles indicating the relationships between the sets. For example, you can create a Venn diagram to show similarities or differences between groups of numbers.

Creating a Diagram

In the following To Do exercise, perform the steps to create a pyramid diagram in the Detail sheet that shows the relationship of book sales at Harborside Books.

To Do: Create a Diagram

1. In the Detail sheet, scroll down to row 35. This is the row where you want to insert a diagram.

2. Click the Drawing button on the Standard toolbar. The Drawing toolbar displays at the bottom of the Excel window.

3. Click the Insert Diagram or Organization Chart button on the Drawing toolbar. The Diagram Gallery dialog box opens, as shown in Figure 13.8.

4. Click the Pyramid Diagram in the second row, first column. Then click OK. A pyramid diagram object and the Diagram toolbar appear, as shown in Figure 13.9. You should see placeholder text in three elements in the pyramid. You click in the Click to add text placeholder text in an element and then type a name in the empty element.

5. Click in the top triangle placeholder text, type **Hard Cover**. Click in the middle element placeholder text and type **CD**. Click in the bottom element placeholder text and type **Web Site**.

6. Click in any cell to deselect the diagram. Your diagram should look similar to the one in Figure 13.10.

▼ To Do

13

FIGURE 13.8
The Diagram Gallery dialog box.

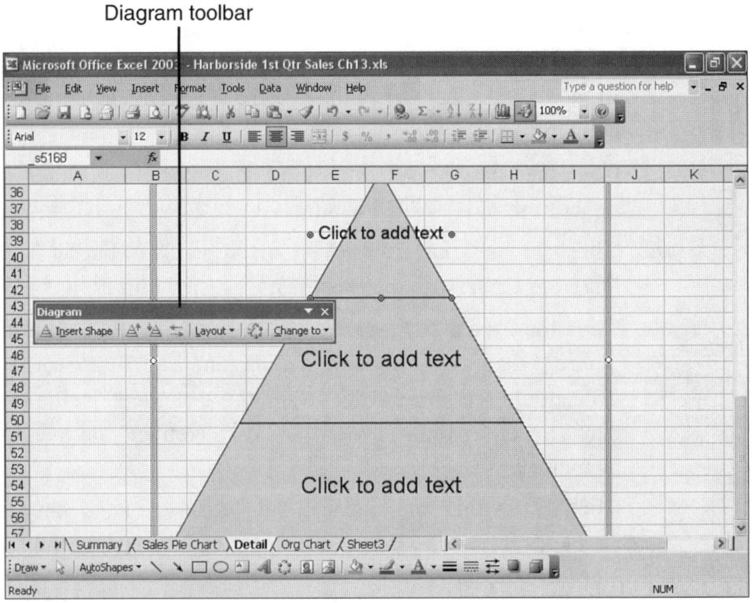

Cycle Diagram

Organization Chart

Radial Diagram

Pyramid Diagram

Venn Diagram

Target Diagram

FIGURE 13.9
A pyramid diagram object with place-holder text.

Diagram toolbar

FIGURE 13.10

A pyramid diagram object.

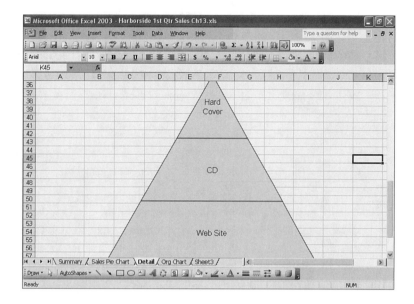

Modifying a Diagram

When you create a diagram on a worksheet, Excel displays the Diagram toolbar on the worksheet. If the diagram is not selected, click on the diagram and the Diagram toolbar will appear. This toolbar contains the tools you need to make changes to your diagram and enhance its appearance. Figure 13.11 shows the tools on the Diagram toolbar.

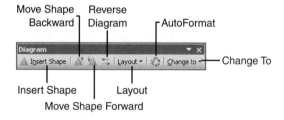

FIGURE 13.11

The Diagram toolbar.

13

Table 13.1 lists the tools on the Diagram toolbar and describes their purpose.

TABLE 13.1 Diagram Tools on the Diagram Toolbar

Diagram Tool	What It Does
Insert Shape	Lets you add AutoShapes to the diagram.
Move Shape Backward	Moves a shape to appear behind all of the other objects.
Move Shape Forward	Moves a shape to appear at the very front of the worksheet.
Reverse Diagram	Reverses the order of elements from left to right or vice versa in the diagram.
Layout	Lets you fit, expand, scale, and change the layout of the diagram.
AutoFormat	Add color and shadows to the elements, and change the line style and color of the lines.
Change To	Lets you select a different diagram type.

To add shapes or elements, select the shape on the diagram that you want to add the new shape beneath or next to, and then click Insert Shape on the Diagram toolbar. For example, if you want to add another element beneath the triangle at the top of the pyramid, click the triangle in the pyramid, and then click Insert Shape on the Diagram toolbar. An element with placeholder text appears beneath the triangle in the pyramid. Then you can fill in the text in the element.

To delete a shape or element, select it and then press the Delete key. You should no longer see the shape or element in the diagram.

A diagram is treated as an object in an Excel worksheet. Therefore, you can move and resize the diagram, just as you would any object in Excel.

To move the diagram, point to the diagram border in the worksheet and, when you see a four-headed arrow, drag the diagram to the new location.

If you want to resize the diagram in the worksheet, move the mouse pointer to a side border or corner until you see a double-headed arrow. Then drag the border to stretch or shrink the diagram.

Formatting a Diagram

After you add and remove shapes and elements in your diagram, you can format it with the AutoFormat command on the Diagram toolbar.

The next To Do exercise shows you how to add color, a shadow to the boxes, and change the line style and color of the lines.

To Do: Format a Diagram

1. Click the AutoFormat button on the Diagram toolbar. The Diagram Style Gallery dialog box appears, as shown in Figure 13.12.

FIGURE 13.12

Choices in the Diagram Style Gallery.

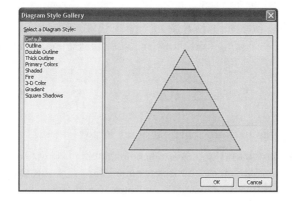

2. Click on different styles in the Diagram Style list to see which format you like best. When you find the one you like, click on the style and click Apply. The diagram style in Figure 13.13 is 3-D Color.

FIGURE 13.13

A pyramid diagram formatted with 3-D Color Autoformat.

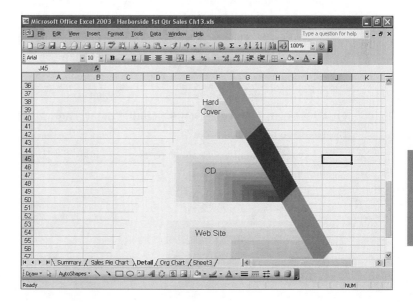

3. Click in any cell to deselect the diagram. Notice that the lines and colors in the diagram have a new style and look.

Summary

During this hour you learned about Excel's other chart types—from org charts to picture charts, and diagrams. You are to be commended for working through the To Do's and absorbing as much as you can to produce some fine-looking professional charts.

In the next hour, you learn how to work smarter in Excel by using multiple workbooks, customizing Excel, linking worksheets and workbooks, protecting your data, and using add-ins.

Q&A

Q Why is Organization Chart not in my Picture menu?

A Okay, no problem. The program is not installed. Use the Add/Remove Programs panel in the Windows Control Panel and your Microsoft Office or Microsoft Excel CD-ROM software to install Organization Chart.

Q Why couldn't I find any pictures to represent the data in my chart?

A Make sure you look in all the folders that contain pictures. The pictures are usually stored in the My Pictures subfolder under the My Documents folder or the Clip Art subfolder under Program Files, Microsoft Office, Office. If you can't find them in either place, install pictures from your Microsoft Office or Microsoft Excel CD-ROM software. Or, you can import the pictures from the Web.

Q How do I change the color of an individual shape or element in my diagram?

A Select the shape or element you want to change, click the Fill Color button on the Drawing toolbar, and pick any color you want.

Q An element in my diagram is pointing the wrong way. How do I change the direction of that element?

A Select the element you want to reverse, and click the Reverse Diagram button on the Diagram toolbar.

PART IV

Advanced Excel Techniques

Hour

Hour 14

Working Smarter

The topics of this hour are as follows:

- How to arrange workbooks
- How to move between workbooks
- How to copy and move data between workbooks
- How to create formulas that refer to other workbooks and worksheets
- How to create links between worksheets and workbooks
- How to customize Excel
- How to protect your data
- What Excel add-ins are

This hour gives you the information you need to create formulas that link data from other worksheets and workbooks, customize Excel, protect your data, and use Excel add-ins.

At the end of this hour, you'll be working smarter in Excel with some very useful tools at your fingertips.

Working with Multiple Workbooks

In some situations, you might have more than one workbook open at a time. You can open as many workbooks as will fit in your computer's memory. However, when you open multiple workbooks, you need to know how to manage them. You can arrange them in various ways on your screen and then move between them in a snap to get to the workbook you want. You can even copy and move data between workbooks instead of typing the same data over and over into multiple workbooks.

Arranging Workbooks

Suppose that you want to see all the open workbooks at one glance. You can do just that by arranging them on the screen for easy viewing. Excel makes it easy to have multiple workbooks open and to avoid getting lost in the maze. With the help of Excel's Window Arrange command, you can arrange workbooks in windows in four ways:

- Tiled—Arranges the open workbooks in small windows displayed in a tiled fashion on the screen
- Horizontal—Displays the open workbooks in windows as horizontal bands across your workspace
- Vertical—Organizes the open workbooks in windows as vertical bands in your Excel window
- Cascade—Layers the open workbooks in windows on the screen

Follow the instructions in the next To Do exercise to arrange workbooks in all four ways. You start by opening the Sales 1st Qtr workbook, and then you save the workbook with a different name to create two more workbooks, Sales 1st Qtr 2 and Sales 1st Qtr 3. Be sure to have the Sales 1st Qtr workbook open before you begin the exercise.

To Do: Arrange Workbooks

1. Choose File, Save As. Name the workbook Sales 1st Qtr 2 and click Save.
2. Choose File, Save As. Name the workbook Sales 1st Qtr 3 and click Save.
3. Open the Sales 1st Qtr workbook.
4. Open the Sales 1st Qtr 2 workbook. Now you should have all three workbooks open: Sales 1st Qtr, Sales 1st Qtr 2, and Sales 1st Qtr 3. When you arrange workbooks, all the workbooks you want to use must be open.
5. Choose Window in the menu bar and click Arrange. The Arrange Windows dialog box appears, as shown in Figure 14.1.

FIGURE 14.1

The Arrange Windows dialog box.

▼ 6. If necessary, select Tiled and then click OK. Excel should place your workbooks in the arrangement you selected; in this case, your workbooks should appear in small windows in a tiled effect (see Figure 14.2).

FIGURE 14.2

Tiled workbooks.

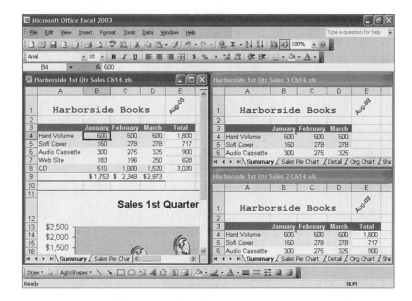

7. Choose Window, Arrange; select Horizontal; and click OK. Excel arranged your workbooks in windows as horizontal bands across the workspace (see Figure 14.3).

FIGURE 14.3

Horizontal arrangement.

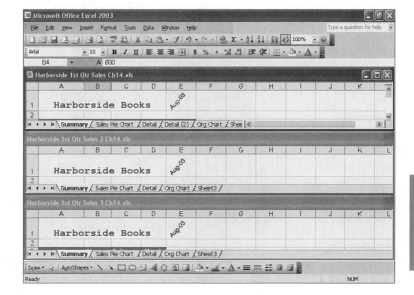

14

▼

▼   8. Choose Window, Arrange; select Vertical; and click OK. You should see your
           workbooks arranged in windows as vertical bands in the Excel window (see
           Figure 14.4).

FIGURE 14.4

Vertical arrangement.

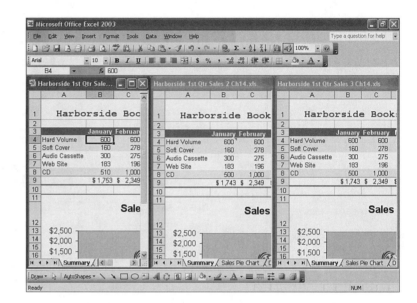

        9. Choose Window, Arrange; select Cascade; and click OK. Your workbooks should
▲   appear in layers in the Excel window (see Figure 14.5).

FIGURE 14.5

Cascaded workbooks.

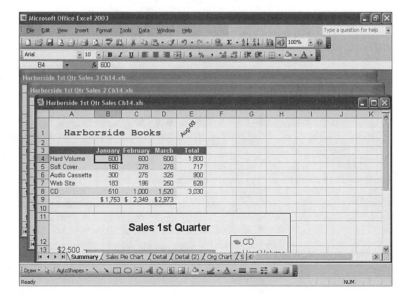

Moving Between Workbooks

Regardless of whether you decide to arrange the open workbooks or just leave them on top of each other in the order in which you opened them, you can move among open workbooks very easily. Excel provides several quick ways to get to the workbook you want. You can use the mouse, shortcut keys, or the Window menu to move to the workbook of your choice. Here are your choices for moving between open workbooks:

- Click a visible part of a workbook window.
- Press Ctrl+F6 or Ctrl+Tab to move from one workbook window to another.
- Click Window in the menu bar. At the bottom of the Window menu is a list of workbook names, allowing you to switch to any open workbook. Simply select the name of the workbook you want to display.

Perform the steps in the next exercise to move between workbooks. You should be using three workbooks: Sales 1st Qtr, Sales 1st Qtr 2, and Sales 1st Qtr 3. Be sure to have all three workbooks open before you begin the exercise.

To Do: Move Between Workbooks

1. Double-click the Sales 1st Qtr workbook title bar. The workbook should appear in a full-size window onscreen.

2. Press Ctrl+F6 to move to the next open workbook (Sales 1st Qtr 2).

3. Press Ctrl+F6 to move to the other workbook (Sales 1st Qtr 3).

4. Click Window in the menu bar. The Window menu appears with a list of workbook names at the bottom of the menu, as shown in Figure 14.6. The check mark next to Sales 1st Qtr 3.xls indicates that the workbook is active.

5. Choose Sales 1st Qtr 3 from the Window menu. The workbook you selected should appear in a full-size window onscreen.

6. Close the Sales 1st Qtr 3 workbook. If you're asked to save any changes, click No.

▼ To Do

▼

14

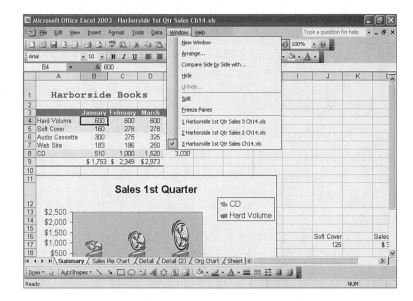

FIGURE 14.6

Workbook names on the Window menu.

Copying Data Between Workbooks

With Excel's Copy command, you can even copy data from one workbook to another. For example, you open two workbooks: one that contains a quarterly budget and another with the annual budget. To make things easier, you might want to copy the first-quarter projected budget figures in the first workbook to the second workbook. The original data in the first workbook remains intact. A copy of the data appears in the second workbook.

To copy data between workbooks, open both workbooks. Select the data in the first workbook and click the Copy button on the Standard toolbar. To switch between workbooks, you can use any of the methods mentioned in this hour. One of those methods is clicking Window in the menu bar and choosing the second workbook at the bottom of the Window menu. Select the sheet and click in the cell where you want the data to appear. Click the Paste button on the Standard toolbar. Excel copies the data to the second workbook.

The instructions in the following To Do exercise help you practice copying data from one workbook to another. You're going to work with two workbooks: Sales 1st Qtr and Sales 1st Qtr 2. Be sure to have these workbooks open before you start step 1. In the exercise, you first enter data in the Sales 1st Qtr workbook and then copy the data to the Sales 1st Qtr 2 workbook.

To Do: Copy Data Between Workbooks

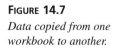

1. In the Sales 1st Qtr workbook, in the Summary sheet, in cell E3, type **Total** and press Enter. Excel formats the text with the AutoFormat color and font style. In cell E4, double-click the AutoSum button on the Standard toolbar. The total for row 4 appears in cell E4.

2. Drag the fill handle in cell E4 down to cell E8. The totals appear in column E.

3. Select cells E3:E8.

4. Click the Copy button on the Standard toolbar.

5. Press Ctrl+F6 to switch to the Sales 1st Qtr 2 workbook.

6. In the Summary sheet, click cell E3.

7. Click the Paste button on the Standard toolbar. The data you copied and pasted into the second workbook should appear starting in row 3, as shown in Figure 14.7.

FIGURE 14.7

Data copied from one workbook to another.

Data you copied in cells E3:E8

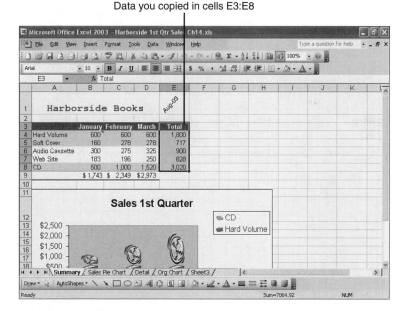

Moving Data Between Workbooks

Moving data between workbooks is similar to copying data between workbooks. Select the data in the first workbook and click the Cut button on the Standard toolbar to cut the data; when you switch to the second workbook, click the Paste button on the Standard toolbar. Excel removes the data from the first workbook and places it in the second workbook.

14

The fast way to move data between workbooks is to use the drag-and-drop method. First, open the workbooks you want to use for the move. Choose Window, Arrange and select the Tiled option. Click OK to arrange the windows so that a small portion of each one appears onscreen. Select the tab of the worksheet(s) you want to copy. Move the mouse pointer over one of the selected tabs, click and hold the mouse button, and drag the tab to its new location. When you release the mouse button, the worksheet moves to the other workbook.

Working with Formulas That Reference Other Workbooks and Worksheets

Because a workbook can contain multiple worksheets, you might need to reference a cell in another worksheet or even another workbook file. No problem! As long as you follow the proper syntax, you can type a formula that contains a reference to any file.

If the cell is contained in another worksheet in the current workbook, you need to include the sheet name followed by an exclamation point (!) and then the actual address of the cell. Blank spaces are not allowed. For example, Sheet4!A75, points to cell A75 on Sheet 4 of the current workbook. Anytime you reference another worksheet in the workbook, you must include the exclamation point. If you've renamed a worksheet from its default sheet name, use the sheet name and an exclamation point.

If a referenced sheet name contains spaces, enclose the sheet name in single quotes. For example, 'Jan Sales'!A21. The exclamation point character follows the second quote.

Although you can type a cell reference to another worksheet, it's easier to use the mouse. If you need to reference a cell on another sheet as you're building a formula, click the appropriate sheet tab and then point to the cell you want to use. Excel places the sheet name and cell reference, using perfect syntax, into the formula.

You can reference cells that are not currently visible in the worksheet by scrolling to the cell with the scrollbars. You can even reference a cell in another sheet by clicking the sheet tab and then clicking the cell you want to include.

You can also reference a cell from another workbook. It's best to point to the cell you want to use, rather than worry about making sure that you've used the correct syntax.

Make sure that you open the workbook(s) that contain the cells you want to reference before you begin.

Begin the formula by clicking the Edit Formula button so that the formula appears in the Formula palette. As you construct the formula, switch to the open worksheet by clicking the Window menu, and navigating to the worksheet and cell. After you click the cell you want, use the Window menu and click the file that contains the formula you're working on. When you're done building the formula, click the OK button on the Formula palette.

Creating Links Between Worksheets and Workbooks

Linking is the process of dynamically updating data in a worksheet from data in another source worksheet or workbook. When data is linked, the linked data reflects any changes you make to the original data.

Linking is accomplished through special formulas that contain references known as *external references*. An external reference can refer to a cell in a different worksheet in the same workbook or to a cell in any other worksheet in any other workbook.

Excel lets you links data from other worksheets and workbooks in these ways:

- Reference another worksheet in a linking formula using sheet references
- Reference several worksheets in a linking formula using 3D references
- Reference another workbook in a linking formula

When you build a linking formula, you type the formula in the cell where you want the results to appear.

Referencing Another Worksheet in a Formula

If you have a lot of data and you create many worksheets to store this data, you might have occasions when a formula in one worksheet needs to use data from another sheet. These formulas are called *sheet references*. They're useful because you don't have to create redundant data in numerous sheets.

To refer to another cell in another sheet, place an exclamation mark between the sheet name and cell name. The syntax for this type of formula looks like =SHEET!Cell. Use the correct sheet name in place of SHEET if you have named the sheet.

The next exercise helps you build a linking formula to reference a cell on another sheet.

14

To Do: Create a Link Between Worksheets in a Formula

1. Press Ctrl+F6 to move to the Sales 1st Qtr workbook. In the Detail sheet, in cells B5:B9, enter the following numbers: **100**, **125**, **150**, **215**, **185**. Then, widen column A to accommodate the long entry in cell A6.

2. In the Summary sheet, click cell J16. Type **Soft Cover** and press Enter.

3. Cell J17 will contain the linking formula. Type =.

4. Click the Detail sheet tab.

5. Click cell B6.

6. Press Enter. Excel calculates the formula.

> If you know which cells you want to reference, you can type the entire linking formula in a cell. If you're not sure of the cell address that you want to reference on another sheet, you can start writing your formula and switch to the sheet that you want to reference when you get to that part of the formula. Then click the cell or range of cells that you want in your formula. The cell or range reference appears automatically in your formula. You can then finish your formula and press Enter to calculate.

7. Click cell J17. Now you should see the linking formula =Detail!B6, which links the data in cell B6 on the Detail sheet to cell J17 on the Summary sheet. The formula bar contains the formula, and the correct answer is 125, as shown in Figure 14.8.

> When a sheet name contains spaces, such as Sales 2004, you need to place single quotation marks around it when you are making sheet references, as in 'Sales 2004'.

Linking formula

FIGURE **14.8**

A linking formula that references another sheet.

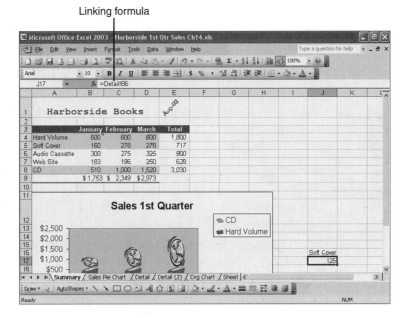

Linking Several Worksheets

What if you have a formula that needs to reference a cell range that has two or more sheets in a workbook? This might happen if you have identical worksheets for different budgets, sales teams, or regions. You also might have several different worksheets that have totals calculated and entered in identical cell addresses. You can then add all these totals to get a grand total by referencing all the sheets and cell addresses in one formula.

When you have cell ranges such as this, Excel refers to them as *3D references*. A 3D reference is set up by including a sheet range, which names the beginning and end sheets, and a cell range, which names the cell to which you are referring. A formula that uses a 3D reference that includes Sheet1 through Sheet5 and the cells A4:A8 might look something like this: =SUM(SHEET1:SHEET5!A4:A8).

Another way to include 3D references in your formulas is to click the worksheets that you want to include in your formula. To do this, start your formula in the cell where you want the results. When you come to the point where you need to use the 3D reference, click the first worksheet tab that you want to include in your reference, hold down Shift, click the last worksheet that you want to include, and select the cells you want to reference. When you finish writing your formula, press Enter.

14

The next exercise helps you build a linking formula to reference a cell on another sheet. Before you create the formula, you'll need to copy the Detail sheet so that you have two sheets of data to calculate.

To Do: Create a Link Between Multiple Worksheets in a Formula

1. Click the Detail sheet. Point to the Detail Sheet tab, hold down the Ctrl key, and drag to the Org Chart tab. Excel duplicates the Detail sheet, creating a new sheet with the name Detail (2).

2. Click the Detail (2) sheet tab and then click cell A4. Then type **New York** and press Enter.

3. Click the Detail sheet tab and then click cell C15. Then type **Boston and New York** and press Enter.

4. Cell C16 will contain the linking formula. Type **=SUM('Detail:Detail (2)'!B5:B9)**. Be sure to type a space between Detail and (2).

5. Press Enter.

Another way to include 3D references in your formulas is to use the mouse and click the worksheets that you want to include in your formula. To do so, start typing your formula in the cell where you want the answer to appear. When you get to the point where you need to use the 3D reference, click the first worksheet tab that you want to include in your reference, press and hold the Shift key if the worksheets are consecutive, click the last worksheet that you want to include, and select the cells you want to reference. If the worksheets are nonconsecutive, press and hold the Ctrl key, click the worksheets you want to include, and select the cells you want to reference. When you finish entering your formula, press Enter.

6. Double-click cell C16. In this cell, you should see the linking formula =SUM('Detail:Detail (2)'!B5:B9), which links the data in the range of cells B5 through B9 on the Detail sheet through the Detail (2) sheet. The Formula bar contains the formula, and the correct result is 1550, as shown in Figure 14.9.

7. Press Enter to deselect cell C16.

FIGURE **14.9**

A linking formula that references several sheets.

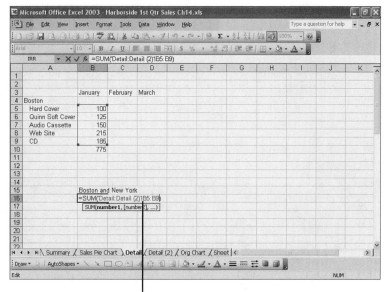

Linking worksheets formula

Linking Workbooks

When you are linking workbooks, the workbooks have some special names that you need to know about. The workbook that contains a linking formula is the dependent workbook, and the workbook that contains the linked data is the source workbook.

If you're referencing a cell in another workbook, the syntax is [Book]Sheet!Cell. When you enter a linking formula to reference a cell in another workbook, include the workbook name enclosed in brackets, the sheet name followed by an exclamation mark (!), and the cell reference.

In the next To Do exercise, you use the Window command to switch between two open workbooks, Sales 1st Qtr and Sales 1st Qtr 2. Perform the steps that follow to build a linking formula that links the workbooks.

To Do: Create a Link Between Workbooks in a Formula

1. In the Sales 1st Qtr workbook, click the Summary Sheet tab. This workbook will contain the linking formula.

2. Click cell L16. Type **Sales 1st Qtr & Sales 1st Qtr 2** and press Enter.

3. Cell L17 will contain the linking formula. Type =, click cell B9, and type +.

4. Click Window in the menu bar and select the Sales 1st Qtr 2 workbook.

14

▼ 5. In the Summary sheet, click cell B9. This cell contains the data you want to link to the first workbook.

6. Press Enter.

7. Double-click cell L17. In cell L17, you should see the linking formula =B9+'[Sales 1st Qtr 2.xls]Summary'!$B$9, which links the data in cell B9 on the Summary sheet of the Sales 1st Qtr 2 workbook. The Formula bar contains the formula, and the correct result is $3,486.82, as shown in Figure 14.10.

▲ 8. Press Enter to deselect cell L17.

FIGURE 14.10

A linking formula that references another workbook.

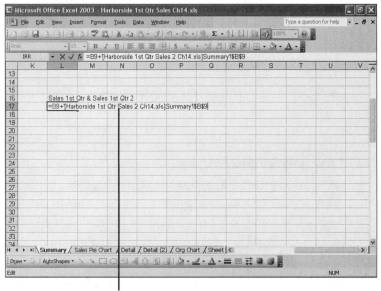

Linking workbooks formula

Updating Links

When you are working with multiple workbooks and linking formulas, you need to know how the links are updated. If you change data in cells that are referenced in linking formulas, will the formula results be updated automatically? Yes, as long as both workbooks are open.

If the data in the source workbook is changed while the dependent workbook—the one that contains a linking formula—is closed, the linked data is not immediately updated. The next time you open the dependent workbook, Excel asks whether you want to update the data. To update all the linked data in the workbook, choose Yes. If you have links that are manually updated or you want to update the links yourself, choose No.

To Do: Update Links Manually

1. Press Ctrl+F6 to switch to the Sales 1st Qtr 2 workbook. Then close the workbook and remember to save the changes.

2. In the Sales 1st Qtr Workbook, click cell B8.

3. Type **510** and press Enter.

4. Select Edit, Links. The Edit Links dialog box opens, as shown in Figure 14.11. The Source File list box contains a list of all linking resources used in the active workbook. The link reference you want to update, in this case, Sales 1st Qtr 2, is already selected. The status of the source file is Unknown.

FIGURE 14.11
The Edit Links dialog box.

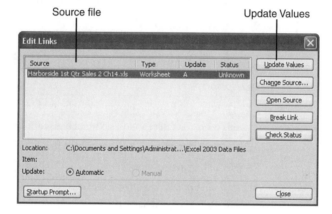

5. Click Update Values. The status of the source file changes from Unknown to OK.

 The Update Values button in the Links dialog box is available only if the source workbook is not already open and if any linked formulas have been changed since the last update. In the Edit Links dialog box, you can click the Change Source button to change the link reference. Or you can open the source worksheet by clicking the Open Source button in the Edit Links dialog box.

6. Click Close. The linked formula in cell L17 is updated from $3,486 to the new value of $3,496.

Customizing Excel

You can customize Excel to change they way things look in the Excel window when you start the program. The startup options in the Customize dialog box let you personalize

14

menus and toolbars, set the icon size, list font names in their font, show ScreenTips on toolbars, and change menu animations.

Customizing Toolbars

Excel offers several toolbars to save you time in choosing commands. The Standard toolbar and Formatting toolbar appear at the top of the screen. Earlier in this book, you learned that other toolbars appear when you create a template, a picture, a chart, and an org chart. The toolbars listed in Table 14.1 are available when you need them.

 The 3-D Settings and Shadow Settings toolbars are not visible on the toolbar menu but can be found in the Customize menu.

TABLE 14.1 Excel's Toolbars

Toolbar	Description
Standard	Contains tools for Excel's most commonly used features.
Formatting	Contains tools for Excel's most commonly used formatting commands.
Borders	Contains tools for drawing borders around individual cells and groups of cells.
Chart	Changes and formats a chart.
Control Toolbox	Creates dialog boxes and other Excel control objects.
Drawing	Contains tools for drawing objects.
External Data	Lets you work with data you imported from an external database.
Forms	Contains tools for creating your own fill-in forms.
Formula Auditing	Lets you troubleshoot, check data in, and trace source cells in formulas.
List	Contains tools for working with lists.
Picture	Lets you alter a picture.
PivotTable	Contains tools for working with pivot tables.
Protection	Gives you tools for locking cells, and protecting a worksheet and workbook.
Reviewing	Lets you review changes, highlight changes, and accept or reject changes on worksheets you share with others.
Task Pane	Displays the last task pane you used such as Home, Help, Search, Clip Art, Clipboard, and New Workbook.
Text to Speech	Provides speech playback tools for listening to a computer-generated voice read the data you entered on a worksheet.
Visual Basic	Contains tools for writing and editing instructions in Visual Basic.

TABLE 14.1 continued

Toolbar	Description
Watch Window	Displays a toolbar that shows you cells and their formulas allowing you to check them for any errors.
Web	Gives you tools for browsing the Web.
WordArt	Contains tools for editing and formatting WordArt text.
XML	Provides tools for opening and saving any properly-structured XML file, creating Web queries to properly structured XML data sources, and saving entire workbooks as XML worksheets.

If you want to show or hide a toolbar, choose View, Toolbars. On the Toolbar menu, a check mark appears next to a toolbar that is displayed. To show or hide a toolbar, click a toolbar name in the menu. Excel displays or hides the toolbar in the Excel window.

> To use the Toolbar shortcut menu to hide or display a toolbar, right-click any toolbar. The Toolbar shortcut menu appears. A check mark appears next to each toolbar that is currently displayed. Choose a toolbar on the menu that you want to hide or display.

After you display the toolbars you need, you may position them in your workspace so that they are most convenient for you. To move toolbars to a new location on the screen, look at the vertical line that appears at the left edge of a docked toolbar. When you point to the vertical line, the mouse pointer changes to a four-headed arrow, which indicates that you can move the toolbar. Hold down the mouse button and drag the toolbar to a new location. You can drag it to a dock or let it float anywhere in the window.

If you decide to drag the toolbar to a dock, you can position it in one of four toolbar docks:

- Between the Formula bar and menu bar
- On the left side of the Excel window
- On the right side of the Excel window
- At the bottom of the Excel window

When you find a dock, the toolbar outline changes from square to rectangular. Then you can release the mouse button.

14

If a toolbar contains a drop-down list (such as the Zoom tool in the Standard toolbar and the Font tool in the Formatting toolbar), you cannot drag it to a left or right toolbar dock. If you do, you lose the tools that contain a drop-down list.

If there are too many or not enough options on an Excel toolbar, you can edit the toolbar. And if necessary, you can even design your own. Select View, Toolbars, Customize to add, remove, and move buttons to get the toolbar just the way you want it.

In addition to customizing toolbars, you can customize the way your menus appear when you select a menu command. For example, you can choose an animation option that causes a menu to display with special effects, such as random, unfold, and slide effects.

You can create a shortcut to a workbook by creating a shortcut icon for your workbook. The icon appears on your Windows desktop. Then, when you click the shortcut icon, Windows opens both Excel 2003 and your workbook.

Changing Startup Options

Excel's Customize command lets you change the startup options for Excel. These options determine how things look on your screen when you start Excel. The startup options are self-explanatory:

- Standard and Formatting Toolbars Share One Row
- Large Icons
- List Font Names in Their Font
- Show ScreenTips on Toolbars

There are several startup options that are turned on by default: Standard and Formatting Toolbars Share One Row, Menus Show Recently Used Commands First, List Font Names in Their Font, and Show ScreenTips on Toolbars. The other startup options are turned off.

The figures in this book show full toolbar menus, and if your toolbars and menu options are turned on, you won't see all of the options we show. Personalized toolbars and menus are there specifically to ease their use, especially for beginning users. You don't have to turn them off if you find them easier to use right now. When you are feeling confident with using Excel's toolbars and menus, feel free to change the toolbar and menu options in the Customize dialog box.

To change any startup options, choose Tools, Customize. The Customize dialog box appears. Click the Options tab, as shown in Figure 14.12.

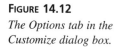

FIGURE 14.12

The Options tab in the Customize dialog box.

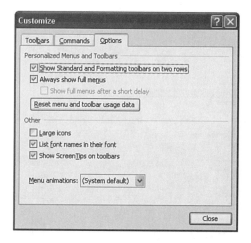

A check mark in a check box indicates that the option is turned on. An empty check box indicates that the option is turned off. Choose any options you want and then click Close. The next time you start Excel, the screen will display the startup options you selected.

Designing a Custom Toolbar

One great thing about Excel is that you can design a custom toolbar that provides all the options you need to perform tasks in Excel with ease.

The upcoming To Do exercise builds a toolbar that contains three tools: Save, Undo, and Spelling.

To Do: Build Your Own Toolbar

1. Choose View, Toolbars, Customize. The Customize dialog box opens.

2. Click the Toolbars tab. This tab contains options for creating and editing toolbars, as shown in Figure 14.13.

3. Click the New button. The New Toolbar dialog box pops open.

4. In the Toolbar Name box, type **My Toolbar**. You are giving this name to your toolbar.

5. Click OK. This step saves the toolbar name and places it at the bottom of the Toolbars list. A check mark appears in the check box, which indicates that the toolbar is displayed. You should see an empty toolbar with the name My in the title bar. The rest of the name couldn't fit just now. As you add buttons, you can see more of the name, or you can resize the toolbar with the mouse. You want to add buttons to the toolbar.

▼ To Do

14

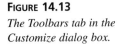

FIGURE 14.13

The Toolbars tab in the Customize dialog box.

6. Click the Commands tab. You should see a Categories list and a Commands list, as shown in Figure 14.14. The Categories list contains the command names, and the Commands list shows the icons that represent the commands. The File category is already selected and is the category you want for the File, Save command.

FIGURE 14.14

The Commands tab in the Customize dialog box.

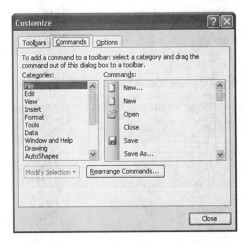

7. In the Commands list, click Save. Excel displays a highlighted bar across the command, indicating that it is selected.

▼ 8. Point to the Save command in the Commands list and drag the command to the My Toolbar toolbar. The Save button appears on the toolbar. As you drag, Excel displays a small button and a plus sign (+), indicating that you are copying the button.

9. In the Categories list, click Edit. The icons for the Edit command appear in the Commands list.

10. In the Commands list, click Undo.

11. Point to the Undo command in the Commands list and drag the command to the My Toolbar toolbar. The Undo button appears on the toolbar. One more button to go!

12. In the Categories list, click Tools. The icons for the Tools command appear in the Commands list.

13. In the Commands list, click Spelling.

14. Point to the Spelling command in the Commands list and drag the command to the My Toolbar toolbar. The Spelling button appears on the toolbar. Now you should have three tools on the toolbar. You're done!

15. Click the Close button to close the Customize dialog box. Your toolbar should resemble the toolbar in Figure 14.15.

Custom toolbar

FIGURE 14.15

The custom toolbar.

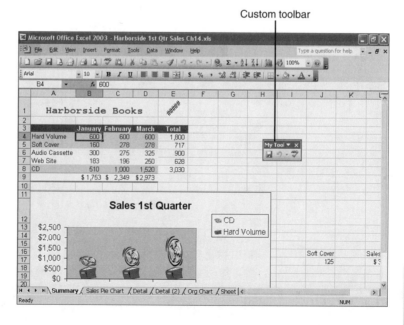

14

▲ 16. Click the Close button on the custom toolbar to close the toolbar.

To delete a custom toolbar, choose View, Toolbars, Customize; alternatively, right-click any toolbar or anywhere in the toolbar area, and then choose Customize. In the Customize dialog box, click the Toolbars tab; choose the custom toolbar you want to delete; then click the Delete button in the Customize dialog box. Click Yes to confirm the deletion. Excel removes the toolbar from the list, and the toolbar is no longer available.

Editing an Existing Toolbar

Why would you want to edit an existing toolbar? The primary reason is to tailor an existing toolbar so that it contains only the buttons you really need for the commands you use most frequently. That way you have a toolbar that offers tools just for the type of work you do in Excel. When you edit an existing toolbar, you add or remove buttons and move buttons to the most convenient location on the toolbar.

In Excel, adding and removing buttons is a cinch. Just click the Toolbar Options down arrow button at the right end of a toolbar. Next click the Add or Remove Buttons menu, and then click the name of the toolbar on the menu. For example, Standard or Formatting. A menu of icons with their commands appears, as shown in Figure 14.16.

Figure 14.16

The Add or Remove Buttons menu for the Standard toolbar.

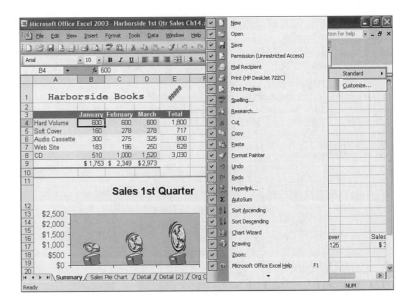

A check mark appears next to the commands that appear on the toolbar. Click a check mark to tell Excel to remove the button from the toolbar. Click a command that doesn't have a check mark to add the button to the toolbar. When you're done adding and removing tools, click any cell in the worksheet to hide the Add or Remove Buttons menu.

To rearrange buttons on a toolbar, open the Customize dialog box, click the Commands tab, and then click the Rearrange Commands button. In the Rearrange Commands dialog box, select the button you want to move, and then click the Move Up or Move Down button until the button is where you want it. Click Close to close the Rearrange Commands dialog box, and then click Close to close the Customize dialog box.

> If you mess up one of Excel's toolbars, there's no need to fret. To restore a toolbar to its original setting, display the Toolbars tab in the Customize dialog box and select the toolbar in the Toolbars list. Click the Reset button. Then close the dialog box. Excel restores the toolbar, displaying its original tools and settings. Custom toolbars, by the way, cannot be reset.

Changing Menu Animations

Normally, the Menu Animation feature is set to None (System Default), which means that when you choose a menu command, nothing special happens. But you can animate your Excel menus by choosing a Menu Animation option that opens and closes a menu with a special effect. Whatever menu animation you choose becomes the setting for menus in all other Office programs.

To animate your menus, choose Tools, Customize and then click the Options tab. In the Menu Animations drop-down list, select one of these options: Random, Unfold, or Slide (see Figure 14.17). Then click Close.

Try out each animation option to find the one you like. If you don't like any of them, you can always opt for no animation by choosing (System Default) in the Menu Animations drop-down list.

Creating a Shortcut to a Workbook

If you use a particular workbook frequently, you might want to keep that workbook conveniently at your fingertips on your Windows desktop. That way, you can open the workbook quickly and easily at any time directly from the desktop. You won't have to open Excel and then open the workbook, thereby reducing the number of steps involved in opening the workbook.

14

FIGURE 14.17

The Menu Animations options.

Menu animations choices

An icon with a small arrow in the lower-left corner represents the shortcut. The "shortcut" arrow indicates that you can use an icon as a shortcut to an object. In this case, the object is a file within an application.

Double-clicking the shortcut icon opens the object to which the shortcut is pointing. For example, you create a shortcut to the Sales 1st Qtr workbook by placing a Sales 1st Qtr shortcut icon on the Windows desktop. Then, when you double-click the shortcut icon, Windows opens Excel 2003 and the Sales 1st Qtr workbook.

To create a shortcut icon, follow the steps in the To Do exercise. In this exercise, you create a shortcut icon for the Sales 1st Qtr workbook.

To Do: Create a Shortcut to a Workbook

1. Click the Open button on the Standard toolbar.

2. In the file list, locate Sales 1st Qtr and click it.

3. Right-click Sales 1st Qtr. A shortcut menu pops up.

4. Choose Send To, Desktop (Create Shortcut) (see Figure 14.18).

5. Close the Open dialog box.

6. Click the Minimize button in the upper-right corner of the Excel window. At the top of the desktop, you should now see the shortcut icon called Shortcut to Sales 1st Qtr.

7. Click the Microsoft Excel button on the Windows taskbar to display the full-size Excel window.

FIGURE 14.18

Sending the shortcut to the Desktop with the shortcut menus.

To delete a shortcut icon, click the icon to select it and then press the Delete key. You are prompted to confirm the deletion. Choose Yes to delete the shortcut icon, and it disappears.

Protecting Your Data

If a worksheet contains cells you do not want changed, you can lock them so that they cannot be edited or deleted. You can also add a password to a sheet or workbook to protect the entire sheet or workbook.

If you have columns and rows that you do not want anyone to see or change, you can hide the columns and rows and then display them again whenever you wish.

Locking Cells

To set cell protection, perform the steps in the To Do exercise. You want to lock all the cells in your worksheet except for the numbers for March in column D.

14

To Do: Lock Cells

1. In the Summary sheet, select cells D4:D8. You want to protect these cells from being locked.

2. Choose Format, Cells. The Format Cells dialog box appears.

3. Click the Protection tab, as shown in Figure 14.19. A check mark appears in the Locked check box, which means that all cells are locked.

4. Click the Locked check box. This step removes the check mark, which indicates the selected cells will not be locked.

FIGURE 14.19

The Protection tab in the Format Cells dialog box.

Locked   Protection

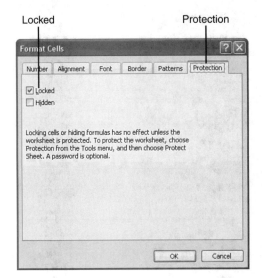

5. Click OK.

6. Click any cell in column C and type anything. Excel permits you to do so because the worksheet is not protected from changes. For cell or object protection to be in effect, you must turn on worksheet protection. You will learn how to do this in the next section.

▲ 7. Click the Undo button on the Standard toolbar to reverse the change.

For cell or object protection to be in effect, you must turn on worksheet protection.

Protecting a Worksheet

By default, cells are locked, but the worksheet protection is not on. You can unlock all the cells you want to change and then turn on worksheet protection.

To protect the worksheet, choose Tools, Protection, Protect Sheet. Excel displays the Protect Sheet dialog box, as shown in Figure 14.20.

FIGURE 14.20

The Protect Sheet dialog box.

You can protect the sheet for selecting, formatting, inserting, deleting, sorting, AutoFilter, PivotTable reports, objects, and scenarios. By default, the worksheet and contents of locked cells is protected, along with the act of selecting locked and unlocked cells is protected. A password is optional. Choose OK to protect the worksheet.

Now, to test whether the cells are locked, click cell C4, type **950**, and press Enter. Notice that when you try to edit locked cells, an alert box tells you that locked cells cannot be changed. Choose OK to clear the alert box. Excel prevents you from making the change to the cell because the cell is locked and the worksheet is protected.

Now try to type a number in cell D4. Can you do it? The answer should be yes. Excel allows you to type in a cell that is not locked.

To turn off worksheet protection, choose Tools, Protection, Unprotect sheet.

Protecting the Workbook

You might want to protect the structure of a workbook and the windows. Here are the structure elements you can protect in a workbook:

- Viewing hidden worksheets.
- Changing the names of worksheets.

14

- Moving, deleting, hiding, or worksheets.
- Inserting new worksheets or chart sheets. You can add an embedded chart to an existing worksheet with the Chart Wizard.
- Moving or copying worksheets to another workbook.
- In a PivotTable report, displaying the source data for a cell in the data area, or displaying page field pages on separate worksheets.
- Creating a scenario summary report.
- Using the analysis tools in the Analysis ToolPak that inserts results on a new worksheet.
- Recording new macros.

Here are the windows elements you can protect in a workbook:

- Changing the size and position of the windows.
- Moving, resizing, or closing the windows.

You can assign a password (optional) so that users need a password to change the structure of, or windows in, the workbook.

To protect a workbook, click Tools in the menu bar and choose Protection, Protect Workbook. Excel opens the Protect Workbook dialog box, as shown in Figure 14.21.

FIGURE 14.21

The Protect Workbook dialog box.

To select the elements you want to protect, click in the Structure check box to protect the worksheets in the workbook. Click in the Windows check box so that the size and position of the windows cannot be changed. If you want, type a password in the Password box, click OK, and type the password again. Click OK.

When you want to unprotect the workbook, choose Tools, Protection, Unprotect Workbook. The Unprotect Workbook dialog box opens. Enter the password and then click OK. Your workbook is now unprotected.

Remember your password. If you forget it, you cannot unprotect your work-book. Also, passwords must be entered in the exact upper- and/or lowercase letters.

Hiding and Displaying Rows and Columns

A worksheet might contain columns and rows that you don't want to appear on the worksheet. If so, you can easily hide columns and rows with the Hide command or with the mouse. Remember that hidden elements don't print when you print the worksheet.

To use the Hide command to hide columns, select the column you want to hide by clicking the column header (the column header contains the column letter). You can hide additional columns by pressing the Ctrl key while clicking each column header. Then choose Format, Column, Hide. If you hide column C, for example, only columns A, B, D, E, and so on are visible (see Figure 14.22). A dark gray border between columns B and D replaces column C in the column header.

FIGURE 14.22

Column C is hidden.

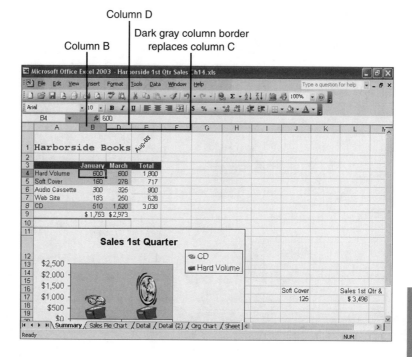

14

To display hidden columns, highlight the two columns on either side of the hidden column. For instance, if column C is hidden, highlight columns B and D. Choose Format, Column, Unhide. Excel displays the hidden column.

Here's how you can use the mouse to hide and unhide columns:

- To use the mouse to hide a column, point to the column's right border. Drag the right column border past the left column border. The column disappears.

- To unhide a column with the mouse, point to the left border of the column heading to the right of the hidden column. For example, if column C is hidden, point to the left border of column heading D. When the mouse pointer border turns into a double-lined border, drag the column border to the right.

To use the Hide command to hide rows, select the row you want to hide by clicking the row header (the row header contains the row number). After selecting one row, you can select other rows by pressing the Ctrl key while clicking each row header. Then choose Format, Row, Hide. If you hide row 3, for example, only rows 1, 2, 4, 5, and so on are visible. A dark gray border replaces the hidden row in the row header (see Figure 14.23).

FIGURE 14.23

Row 3 is hidden.

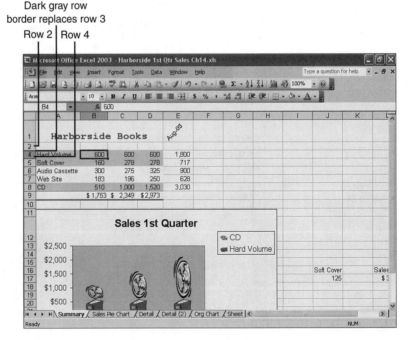

Dark gray row
border replaces row 3
Row 2 | Row 4

To display hidden rows, highlight the rows above and below the hidden row. For instance, if row 3 is hidden, highlight rows 2 and 4. Choose Format, Row, Unhide. Excel displays the hidden row.

Here's how to use the mouse to hide and unhide rows:

- To use the mouse to hide a row, point to the row header's bottom border. Drag the bottom row border past the top row border. The row disappears.

- To unhide a row with the mouse, point to the dark gray borderline between two row headings next to the hidden row. For example, if row 3 is hidden, point to the dark gray borderline between row headings 2 and 4. Move the mouse down slightly until you have a double-lined border mouse pointer and then drag the row border down. The hidden row appears.

Protecting Your Files

Anyone can sit down at your computer and look through your files. Maybe you share your home computer with other family members who can open your files. In today's computing climate, most offices and corporations work over a computer network. A network offers many advantages, including the capability to print your work to several different printers and to share your work with others. However, working on a network means that other people can access the files you create.

The people who can view your files can also change and delete them. If you're working with sensitive or personal data or you don't want someone to alter your files, you might consider protecting them in a few different ways.

Setting a File Password

Anytime you want to protect a workbook from prying eyes, you can require a password on the file. However, before you set up file passwords, check with your network administrator to make sure that passwords are allowed. Some networks frown on user-created file passwords and provide other options for securing data.

If you set up a file password, make sure it's one that you can remember. Passwords are serious business; if you lose or forget the password, your file becomes inaccessible to you. "Cracking" a password is almost impossible.

Play it safe: Jot down the password you assign to a file and store it in a safe place. Make sure that one of your co-workers or your network administrator knows where to find the password in an emergency.

14

To Do: Set a File Password

1. When the file you want to protect is on the screen, click File, Save As. The File Save As dialog box appears.

2. Click the Tools button on the Save As toolbar and choose General Options. The Save Options dialog box appears.

3. Type the password in the Password to Open text box. For security purposes, the letters you type are shown as symbols, as shown in Figure 14.24. Click OK when you're done typing.

The password you enter is hidden by asterisks.

FIGURE 14.24

The Save Options dialog box where you enter a password.

4. The Confirm Password dialog box appears, asking you to re-enter the password, as shown in Figure 14.25. Type the password exactly as you typed it before and then click OK. Excel returns you to the Save As dialog box.

FIGURE 14.25

Confirm the password by typing it again.

5. Click the Save button to save the file and enable the password-protection option. Choose Yes when asked whether you want to replace the existing file.

The next time you open the file, you'll be prompted for the password. If you share the password with others, they too will be able to open the file.

Assigning Modification Rights

If you're working on very sensitive data, you can include an even greater level of security to password-protected files. In addition to assigning a general password, you can add a password that allows only certain people to modify the file. That way, you can ensure that the data in the workbook can be changed by only a select group.

To assign a modification password, click File, Save As. Click the Tools button on the Save As toolbar and select General Options. Type a password in the Password to Modify box and click OK. Type the password again in the Reconfirm dialog box and click OK. When you return to the Save As dialog box, click Save to save the changes you made to the file. Choose Yes when asked whether you want to replace the existing file.

The next time the file is opened, you will be prompted for your password. After you enter your password, a box, similar to the one shown in Figure 14.26, appears. If the correct password is not entered, the user will be able to look at the file, but not modify the data.

FIGURE 14.26

Password dialog box.

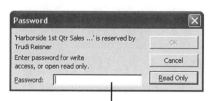

The password is needed to modify the data.

Loose lips sink ships! If the data in your files is sensitive enough to warrant password protection, make sure you provide the passwords to only the people who need to see the files.

Always check with your supervisor or network administrator before you add passwords to your worksheets. In a collaborative work effort, passwords can sometimes create unwanted problems.

Creating a Read-Only File

To protect your data without setting file passwords, you can turn on the read-only option. A read-only file doesn't need password protection. To assign the read-only option, check the box next to Read-Only Recommended in the Save Options dialog box.

After the read-only option is assigned, anyone who opens the file will see the warning box shown in Figure 14.27. When the file is open, the words Read Only appear in parenthesis next to the filename on the title bar.

14

FIGURE 14.27

The Read-Only warning box specifies that the file should not be changed.

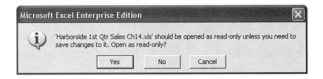

Unfortunately, the Read-Only option only recommends that users should view the contents of the file and not make changes. Any changes can be saved to a new file with a different name. If someone clicks No in the Read-Only warning box while opening the file, the file opens normally and changes can be made and saved to the original file.

Saving Your Workspace

Sometimes you open one workbook. Other times, you might need to open several workbooks and switch between them. After you arrange the workbooks on your screen, consider using the Save Workspace command. The Save Workspace command saves the open workbooks plus their present location on your computer screen.

To use this command, click the File menu and choose Save Workspace. The Save Workspace dialog box opens, as shown in Figure 14.28. In the File Name box, type a name for the workspace file. Workspace files have the extension .XLW. Then click Save.

FIGURE 14.28

Use the Save Workspace dialog box to save your arranged workbooks in a workspace file.

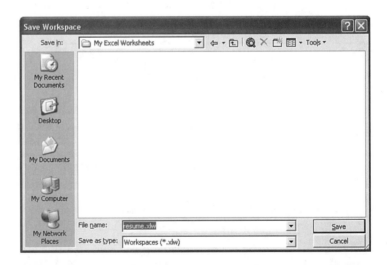

You open a workspace file as you would any Excel file. Just click the Open button on the Standard toolbar, and double-click on the workspace file. Excel opens the file and arranges the workbooks the way you had saved them.

Using Excel Add-ins

From time to time, you might have noticed the Add-Ins item on the Tools menu and wondered what that option does. Excel add-ins are worksheet tools that bring more power to your desktop. Table 14.2 lists the Excel add-ins and explains what they do.

TABLE 14.2 Excel's Add-ins

Add-in	What It Does
Analysis ToolPak	Gives you several worksheet functions and macro functions for financial and scientific data analysis for use in a workbook, the Function Wizard, and the Tools menu.
Analysis ToolPak VBA	Provides developers with Analysis ToolPak syntax tools and functions for financial, statistical, and engineering analysis.
Conditional Sum Wizard	Assists you with summing data in lists.
Euro Currency Tools	Lets you format values as euros and provides the EUROCONVERT worksheet function for converting currencies.
Internet Assistant VBA	Allows developers to publish Excel data to the Web by using Excel 97 Internet Assistant syntax.
Lookup Wizard	Allows you to create formulas to find data in Excel tables.
Solver Add-in	Lets you determine answers to complex what-if questions or equations by analyzing cells and determining the optimum value adjustments to arrive at a desired result.

Determining Whether an Add-in Is Installed

If you want to know whether an add-in is installed, choose Tools, Add-Ins. The Add-Ins dialog box appears, as shown in Figure 14.29.

A list of add-ins that are available in Excel appears in the Add-Ins Available list box. If a check mark appears in the check box next to the add-in feature in the Add-Ins Available list, your add-in is installed. If a check box is empty, that add-in isn't installed.

If you want to install an add-in, use the Add/Remove Programs feature in the Windows Control Panel and your Microsoft Office or Microsoft Excel installation CD-ROM.

14

FIGURE **14.29**

The Add-Ins dialog box.

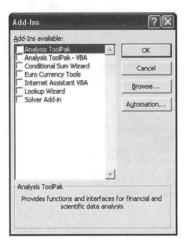

Summary

In this hour, you gained a working knowledge of the Excel tools that will help you work smarter in Excel. Excellent job!

The next hour brings you detailed information on Excel's functions.

Q&A

Q I built a linking formula to link data on several sheets, Budget 2003, Budget 2004, and Budget 2005. Excel informed me that my formula is wrong. What next?

A When the sheet name contains spaces, such as Budget 2003, you need to place single quotation marks around it when you are making sheet references.

Q Why didn't Excel update the data in my linked workbooks?

A If both the source and dependent workbooks are open, Excel updates the links automatically. The Update Now button in the Links dialog box is available only if the source workbook is not already open and if any linked formulas have been changed since the last update. Choose Edit, Links and then click the Update Values button in the Edit Links dialog box to update the data in both workbooks.

Q How do I delete a custom toolbar that I no longer use?

A Right-click the custom toolbar and choose Customize. In the Customize dialog box, choose the custom toolbar you want to delete and then click the Delete button in the Customize dialog box. Click Yes to confirm the deletion. Excel removes the toolbar from the list, and the toolbar is no longer available.

Q I messed up my Standard toolbar and want to restore the original buttons. Is that possible?

A Absolutely. Choose View, Toolbars, Customize. Choose the Toolbars tab in the Customize dialog box and select the Standard toolbar in the Toolbars list. Click the Reset button and click Close. Excel should restore the Standard toolbar, displaying its original tools and settings.

Q How do I remove a workbook shortcut icon from my Windows desktop?

A Click the shortcut icon to select it and then press the Delete key. Click Yes to confirm the deletion. Excel removes the shortcut icon from the desktop.

Q I locked the cells I want to protect, and I can still change the entries in those cells. What should I do?

A You also need to protect the worksheet by choosing Tools, Protection, Protect Sheet. In the Protect Sheet dialog box, choose any options you want. A password is optional. Then click OK.

Q I know I'm typing the correct password on a protected file, but Excel won't accept the password. What am I doing wrong?

A Are you sure you're typing the correct password? If so, are you typing the password with the correct case. Excel passwords are case sensitive. Try it again.

Q I copied cells from one workbook to another and now some of the cells contain #REF!. What happened?

A Evidently you copied a formula that contains a reference to a cell that is invalid. This means you probably deleted a referenced cell.

14

HOUR **15**

Using Functions

The highlights of this hour are

- Why you should use Excel functions
- How to use the Insert Function dialog box
- How to use the Formula palette
- What you should know about financial functions
- How to use date and time functions
- How to use logical functions
- How to use lookup functions

Hour 5, "Letting Excel Do the Math," explained the uses of simple worksheet functions and showed examples of some functions in action. The text lists each function and indicates where to include arguments. If you've read Hour 5, you have a basic understanding of the purpose of functions and how they work.

This hour explains the use of the Insert Function dialog box and Formula palette, which makes it easier to use the more complex Excel functions. In addition, this session includes an extensive listing of many important Excel functions and gives you an opportunity to use some of them in the To Do exercises.

Advantages of Excel Functions

Functions are tools you can use to analyze data and get information. In other words, functions help answer your questions so that you can evaluate and examine your business and make projections.

Understanding How Functions Work

Excel uses straightforward formulas to perform simple calculations, such as adding or subtracting, on a number or series of numbers. For example, the formula =SUM(B4:B8) inserts the sum of the numbers contained in the range B4 to B8 into the cell containing the formula. These simple formulas are the foundation of many functions. Other functions combine several formulas or procedures to achieve a desired result.

Functions should be entered in the following basic order:

1. Start a function with an equal sign (=).
2. Enter the function name.
3. Include information about a cell or range of cells to be analyzed.
4. Enter arguments about what to do with the selected range of cells.

Some functions require additional information, which is discussed in this hour. For instance, the following is the format for the ADDRESS function, which returns a value about a cell address in a worksheet:

```
=ADDRESS(row_number,column_number,absolute_number,a1,sheet_text)
```

The arguments row_number and column_number are required arguments, and the remainder of the arguments are optional.

Some functions allow a variable number of arguments. For example, you can use as many arguments in the SUM function as necessary. You can include a maximum of 1,024 arguments in a function, providing that no single string of characters in the function statement exceeds 255 characters.

You can enter functions into your worksheets manually, with a macro, or by using the Insert Function dialog box and the Formula palette.

Using the Insert Function Dialog Box and Formula Palette

15

Excel's Insert Function dialog box and Formula palette make it easier for you to use and understand functions by organizing them into logical categories and by prompting you to complete the arguments required to make the function return a correct value.

The Insert Function dialog box and Formula palette can be accessed in several ways:

- Click the Insert Function button (the fx button)) on the Formula bar.
- Click Insert in the menu bar and choose Insert Function.
- Press Shift+F3.
- Type the equal sign (=) and name of the function in a cell and press Ctrl+A. Then enter the arguments in the Function Arguments dialog box.
- Click the Function down arrow button at the far left end of the Formula bar and select a function from the Function list.

When you use any of these methods except for the last two in the list (the Insert Function button [the fx button] on the Formula bar), Excel displays the Insert Function dialog box, as shown in Figure 15.1.

FIGURE 15.1

The Insert Function dialog box.

From this dialog box, you choose a function, click OK, and the Function Arguments dialog box opens (see Figure 15.2).

The most recently used category of functions appears in the Category list in the Insert Function dialog box. This feature is especially handy when you use a particular group of functions frequently. The list changes and keeps the last 10 functions you used. When a function is highlighted in the list on the right, its name, a brief description, and its arguments are displayed below the Category list.

FIGURE 15.2

The Function Arguments dialog box.

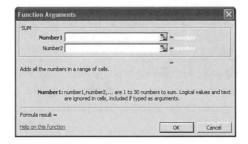

After you select a function in the Insert Function dialog box, just click OK. This brings you to the second step, which is entering arguments or instructions for calculation in the Function Arguments dialog box.

You can use the keyboard or the mouse to enter arguments that require cell addresses or ranges. Other arguments that are not associated with specific cells on the worksheet must be entered manually. Some arguments are required for a value to be returned, and some are optional. Arguments that are required appear in bold. Optional arguments appear in regular typeface. In Figure 15.2, you enter a range of cells in the Number 1 text box.

> If you need help with a particular function while you're in the Function Arguments dialog box, click the Help button. Excel's Help Assistant walks you through the particular function with which you are working.

Financial Functions

Financial functions are used for various financial calculations involving interest rates, loan terms, present values, and future values. Financial functions are essential for performing in-depth financial analysis of purchases, investments, and cash flow.

DDB

The DDB function calculates depreciation using the double declining balance method, which accelerates the rate of depreciation early in the life of an asset. When the asset's book value depreciates to the salvage value, depreciation stops.

The basic format for the DDB function looks like this:

```
DDB(cost,salvage,life,period,factor)
```

Enter values (cell references or constant values) for the initial cost, the salvage value, the life of the asset, and the period for which depreciation is being calculated. The life and period should both be in the same time measurement, such as years, months, or days. Optionally, you can enter a factor for the rate of depreciation. If you do not enter a factor, the DDB function assumes a factor of 2 (that is, double declining).

For example, suppose you are depreciating an asset over a 10-year life and want to calculate the depreciation in year 10. The cost (10,000) is in cell A5, and the salvage value (500) is in cell A6. The formula with the DDB function and the result of the calculation is

=DDB(A5,A6,10,10)   268.44

FV

FV is the future value. The syntax for the FV function looks like this:

=FV(interest rate,periods,payment amount,present value,type)

FV calculates the future value of an investment after payments have been made at a particular rate over a particular amount of time. The function finds the total dollar value of an investment after the investment has matured. Enter the interest rate as the periodic rate (usually a monthly or yearly rate). The periods argument contains the number of periods that the investment is active. You should use the same type of period for this argument and the interest rate (in months, years, and so on). The payment amount is the amount of each payment to the investment and represents a regular amount. The present value is the starting value of the investment. The type indicates whether payments are made at the beginning or end of the period. Entering 1 indicates the beginning and 0 indicates the end. Of course, any of these arguments can be cell references.

Remember that cash paid out must be shown as a negative number, and interest or cash received is a positive number. Therefore, if you are calculating the future value of a savings account, the present value (amount deposited) and the payment amount (monthly deposits) are negative numbers because they are "paid out" to the investment.

Consider the following example of a formula with the FV function and its result:

=FV(12%/12,120,-125,0, 1)   29042.38

Notice that the annual interest rate is converted to a monthly (periodic) rate using the formula 12%/12 and that the term and payment values reflect the same type of period (months). The result shows that you will have $29,042.38 after 10 years (120 months) of depositing $125 monthly at a 12% annual interest rate.

IPMT

This financial function calculates the interest paid for a particular payment given the interest rate, the number of periods in the term, and the present value. Specify the period for which you want to determine the interest being paid. The `type` determines whether payments are made at the beginning (`1`) of the period or at the end (`0`). The syntax for the `IPMT` function is

```
=IPMT(rate,period,periods,present value,future value,type)
```

`rate` is the interest rate per period. `period` is the period for which you want to find the interest, and must be in the range `1` to `nper`. `periods` is the total number of payment periods in an annuity. `present value` is the lump-sum amount that a series of future payments is worth right now. The `future` value is a cash balance you want to attain after the last payment is made. If you omit the future value, Excel assumes the future value is `0`. The future value of a loan, for example, is `0`. `type` is the number 0 or 1 and indicates when payments are due. If you omit the type, Excel assumes the type is `0`. If payments are due at the end of the period, set the type to `0`. If the payments are due at the beginning of the period, set the type to `1`.

Make sure that you are consistent about the units you use for specifying rate and periods. For instance, if you make monthly payments on a three-year loan at 10% annual interest, use `10%/12` for `rate` and `3*12` for `nper`. If you make annual payments on the same loan, use `10%` for `rate` and `3` for `nper`. For all the arguments, cash you pay out, such as deposits to savings, is represented by negative numbers. Cash you receive, such as dividend checks, is represented by positive numbers.

For example, the following formula calculates the interest due in the first month of a three-year, $10,000 loan at 10% annual interest:

```
=IPMT(0.1/12,1,36,10000)
```

The interest due in the first month of the loan is $83.33.

NPER

`NPER` calculates the number of required pay periods for an investment based on periodic, constant payments, and a constant interest rate. The syntax for the `NPER` financial function is

```
=NPER(rate,payment,present value,future value,type)
```

`rate` is the interest rate per period. `payment` is the amount of each payment to the investment and represents a regular amount. `present value` is the lump-sum amount that a series of future payments is worth right now. The `future` value is a cash balance you want to attain after the last payment is made. If you omit the future value, Excel assumes the future value is `0`. The future value of a loan, for example, is `0`. `type` is the number `0` or 1 and indicates when payments are due. If you omit the type, Excel assumes the type is 0. If payments are due at the end of the period, set the type to 0. If the payments are due at the beginning of the period, set the type to 1.

For example, suppose you want to buy a boat. The cost of the boat is $4,500, and the bank will loan you the amount. You know you can afford to pay $125.00 at the beginning of each month if you borrow the money. How many monthly payments will you have to make to pay off a $4,500 loan at 8% yearly interest? The following NPER function will calculate the number of monthly payments:

```
=NPER(0.08/12,-125,4500,0,1)
```

The number of monthly payments is 40.9, and rounded up, is 41.

NPV

The NPV function calculates the net present value of a series of cash-flow transactions or an investment based on a series of periodic cash flows and a discount rate. rate is the periodic interest rate of an investment of equivalent risk, and the range is the range of cells containing the cash incomes or outflows. If you are the investor or lender, remember that the loan paid out is negative and the payments in are positive. If the result is a positive number, the investment can be considered a good one. The basic format of the NPV function is

```
=NPV(rate,range)
```

What if you consider an investment in which you pay $10,000 one year from today and receive an annual income of $3,000, $4,200, and $6,800 in the next three years. Assuming an annual discount rate of 10%, the net present value of this investment is

```
NPV(10%,-10000,3000,4200,6800)
```

The net present value is $1,188.44.

PMT

The PMT function calculates the periodic payment when you enter the interest rate, periods, and principal as arguments:

```
=PMT(rate,periods,principal)
```

The following To Do exercise shows you how to set up and use loan calculations. Excel provides a number of functions for calculating loan amounts. There are four parts of a loan: the principal amount, periodic interest rate, periodic payment, and number of payments (or term).

The purpose of the worksheet is to calculate any one of these amounts when you know the other three. For example, you can calculate the monthly payment amount when you know the principal, interest rate, and term. You'll be entering data in a blank worksheet to prepare for calculating the monthly payment.

To Do: Calculate the Monthly Payment

1. Enter data into a new worksheet to match the data in the worksheet shown in Figure 15.3. For the interest amount, be sure to type **0.6** and to format the number with the Percent Style tool on the Formatting toolbar.

2. Suppose you want to calculate the monthly payment amount using the worksheet from Figure 15.3. Simply enter the formula **=PMT(D5/12,D7,D4)** into cell D6 as shown in Figure 15.4. In this case, you would enter values for the interest rate, periods, and principal only.

FIGURE 15.3

The beginning of a loan-calculation work-sheet.

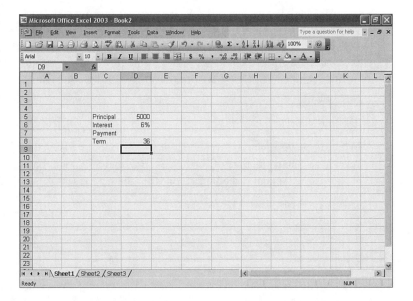

Notice that the interest rate is entered as the periodic rate. This periodic rate should be for the same time periods entered in the `periods` argument. In the example, the term is **36** months (36 `periods`), so you've entered the monthly interest rate. If you know only the annual interest rate, simply divide the annual rate by 12 to get the monthly rate. Or you can enter the formula `=12%/12` to calculate the periodic rate from the annual rate.

The result in cell D6 should be (\$152.11). The formula in the Formula bar should read =PMT(D6/12,D8,D5). Notice that the payment amount appears as a negative because it represents cash out. When using sums you have borrowed, the principal is positive (cash in) and the payment is negative (cash out). For sums loaned, the principal is negative and the payment is positive.

FIGURE 15.4

Example of calculating the payment of a loan.

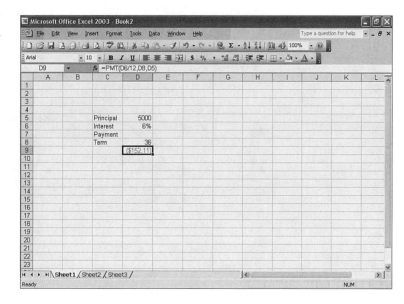

PPMT

The PPMT function calculates the amount of principal being paid during any of the payment periods, given the periodic interest rate and number of periods. A complete example of using this function to view the principal amount of each payment appears later in this section. The PPMT function looks like this:

```
=PPMT(rate,period,periods,present value,future value,type)
```

Given the rate, period, and principal, PPMT calculates the principal payment for any given payment number. The format for the PPMT function is

```
=PPMT(rate,payment number,periods,principal)
```

Follow the steps in the To Do exercise to calculate the amount of interest and principal paid at each payment. As you might already know, you pay more interest at the beginning of a loan than at the end. The proportion of interest to principal is different for each payment. You can use the PPMT function to determine how much principal is being paid with each payment. You start by entering data in the same worksheet used in the previous exercise in preparation for using the PPMT function.

To Do: Calculate How Much Principal Is Paid with Each Payment

1. Enter the heading, column headings, and payment numbers from 1 to 36 (or whatever the term requires) down column C, as shown in Figure 15.5. Figure 15.5 also shows some basic formatting applied to the worksheet, including the border around the table of values and some number formats.

FIGURE 15.5

Enter the payment numbers on the worksheet.

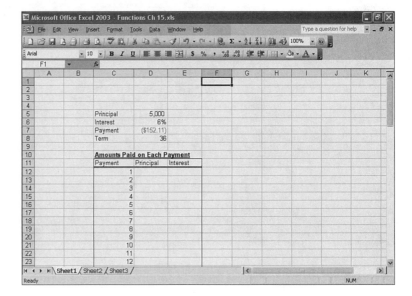

2. The first formula calculates the interest paid at the first payment. In cell D12, enter the formula `=PPMT($D$6,C12,$D$8,$D$5)`.

   The result should be (`$41.97`). Notice that all the references are absolute except the payment number, which is copied down column D to produce each payment.

3. Enter the formula `=$D$7-D12` for the interest amount in cell E12.

   This formula simply takes the payment amount and subtracts the PPMT amount for each payment number. You can see that the first payment consists of `$41.97` of principal and `$110.14` of interest.

4. To view the remaining payments, select D12:E12 and use the fill handle to fill the range D13:E47. The result should look something like Figure 15.6.

5. Use the SUM function to total each column at the bottom.

6. Add the two totals for the entire amount of the loan, including principal and interest. The totals are shown in Figure 15.7.

FIGURE 15.6
Payment formulas.

Amount paid to principal

Payment number   Amount paid to interest

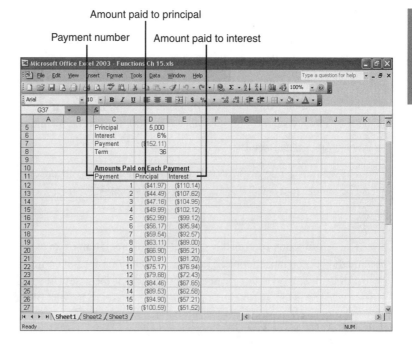

Total interest

FIGURE 15.7
Adding totals.

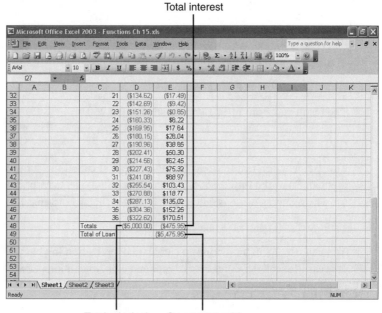

Total principal   Grand total paid

RATE

The RATE function calculates the interest rate or discount rate for a loan or investment when you enter the term, payment, and principal as arguments:

```
=RATE(term,payment,principal)
```

An example of using the RATE financial function is to calculate the rate of a four-year $8,000 loan with monthly payments of $200. Here's the formula:

```
=RATE(48, -200, 8000)
```

The result is a rate of 0.77%. This is the monthly rate, because the period is monthly. The annual rate is 0.77%*12, which equals 9.24%.

SLN

The SLN function returns the straight-line depreciation of an asset for one period. This method accelerates depreciation at a constant rate for the entire life of the asset. Enter the initial cost, the salvage value, and the life of the asset (in years). cost is the initial cost of the asset. salvage is the value of the asset at the end of the depreciation. Life is the number of periods over which the asset is being depreciated. The syntax of an SLN function looks like the following:

```
=SLN(cost,salvage,life)
```

An example of the SLN function is calculating the straight-line depreciation for a truck that costs $30,000, which has a useful life of 10 years and a salvage value of $7,500. The SLN formula would look like this:

```
=SLN(30000,7500,10)
```

The result is a straight-line depreciation of $2,250.

SYD

The SYD function is a third depreciation method called the sum of the years' digits method. Enter the initial cost, the salvage value, the life of the asset, and the period for which depreciation is calculated. The SYD function format has this syntax:

```
=SYD(cost,salvage,life,period)
```

You can use the SYD function to calculate depreciation in year 10 when the asset has a 10-year life, cell A5 contains 10,000, and cell A6 contains 500. The formula and its result are as follows:

```
=SYD(A5,A6,10,10)      172.73
```

Date and Time Functions

Date and time functions are used specifically for date and time math calculations and conversions. Date math and time math have the capability to calculate elapsed time, add time to a given date or time, or calculate the difference between two dates or times. The following functions are used for these calculations. For more information about date math, see Hour 9, "Changing the Look of Values."

DATEVALUE

This function converts a text string into a valid date (in other words, a date serial number). The text string must contain data that is recognizable as a date. The function recognizes text entered in any of the date formats shown in the Number tab in the Format Cells dialog box, when you choose the Date category. You can specify any date from January 1, 1900 to February 6, 2040. The format of a DATEVALUE function is

```
=DATEVALUE(text)
```

An example of the DATEVALUE function and its result is

```
= DATEVALUE (B5), where B5 contains     1/25/91
```

The result, 31801, is the number of days between 1/1/00 and 1/25/91.

DAY, MONTH, and YEAR

These functions return the day, month, or year corresponding to a specified date. The date variable can be any valid date entered as the number of days elapsed since January 1, 1900. The value can also be a reference to a cell containing a valid date, or it can be any date expression resulting in a valid date. These functions break a date into its various portions. The following syntax is used for the DAY, MONTH, and YEAR functions:

```
=DAY(date)MONTH(date)YEAR(date)
```

Suppose cell B2 contains the date 2/24/91. Here are some examples of these functions and their results:

```
DAY(B2)        24

MONTH(B2)      2

YEAR(B2)       1991
```

NOW

The NOW function pulls the current date and time from the DOS startup date and time. The value is returned as a number with a decimal value, as in 2245.2025. The integer part of this number represents the date (in "days elapsed" format) and the fractional part represents the time (in "time elapsed" format). The NOW function's format is

```
=NOW( )
```

There is no argument for the function. You can simply format the value into a date using any of the date formats in the Number tab in the Format Cells dialog box, when you choose the Date category. Or you can format the value into a time using the time formats in the Number tab in the Format Cells dialog box, when you choose the Time category. You can also use the TRUNC function to separate the two portions, as in =TRUNC(NOW( )). This formula strips off the decimal portion of the date/time serial number, turning it into a date only. You can then format this date or use the DAY, MONTH, and YEAR functions to split the value even further.

TIMEVALUE

The TIMEVALUE function converts a text string into a valid time. The text string must be recognizable as a time entry. It should resemble any of the time formats in the Format Number command. The result is displayed in the "time elapsed" format but can be formatted with the Format Number command. Enter times as text strings by typing them in two or three parts (for example, 12:30 or 12:30:15) or by including the AM/PM (for example, 12:30:00 AM). The format for the TIMEVALUE function is

```
=TIMEVALUE(text)
```

The following is an example of the function and its result:

```
=TIMEVALUE(B4), where B4    0.9828125contains '11:35:15 PM'
```

The numerical result can be formatted as the valid time 11:35:15 PM.

WEEKDAY

This function converts a serial number to a day of the week as a value from 1 to 7. The value 1 equals Sunday, 2 equals Monday, and so on. To format this value as the appropriate day name, use the Format Cells command and, on the Number tab, specify the custom date format "dddd" by choosing the Custom category to create the format.

The syntax for the WEEKDAY function looks like this:

```
=WEEKDAY(date)
```

An example of this function and its result is

```
=WEEKDAY(1/1/91)   6
```

The 6 can be formatted as the weekday name Thursday using the `"dddd"` format.

Logical Functions

Logical functions are used to create logical tests. A test enables a formula to make a decision based on particular data. A test can determine whether a value is greater than 25, and the formula making the test can perform one function if true, and another if false.

IF

The most common and useful logical function is the `IF` function, which allows you to develop several kinds of tests based on the operators used in the test statement. `IF` is often combined with other logical functions to create more specific tests. The syntax for the `IF` function looks like this:

```
=IF(condition,value if true,value if false)
```

The `IF` function tests that a condition is true or false. If the condition proves true, one value is returned. If the condition proves false, another value is returned. To prove a condition true or false requires a relational operator. Excel offers several:

- `>` Is greater than
- `<` Is less than
- `=` Is equal to
- `>=` Is greater than or equal to
- `<=` Is less than or equal to
- `<>` Is not equal to

In the following example, you can substitute any of these operators for the one given:

```
=IF(A1=A2,"Right","Wrong")
```

If the value of `A1` is equal to that of `A2`, the formula returns `Right`. Otherwise, the formula returns `Wrong`. The value if true and the value if false can be any constant value, cell reference, or formula.

Perform the steps in the upcoming To Do exercise to build a logical formula to test a condition and show results with the words `Yes` and `No`. Then you copy the formula to a column to test the condition for all the sales data. The results in the last column show either the word Yes or No in each cell that contains a logical formula. You start by entering data in a blank worksheet to prepare for building a logical formula.

To Do: Build a Logical Formula

1. Click the Sheet2 tab. Enter the data into Sheet2 to match the data in the worksheet shown in Figure 15.8. You need to widen column C and format the numbers in column D with the Comma Style with zero (0) decimal places.

2. Click cell E2.

3. Type =IF(.

4. Click cell D2.

5. Type >50000,"Yes","No").

6. Press Enter.

7. Click cell E2 and point to the fill handle.

8. Drag the fill handle to copy the logical formula down to cell E8.

FIGURE 15.8

Sales quota data for building a logical formula.

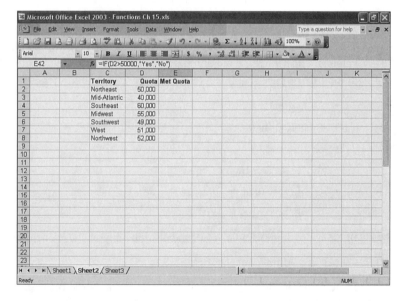

9. Click any cell to deselect the range.

Excel shows the word Yes or No in each cell that contains a logical formula, as shown in Figure 15.9.

FIGURE 15.9

Logical formula results.

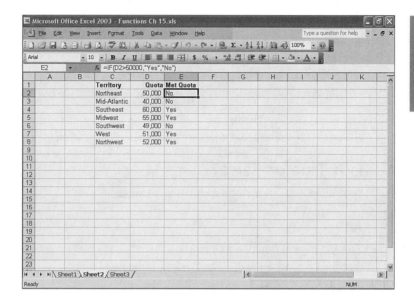

15

ISBLANK

This function tests whether a cell is blank. If the specified cell is blank, a value of TRUE is returned; otherwise, FALSE is returned. The referenced cell can be any valid cell in the worksheet. The ISBLANK function is commonly used with the IF function to test for a blank cell and then perform some action based on the outcome. For example, you can use ISBLANK with IF to print a message next to cells that need to be filled in and then remove the message after the data is entered.

The ISBLANK function's format is

```
=ISBLANK (cell)
```

The corresponding formula follows:

```
=IF(ISBLANK(B5) = FALSE, "", "Please enter the amount in cell B5")
```

ISERR

This function tests whether a specified cell contains an error. If so, then a value of TRUE is returned. Otherwise, FALSE is returned. The ISERR function is commonly used with the IF function to "trap" errors in the worksheet and allow control over the result of the error. Normally, any calculation that references a cell containing an error causes #VALUE! or some other error message to be returned. But using the ISERR function, you can pinpoint the error.

The syntax for the ISERR function is

=ISERR(cell)

For example:

=IF(ISERR(B5) = TRUE, "Invalid entry in cell B5", B5*B6)

This formula tests whether the value of B5 is an error. If so, the phrase Invalid entry in cell B5 is returned. Otherwise, the desired calculation is performed.

Is It True or False?

TRUE and FALSE return TRUE and FALSE as values.

AND

The AND logical function returns the value TRUE if all of its arguments are true; otherwise it returns the value FALSE. The syntax for the AND function is

=AND(Condition 1,Condition 2...)

You can test up to 30 conditions with the AND function. Typically, you use the AND function with the IF function to return a value based on more than one condition.

For example, there are only two possible grades for marking a student mid-term and final term papers: P (Pass) and F (Fail). To pass the course, a student must have a mark that is >=50 for each term paper. The AND function combined with the IF function would look like this:

=IF(AND(B2>=50,C2>=50,"P","F")

Cell B2 contains 51 and cell C2 contains 95. The AND function tests whether both marks satisfy this condition. If both marks are >=50, the return value of the AND function will be TRUE, and the IF function's value of P (Pass) will appear in the cell. Otherwise the return value of the AND function will be FALSE, and the IF function's value of F (Fail) will appear in the cell.

OR

The OR logical function returns TRUE if one or more of its arguments is true; otherwise it returns FALSE. The syntax for the OR function is

=OR(Condition 1,Condition 2...)

You can test up to 30 conditions with the OR function. Typically, you use the AND function with the IF function to return a value based on more than one condition.

15

Typically, you use the AND function with the IF function to return a value based on more than one condition.

For example, there are only two possible grades for marking a student mid-term and final term papers: P (Pass) and F (Fail). To pass the course, a student must have a mark that is >=50 for either term paper. The OR function combined with the IF function would look like this:

```
=IF(OR(B2>=50,C2>=50,"P","F")
```

Cell B2 contains 51 and cell C2 contains 95. The OR function tests whether either mark satisfies this condition. If either mark is >=50, the return value of the OR function will be TRUE, and the IF function's value of P (Pass) will appear in the cell. Otherwise the return value of the OR function will be FALSE, and the IF function's value of F (Fail) will appear in the cell.

NOT

NOT reverses the logic of an argument. True arguments become false and vice versa. The format of the NOT function looks like

```
=NOT(logical)
```

The NOT function returns the value TRUE if the logical argument is false. Conversely, the NOT function returns the value FALSE if the logical argument is true. Use the NOT function when you want to make sure a value is not equal to one particular value.

Suppose you are told that you need to create a formula that does something if the city is Boston or New York. An approach would be to specify that you're interested in cities that are not Denver. This way, all cities that are not Denver will return TRUE. Here's an example of using the NOT function:

```
=Not(B5="New York")
```

The NOT function returns TRUE if B5 contains anything except New York.

How to Use Lookup Functions

Lookup functions search for values within tables or lists. Each lookup function uses a different method for searching and returning values. Each method is suited for a particular task. Anytime your worksheet uses tables to hold values, such as tax tables or price tables, you can employ a lookup function for added power in the application.

VLOOKUP and HLOOKUP

These two lookup functions search for values in tables based on a lookup value, the value you are trying to match. For example, a tax table contains tax rates based on income. Income is the lookup value. VLOOKUP searches vertically in a column of values and then returns a corresponding value from the table. HLOOKUP searches horizontally in a row of values and then returns a corresponding value from the table.

If the lookup range within the specified table range contains text strings, the search variable must also be a text string. In such cases, the lookup function must be able to find an exact match for the specified information, including upper- and lowercase letters. If no match is found, the function returns the error #VALUE!. The data in the table (that is, the value to be returned) can be numeric values or text. The syntax for the HLOOKUP function is

```
=HLOOKUP(value,range,row offset)
```

As an example, suppose you have a table of prices for merchandise and want to search that table for item number 125. When item number 125 is located in the table, the price of the item is returned.

The VLOOKUP function searches vertically in a column of values and then returns a corresponding value from another table column. The function works like this:

```
=VLOOKUP(value,table range,offset)
```

An example of a vertical lookup function is

```
=VLOOKUP(B2,A4:B10,2)
```

The value is the number or text in the first column of the table that you are trying to match with corresponding information. It can be any number, text, cell reference, or formula. For the Figure 15.10 example, the value was entered as the cell reference B2 so that any number entered into cell B2 becomes the value for the lookup. The table range is the worksheet range containing the table. The first column of this range, called the lookup column, should include the list of values for which you will be searching. The table can then include as many more columns as necessary to contain all information. Additional columns are called offset columns, and they contain the cells with information you want to return when you select a value from the lookup column. When entering the VLOOKUP formula, the lookup column is referred to as offset 1, the next column is offset 2, and so on.

FIGURE 15.10

Using the VLOOKUP function.

15

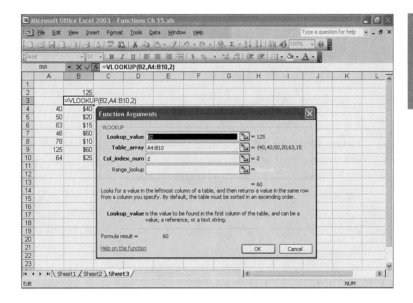

When the function finds the lookup value in the lookup column, it remembers the row position of the lookup value. Then the function searches across the table to return information from the column specified by the offset value listed in the formula. The lookup formulas in cells B3, C3, and D3 return information from each of the columns of the table, using the following functions:

```
=VLOOKUP(B2,A4:D10,2)
```

```
=VLOOKUP(B2,A4:D10,3)
```

```
=VLOOKUP(B2,A4:D10,4)
```

Notice that the formulas are almost identical; the only difference is that they contain different offset values, selecting values from different columns along one row of the table.

When you create lookup tables and the lookup formulas that use them, keep some basic rules in mind. First, the values in the lookup column must be in ascending order (sorted). If the values are text, they must be in alphabetical order. If the lookup column is not in ascending order, the function might return incorrect values. Excel searches the lookup column until it finds a direct match. If a direct match cannot be found, the closest value smaller than the search variable is used. Therefore, if a lookup value is greater than all values in the table, the last value in the table is used because it's the largest. If the lookup value is smaller than all values in the table, the function returns the error #VALUE!.

If the lookup column contains text, the lookup function must be able to match the lookup value exactly, including upper- and lowercase letters. When no match is found, the function returns the error #VALUE!. Even if the lookup column contains text, the offset columns can contain numeric values or text.

Lookup Wizard

Excel's Lookup Wizard can step you through searching for values in tables based on a lookup value, the value you are trying to find. As an example, if you have a price table that contains prices for merchandise based on item numbers, price is the lookup value. What if you want to search that table for item number 50? The Lookup Wizard searches vertically in a column of values and horizontally in a row of values, finds the value at the intersection of the column and row, and then returns that value from the table. For instance, the price of item number 50 is returned and copied into a cell on the worksheet.

Excel can copy the results in two ways:

- Copy just the lookup formula with its result into a cell.
- Copy the lookup formula with its lookup parameters (the column label, the row label, and the formula with its result).

The next exercise enables you to practice using the Lookup Wizard to find the interest on payment number 10. You'll be working with the Amounts Paid on Each Payment table in Sheet1 again.

To Do: Look Up a Value with the Lookup Wizard

1. Click the Sheet1 tab.
2. Select C11:E47, which is the range you want to search.

> Make sure you include the column and row headings in the range you select. The Lookup Wizard refers to column headings as column labels and row headings as row labels.

3. Click Tools in the menu and choose Lookup. The Lookup Wizard–Step 1 of 4 dialog box appears, as shown in Figure 15.11. You should see the selected range $C$11:$E$47 in the dialog box. This range is the one you want.

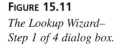

FIGURE 15.11

*The Lookup Wizard–
Step 1 of 4 dialog box.*

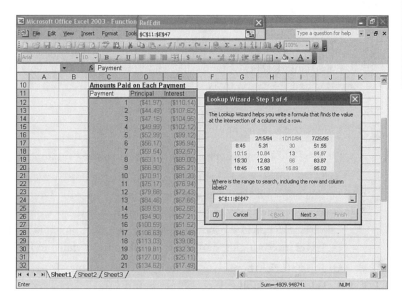

If the Lookup Wizard is not on your Tools menu, the add-in Lookup Wizard was not installed on your computer. To install the Lookup Wizard, choose Tools, Add-Ins. Scroll down the list until you see the Lookup Wizard and click its check box. Click OK. Excel displays instructions for installing the Lookup Wizard add-in from the Microsoft Office or Microsoft Excel CD-ROM.

4. Click the Next button. The Lookup Wizard–Step 2 of 4 dialog box pops up.

5. In the Which Column Contains the Value to Find box, choose Interest. This step selects the column label.

6. In the Which Row Contains the Value to Find box, choose Payment. This step selects the row label.

7. Click the Next button. The Lookup Wizard–Step 3 of 4 dialog box shows up. The Copy Just the Formula to a Single Cell option should be selected. You want this option. You should also see the return value of E21, which is the item number that the Lookup Wizard found in the table.

8. Click the Next button. The Lookup Wizard–Step 4 of 4 dialog box should appear.

9. Click cell C52. This step tells Excel where to copy the formula.

10. Click the Finish button. Excel shows the result $81.20 in cell C52.

Summary

This hour gave you a solid introduction to many of Excel's sophisticated functions. Your completion of this challenging hour is to be commended.

The next hour teaches you how to check for errors on your worksheets with Excel's auditing and validation tools.

Q&A

Q Why did Excel insert a plus sign next to the function name I entered?

A If you access the Function Arguments dialog box by typing an equal sign and the function name in a cell and then pressing Shift+F3, typing the name in lowercase validates the function name. If the function name you entered is correct, Excel converts it to uppercase automatically. If the function name is incorrect or invalid, Excel inserts a plus sign and leaves the invalid name in lowercase.

Q I got stuck when I was working with a complex function in the Function Arguments dialog box. What should I have done?

A If you need help with a particular function while you're in the Formula palette, click the Help button. Excel's Office Assistant walks you through either the Formula palette or the particular function with which you are working.

Q The Lookup Wizard doesn't appear on my Tools menu. What next?

A The Lookup Wizard is an add-in. You need to install the Lookup Wizard from the Microsoft Office or Microsoft Excel CD-ROM with Add/Remove Programs in the Windows Control Panel.

Q I selected the data in my table and used the Lookup Wizard to search for a value. Why didn't I get the results I wanted?

A Make sure you include the column and row headings in the range you select. The Lookup Wizard refers to column headings as column labels and row headings as row labels.

Hour **16**

Auditing and Validating Your Work

The topics of this hour include the following:

- How to audit formulas
- How to validate data
- How to circle invalid data
- How to use constants and formulas
- How to define label ranges

In this hour, you learn auditing terms, use the Formula Auditing toolbar, check and review worksheet data, learn how values are determined, and track problems in formulas. You'll also use the Data Validation command to validate the data in your worksheets and circle any invalid data so that you can make the corrections.

When this hour ends, you'll be auditing and validating the data in your own worksheets to catch errors. By doing the exercises in this hour and using Excel's formula auditing and validation tools, you'll discover how quick and easy it is to audit and validate your work.

Auditing Workbooks

The auditing features are some of the most useful tools in Excel. These tools can help you detect problems in your worksheet formulas. Excel supplies a Formula Auditing toolbar to help you find errors on your worksheets, attach comments to cells, and track problems in your worksheet formulas.

Using auditing tools can help you understand, visualize, and troubleshoot the relationships among cell references, formulas, and data.

When you're auditing formulas in your worksheets, you might want to use the Go To Special command to quickly search for comments, precedents, dependents, or any other auditing information. The Go To Special command helps you find the following information while auditing your worksheets:

- Comments
- Constants
- Formulas that meet particular criteria
- Blank cells
- Cells in the current region or array
- Cells that do not fit a pattern in a row or column
- Precedents
- Dependents
- Last active cell in your sheet
- Visible cells
- Objects

To use the Go To Special command, simply press F5 (Go To) and click the Special button in the Go To dialog box. In the Go To Special dialog box, select the item you want to go to and click OK. Excel highlights the cells on the worksheet that correspond to the item you selected in the Go To Special dialog box.

Understanding Dependents and Precedents

Before you audit a worksheet, you should be familiar with the following auditing terms:

- Constant—Cells with contents that are that are used by other cells that contain formulas. In Excel, cells containing values that do not begin with an equal sign are constants, whether they are numbers or text.
- Dependent—Cells that contain formulas that refer to other cells.

- Error—Values that result from an incorrect cell reference or formula.

- Precedent—Cells that are referred to directly by a formula.

- Tracer—A visual tool that enables you to find precedents, dependents, and errors in any cell in a worksheet. Tracers are graphic displays, such as arrows, that visually show you where formulas get their values. Tracers show relationships between cells and illustrate precedent and dependent relationships.

Using the Formula Auditing Toolbar

Excel's Formula Auditing toolbar provides tools for auditing data in your worksheets. Figure 16.1 shows the Formula Auditing toolbar. To display the Formula Auditing toolbar, choose Tools, Formula Auditing, Show Formula Auditing Toolbar.

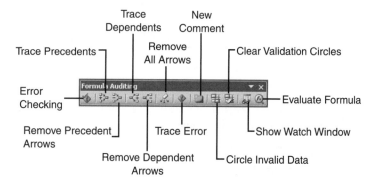

FIGURE 16.1
The Formula Auditing toolbar.

Table 16.1 lists the auditing tools on the Formula Auditing toolbar and describes the purpose of each tool.

TABLE 16.1 Excel's Auditing Tools

Tool	What It Does
Error Checking	Checks for problems in formulas on the worksheet using a set of rules to find common mistakes.
Trace Precedents	Draws arrows from all cells that supply values directly to the formula in the active cell (precedents).
Remove Precedent Arrows	Deletes a level of precedent tracer arrows from the active worksheet.
Trace Dependents	Draws arrows from the active cell to cells with formulas that use the values in the active cell (dependents).
Remove Dependent Arrows	Deletes a level of dependent tracer arrows from the active worksheet.
Remove All Arrows	Deletes all tracer arrows from the active worksheet.

TABLE 16.1 continued

Tool	What It Does
Trace Error	Draws an arrow to an error value in the active cell from cells that might have caused the error.
New Comment	Displays a comment text box next to a cell you selected that will contain text or audio comments.
Circle Invalid Data	Identifies incorrect entries with circles. Incorrect entries are values outside the limits you set by using the Data Validation command.
Clear Validation Circles	Hides circles around incorrect values in cells.
Show Watch Window	Displays the Watch Window toolbar, allowing you to watch cells and their formulas, even when the cells are not in view.
Evaluate Formula	Displays the parts of a nested formula, which tests cell contents and helps you make decisions based upon the results. Evaluates the order in which the nested formula is calculated.

Using Error Checking

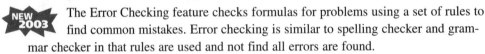 The Error Checking feature checks formulas for problems using a set of rules to find common mistakes. Error checking is similar to spelling checker and grammar checker in that rules are used and not find all errors are found.

You can turn the error checking rules on or off individually. To do so, choose Tools, Options, and click the Error Checking tab (see figure 16.2). By default, background error checking is turned on. That way, Excel immediately checks for formula errors on the worksheet as you work. If you choose to turn off the background error-checking feature, you can check for formula errors one at a time like a spelling checker.

Another error checking option is to reset all previously ignored errors so that they appear again. To set this option, click the Reset Ignored Errors button. Select the rules you want to turn on or off and click OK.

When Excel finds a problem with a formula, a green triangle appears in the upper left corner of the cell that contains the formula.

If you turned off background error checking and decide to check for errors in formulas manually, click the Error Checking button on the Formula Editing toolbar and Excel will display the green triangle in the cell with the problem.

When error checking finds a formula with a problem, you should see options for resolving the problem. You can either select one of the options or ignore the problem. If you ignore a problem, it does not appear in subsequent error checks.

FIGURE 16.2

The Error Checking tab in the Options dialog box.

Enable Background Error Checking

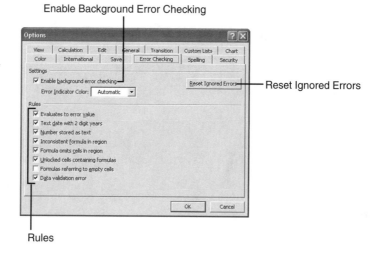

Reset Ignored Errors

Rules

Using Tracer Arrows

When you audit a worksheet to trace the precedents or dependents of a cell, Excel displays the following tracer arrow symbols on your worksheet:

- Blue or solid arrow—Indicates direct precedents of the selected formula.
- Red or dotted arrow—Indicates formulas that refer to error values.
- Dashed arrow attached to a spreadsheet icon—Refers to external worksheets.

Before you use tracer arrows to audit your worksheet, you need to verify that the Hide All option is not selected in the Options dialog box. When the Hide All option is not selected, Excel displays the tracer arrows on your worksheets. If the option is selected, Excel does not display any tracer arrows when you audit your worksheets.

To verify that the Hide All option is turned off, choose Tools, Options. In the Options dialog box, click the View tab if necessary. In the Objects section, verify that the Hide All option button is not selected and that the Show All option button is selected (displays with a black circle in the radio button), as shown in Figure 16.3. Click OK. Now you're all set to audit your worksheet using tracer arrows.

Go through the steps in the next To Do exercise to trace precedents and dependents with tracer arrows. The first step is to display the Formula Auditing toolbar. You need to work with the My Budget workbook for the entire hour, so be sure to open it before you start the exercise. If you are prompted to update linked information, choose Yes.

Show All

FIGURE 16.3

*The Show All option
in the Options
dialog box.*

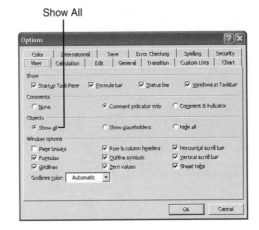

To Do: Trace Precedents Using Tracer Arrows

1. Choose Tools, Formula Auditing, Show Formula Auditing Toolbar. Excel displays
   the Formula Auditing toolbar.

2. To trace the precedents of a cell (to figure out the relationship between a formula
   and its cell references), click the cell that contains the formula you want to trace.
   In this case, click cell B9.

3. Click the Trace Precedents button on the Formula Auditing toolbar. Excel displays
   a tracer arrow on the worksheet, as shown in Figure 16.4.

4. Double-click the point of the tracer arrow (blue or solid arrow) to select the cells
   leading up to the cell at the point end of the arrow. The cells that are referenced in
   the formula are highlighted.

5. Double-click the point of the tracer arrow again to select the cell at the point end of
   the arrow. Excel removes the highlighting from the cells related to the formula.

6. Click cell J17. This cell contains the formula you want to trace.

7. Click the Trace Precedents button on the Formula Auditing toolbar. Excel displays
   a tracer arrow on the worksheet.

8. Double-click the point of the external worksheet arrow (dashed arrow with a
   spreadsheet icon). The Go To dialog box opens (see Figure 16.5).

9. Select the item in the Go To list. Excel displays the spreadsheet reference in the
   Reference box at the bottom of the dialog box. Click OK to confirm your choice.
   Excel should display the selected sheet (Detail sheet tab) and make cell B5 the
   active cell. The active cell references the formula you're tracing.

16

FIGURE 16.4
A precedent tracer arrow on the worksheet.

Precedent tracer arrow   Trace Precedents button

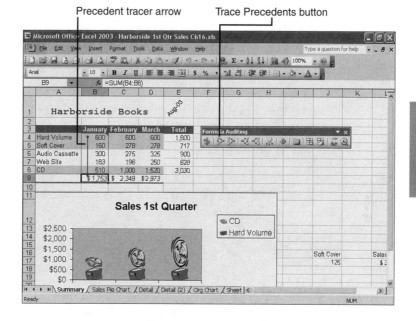

External spreadsheet reference

FIGURE 16.5
The Go To dialog box.

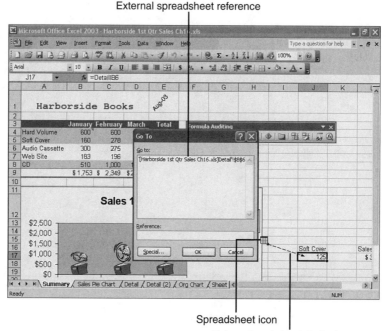

Spreadsheet icon

External worksheet dashed arrow

▼ 10. Click the Summary sheet tab to return to the original worksheet.

11. Click the Remove Precedents Arrows button on the Formula Auditing toolbar to remove one level of tracer arrows. The external spreadsheet tracer arrow and

▲ spreadsheet icon should disappear.

The next exercise shows you how to trace dependents with tracer arrows to determine the relationship between a cell reference and the formula that contains the cell reference. You should be using the Detail worksheet.

To Do: Trace Dependents Using Tracer Arrows

1. Click the cell dependent that you want to trace. In this case, click cell B5.

2. Click the Trace Dependents button on the Formula Auditing toolbar. Excel displays tracer arrows on the worksheet, as shown in Figure 16.6.

3. Double-click the point of the tracer arrow (blue or solid arrow) that points to cell B10 to select the cell at the point end of the arrow. The active cell is now B10.

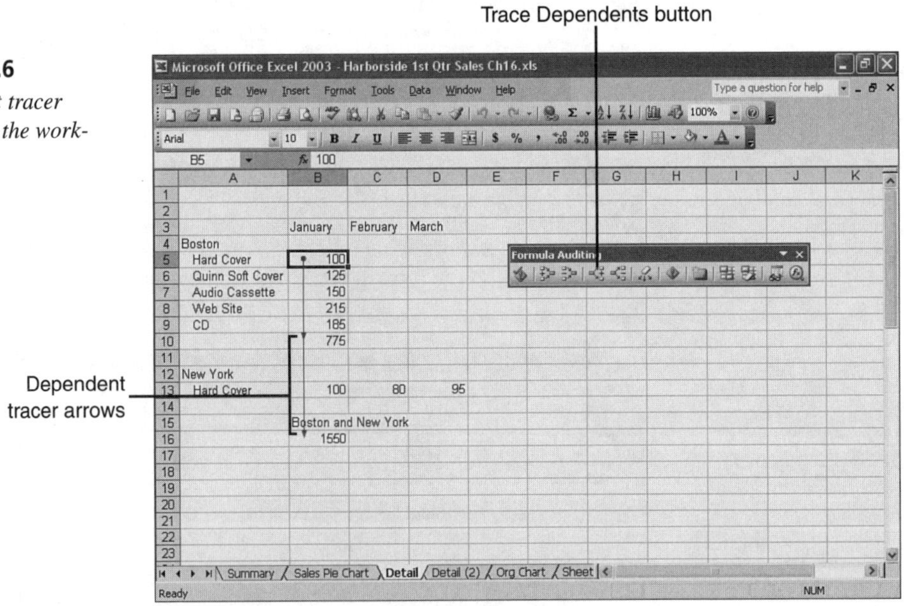

Trace Dependents button

FIGURE 16.6

Dependent tracer arrows on the worksheet.

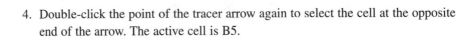

Dependent tracer arrows

▼ 4. Double-click the point of the tracer arrow again to select the cell at the opposite end of the arrow. The active cell is B5.

▼   5. Double-click the point of the tracer arrow (blue or solid arrow) that points to cell
       C23 to select the cell at the point end of the arrow. The active cell is now C23.

    6. Double-click the point of the tracer arrow again to select the cell at the opposite
       end of the arrow. The active cell is B5.

▲   7. Click the Remove Dependent Arrows button on the Formula Auditing toolbar to
       remove the tracer arrows.

Tracing Errors

After tracing precedents and dependents, you can also trace any errors in your worksheet.
If you have formulas that produce errors, Excel's Trace Errors feature can help you find
and correct the errors.

Tracing errors in a worksheet pinpoints the errors so that you can fix them. Some of the
error values that can appear in a cell include the following:

- #DIV/0!—Occurs when you create a formula that divides by zero (0) or divides by
  a cell that is empty.

- #N/A—Happens when you have a value that is not available to a function or a formula.

- #NAME?—Appears when Excel doesn't recognize text in a formula.

- #NULL!—Happens when you specify an intersection of two areas that do not inter-
  sect. For instance, you might have an incorrect range operator (not using a comma
  to separate two ranges, such as =SUM(B1:B8,F4:F8) or an incorrect cell reference.

- #NUM!—Occurs when you use an unacceptable argument in a function that should
  be a numeric argument or when a formula's result is a number that is too large or
  too small for Excel to display. Excel displays values between -1*10307 and
  1*10307.

- #REF!—Happens when a cell reference is not valid, such as when you delete cells
  that refer to formulas or paste cells onto cells that are referred to by other formulas.

- #VALUE!—Appears when you use the wrong type of argument in a function or
  wrong operand in a formula.

The following To Do exercise walks you through tracing an error that appears in a cell.
First you introduce an error by editing a formula to get incorrect results. (Continue working in the Detail worksheet.)

16

To Do: Trace Errors

1. Click cell B10, press F2, and press the End key. Next, type /, click B4, and press Enter. You should see the #DIV/0! error in cell B10. This error value is traceable.

2. Select cell B10 and click the Trace Error button on the Formula Auditing toolbar. Excel displays an error tracer arrow on the worksheet, as shown in Figure 16.7. You should also see a Trace Error icon (diamond with an exclamation point) next to cell B10. If you point to the Trace Error icon, a ScreenTip informs you that the formula or function is dividing by zero or empty cells.

If you click on the Trace Error down arrow, you will see a shortcut menu with commands for fixing the formula error.

3. Double-click the point of the error tracer arrow (red, dotted, blue, or solid arrow) to select the cell at the base of the arrow. The active cell is B4, which is the cause of the error. Cell B4 is empty, which means the cell has a value of zero (0). Zero cannot be a divisor, and you cannot divide by zero. Therefore, Excel displayed the #DIV/0! error result in cell B10.

FIGURE 16.7

An error tracer arrow on the worksheet.

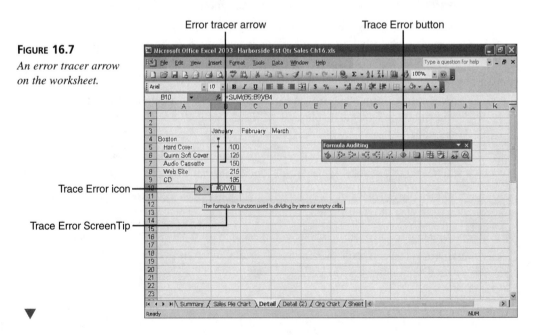

▼   4. Double-click the point of the error tracer arrow again to select the cell at the point
        end of the arrow. Cell B10 is the active cell.

     5. In cell B10, type **=SUM(B5:B9)** to correct the error. Press Enter. The error tracer
        arrow should disappear.

> If you correct an error and the little green triangle doesn't disappear, it
> doesn't mean you didn't fix the error correctly—it means you have another
> error to clear.

16

▲   6. Click the Close (×) button on the Formula Auditing toolbar to close the toolbar.

Validating Input

Excel's Data Validation command lets you perform validation on entries to set up data
validation rules. You can define data that is acceptable for any given cell or range of
cells, and input messages or error alerts that display whenever a validated cell is selected.
Error alerts can display whenever a validated cell is selected or when a user tries to enter
an invalid value. Data Validation only warns you against inputting invalid data—it
doesn't stop you from doing so.

Setting Validation Rules

Follow the steps in the next exercise to set up the data validation rules. You are setting
rules for the Car data in column B on the Detail sheet.

To Do: Set Validation Rules

▼ To Do

1. Click cell A12 on the Detail sheet. Type **New York** and press Enter. In cell A13,
   type **Hard Cover** and press Enter. Click cell A13 and then click the Increase Indent
   button on the Formatting toolbar.

2. In cells B13:D13, type the numbers **49, 80,** and **125.**

3. Select cells B13:D13. This step tells Excel what data you want to validate in the
   worksheet.

4. Choose Data, Validation. The Data Validation dialog box opens, as shown in Figure
   16.8. This exercise uses all three tabs: Settings, Input Message, and Error Alert.

▼

FIGURE 16.8

*The Data Validation
dialog box.*

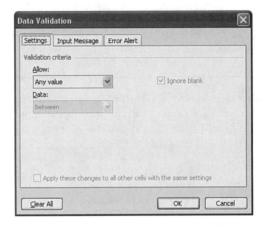

5. First, in the Settings tab, click the Allow drop-down arrow and choose Whole Number.

6. In the Data list, ensure that Between is selected.

7. In the Minimum box, type **50**.

8. In the Maximum box, type **100**.

9. Click the Input Message tab.

10. In the Input Message box, type **Any whole number from 50 to 100**.

11. Click the Error Alert tab.

12. In the Error Message box, type **Hard cover sales are less than 50 or greater than 100**.

13. Click OK to confirm your entries. Excel shows the following text box next to cell B13: `Any whole number from 50 to 100`. The next step is to edit an entry to produce invalid data in a cell.

14. Click cell D13 on the Detail sheet.

15. Type **35** and press Enter. Good job! Your error alert worked. Excel displays the error message **Hard cover sales are less than 50 or greater than 100**.

16. Click the Cancel button to remove the message.

Circling Invalid Data

If your worksheet contains any invalid data, you can identify that data by using the Circle Invalid Data feature. You need to display the Formula Auditing toolbar to use the feature. Excel identifies invalid data by marking the data with a red circle. You can correct the invalid data by typing over the data in the cells that contain a red circle.

The instructions in the following To Do exercise step you through circling and correcting invalid data on your worksheet. First you need to enter invalid data for a car expense in the Detail sheet.

To Do: Circle and Correct Invalid Data

▼ To Do

1. Choose Tools, Formula Auditing, Show Formula Auditing Toolbar. Excel displays the Formula Auditing toolbar.

2. Click the Circle Invalid Data button on the Formula Auditing toolbar. You should see a red circle around the 49 in cell B13 and the 125 in cell D13 (see Figure 16.9). The number 49 in cell B13 is less than 50. The number 125 in cell D13 is greater than 100. Therefore, the data is invalid.

16

Invalid data

FIGURE 16.9

Circle around invalid data.

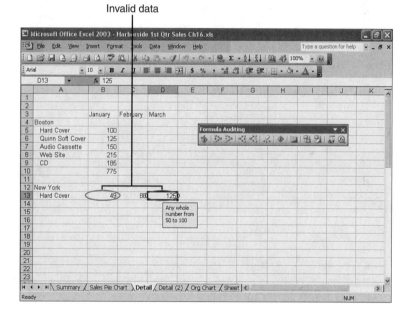

3. Click cell B13 and type **100**. Then press Enter. Click cell D13 and type **95**. Then press Enter. The red circle is removed from both cells.

4. If a red circle still shows in cell B13 and D13, click the Clear Validation Circles button on the Formula Auditing toolbar.

5. Click the Close (×) button on the Formula Auditing toolbar to close the toolbar.

Using Named Constants and Formulas

Constants are cells whose contents are deemed not to be a formula, so those cells whose values do not begin with an equal sign are constants, whether they are numbers or text.

The Formula option selects cells that meet the selection criteria of values returned as numbers, text, logical, or errors.

Using Constants

As you learned at the beginning of this hour, you can use the Go To Special command to find constants.

To do so, just press F5 (Go To) and click the Special button in the Go To dialog box. The Go To Special dialog box appears, as shown in Figure 16.10.

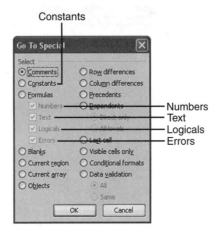

FIGURE 16.10

Selecting constants in the Go To Special dialog box.

In the Go To Special dialog box, select Constants (see Figure 16.10). Excel automatically selects (puts check marks in) all the check boxes under the Formulas option. Therefore, by default Excel finds all constants that are numbers, text, logicals, or errors.

If you want to search for one or more of these constants, click in the check box to remove the check mark for the constants you don't want to find. Leave the check mark in the boxes for constants you want to find. Finally, click OK to confirm your choices.

Excel highlights all the constants on your worksheet, as shown in Figure 16.11. Notice that the formulas are not highlighted. Now you know where the constants are located. Just click any cell to deselect the highlighting.

FIGURE 16.11

Constants highlighted on the Detail worksheet.

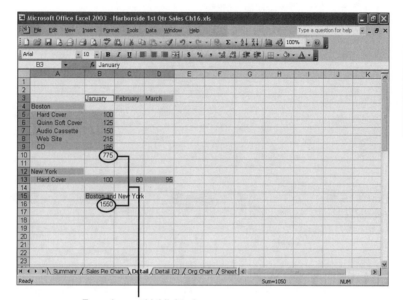

Formulas not highlighted

Using Formulas

The Go To Special command also finds formulas that meet a particular criteria you specify.

To find formulas on your worksheet, press F5 (Go To) and click the Special button in the Go To dialog box. The Go To Special dialog box pops up. Select Formulas. Notice that Excel automatically selects (puts a check mark in) all the check boxes under the Formulas option, as shown in Figure 16.12.

By default, Excel finds all formulas that contain numbers, text, logicals, or errors. To search for one or more of these formulas, click in the check box to remove the check mark for the items you don't want to find. Leaving a check mark next to an item causes Excel to search for that type of formula. Then click OK. Excel should highlight all the formulas based on the criteria you specified in the Go To Special dialog box (see Figure 16.13).

FIGURE 16.12

Selecting formulas in the Special Go To dialog box.

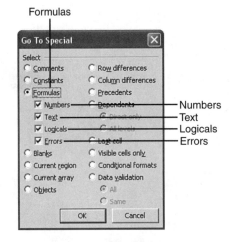

FIGURE 16.13

Formulas highlighted on the Detail worksheet.

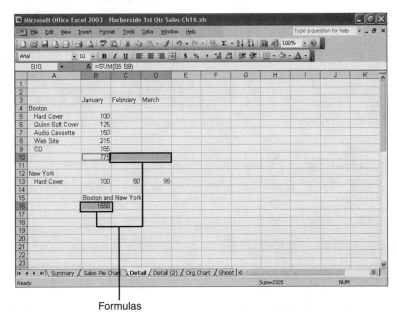

Defining Label Ranges

You can define label ranges on your worksheets so that you can use the label names, instead of cell references, in formulas. You can even specify label ranges that contain row and column labels on your worksheet. Naming a cell or range of cells is a major shortcut for referring to long cell addresses in formulas or row and column labels on worksheets.

Adding Names

To add a name, select the cell or range of cells you want to name. Then choose Insert, Name, Label. The Label Ranges dialog box pops up, as shown in Figure 16.14.

The range you selected appears in the Add Label Range box. Notice the Row labels option is selected. The data in rows 5 through 9 are labels for those rows. Click the Add button to add the label range to the existing list at the bottom of the dialog box. You can select another range on the worksheet, and click the Add button to repeat the process and add as many label ranges as you want. When you're finished labeling your ranges, click OK.

FIGURE 16.14

The Label Ranges dialog box.

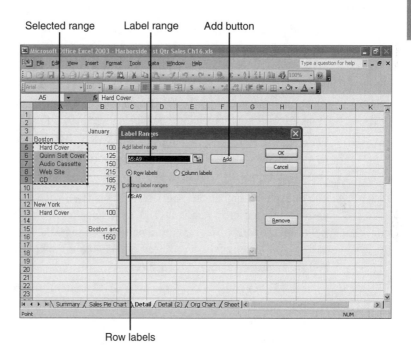

Selected range   Label range   Add button

Row labels

To refer to the label range on your worksheet in a formula, type the formula until you get to the place where you need to insert the label range. Then choose Insert, Name, Label. Double-click the label range in the Existing label ranges list. Excel inserts the range into your formula.

Removing Names

To remove a label range from your worksheet, choose Insert, Name, Label. In the Label Ranges dialog box, click the label range you want to get rid of. Click the Remove button. Excel removes the label range from the list. Then click OK.

Summary

During this hour, you learned a great deal about auditing and validating data in worksheets. Now you can try out these techniques on your own worksheets to make them error-free.

The next hour introduces you to analyzing your data by using the Scenario Manager, working with the Goal Seek tool, and creating reports.

Q&A

Q Why don't the tracer arrows display on my worksheet?

A The Hide All option is probably selected in the Options dialog box. When the Hide All option is not selected, Excel displays the tracer arrows on your worksheets. If the option is selected, Excel does not display any tracer arrows when you audit your worksheets. Choose Tools, Options, and click the View tab. Make sure the Show All option is selected in the Objects section on the View tab.

Q I clicked the Remove Precedents Arrows tool twice on the Formula Auditing toolbar to remove two levels of precedent tracer arrows. Why did Excel remove only one level of arrows?

A The maximum number of tracer arrow levels is two: red and blue. Dependent and precedent tracer arrows are blue and error value tracer arrows are red. Clicking the Remove Precedents Arrows button on the Formula Auditing toolbar removes only one level of tracer arrows. You need to click the Remove All Arrows button to remove all arrows from the worksheet.

Q Why did Excel remove only one level of dependent arrows on my worksheet when I clicked the Remove Dependents Arrows tool twice on the Formula Auditing toolbar?

A Excel displays two levels of tracer arrows: blue arrows for dependent values and red arrows for error values. Clicking the Remove Dependents Arrows button on the Formula Auditing toolbar removes only one level of tracer arrows. You need to click the Remove All Arrows button to remove all arrows from the worksheet.

HOUR 17

Analyzing Your Data

The highlights of this hour include the following:

- How to use the Scenario Manager
- How to use the Goal Seek tool

This hour discusses how you might use the Scenario Manager and the Goal Seek tool to analyze your data. By the end of this hour, you'll be a pro at analyzing your data with some of Excel's most powerful and helpful features.

Using the Scenario Manager

Excel's Scenario Manager feature enables you to analyze your data to see how changing one or more values in the worksheet affects the other cells in the worksheet. This feature comes in handy for figuring out what would happen if certain factors in your business changed.

After you create a simple scenario in this hour, you'll learn about hiding and protecting scenarios to prevent others from making changes to them. Then you will view different scenarios on the worksheet. Finally, you will create a scenario summary to view all scenarios from your worksheets in one report.

Creating Scenarios

In many cases, you use worksheets to perform what-if analysis. After you set up a series of calculations, you can change the values of certain cells to view different scenarios. For example, "What if I sold 15% more products this year? What if I reduce inventory? How would these changes affect my total income?" Being able to anticipate the effect of changes is what makes a spreadsheet so valuable.

The Tools, Scenarios option enables you to substitute one or more values with a range of values and observe how the new values affect the rest of the data in the worksheet. You can ask Excel, "What if the value changes?" and the Scenario Manager instantly shows the substitutions and their effects directly on the worksheet. For instance, perhaps you want to see what happens to your projected income if sales rise or drop, or if you increase or decrease inventory. You can use the Scenario Manager to enter all the possibilities.

Follow the instructions in the exercise to see how the Scenario Manager works. You start by creating a new workbook and entering data to prepare for creating a simple scenario. Your goal is to create the best scenario for projected sales and projected inventory.

To Do: Create a Scenario

1. Create a new workbook and name it Data Analysis.

2. In Sheet1, type the data shown in the worksheet in Figure 17.1. Cell C6 contains the Profit formula, =C3-C4.

3. Click cells C3:C4. These cells contain the data you want to change. You want to create the best scenario for projected sales and projected inventory.

4. Select Tools, Scenarios. The Scenario Manager dialog box opens, as shown in Figure 17.2.

5. To add a new scenario, click the Add button. Excel displays the Add Scenario dialog box (see Figure 17.3), which is where you define the scenario.

6. In the Scenario Name box, type **Best**. Notice that cells C3:C4 appear in the Changing Cells box. These are the cells on the worksheet that this scenario will change.

7. Click OK. Excel opens the Scenario Values dialog box, which is where you enter the input values for the scenario. Each input value is assigned a number. In this case, you have two changing cells, and you should see the numbers 1 and 2 at the left edge of the dialog box.

8. In box 1, you should see **200000**. In box 2, you should see **40000**. These values represent the projected figures for sales and inventory.

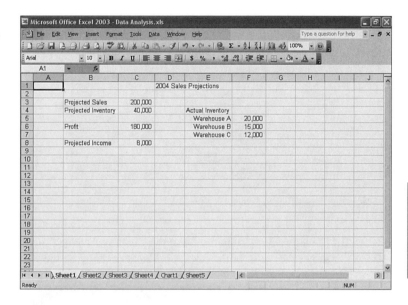

FIGURE 17.1
Setting up a worksheet with values and variables.

FIGURE 17.2
The Scenario Manager dialog box.

9. Click OK to return to the Scenario Manager dialog box.

10. Click the Show button to change the values in the worksheet. Excel displays the input values in the worksheet and recalculates the formulas to reflect the changed values. In this example, note the input values remained the same when you clicked the Show button. There were no changes to the values on the worksheet because the input values, 200,000 and 400,000, were the best scenario numbers you selected for the scenario.

11. Add another scenario for cells C3:C4 and name it Worst. For scenario values, enter **1000** in box 1 and **500** in box 2. Show the values on the worksheet.

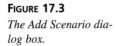

FIGURE 17.3

The Add Scenario dialog box.

12. Click the Close button to close the Scenario Manager dialog box. Figure 17.4 shows the result of the Scenario Manager changing the worksheet.

FIGURE 17.4

Result of the Scenario Manager changing the worksheet.

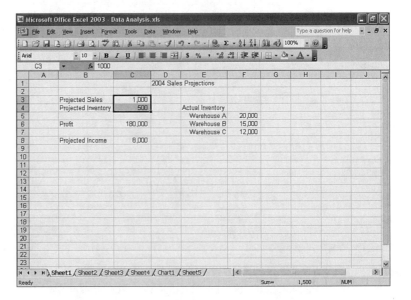

You can enter all kinds of possibilities by creating other scenarios with different input values to see different results. To do so, repeat the steps for creating a scenario using the new input values as the changing cells. The Scenario Manager begins its calculations using the new cell values. For instance, you can decrease sales and increase inventory to create the worst scenario, or you can increase both sales and inventory to create a better scenario. Changing these values can result in other scenarios.

Hiding and Protecting Scenarios

You can hide a scenario to prevent others from seeing sensitive or confidential information in the scenario. A hidden scenario does not appear in the Scenarios list in the Scenario Manager dialog box.

You can also protect your scenario from changes. By default, the Prevent Changes option is on, thereby preventing anyone from making changes to the scenario. However, you can turn it off to allow changes.

When you add or edit a scenario, you can hide or protect it. To do so, choose Tools, Scenarios. In the Scenario Manager dialog box, click the Add button or Edit button. The Add Scenario or Edit Scenario dialog box appears. Figure 17.5 shows the Edit Scenario dialog box.

17

FIGURE 17.5
The Edit Scenario dialog box.

Prevent Changes   Hide

At the bottom of either dialog box, in the Protection section, click the Hide check box to hide the scenario. If you want to protect the scenarios, leave the check mark in the Prevent Changes check box. If you want to unprotect the scenario and allow changes, click the check box to remove the check mark in the Prevent Changes box. Then click OK to confirm your choices. Click Close in the Scenario Manager dialog box to return to the worksheet.

Viewing a Scenario

Suppose you want to play out different scenarios you had created in order to make some business decisions. You can view each scenario you added and then analyze the sets of data in the scenarios. To do so, choose Tools, Scenarios. Select a scenario in the Scenarios list and click Show. Repeat the step to view different scenarios.

Creating a Scenario Summary Report

If a summary of the scenarios is really what you're interested in, and you'd like to view all your results on one sheet, you can get there directly with the Scenario Summary feature.

To create a scenario summary, choose Tools, Scenarios. In the Scenario Manager dialog box, click the Summary button. The Scenario Summary dialog box opens, as shown in Figure 17.6.

FIGURE 17.6

The Scenario Summary dialog box.

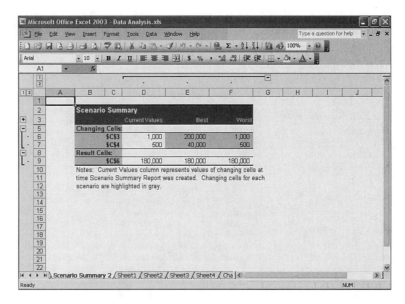

Select the Scenario Summary option and click OK. Excel displays the scenario summary on a new sheet before the Sheet 1 tab. The new sheet is called Scenario Summary, as shown in Figure 17.7.

You should see a tree structure to the left of the row heading numbers in the Scenario Summary sheet. There are minus signs and plus signs for collapsing and expanding report sections. Click on a minus sign (–) to hide the section in the report. Click on a plus sign (+) to expand the section in the report.

You can print the report as you would any worksheet by using the File, Print command.

If you want to delete the report, click the Scenario Summary sheet tab, and choose Edit, Delete Sheet. Click Delete to confirm the deletion.

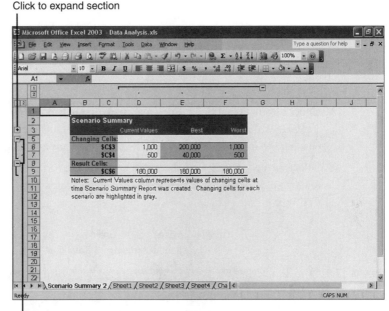

FIGURE 17.7
The Scenario Summary report on a new sheet.

Click to expand section

Click to collapse section

Using the Goal Seek Tool

Goal Seek is a useful tool that you can use to achieve a certain value in a cell that contains a formula. The way you do that is to adjust the value of another cell that has a direct effect on the original cell. If I can afford $400 a month, what could I borrow? You can use Goal Seek to see how much you can borrow to make the payment of $500 per month.

How the Goal Seek Tool Works

The following To Do exercise shows you how Goal Seek works. You need to enter data on Sheet2 in the Data Analysis workbook to prepare for using Goal Seek.

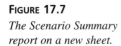

To Do: Use the Goal Seek Tool

1. In Sheet2, type the data shown in the worksheet in Figure 17.8. For the worksheet to look just like the one in the figure, left-align cells C6:C9 and format cells E6:F9 with two decimal places. In the Total column, the following cells contain these formulas:

▼

- F6: =E6*C6

- F7: =E7*C7

- F8: =E8*C8

- F9: =E9*C9

- F11: =SUM(F6:F10)

2. Choose Tools, Goal Seek. The Goal Seek dialog box opens, as shown in Figure 17.9. Here's where you tell Excel which cell contains the formula you want to change, the input value, and the cells that you want to change.

3. Select the cell on the worksheet that contains the formula whose result you want to change. If necessary, click cell F11. The cell reference F11 appears in the Set Cell box.

FIGURE 17.8

Setting up a worksheet with values and totals.

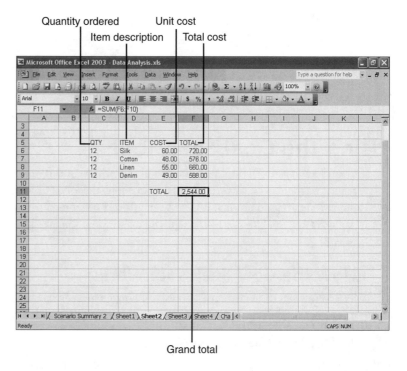

4. The value you want the formula to reflect needs to be entered in the To Value box. Click in the To Value box and type **5000**. This step tells Excel to reach a different grand total of **5000**.

5. Now you need to tell Excel which cell contains the data you want to change. We want Goal Seek to change the quantity ordered for silk. Click in the By Changing Cell box, click the worksheet, and select cell C6. Cell C6 appears in the By

▼

▼ Changing Cell box. This step tells Excel to reach a different quantity for silk, given a grand total of 5000.

FIGURE 17.9
The Goal Seek dialog box.

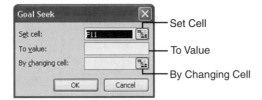

6. Click OK. The Goal Seek Status dialog box pops open, as you see in Figure 17.10. This dialog box gives you several options: stepping through an operation, pausing operations, and seeking additional help. You also see the cell information, the target value, and the current value. As Goal Seek works, you can see the result and step through, pause, or change it as you go.

7. Click OK. Goal Seek places the value found into the specified cell.

8. If this value isn't the one you want, restore the original value by clicking the Undo button on the Standard toolbar.

9. If you can't decide what to do, click the Redo button on the Standard toolbar to
▲ recalculate the goal seek you just undid.

17

Target value

FIGURE 17.10
Goal Seek Status dialog box.

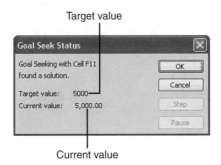

Current value

Using Goal Seek on Chart Data

If the value of a data marker (data series) on a chart was generated from a formula, you can change the values in a chart by using the Goal Seek tool. More specifically, you can alter the values generated from formulas in a worksheet in 3D Surface, Radar, and Area charts by using the Tools, Goal Seek option on the worksheet.

The next exercise walks you through using Goal Seek on chart data. In Sheet2, you create a 3D Area chart, using the Chart Wizard to illustrate the items and totals. Then you use Goal Seek to change the chart data for the silk item.

To Do: Use Goal Seek on Chart Data

▼ To Do

1. In Sheet2, select cells D5:D9. Hold down the Ctrl key and select cells F5:F9. This step tells Excel to chart the data in the Item and Total columns.

2. Use the Chart Wizard tool on the Standard toolbar to create a 3D Area chart on Sheet2, and accept all the defaults in the Chart Wizard dialog boxes. If you need help building the chart, refer to Hour 12, "Adding a Chart." Figure 17.11 shows the 3D Area chart. Now you can use Goal Seek to change the data in the chart. You want to change the data for the silk item.

3. Click cell F6. This cell contains the formula whose result you want to change.

FIGURE 17.11

The 3D Area chart on the worksheet.

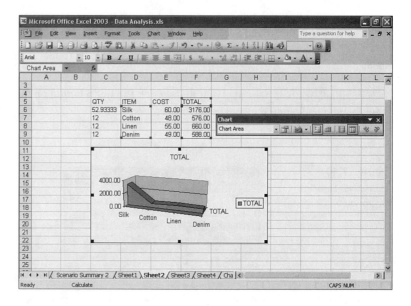

4. Choose Tools, Goal Seek. The Goal Seek dialog box opens. In the Set Cell box, you should see cell F6. This cell contains the formula whose result you want changed.

5. The value you want the formula to reflect needs to be entered in the To Value box. Click in the To Value box and type **1000**. This step tells Excel to reach a different total of **1000**.

▼

▼ 6. Now you need to tell Excel which cell contains the data you want to change. You want Goal Seek to change the quantity ordered for silk. Click in the By Changing Cell box, click the worksheet, and select cell C6. Cell C6 appears in the By Changing Cell box. This step tells Excel to reach a different quantity for silk, given a grand total of 1000.

> When you use the Goal Seek tool to change the values in a chart, you can change the value of only one cell.

7. Click OK. The Goal Seek Status dialog box pops open. Goal Seek found a solution.

8. Click OK. Goal Seek places the value found into the specified cell and updates the 3D Area chart. Notice that the silk area on the chart decreased to 1000, as shown in Figure 17.12.

FIGURE 17.12

Changed data in the 3D Area chart.

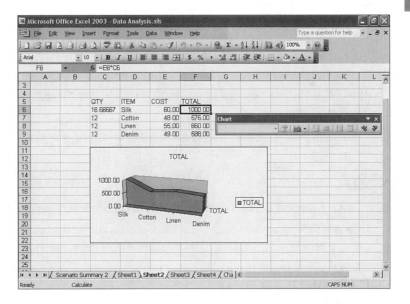

9. If this value isn't what you want, restore the original values by clicking the Undo button on the Standard toolbar.

10. If you can't decide what to do, click the Redo button on the Standard toolbar to recalculate the Goal Seek you just undid.
▲

17

Common Goal Seek Errors

Here are some of the common Goal Seek errors that might occur before you reach a solution:

- You interrupted the Goal Seek process.
- You entered the wrong cell reference in the Set Cell box. The cell that contains the formula you want to change should appear in the Set Cell box.
- You specified the wrong value in the To Value box.
- The cell reference you entered in the By Changing Cell box is a range of cells. Goal Seek can change only one cell for you.

When Goal Seek stops before a solution is found, an error message appears in the Goal Seek Status dialog box. Click the Pause button, make any changes you desire, and then try goal seeking again by clicking the Continue button.

Summary

You worked hard during this hour to grasp the concepts and instructions for analyzing data with Excel's sophisticated Scenario Manager and Goal Seek tools. Your hard work will pay off the first time you need to analyze data on the job. You can always refer to this session for help in setting up your worksheets and using the data analysis tools. These tools will impress your boss and co-workers, as well as help you reach the results you want.

In the upcoming hour, you delve into using pivot tables to restructure your data into tables that calculate formulas and display data just the way you want it to look.

Q&A

Q I want to hide sections in my Scenario Summary report. What should I do?

A Click on a minus sign (–) in the tree structure to the left of the row heading numbers in the Scenario Summary sheet. Excel hides the section in the report.

Q Can I pause the goal-seeking process so that I can stop and start whenever I want?

A Clicking the Pause button changes the choices in the Goal Seek Status dialog box to Stop and Continue.

Q Can I use the Goal Seek tool to change the value of two cells in a 3D Area chart?

A Sorry. When you use the Goal Seek tool to change the values in a chart, you can change the value of only one cell.

HOUR **18**

Working with Pivot Tables

The topics in this hour are as follows:

- What you should know about pivot tables
- How to build a pivot table
- How to modify a pivot table
- How to work with PivotTable reports
- How to build a PivotChart

In this hour, you get to know a very powerful data analysis tool in Excel—the PivotTable. You can use a pivot table to summarize large amounts of information in a friendly, informative, interactive worksheet table. Also, you can create a PivotChart from pivot table information.

At the conclusion of this hour, you'll be creating simple pivot tables and charts to analyze vast amounts of data in your daily work.

What Is a Pivot Table?

A pivot table lets you analyze, summarize, and manipulate data in large lists, databases, worksheets, workbooks, tables, or other collections of data. Pivot tables offer flexible and intuitive analysis of data. It's called a *pivot table* because you can move fields with the mouse to provide different types of summary lists; that is, the table can change, or "pivot."

Although the data that appears in pivot tables looks like any other worksheet data, you cannot directly enter or change the data in the data area of a pivot table. The pivot table is linked to the source data, and what you see in the cells of the table are read-only amounts. However, you can change the formatting (Number, Alignment, Font, Border, Patterns) and choose from a variety of computation options such as SUM, AVERAGE, MIN, and MAX.

You can create a pivot table from several sources. The default, and most common choice, is to create a pivot table from an Excel list or database. You can also create a pivot table from an external data source, such as an Access database, multiple consolidation ranges, or another pivot table.

A Pivot Table Example

Suppose you have a list of magazine advertisements. A simple pivot table is useful for tracking the magazine advertisements for an accounting firm. Figure 18.1 shows an example of a worksheet with a list of magazine advertisements. It contains the month, magazine, and number of responses and new accounts. Figure 18.2 shows a typical pivot table for tracking the magazine advertisements.

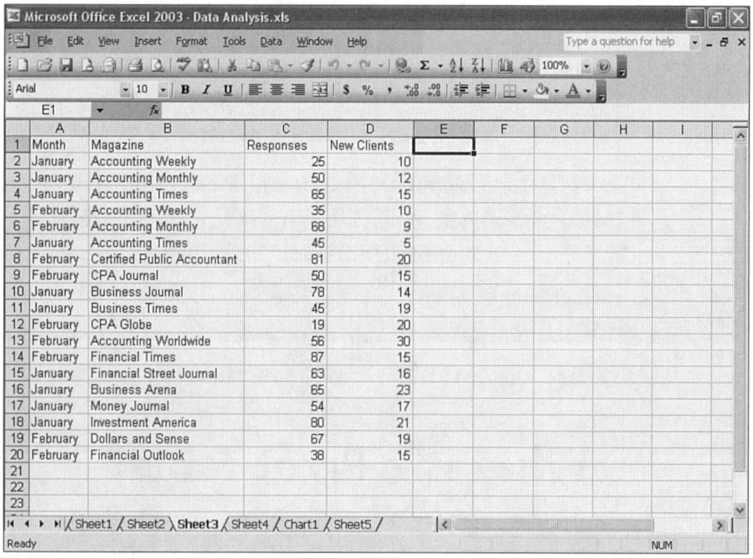

Month	Magazine	Responses	New Clients
January	Accounting Weekly	25	10
January	Accounting Monthly	50	12
January	Accounting Times	65	15
February	Accounting Weekly	35	10
February	Accounting Monthly	68	9
January	Accounting Times	45	5
February	Certified Public Accountant	81	20
February	CPA Journal	50	15
January	Business Journal	78	14
January	Business Times	45	19
February	CPA Globe	19	20
February	Accounting Worldwide	56	30
February	Financial Times	87	15
January	Financial Street Journal	63	16
January	Business Arena	65	23
January	Money Journal	54	17
January	Investment America	80	21
February	Dollars and Sense	67	19
February	Financial Outlook	38	15

FIGURE 18.1
List of magazine advertisements for an accounting firm.

FIGURE 18.2

Typical pivot table.

	A	B	C	D
1	Magazine	(All)		
2				
3	Sum of New Clients	Month		
4	Responses	January	February	Grand Total
5	19		20	20
6	25	10		10
7	35		10	10
8	38		15	15
9	45	24		24
10	50	12	15	27
11	54	17		17
12	56		30	30
13	63	16		16
14	65	38		38
15	67		19	19
16	68		9	9
17	78	14		14
18	80	21		21
19	81		20	20
20	87		15	15
21	Grand Total	152	153	305
22				
23				

In this hour, you learn how to create a pivot table just like the one in Figure 18.2.

Learning the PivotTable Lingo

Here is some PivotTable lingo that you need to know before you work with pivot tables.

- **Item**—An item label is a subcategory of a PivotTable field and is derived from unique entries in a database field or in a list column. Items appear as row or column labels or in the lists for page fields in a pivot table report.

- **Row field**—Row field labels have a row orientation in a pivot table report and are displayed as row labels. Appears in the ROW area of a pivot table report layout.

- **Column field**—Column field labels have a column orientation in a pivot table report and are displayed as column labels. Appears in the COLUMN area of a pivot table report layout.

- **Data field**—Data fields from a list or table contain summary data in a pivot table, such as numeric data (statistics, sales amounts, text). Summarized in the DATA area of a pivot table report layout.

- **Page field**—Page fields filter out the data for other items and display one page at a time in a pivot table report.

It's important to know what you want to do with your data in a PivotTable report. You need to know what you want to see. You might find it helpful to put what you want to learn in a series of questions. For example:

- How many new clients did we gain in January?
- Which magazine provided the highest number of new accounts for February?
- What's the average number of responses from the magazine advertisements?

Building a Pivot Table

You can build a simple pivot table with the Data, PivotTable and PivotChart Report option, which displays a series of PivotTable Wizard dialog boxes. The wizard steps you through the process of creating a pivot table, and you get to see a basic breakdown of the data you have in your Excel list or database. A diagram with the labels PAGE, COL-UMN, ROW, and DATA appears, and you just drag field buttons onto the diagram. This step tells Excel about the data you want to analyze with a pivot table.

Perform the steps in the following To Do exercise to create a pivot table from an Excel list. Get ready to use the Data Analysis workbook you used in Hour 17, "Analyzing Your Data."

To Do: Build a Pivot Table

1. In Sheet2 in the Data Analysis workbook, type the data shown in the worksheet in Figure 18.3. Click any cell in the list. Now the active cell is within the list, and Excel knows that you want to use the data in the Excel list to create a pivot table.

2. Choose Data, PivotTable and PivotChart Report. If the Office Assistant asks whether you want help with pivot tables, choose No. The PivotTable and PivotChart Wizard—Step 1 of 3 dialog box opens, as shown in Figure 18.4. From this point, until the pivot table appears in the worksheet, you are working in the PivotTable Wizard.

3. In the Where Is the Data That You Want to Analyze? area, choose Microsoft Excel List or Database if it's not already selected. This step tells Excel the source of the tabular data.

4. In the What Kind of Report Do You Want to Create? area, choose PivotTable. Now Excel knows that you want to create a pivot table.

5. Click the Next button. The PivotTable and PivotChart Wizard—Step 2 of 3 dialog box opens. In the Range box, the range should be $A$1:$D$20, which defines the data range you want to use for the pivot table. The range should include the columns headings in row 1.

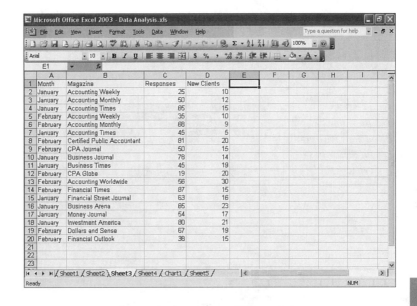

FIGURE **18.3**

The data you need to enter in an Excel list.

FIGURE **18.4**

The PivotTable and PivotChart Wizard—Step 1 of 3 dialog box.

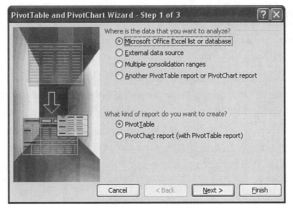

18

If the range is incorrect, click in the Range box and type the correct cell references. A quick way to specify the range in the Range box is to highlight the range in the worksheet.

6. Click the Next button. The PivotTable and PivotChart Wizard—Step 3 of 3 dialog box opens. You use this dialog box to tell Excel whether to place the pivot table on an existing or new worksheet. In this case, you want to place the table on a new worksheet.

▼   7. If necessary, choose New Worksheet.

    8. The next step is to design the layout of the pivot table. Click the Layout button. Excel opens the PivotTable and PivotChart Wizard—Layout dialog box, as shown in Figure 18.5.

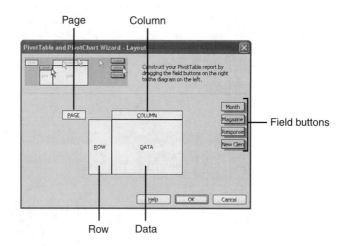

FIGURE 18.5

The PivotTable and PivotChart Wizard— Layout dialog box.

The fields appear on buttons to the right in the dialog box. These currently are the column fields. The four areas you can define to create your pivot table are ROW, COLUMN, DATA, and PAGE.

You drag the field buttons to the areas to define the layout of your pivot table. For example, to summarize the values in a field in the body of the table, place the field button in the DATA area. To arrange items in a field in columns with the labels across the top, place the field button in the COLUMN area. To arrange items in a field of rows with labels along the side, place the field button in the ROW area. To show data for one item at a time, one item per page, place the field button in the PAGE area.

    9. Drag the Month button to the PAGE area.

  10. Drag the New Clients button to the DATA area.

  11. Drag the Responses button to the ROW area.

  12. Drag the Magazine button to the COLUMN area.

  13. Click OK to return to the PivotTable and PivotChart Wizard—Step 3 of 3 dialog box. Then click the Finish button. The PivotTable Wizard places the table in the new worksheet called Sheet4, as you can see in Figure 18.6. Also, the PivotTable

▲   toolbar and the PivotTable Field List should appear.

FIGURE 18.6

The pivot table, PivotTable toolbar, and PivotTable Field List.

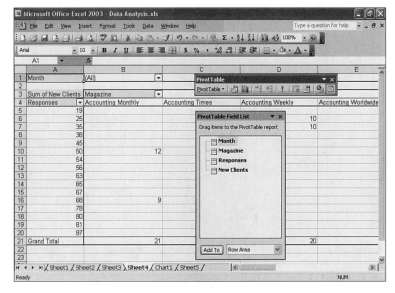

Modifying a Pivot Table

18

After you build a pivot table, you can make changes to it any time. For example, if you want to examine the new clients for a particular month, you need to change the Month field. Use the drop-down list to the right of the field name. Select a month and click OK. This step selects and deselects new clients in the list, and Excel instantly displays new clients broken down by more or less magazines in the DATA area of the pivot table. You also should see the grand total dollar amounts by magazine at the bottom of each item. At the bottom of the table, you should see the grand total for new clients to all magazines.

You can use this report to analyze your data in various ways. For instance, click the PivotTable down arrow button on the PivotTable toolbar, choose PivotTable Wizard, and click the Layout button. Drag the buttons off the diagram, and arrange the fields like this: Magazine in the PAGE area, Month in the COLUMN area, New Clients in the DATA area, and Responses in the ROW area. The completed PivotTable dialog box should look like the one in Figure 18.7.

The pivot table now illustrates sales by cost for each item. All items are selected in the column field, and you should see the total item quantity for all the items. You can use the Cost row field to restrict cost shown to each individual item. Figure 18.8 shows the pivot table derived from rearranging the data.

FIGURE 18.7

Rearranging data in the PivotTable and PivotChart Wizard dialog box.

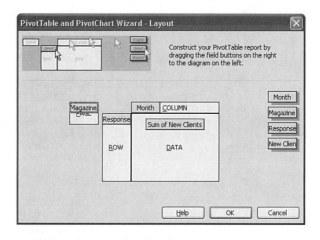

FIGURE 18.8

Rearranged data in the pivot table.

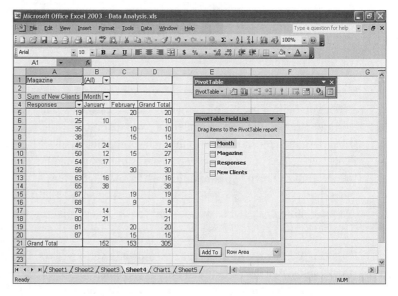

The PivotTable toolbar provides tools for working with pivot tables. Table 18.1 lists those tools and what they can do for you.

TABLE 18.1   PivotTable Tools

Tool	What It Does
PivotTable	A menu that contains commands for working with a pivot table.
Format Report	Enables you to format the pivot table report.
Chart Wizard	Enables you to create a chart using the data in the pivot table.
Hide Detail	Hides the detail information in a pivot table and shows only the totals.

TABLE 18.1   continued

Tool	What It Does
Show Detail	Shows the detail information in a pivot table.
Refresh External Data	Allows you to refresh the data in the pivot table after you make changes to data in the data source.
Include Hidden Items in Totals	Lets you show the hidden items in the totals.
Always Display Items	Always shows the field item buttons with drop-down arrows in the pivot table.
Field Settings	Displays the PivotTable Field dialog box so that you can change computations and their number format.
Hide Field List	Hides and shows the PivotTable Field List window.

Below the buttons on the PivotTable toolbar, you should see the PivotTable Field List window. The field buttons that you dragged to the PAGE, ROW, COLUMN, and DATA areas in the PivotTable diagram appear in the window. You can drag a field button from the window to the PivotTable at any time to rearrange the data in your pivot table.

Some other changes you might want to make to your pivot table include removing and adding fields in the pivot table. To remove fields, drag the field item buttons off the PivotTable. Excel indicates in the pivot table exactly where you should place a field button. For example, in the PAGE area, you should see "Drop the page field here." To add fields to the pivot table, drag the fields from the PivotTable Field List window into the PAGE, COLUMN, ROW, and DATA areas marked on the PivotTable. By using the PivotTable Field List window, you can build new or different pivot tables in a snap.

You can change the computation for the numbers. By default, the numbers are added with the SUM function, but you can change to AVERAGE, MIN, or MAX. For example, if you want to average the numbers instead of summing them, double-click the Sum of New Clients button in the DATA area. The PivotTable Field dialog box opens, as shown in Figure 18.9.

FIGURE 18.9

The PivotTable Field dialog box.

18

Choose Average and click OK. Excel changes the Sum of New Clients to Average of New Clients.

> To change the format of numbers in a PivotTable, open the PivotTable Field dialog box, click the Number button and choose a number format. Click OK.

If you want to group PivotTable items and create a new field for the items as a group, select the cells you want to group. Choose Data, Group and Outline, Group. Excel creates a new field that contains the selected items.

To group items automatically, select one item in a field. Choose Data, Group and Outline, Group. In the Group Dialog box, in the By list, select the grouping options you want. Then click OK. Excel creates the groups based on the options you selected.

Working with Pivot Table Reports

Excel doesn't allow you to edit data in a pivot table report, because it maintains a link to the source data. But you can update the source file to pass any new or changed information to the pivot table. For example, any new clients will show up on the pivot table if you enter them into the source Excel list on the worksheet. After you change the source data, click the Refresh External Data button on the PivotTable toolbar. Excel returns any new or changed information to your table.

What if you want to change the orientation of the table? No problem. Just drag the field button to the new location. For instance, if you want to see the Month data in a row instead of a column, drag the Month field button from its place in the COLUMN area into the ROW area. Excel will automatically reformat the pivot table, reflecting the new information. You don't have to use the PivotTable Wizard dialog box here. Just make the change in the pivot table directly.

Another thing you can change in a pivot table report is a field name. Just click a field name in the pivot table and type over it with the new field name.

The totals in the table are computed for each subcategory in the row and for the column. When you add another row field, the pivot table displays a new subtotal field on the row. The same happens with column data. The data in every row and every column is totaled. There is a grand total field for the table, too.

If you want to hide the detail data in the pivot table report and show only the totals, select the data cell and click the Hide Detail button on the PivotTable toolbar. To switch back to showing the detail, click the Show Detail button on the PivotTable toolbar.

Building a PivotChart

A PivotChart is basically a column chart (by default) that is based on the data in a pivot table. You can change the chart to a different chart type if desired.

The next To Do exercise creates a PivotChart from an Excel list. You need to use the Excel list you created on Sheet2 earlier in this hour.

To Do: Build a PivotChart

▼ To Do

1. Click the Sheet3 tab and click any cell in the Excel list. This step tells Excel that you want to use the data in the Excel list to create a PivotChart.

2. Choose Data, PivotTable and PivotChart Report. If the Office Assistant asks whether you want help with pivot tables, choose No. The PivotTable and PivotChart Wizard—Step 1 of 3 dialog box opens. From this point, until the PivotChart appears in the worksheet, you are working in the PivotTable and PivotChart Wizard.

3. In the Where Is the Data That You Want to Analyze? area, choose Microsoft Excel List or Database if it's not already selected. This step tells Excel the source of the chart data.

4. In the What Kind of Report Do You Want to Create? area, choose PivotChart (with PivotTable), shown in Figure 18.10. Now you've told Excel that you want to create a PivotChart with a pivot table.

18

FIGURE 18.10

The PivotTable and PivotChart Wizard— Step 1 of 3 dialog box.

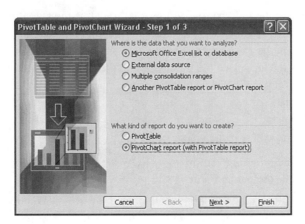

5. Click the Next button. The PivotTable and PivotChart Wizard—Step 2 of 3 dialog box shows up. In the Range box, the range should be $A$1:$D$20, which defines the data range you want to use for the PivotChart.

▼

> If the range is incorrect, click in the Range box and type the correct cell references. A quick way to specify the range in the Range box is to highlight the range in the worksheet.

6. Click the Next button. Excel asks whether you want to save memory and combine reports by placing the chart on the same sheet as the pivot table or keep the reports separate by placing the PivotChart on a chart sheet by itself. You want to keep the reports separate.

7. Choose No to separate the reports. The PivotTable and PivotChart Wizard—Step 3 of 3 dialog box opens. You can now tell Excel whether you want to place the PivotChart with pivot table on an existing or new worksheet. You want to place the chart and table on a new worksheet.

8. If necessary, choose New Worksheet.

9. The next step is to design the layout of the pivot table so that Excel can create the chart from the data in the table. Click the Layout button. Excel opens the PivotTable and PivotChart Wizard—Layout dialog box.

   The fields appear on buttons to the right in the dialog box. These currently are the column fields. The four areas you can define to create your pivot table are ROW, COLUMN, DATA, and PAGE.

   You drag the field buttons to the areas to define the layout of your pivot table. For example, to summarize the values in a field in the body of the table, place the field button in the DATA area. To arrange items in a field in columns with the labels across the top, place the field button in the COLUMN area. To arrange items in a field of rows with labels along the side, place the field button in the ROW area. To show data for one item at a time, one item per page, place the field button in the PAGE area.

10. Drag the New Clients button to the DATA area.

11. Drag the Magazine button to the ROW area. Your pivot table diagram should resemble the one in Figure 18.11.

12. Click OK to return to the PivotTable and PivotChart Wizard—Step 3 of 3 dialog box. Then click the Finish button. The PivotTable Wizard places the chart in the new worksheet called Chart1, as you can see in Figure 18.12. Also, the PivotTable toolbar and PivotTable Field List window should appear. Close the toolbar and the window.

FIGURE 18.11
The PivotTable and PivotChart Wizard— Layout dialog box.

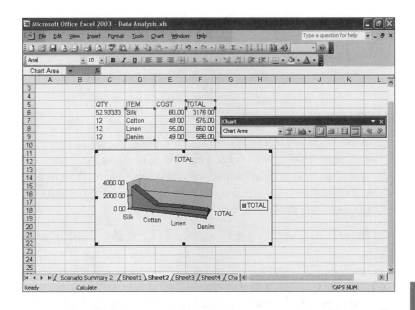

FIGURE 18.12
The PivotChart.

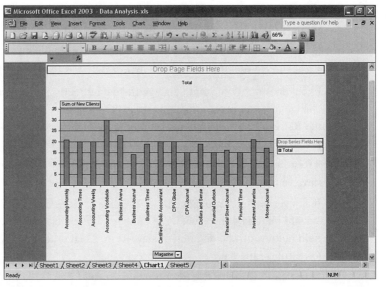

18

Creating a Chart from PivotTable Report Data

What if you don't want to create a PivotChart that interacts with the data in the PivotTable report? You can create an ordinary, non-interactive chart to represent the pivot table data. To do so, select the data in the PivotTable report that you want to include in your chart. If you want to include field button data in the first row and column of the PivotTable report, select the data by dragging from the bottom right corner of the data.

Click the Copy button on the Standard toolbar. Click in a cell in a blank area. Choose Edit, Paste Special. Click Values, and then click OK. Create your chart using the Chart Wizard. For instructions on how to use the Chart Wizard, see Chapter 12, "Adding a Chart."

Summary

In this hour, you learned the ABCs of building and modifying pivot tables, and you worked with pivot table reports. When you want to use Excel to manage a list of data, but you're not sure whether Excel can handle everything, give it a try. You have little to lose, because you can always move your data around, from row to column to data and back, and by adding and removing fields from the pivot table.

The next hour teaches you all about integrating Excel with other Office applications.

Q&A

Q The cell references in the Range box in the first PivotTable and PivotChart Wizard dialog box are wrong. What next?

A If the range is incorrect, click in the Range box and type the correct cell references. A quick way to specify the range in the Range box is to highlight the range in the worksheet.

Q I want to change the data in the pivot table, but Excel won't let me. What can I do?

A Excel doesn't allow you to change the data directly in the pivot table, but you can change the data in the source, such as the Excel list. After you make the changes, click the Refresh External Data button on the PivotTable toolbar to update the data in the pivot table, reflecting the changes you made in the source list.

Q After I create a pivot table, can I change the way the data is arranged, or do I have to create a new table?

A It's never too late. You can change the data arrangement by clicking the PivotTable Wizard button on the PivotTable toolbar and then clicking the Layout button. Drag the field buttons off the diagram to start fresh. Then drag the field buttons back to diagram to rearrange the data.

Q What can I do with the field buttons in the PivotTable Field List window?

A You can drag them to the pivot table to change the arrangement of your data quickly.

Q What if I want to show only the totals in my pivot table report?

A After selecting the data item, just click the Hide Detail button on the PivotTable toolbar to show only the totals and hide the detail information. When you want to display the detail again, click the Show Detail button on the PivotTable toolbar.

HOUR 19

Integrating Excel with Other Office Applications

The subjects covered in this hour include the following:

- How to link and embed objects
- How to insert objects from the menu and the Clipboard toolbar
- How to create hyperlinks
- How to send Excel documents via email with Outlook

After you learn how to use Excel, and if you already know how to use Word and Outlook, you can use Microsoft Office to share information between applications.

This hour introduces you to linking and embedding objects, inserting objects that you create in other applications, creating hyperlinks between Office applications, and how to send Excel documents via email using Microsoft Outlook.

When this hour is over, you'll know how to integrate Excel with other Office applications, making it easy to share data between word processing, spreadsheet, and personal information manager programs.

Using Objects in Excel

Sharing data between applications is called *Object Linking and Embedding*, more commonly known as *OLE*. This might sound complicated, but it isn't. It means there's an object in a document in one Windows application that is linked to or embedded from a document in another Windows application. Many Windows applications let you link and embed information in any of these applications. For example, you can copy a Microsoft Excel chart and put it into a Microsoft Word document.

This feature lets you copy or move information between documents in different applications using drag-and-drop. Both applications must support OLE.

If the object is linked, it appears in your Office document but it is stored outside of your document. Your document holds the link, which is like an address, and when you want to view or print your document, Excel reads the address, fetches the object, and provides it. If the original object is changed, the next time you link to it, you see the changes.

When you take an existing Excel worksheet or chart in a Word document and copy and paste the information or import it into another Word document, you can embed the worksheet rather than linking it. If the object is embedded, it is moved into your document after it's created and becomes a part of your document, just like the text, numbers, and clip art you create while you work in Excel.

By embedding the worksheet as an object, you can double-click the worksheet in Word, and the Word menus and toolbars are temporarily replaced by the Excel menus and toolbars. It's like working in a "super application," in which one window can perform many different types of applications' tasks—word processor to spreadsheet program and back. The advantage is that you can quickly and easily make changes to objects from different applications in the same window. This process is referred to as OLE. Any changes you make to the worksheet are automatically reflected in the worksheet in Word.

Object Linking

Object linking enables you to share data between programs with OLE. You can link Office documents. For example, you can take an existing Excel worksheet and copy and paste its contents or import it into a Word document. Then you can create a link between the Excel worksheet and the Word document so that each time the worksheet is updated in Excel, the worksheet data in Word is automatically updated to reflect any changes.

When you link Office documents, one document is called the *source document* and the other is called the *target document*. The source document contains the information you want to link; the target document receives the linked information. For example, if you want to link an Excel worksheet to a Word document, the worksheet file is the source document and the Word file is the target document.

When you link documents, the source document appears in the target document, but it is not physically there. For instance, you can see an Excel worksheet in a Word document, but the worksheet still resides in Excel.

Follow the steps in the next To Do exercise to link an Excel worksheet to a Word document. You'll be using the Sales 1st Qtr workbook and a blank Word document.

To Do: Link Office Documents

1. First open the Sales 1st Qtr workbook. Be sure to update the links when you open the workbook. Then click the Summary sheet.

2. Now it's time to start Word. Click the Start button on the Windows taskbar, and choose Programs, Microsoft Word. You should see the Word window with a blank document on your screen.

3. With both applications open, let's switch to Excel by clicking the Microsoft Excel button on the Windows taskbar.

4. Select the data in cells A1:D9 in the Summary sheet. This is the source data for linking the worksheet object to the Word document.

5. Click the Copy button on the Standard toolbar.

6. Click the Microsoft Word button on the Windows taskbar to switch to Word.

7. Choose Edit, Paste Special. The Paste Special dialog box appears. The selected range appears at the top of the dialog box in the Source area.

8. In the As list, choose Microsoft Excel Worksheet Object. This tells Word which object you want to place in the Word document.

9. Click the Paste Link option. This tells Excel that you want to create a link between the source data and the Word document. Figure 19.1 shows the Paste Special dialog box with all the selections you should have made.

19

Source range   Microsoft Excel Worksheet Object

FIGURE 19.1

The Paste Special dialog box.

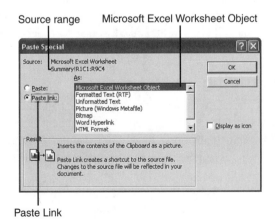

Paste Link

▼   10. Click OK. The Excel worksheet should appear in the Word document as an object
        (see Figure 19.2).

FIGURE 19.2

A linked worksheet in a Word document.

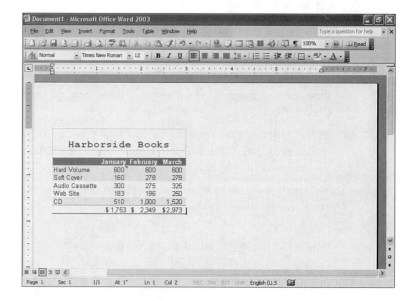

11. Save the Word document by clicking the Save button on the Standard toolbar.
    Name the file My Integration, and click the Save button.

    When you copied cells A1:D9, Excel also copied the entire worksheet. The
    selected cells are the only ones visible, but if you double-click the object, you can
    scroll and see the entire worksheet.

    If you want to change the information in the Excel worksheet object, just double-
    click the worksheet in the Word document. The link switches you to Excel, where
    you make your changes. Next, you can save and close the worksheet. Switch back
    to Word, and you will see that the linked worksheet reflects the changes you made
▲   in Excel.

Object Embedding

Just like linking documents, you have a source document and a target document when
you embed an object in a document. Embedding a document as an object physically
places a document within another document. For example, if you embed an Excel worksheet or chart in a Word document, the worksheet or chart physically resides in Word as
well as Excel.

In the upcoming exercise, you'll see how embedding an Excel worksheet as an object in a Word document is similar to linking Office documents. You'll be using the Sales 1st Qtr workbook and the My Integration document again. Follow the steps in the next To Do exercise to begin embedding an object.

To Do: Embed an Object

▼ To Do

1. In the Word document, press Enter a few times to insert some space beneath the worksheet object, and then press Ctrl+End to move to the bottom of the document. Press Ctrl+Enter to insert a page break. The insertion point should be at the top of page 2 now.

2. Now we'll switch to Excel by clicking the Microsoft Excel button on the Windows taskbar.

3. Press the Esc key to clear the flashing marquee border.

4. Select the data in cells A1:D9 in the Sales 1st Qtr workbook. This is the data that we'll embed in the Word document as an object.

5. Click the Copy button on the Standard toolbar.

6. Click the Microsoft Word button on the Windows taskbar to switch to Word.

7. Choose Edit, Paste Special. The Paste Special dialog box appears. The selected range appears at the top of the dialog box. Leave the Paste option selected.

8. In the As list, choose Microsoft Excel Worksheet Object. This tells Word which object you want to place in the Word document. Figure 19.3 shows the Paste Special dialog box with the selection you should have made.

Source range   Microsoft Excel Worksheet Object

FIGURE 19.3

The Paste Special dialog box.

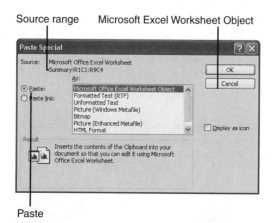

Paste

9. Click OK. The Excel worksheet is now an embedded object in the Word document. Now let's change a couple of numbers in the Excel worksheet and see how Excel treats an embedded object.

▼   10. Double-click the worksheet object. Notice the Word window takes on the appearance of an Excel window, displaying Excel's menus, toolbars, and the formula bar (see Figure 19.4).

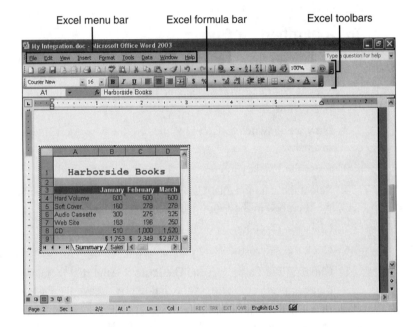

Excel menu bar   Excel formula bar   Excel toolbars

FIGURE 19.4

An embedded worksheet in a Word document.

11. Click cell C6, type **100**, and press Enter. Next, click cell C8, type **200**, and press Enter. This changes two numbers in the Excel worksheet. Notice that the value in the Total row has been updated to reflect the new numbers.

12. Click outside the worksheet. The Word menu and toolbars appear. Notice the worksheet now contains the new numbers and the formulas have been recalculated automatically to reflect the changes you made. It's like magic!

Remember, when you embed a worksheet object, the entire worksheet is really inserted. If you display the wrong worksheet in Word, simply double-click the worksheet in the Word document and click the worksheet tab you want. Then click outside the worksheet area in Word.

13. Close the Word document and save the changes. Then, close Word by double-clicking the Word Control icon in the upper left corner of the Word window. You should
▲   see only the Excel window on your screen.

Inserting Objects

In addition to pictures, you can insert objects created in other applications. For instance, you can insert a joke from the Internet (if you have a connection to the Internet) or a calendar from Calendar Control.

When you choose to insert an object, Excel runs the required application and lets you create the object. When you quit the other application, the object is inserted on the current worksheet or chart.

Inserting an Object from the Menu

This To Do exercise shows you how to insert an object from another application using the Insert, Object command. Use the Sales 1st Qtr workbook for this exercise. We're going to create a simple freehand drawing in the Bitmap Image application and insert the drawing as an object in the Summary sheet.

To Do: Insert an Object from the Menu

1. In the Summary sheet, press Esc to remove the marquee. Select the cell on the sheet where you want the upper-left corner of the object placed. In this case, scroll down to row 35, and click cell C35.

2. Choose Insert, Object. The Object dialog box pops opens, as shown in Figure 19.5. There are two tabs: Create New and Create From File. The Create New tab lets you run another application and create the object. The Create From File tab allows you to insert an object that you have already created and saved.

FIGURE 19.5
The Object dialog box.

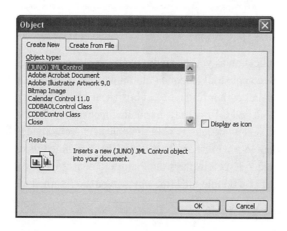

3. Make sure the Create New tab is up front. From the Object Type list, select the program you need to run to create the object. In this case, click Bitmap Image.

4. Click OK. Excel runs the selected application. Now you should see the application window on your screen. The Bitmap Image window appears (see Figure 19.6).

If you want the object to appear as an icon in your worksheet or chart, click the Display as Icon check box. Otherwise the object itself will appear in the worksheet or chart.

FIGURE 19.6
The Bitmap Image window.

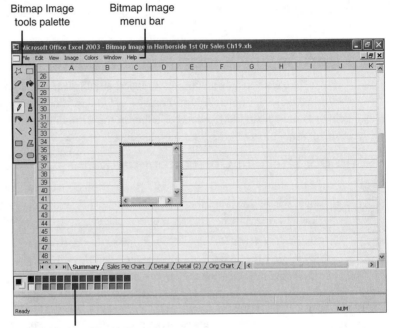

Bitmap Image tools palette

Bitmap Image menu bar

Bitmap Image color palette

5. Use the application as you normally would to create the object. In our case, click the Rounded Rectangle tool (second column, last row) on the Bitmap Image toolbar. Point to the upper-left corner of the object box (near row 36), and click and drag diagonally down to about cell C40 to draw a rounded rectangle. When you're finished, click any cell in the Excel worksheet to save the object, and exit the application. Excel places the object on your worksheet. You should see a rounded rectangle object. When you click the object, Excel displays the Picture toolbar, so that you can make changes to the object. If you double-click the object, you are returned to Paintbrush.

The Create From File tab is similar to using the Insert, Picture command (see Hour 11) because both commands insert an object without running an application.

Using the Clipboard Task Pane

If you want to insert an object using the Clipboard task pane instead of the Insert, Object command, it's easy to do. Create the object in the application and use the Copy command to copy the object to the Clipboard. In Excel, click the worksheet where you want the object to appear. Choose Edit, Office Clipboard to display the Clipboard task pane. Notice the selections on the Clipboard, ready for you to insert as an object in your worksheet (see Figure 19.7).

FIGURE 19.7

The Clipboard task pane.

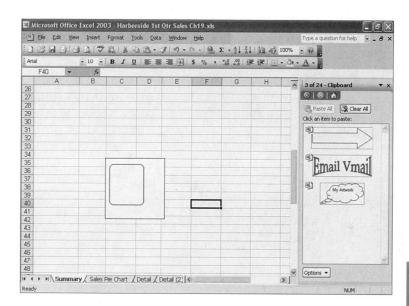

Then click the selection on the Clipboard task pane to paste the object into the worksheet. Excel shows the object in your worksheet.

19

Using Hyperlinks with Other Office Documents

A *hyperlink* is a term that refers to a piece of text or graphic in a document that links to other documents, a location, or element. You can create your own hyperlinks to move to a Word, Excel, PowerPoint, or Access file. You can even link to a specific location in a document or jump to a Web page. When you point to a hyperlink, Word displays the document path (for example, C:\excel\my documents\sales 1st qtr.xls) to which the link points. When you click a hyperlink, Excel moves to the location to which the link points. A hyperlink appears in blue (default color) text in the worksheet.

Hyperlinks are useful when you're distributing your document electronically and expect people to read it onscreen. Make sure that your readers will be able to access the documents to which you link. As an example, if you link a workbook on your local hard drive (C:) instead of a network drive, other people on your network won't be able to jump to the workbook, unless you make the entire contents of your machine available to other users on the network.

You can browse through files on your computer or on a network drive that contain hyperlinks.

Creating the Hyperlink

You need to use the Insert Hyperlink command to create a hyperlink so that you can move among Office documents. Perform the steps in the next exercise to create a hyperlink to move from an Excel worksheet to the Word document. Once again, you'll be using the Sales 1st Qtr workbook and the Word document you created earlier called My Integration.

To Do: Create a Hyperlink

1. Click cell B75 on the Summary sheet. This cell will contain the hyperlink that brings you to the Word document.

2. Choose Insert, Hyperlink. Excel opens the Insert Hyperlink dialog box, as shown in Figure 19.8.

> For faster creation of a hyperlink, press Ctrl+K or click the Insert Hyperlink button on the Standard toolbar to display the Insert Hyperlink dialog box.

3. Click the (Browse for) File button. Choose the folder that contains the file you want to hyperlink, select the file named My Integration, and choose OK.

> If you know the file's pathname, you can enter it in the Type the File or Web Page Name box. For example, C:\My Documents\My Integration.doc.

4. Click OK in the Insert Hyperlink dialog box. The document name is now a hyperlink and appears as blue, underlined text in cell B75.

5. Point to the hyperlink. Notice how the mouse pointer becomes a hand. A ScreenTip containing the filename and path appears below the hyperlink (see Figure 19.9).

▼

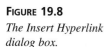

FIGURE 19.8

The Insert Hyperlink dialog box.

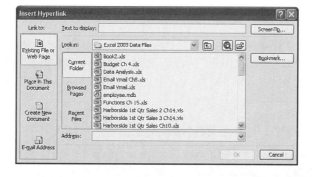

FIGURE 19.9

The hyperlink and ScreenTip with the pathname.

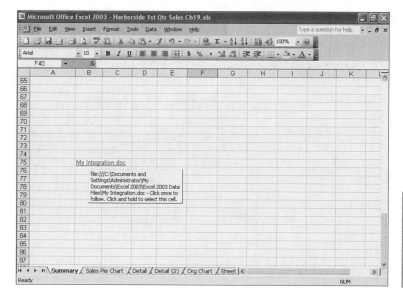

6. Click the hyperlink. Microsoft Word opens and you see the My Integration document.

7. In Word, select File, Exit. This closes the document and Word, and then returns you to the Excel worksheet.

8. Click the Microsoft Excel button on the Windows taskbar. You see the Sales 1st Qtr workbook again. Notice the hyperlink text appears in purple, indicating that the hyperlink is selected.

19

Sending Your Document Via Email with Outlook

You can send your entire Excel workbook, a worksheet, or a selection via email with Outlook directly from Excel. You have a choice to send to either one recipient or to a distribution list of multiple recipients. The nice part is that you don't have to leave Excel to send your documents to others.

Sending to One Recipient

To send an Excel workbook to one recipient, open the workbook you want to send. Choose File, Send To, and select Mail Recipient (as Attachment) or click the E-mail button on the Standard toolbar. Excel's Help Assistant asks if you want to send the entire workbook as an attachment or send the current sheet as the message body. Choose the option you want. If you choose the workbook attachment option, you should see the Outlook message window, illustrated in Figure 19.10.

FIGURE 19.10

Send someone an attached spreadsheet.

Set up the Outlook information requested in the message window, and type your email mail message. Notice that Excel automatically attached the workbook to your email message. Click the Send button to send your message with the attached workbook via Outlook.

If you choose to insert the current sheet in the message body, you will see the Outlook message window, shown in Figure 19.11.

Complete the address information at the top of the message window. Notice that Excel automatically inserted the current sheet into the email message box. Click the Send This Sheet button to send your message with the worksheet as the message body via Outlook.

19

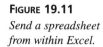

FIGURE 19.11

Send a spreadsheet from within Excel.

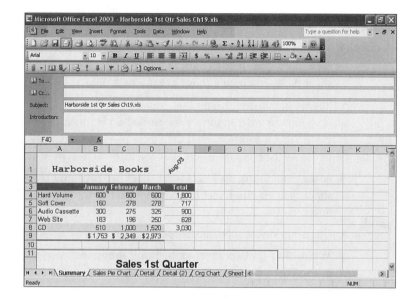

Sending to a Distribution List

You can send an Excel workbook to more than one recipient at once by first opening the workbook you want to send. Choose File, Send To, and select Mail Recipient (as Attachment) or click the E-mail button on the Standard toolbar. Excel's Help Assistant asks whether you want to send the entire workbook as an attachment or send the current sheet as the message body. Choose the option you want. Set up the Outlook information requested in the message window, and type your email message.

Choose the distribution list you want by clicking the To button or the Cc button in the address section of the message window. Notice that Excel automatically attached the workbook to your email message or inserted the current worksheet into the message body. Click the Send button or Send this Sheet button to send your message with the attached workbook or sheet in the message via Outlook to all the recipients on the distribution list.

Summary

Hour 19 has shown you how to integrate Excel with other Office applications. Now that you have some basic knowledge on how to share data between Windows applications, you can refer back to Hour 19 to get the instructions you need whenever you get stuck.

Hour 20 shows you how to automate tasks by creating your own macros.

Q&A

Q When I copied and pasted data from an Excel worksheet into a Word document, and then made changes to the worksheet in Excel, why didn't the worksheet in Word change to reflect the new data?

A Instead of copying and pasting, you need to link the Excel worksheet to the Word document in order to update the worksheet automatically. To do so, select the Edit, Paste Special command and the Paste Link option in the Paste Special dialog box. In the As list box, make sure that Microsoft Excel Worksheet Object is selected.

Q After embedding an Excel worksheet in Word and changing data in the worksheet, why do the Excel toolbars instead of the Word toolbars display onscreen?

A Click outside the worksheet area to display the Word toolbars.

Q What can I do to correct embedding the wrong worksheet from the workbook in my Word document?

A When you embed a worksheet object, the entire workbook is inserted. To display the correct worksheet in Word, double-click the worksheet in the Word document, click the sheet tab you want, and then click outside of the worksheet area in Word.

Q When I tried sending my workbook in an email message via Outlook directly from Excel, why didn't the recipient receive my message?

A Be sure that you're connected and online with Microsoft Exchange or a network. Then try sending the mail again.

Q I cannot find the E-mail button on the Standard toolbar.

A Make sure that Microsoft Outlook is installed on your computer. If it isn't, the E-mail button does not appear on the Standard toolbar.

Hour **20**

Automating Tasks with Macros and Smart Tags

The highlights in this hour are as follows:

- What a macro is and what it can do for you
- How to create a macro
- How to run a macro
- How to fix macro errors
- How to attach a macro to a toolbar
- How to use a macro in other workbooks
- How to prevent macro viruses

During this hour, you will learn how to use macros to simplify your work in Excel, making you more efficient and leaving time for other things you need to do on the job. Macros are not difficult to create and use. They are special instructions that control how Excel functions.

The To Do exercises in this hour show you how to automate Excel through macros. You learn how to create, record, run, edit, and delete macros in one hour. You create a simple macro to change the font and font size of data. When you run this macro, all you have to do is sit back and watch what it does for you. It's that easy.

When this hour ends, and after you're comfortable with the macro tools and features you learn about in this hour, you'll be able to experiment with Excel and simple macros.

What Is a Macro?

As you work with Excel, you might discover yourself repeating many actions and commands. For example, every time you create a new worksheet, you might immediately enter a series of titles (such as months) across one row or format a set of numbers using the currency style.

Although you can make some repetitive work more efficient by using the toolbar or templates (discussed in Hour 6, "Using Excel Templates"), you might find it easier to create a macro to repeat a sequence of actions and commands.

NEW TERM *Macro*—A macro is a sequence of keystrokes, mouse actions, and other commands that you record for later use.

You store macros in a macro sheet, a special type of Excel worksheet that is very similar to a regular worksheet. You must have a macro sheet open to be able to use the macros written in that file.

Each macro has three parts:

- Macro name
- Macro shortcut key
- Macro steps

The *macro name* is a description you use to manage and run the macro. For example, a macro you create to change the font for data on the worksheet can be called Font_change.

The macro shortcut key is an optional key combination you can use to run the macro. For example, you can assign the shortcut key Ctrl+Shift+F to run the Font_change macro.

The macro steps are simply the commands expressed in the Visual Basic language that execute when you run the macro. These steps are a list of instructions that Excel executes in sequence, starting from the first line and moving down to the last line.

The first command should be Sub, a special command that tells Excel the macro has begun its operation. The last command should be End Sub, a special command that tells Excel the macro has finished its operation. For example, examine the macro in Figure 20.1. Notice the three parts to the macro.

Macro name   Macro shortcut key

FIGURE 20.1

Macro instructions for changing the font.

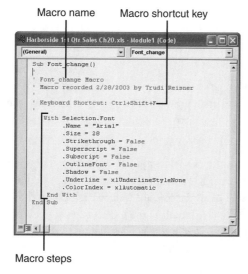

Macro steps

Macros are useful for automating repetitive or complex tasks. Although a macro is a series of programming instructions, you do not need to know anything about programming to create one. Excel offers a macro-recording feature that translates your actions into macro instructions.

Creating a Macro

By recording a series of macro instructions into a macro module or macro sheet in a workbook, you can tell Excel to perform any series of commands or actions for you. A macro can take the place of any mouse or keyboard action that you can perform in Excel. That is, a macro can cause Excel to accomplish a task by itself. You simply record a macro that shows Excel what you want to accomplish. Then Excel can repeat the task at any time.

You can create a macro by manually typing the instructions in a macro sheet or by choosing Tools, Macro, Record. Manually creating a macro requires you to carefully write down each step of the macro in the macro sheet. A single misspelling can affect the operation of the macro. Choosing Tools, Macro, Record, on the other hand, simply records each movement and action you take while using Excel. When you have completed the action, you stop recording by choosing the Stop Recording button on the Stop Recording toolbar. If you make a mistake while recording your macro, you can edit the macro later.

20

For most purposes, then, you should use Tools, Macro, Record to create macros. This method ensures that your macro will work when you use it.

Naming the Macro

A macro name can have up to 256 characters with no spaces. It's best to make your macro names meaningful and short so that you and others can quickly discern which macro to use. You name the macro right after you select Tools, Macro, Record New Macro.

The default macro name that Excel assigns to a macro is the word Macro followed by a number that looks like this: Macro1, Macro2, and so on. The name appears highlighted in the Macro Name box when the Record Macro dialog box first appears. That way, you can easily type right over the default name with any name you want. Remember, a name cannot contain spaces. If you enter a space anywhere in the name, Excel will not accept the macro name.

Selecting a Keyboard Shortcut

All macro shortcut keys must include the Ctrl key in combination with one other keyboard key. You can also use the Shift key in combination with the Ctrl key when assigning the shortcut key. For instance, you might assign the key combination Ctrl+Shift+F to run the Font_change macro.

Excel reserves many Ctrl shortcut key assignments for its own use. Excel will tell you when a combination key is already assigned and won't let you use an existing shortcut key. To avoid conflicts with these existing key assignments, you should use the Ctrl+Shift key combination for your shortcut keys.

Describing the Macro

An optional step is to enter a description of your macro to explain its function. A description can be helpful for you and others who use the macro. The default description contains the date you created or last modified the macro and your user name. In the example of the Font_change macro, you might want to explain that the macro changes the font and font size for data.

Recording the Macro

A macro is recorded on using the currently selected tab of the current worksheet. When you record a macro, Excel displays the Stop Recording toolbar that contains two buttons: Stop Recording and Relative Reference. The Stop Recording button does just what it says—it stops the recording of a macro. The Relative Reference button allows you to switch between relative and absolute references. By default, Excel records absolute cell references unless you click the Relative Reference button on the Stop Recording toolbar to specify that a cell or range of cells should be a relative reference. When you choose relative reference, the Relative Reference button appears depressed on the toolbar. Click the Relative Reference button again to switch back to absolute reference. The button no longer appears depressed.

This To Do exercise guides you through creating a macro called Font_change that changes the font and font size for data on your worksheet. You should be using the Sales 1st Qtr workbook you've worked with before.

To Do: Create and Record a Macro

1. Open the Sales 1st Qtr workbook. This workbook will contain the macro. Click cell B80 so that when you perform actions to record the macro, it will not change anything you didn't intend to change.

2. Choose Tools, Macro and click Record New Macro. The Record Macro dialog box pops up, as shown in Figure 20.2. You should see the default macro name Macro1 in the Macro Name box. You want to change that name to Font_change.

FIGURE 20.2
The Record Macro dialog box.

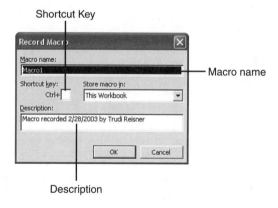

Shortcut Key

Macro name

Description

3. In the Macro Name box, type **Font_change**. This step names the macro.

4. Press Tab. In the Shortcut Key box, hold down Shift and type **F**. This step assigns the shortcut key Ctrl+Shift+F to the macro.

When you run the macro, press the appropriate letter key along with the Ctrl key, without pressing the Shift key, unless the Shift key is part of the shortcut key sequence. For example, Ctrl+Shift+F.

20

5. Click OK. The Record Macro dialog box disappears. Notice the recording indicator in black letters at the left end of the status bar at the bottom of the Excel window. From this point on, until you choose Stop Recorder, Excel stores every action and command on a macro sheet. Also note the Stop Recording toolbar that contains two buttons: Stop Recording and Relative Reference. Figure 20.3 shows you what your worksheet looks like just before you begin to record a macro.

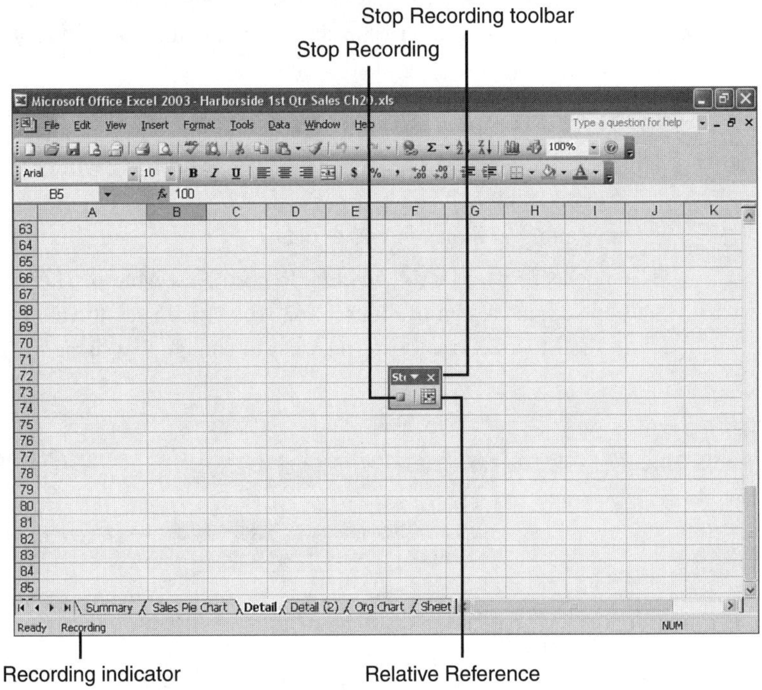

FIGURE 20.3

Recording a macro.

6. Click the Font drop-down arrow on the Formatting toolbar and choose Arial.

7. Click the Font Size drop-down arrow on the Formatting toolbar and choose 22. Now you're finished recording the macro, so stop the recorder.

8. Click the Stop Recording button on the Stop Recording toolbar. Excel hides the toolbar and stops recording the macro. You can tell because the Recording indicator in the status bar disappears. You have now recorded a macro that changes the font and font size for data on the worksheet.

9. Save the workbook. This step saves your macro, too.

Saving the Macro

When you save your workbook, Excel saves your macro on the macro sheet with the workbook. You don't have to do anything else to save the macro. If you accidentally close the workbook without saving changes, Excel doesn't save the macro. You have to start all over and re-create the macro.

Running the Macro

After you create a macro, you can use it to repeat its commands. Excel offers many ways to run a macro. Here are the two most common methods for running a macro:

- Select Tools, Macro, Macros, Run.
- Use the macro shortcut key (if you defined one).

The quickest way to run the macro is to use the macro shortcut key. If the macro doesn't have a shortcut key assigned to it, you must use Tools, Macro, Macros, Run.

In the following To Do exercise, you run the macro you just created by using the macro name, Font_change.

To Do: Run the Macro

1. First select cell A1 in the Summary sheet. This data in this cell needs a font change.

2. Choose Tools, Macro, Macros. The Macro dialog box appears, as shown in Figure 20.4.

3. In the Macro dialog box, select Font_change.

4. Click Run. Excel runs the Font_change macro by changing the title in the worksheet to a 22-point Arial font.

Macros   Run

FIGURE 20.4
The Macro dialog box.

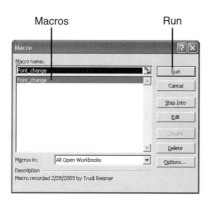

20

If you want to run the macro using a shortcut key, just press the shortcut key you assigned to the macro. Before testing the Font_change macro, select cell J16. Then, to run the Font_change macro, press Ctrl+Shift+F. Excel should format the data in cell J16 with the 22-point Arial font. Macros are powerful, aren't they? You'll have to make column J wider to accommodate the long entry in cell J16.

> You can stop a macro while it's running by simply pressing the Esc key. Excel stops the macro before it completes its actions.

Fixing Macro Errors

Macros don't always work perfectly. That is, you might make a mistake while recording the macro, or you might leave out a step. You don't need to worry about a macro that displays an error message because you can always fix those macro errors in Excel by editing, adding, and removing commands from the macro instructions.

A macro might need additional commands or actions, or you might want to delete some command or action from the macro. What if you want to make changes to existing macro commands and actions or correct errors in a macro that doesn't run properly? No problem. You can make any of these changes to a macro by editing the macro.

Looking at Macro Code

Macro instructions are written in Visual Basic, a fairly easy-to-use programming language. With the macro sheet in view onscreen, you can use Excel's editing commands to make changes to the Visual Basic instructions. You can remove macro commands, edit the specific contents of a cell in the macro worksheet, or even insert new commands into the middle of a macro. Of course, some changes require knowledge of Visual Basic. Specific commands that relate to actions that you want are described in the Microsoft Excel manual that comes with the software.

You can view macro code in the macro sheet by switching to that sheet. To open the macro sheet, choose Tools, Macro, Macros. In the Macro dialog box, select the Font_change macro. Click the Edit button.

> Another way to look at macro code is to choose Tools, Macro, Visual Basic Editor, or press Alt+F11.

The Microsoft Visual Basic window appears, as shown in Figure 20.5. You should see the Visual Basic toolbar and three window panes:

- Project—VBAProject
- Properties—Sheet1
- Visual Basic Instructions

At the far right end of the Visual Basic toolbar, notice the line and column indicator: Ln X and Col X. These indicators tell you the line and column where the insertion point is located in the active pane. To activate a pane, simply click the pane.

FIGURE 20.5

The Microsoft Visual Basic window.

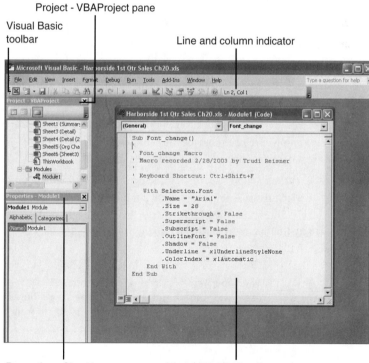

Editing the Macro

You can insert a command manually, remove a command, or edit a macro command on the macro sheet to make changes to the macro. You'll work with the Visual Basic Instructions pane on the right to make your changes. To get a better view of what you're doing in the Visual Basic Instructions pane, click the Maximize button in the upper-right corner of the pane. Excel enlarges the pane so that you see more macro instructions.

The To Do exercise coming up helps you edit the macro. You change the macro's font size from 22 point to 28 point.

To Do: Edit the Macro

1. Click anywhere in line 10 in the Visual Basic Instructions pane, which states Size = 22. This step activates the pane and positions the insertion point where you want to make a change.

2. Click and drag over the number 22 to select it.

3. Type **28**.

> Remember, the line and column indicators on the Visual Basic toolbar can always tell you where the insertion point is in the active pane.

4. Click the Save button on the Visual Basic toolbar. This step saves the changes you made to the macro.

5. Click the Close (×) button in the upper-right corner of the Microsoft Visual Basic window. This step closes the window and returns you to the workbook. Now you can test the change you made to the macro.

6. Click the Detail sheet tab and click cell A1, which contains the title. Press Ctrl+Shift+F. The macro applies the 28-point Arial font to the text in the selected cell. Your macro works perfectly! You'll have to make column A wider and row 1 taller to accommodate the large entry in cell A1.

> When you want to delete a macro, choose Tools, Macro, Macros. Select the macro you want to get rid of. Click the Delete button and choose Yes to confirm the deletion. Excel removes the macro from the Macro name list.

Fixing a Macro with Step Mode

When a macro doesn't work, the process of trying to find the problem and fixing it is called *debugging*.

When you use Step Mode to debug a macro, Visual Basic displays a yellow arrow in the left border of the Visual Basic Instruction pane and highlights in yellow the macro instruction on the line it's pointing to. Read the instruction carefully to see whether it contains any errors, including typos.

To use Step Mode to debug a macro, in the Macros dialog box, select the macro you want to debug. Click Step Into. If you're already in the Visual Basic Editor, choose Debug in the Visual Basic menu bar. Then you have three Step Mode choices:

- Step Into—Moves the Step Mode pointer into the instructions and executes code one statement at a time.

- Step Over—Moves the Step Mode pointer into the Code window and executes code one procedure or statement at a time.

- Step Out—Executes the remaining lines of a procedure in which the current execution point is located.

Use these Step Mode commands to step through the macro instructions and pinpoint the location of any errors.

Attaching a Macro to a Toolbar

As you build macros, you might not remember the macro names or even their shortcut names. You can use Tools, Macro, Run to choose the macros, but this method requires you to continually pull down the menu and scroll through the list of names in the Macro dialog box. A more efficient way to run a macro is to assign it to a button on a toolbar. Assigning a macro to a button makes the macro run whenever you click the button with your mouse. Attaching macros to a toolbar is a quick way to organize your macros so that any user can easily run them.

The next To Do exercise shows you how to attach a macro to the Standard toolbar for the Detail sheet.

To Do: Attach a Macro to a Toolbar

1. In the Detail sheet, choose Tools, Customize. The Customize dialog box appears.

2. Click the Toolbars tab. The Standard toolbar check box should have a check mark in it. The check mark means that the Standard toolbar is currently displayed, and you can make changes to it. You're going to attach the macro to this toolbar.

3. If the button you want to run the macro from is not on a toolbar, click the Commands tab and then click Macros in the Categories list.

4. In the Commands list, you should see the Custom Button with a smiley face next to it, as shown in Figure 20.6. Drag the Custom button onto the Standard toolbar, placing the button between the Zoom box and the Help button at the far right end of the toolbar. You should see a thick border surrounding the Custom button with the yellow smiley face on it. Close the Custom dialog box.

▼ To Do

20

FIGURE 20.6

The Macros category and Custom Button command.

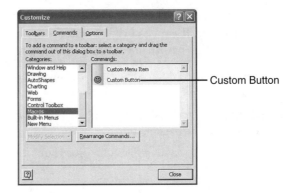

Custom Button

5. Click the Custom toolbar button. The Assign Macro dialog box opens, as shown in Figure 20.7.

FIGURE 20.7

The Assign Macro dialog box.

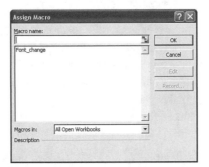

6. Click the Font_change macro name. This step enters the name of the macro in the Macro Name box.

7. Click OK. Excel attaches the macro to the Custom button on the Standard toolbar. Click the Close button to close the Customize dialog box. Now you want to test the new macro button on the toolbar.

8. Select cell A4. Click Custom Button on the Standard toolbar. Bingo! Excel changes the font and font size for the data you selected on the worksheet. You should see the 28-point Arial font.

Another way to run a macro is to assign it to a graphic object on the worksheet. To do so, right-click on the graphic, and choose Assign Macro. In the Assign Macro dialog box, select a macro in the Macro Name list and click OK. Click any cell to deselect the graphic object. Now when you move the mouse pointer over the graphic, the pointer is a hand pointer. Click the graphic and Excel runs the macro you assigned to the graphic.

Using a Macro in Other Workbooks

It's important to know what goes on behind the scenes when you create a macro. When you create a macro, Excel stores your keystrokes and mouse actions as a set of instruction on a macro sheet. You can tell Excel to store the instructions in one of the following places:

- The active workbook
- A new workbook
- Personal Macro workbook

Excel stores your macro in the active workbook by default. If your macro works only on the current workbook, store the macro in the active workbook. If your macro works in a new workbook, create a new workbook and store your macros there. If your macro works on any workbook in Excel, store that macro in the Personal Macro workbook. The macros in a Personal Macro workbook are available every time you start Excel. You can open the Personal Macro workbook at any time to display the macro sheet.

When you record a macro and choose Tools, Macro, Record New Macro, Excel opens the Record Macro dialog box. This dialog box is where you can specify where you want to store your macros. Click the Store Macro In drop-down arrow to look at the choices, as shown in Figure 20.8.

20

FIGURE 20.8
Choices for where to store your macros.

Select an item in the list and continue creating the macro. Excel stores your macros in the place you specify.

Understanding Macro Viruses

You've probably heard a lot of talk about viruses that your computer can catch from other computers on a network, the Internet, or disks. But what if your macros contain viruses? Viruses can contaminate your macros if the workbook is from an unsecure network or Internet site.

To prevent your computer from becoming contaminated with macro viruses, you can display a warning message whenever you try to open a workbook that contains a macro. This warning message always appears whether or not the macro actually has a virus. When the message displays, try to make sure that you know and trust the source of the workbook before you continue.

To check workbooks for macro viruses and display that warning message, choose Tools, Macro and then select Security. The Security dialog box opens, as shown in Figure 20.9. The Security Level tab should be up front. If it isn't, click the tab.

FIGURE 20.9

The Security Level tab in the Security dialog box.

The High option lets you run signed macros from trusted sources. Unsigned macros are automatically disabled when you choose the High option. Choose the Medium option and click OK. Medium security displays the virus warning message. The Low option does not check workbooks for macros that might contain a virus. Therefore, the low security does not display the warning message. Now click OK.

When you open a workbook that contains macros and the security level is medium, Excel displays the warning message that's in Figure 20.10. If you click Disable Macros, Excel ignores the macros in the workbook. If you click Enable Macros, Excel lets you use the macros in the workbook.

FIGURE 20.10

The macro virus warning message.

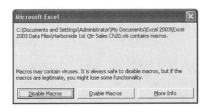

Working with Smart Tags

You can control automatic changes to your worksheet with smart tags. A smart tag is a button that pops up on the screen when you perform certain Excel operations, as described in Table 20.1.

Figure 20.11 shows an example of a smart tag button.

AutoFill Smart Tag

FIGURE 20.11

Smart tag button.

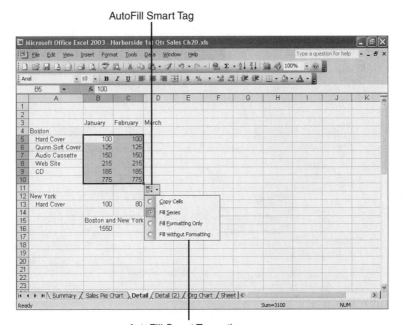

AutoFill Smart Tag options

TABLE 20.1 Smart Tags

Button	Name	How It Works
	AutoFill Options	After you perform a fill operation, such as dragging the fill handle, this smart tag provides options for filling cells.
	Insert Options	After you insert cells, rows, or columns, this smart tag provides formatting options.
	Paste Options	After you paste data, this smart tag specifies how moved or pasted items should display. For example, original formatting, with or without formatting, or with different formatting.
	Smart Tag Actions	Lists information options for a cell that contains data recognized by Excel, such as a stock symbol.
	Trace Error	If you assign an invalid formula to a cell, this smart tag lists error checking options.

When you see a smart tag, hover the mouse pointer over the smart tag button and click the down arrow next to the button to display a menu. Choose an option on the menu to modify the previous operation or obtain additional information.

To display labels for smart tags, you need to turn on the smart tags feature. To do so, choose Tools, AutoCorrect Options. Click the Smart Tags tab, and select the Label data with smart tags check box (see Figure 20.12). Select any smart tags in the Recognizers list. If you want to embed the smart tags in the workbook, select the Embed smart tags in this workbook check box. Then click OK.

When you roll the mouse pointer over a cell that contains a date, financial symbol, or a person's name from a recent Microsoft Outlook email, you will see the Smart Tag. Click the Smart Tag down arrow to see a list of options.

With the Smart Tag Actions and Trace Error smart tags, Excel displays a smart tag indicator in a cell to let you know that the smart tag is available. A smart tag indicator is a small triangle that appears in one of the corners of the cell. When you select a cell with a smart tag indicator, Excel displays the smart tag.

Label data with smart tags

FIGURE 20.12
AutoCorrect Options dialog box.

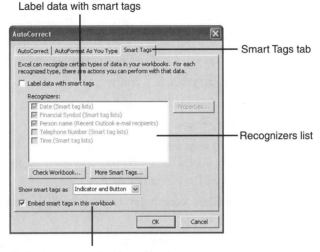

Smart Tags tab

Recognizers list

Embed smart tags in this workbook

Summary

This hour covered the basics for building and working with macros and understanding smart tags. Now you can create your own simple macros. You must have some idea now of which macros you need to automate the repetitive tasks you perform. When you're ready, you can graduate to building complex macros with advanced macro instruction. Who knows? Maybe this hour motivated you to learn Visual Basic; if so, you'll be automating a lot more Excel tasks than you ever dreamed of.

Building and working with an Excel database is discussed in the next hour. An Excel database can store lots of information and is flexible enough to retrieve and display, with a few commands or clicks of a mouse button, only the data you want to see.

Q&A

Q After I assigned the shortcut key letter "a" to my macro, why couldn't I run it?

A Macro shortcut key letters are case sensitive. If you assigned a lowercase letter shortcut key to your macro, make sure the Caps Lock key is turned off when you want to use the lowercase letter to run your macro.

20

Q **After recording the wrong actions and commands in my macro and realizing it halfway through the recording process, is it possible to scrap the macro?**

A Yes. Click the Stop Recording button on the Macro toolbar and choose Tools, Macro, Macros. Then delete the macro and start again.

Q **Can I stop my macro while it is running?**

A Sure. Just press the Esc key to stop the macro before it completes its actions.

Q **Why can't I use my macro in a workbook I opened?**

A You probably stored your macro in the active workbook. If you store your macro in the Personal Macro workbook when you create your macro, Excel makes the macro available to all Excel workbooks.

Q **After I chose the High security level option for Excel macros, why can't I run my macros?**

A High security sometimes disables macros, and you cannot run them. Change the security level to Medium, close the workbook, and then open the workbook again. You should see the macro virus warning message. Choose Enable Macros so that you can run your macros.

Q **Why doesn't the smart tag for a stock symbol display in my worksheet?**

A You need to turn on the smart tag feature for financial symbols. Choose Tools, AutoCorrect Options, click the Smart Tags tab, and select the Label data with smart tags check box. In the Recognizers list, make sure Financial Symbols is checked. Then click OK.

PART V

Creating and Using Databases in Excel

Hour

Hour **21**

Building an Excel Database

This hour covers the following topics:

- Database concepts
- How to structure a database
- How to create a database
- How to enter data in the database
- How to add data to the database
- How to search for data
- How to save the database

This hour introduces Excel databases. You learn about database concepts and how to plan and build a database, as well as how to enter and add data in a database, search for specific data, and save the database. At the end of this hour, you'll know enough about databases to build one of your own.

Basic Database Concepts

In your earlier work with Excel, you created worksheets to store and summarize information or data. Often you organize this information so that you can easily find the entries for a series of values, or calculate the totals for a group of numbers.

In Excel, a database is simply a more organized set of data. By organizing the data into a database, you can use the built-in database commands to find, edit, and delete selected data without manually scrolling through the information.

NEW TERM   *Database*—A tool you use to store, organize, and retrieve information. Excel treats the database as a simple list of data. You enter the database information just as you would enter data into a worksheet. When you select a command from the Data menu, Excel recognizes the list as a database.

Suppose you want to save the names and addresses of all the people on your holiday card list. You can create a database for storing the following information for each person: first name, last name, address, and so on. Each piece of information is entered into a separate field (cell) in the list. All the fields for one person in the list make a record. In Excel, a cell is a field, and a row of field entries makes a record. The column headings in the list are called *field names* in the database.

Figure 21.1 shows the organization of an Excel database.

FIGURE 21.1

Sample database.

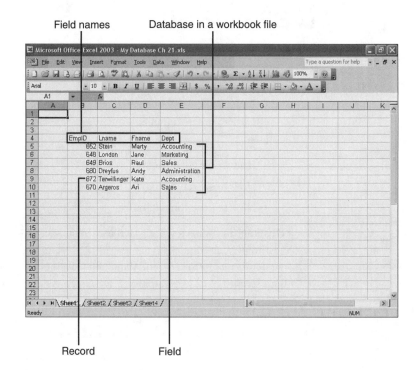

Before you work with a database, you should know these database terms:

- File—A collection of related data.
- Field—A column in the database.
- Field name—A column heading in a database. Excel uses the term column label.
- Record—A row in the database.

After you learn the database terms, here are two more things to think about when creating a database:

- Designing the database on paper
- Building the database with the field names and records

Starting with a Plan

Before you consider building a database in Excel, you need to plan how you want to structure the database. Whether you just think about the plan or write it down on paper, it's advisable to have a plan. That way, you'll save yourself a lot of time and effort because you are less likely to build a database that doesn't work for you.

Structuring Your Database

Consider these helpful questions and answers before structuring your database:

What is the size of the database going to be when I'm finished with it? Well, Excel gives you plenty of room on a worksheet. The size of the database can be as large as your worksheet, 256 columns by 65,536 rows.

What should I know about field names in relation to structuring my database? The field names must be placed in the first row of the database and must contain text. You cannot use values as field names. You can use a field name with a maximum of 255 characters; however, you should try to use shorter names because you can manage the database columns more easily.

How should I handle the records in my database? Each record must have the same number of fields. But you don't have to fill in each field of the record.

How does Excel handle spaces in data that I enter in the database? Excel doesn't deal with spaces at all. First of all, you cannot use spaces in a field name, and you shouldn't use extra spaces in a record entry. That is, don't "pad" an entry with extra spaces at the beginning or end of an entry.

21

Do I need to be concerned with upper- and lowercase letters? Excel's answer to this question is no. You can use any combination of uppercase and lowercase letters in your field names and records. Excel ignores capitalization when sorting or searching a database.

Can you plan on using formulas to calculate data in your database? Sure you can. You can create computed fields that evaluate other fields in the database, such as a Total field that would be equal to the Cost field times the Quantity field.

Creating a Database

You build your database by entering the information into your worksheet. Enter the field names into the first row and then enter the information under the row of field names, which are your records. Now you have yourself a database.

Follow the steps in the following exercise to create a database from scratch. Use a new workbook for your database. Before you start the exercise, create a new workbook and name it My Database.

To Do: Create a Database

1. The first step toward building a database is to enter the field names. In the My Database workbook on Sheet1, select cells B4:E4. This range is where you will enter the field names for your database.

> Selecting the range for the field names allows you to use the Enter key to enter the field names and move to the next cell, moving across the row. That way, you don't have to use the Tab key to move to the right each time you enter data in a cell. When you enter data in the last selected cell and press Enter, Excel makes the first selected cell active again.

2. Type **EmpID** and press Enter.
3. Type **Lname** and press Enter.
4. Type **Fname** and press Enter.
5. Type **Dept** and press Enter.
6. Save the workbook.
7. Click any cell to deselect the range. Your field names should look like the ones in Figure 21.2.

FIGURE 21.2

Field names.

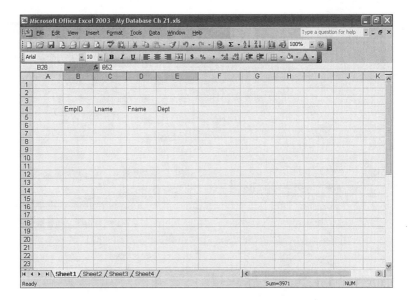

Entering and Adding Data

After you create your database, you can enter your records and add more records to it any time. You append these records at the end of the current database. To make adding these records easier, you can do one of the following:

- Use a data form
- Enter the data directly in the cells on the worksheet

Working with a Data Form

The data form is a dialog box that you use to review, add, edit, and delete records in a database. This dialog box shows one record at a time, starting with the first record. Each field name has a text box that you use to enter a new word or value.

The data form also has several buttons on it that you can use to move through the database, add or delete a record, or find a particular set of records.

Here's how you create a data form. Click any cell in the database. In the My Database file, click any cell in row 4, which contains the field names. Choose Data, Form. Excel displays a message (see Figure 21.3) asking you where your column labels (field names) are in the worksheet.

21

FIGURE 21.3

The column labels message.

Click OK. This step tells Excel that you want to use the first row of the selection or list as labels and not as data. Excel displays the data form in a dialog box, as shown in Figure 21.4. The dialog box's title bar contains the name of the database sheet, in this case, Sheet1. You should see field names, field text boxes, a scrollbar, the record number indicator, data form buttons, and navigation buttons.

FIGURE 21.4

The data form.

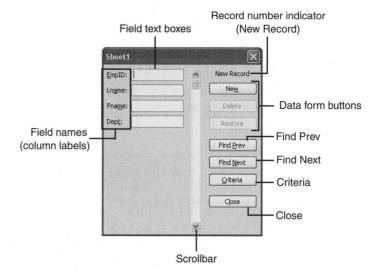

Using the Form

The New button in the data form lets you add new records to your database. Each time you click New or press Enter, Excel adds a new, blank record to the database.

In the data form, you should see a new record with blank boxes next to the field names. Type the data in the boxes, using the Tab key to move to each box. You can use the data that appears in Figure 21.5 to enter the data for one record.

FIGURE 21.5

Entering data in the data form.

When you're finished typing the information in the boxes, click the New button or press Enter. Excel adds the new record to the database and presents a blank data form.

Excel adds the new records at the end of your database, starting with the first blank row beneath the last row in the database. You should see the first record in row 5, right below the field names in your database.

> Be sure to save your database file often when adding new records to the database. Losing a large amount of data, or for that matter, any amount of data, could cause a headache because you would have to retype that data into the worksheet.

Navigating Through Records in the Form

To move around in the data form, you can use either the scrollbar in the middle of the dialog box or the navigation buttons on the right side of the data form. Here are the navigation possibilities:

- Scrollbar—Displays the first record in the database when you drag the scroll box to the top and displays the last record when you drag the scroll box to the bottom; displays each record as you click the up or down scroll arrow.
- Find Next—Displays the next record in the database.
- Find Prev—Displays the previous record in the database.

21

When you have a substantial number of records in your database, use the navigational tools in the data form to move around your database. But try using the navigational tools now so you'll see how they work.

Drag the scroll box to the top of the scrollbar or click the up scroll arrow. The boxes contain information for the first record. You can tell that you are viewing record 1 because the record indicator in the upper-right corner of the data form reads 1 of 1. The indicator always shows you the current record you are viewing and the total number of records.

To get back to the new, blank record, drag the scroll box to the bottom of the scrollbar or click the down scroll arrow. The record indicator shows New Record now.

When you're through with the form, click the Close button in the data form. The data form disappears.

Adding Data Directly to the Worksheet

The second method for adding data is very simple. Just type the data directly into your worksheet. Enter the necessary information to create the database entries.

Use the data in Figure 21.6 to add records to your database directly to the worksheet.

FIGURE 21.6

Entering data directly to the worksheet.

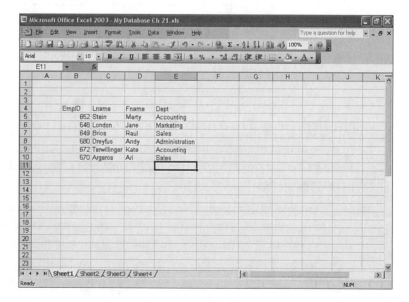

The records appear in the rows beneath the field names. Rows 5 through 10 contain data, and now you should have six records in your database. Widen any columns if necessary.

You could widen columns C and E to make the data easier to read.

When you enter data directly on the worksheet, you should save your database file periodically and often. If you lose this data, your hard work would be for nil and could cause a bad day. You'll have to enter that data again.

Searching for Data

After you enter data into the database, you can use the criteria form or Excel's AutoFilter feature to search for data. The criteria form lets you use comparison criteria in two ways to find records: (1) enter matching data, or (2) use comparison operators.

Entering Matching Data Criteria

You can find specific records using a criteria form, which is a subset of the data form, to create a special criteria record. You enter a word, phrase, or value into the criteria record. This type of criteria is a comparison criteria.

You can also use the following wildcards, which are characters that represent information you don't know or information that is common to many records, when specifying criteria:

- A question mark (?) represents a single character.
- An asterisk (*) represents multiple characters.

For example, you can use the ? wildcard to find everyone whose three-digit department code has 30 as the last two digits by typing **?30**. Or you can use the * wildcard to find everyone whose last name begins with a B by typing **B*** in the Lname field.

After you create the criteria record, the Find Prev and Find Next buttons in the data form jump only to the record that matches the criteria.

The next To Do exercise helps you set up a criteria record that uses the criteria form to search for specific data. You'll search for all last names that begin with a D.

To Do: Set Up and Use a Criteria Form with Matching Data

1. Select any cell in your database. This step selects a cell within the list you want to search.
2. Choose Data, Form. Click the Criteria button. The criteria form pops up, which looks similar to the data form, as shown in Figure 21.7. You should see field

▼ To Do

21

▼   names, field text boxes, the Criteria indicator in the upper-right corner, criteria
           form buttons, and navigation buttons.

FIGURE 21.7
The criteria form.

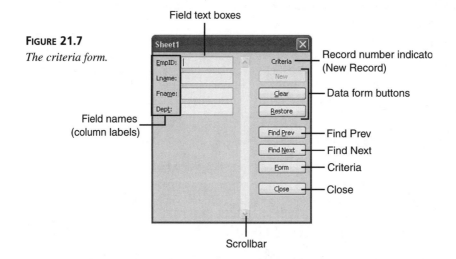

Field text boxes

Field names
(column labels)

Record number indicato
(New Record)

Data form buttons

Find Prev

Find Next

Criteria

Close

Scrollbar

3. You want to use the * wildcard to search for all last names that begin with the letter D. Click the LName box and type **D***. Entering * with the letter D tells Excel to
   find any entry whose last name starts with a D.

4. To use the data form criteria record, click the Find Next button. The fourth record
   displays in the data form because the last name is Dreyfus.

5. Click the Find Next button again. You hear a sound, which indicates that no more
▲ records match the criteria.

Clearing Criteria

It's a good idea to clear the information from the criteria record when you're done finding the matching records. Otherwise, as you continue to use the data form, Excel uses the
same criteria when you click the Find Prev and Find Next buttons.

To remove the criteria, click the Criteria button in the data form. You should see the criteria form. Click the Clear button. Excel removes all the information from the criteria
record. If you want to restore the criteria, you can click the Restore button. Click the
Close button to close the data form.

Using Comparison Operators

You can also search for a condition that must be evaluated, such as all records containing medical benefits less than $5,000. You can use the following comparison operators in Excel search criteria:

- = (equal to)
- \> (greater than)
- \< (less than)
- \>= (greater than or equal to)
- \<= (less than or equal to)
- \<> (not equal to)

To use a comparison operator to search for records containing medical benefits greater than $5,000, you would enter **>5000** in the MedBene field in the criteria form.

In the following To Do exercise, you create a criteria record using the data form to search for all employee ID numbers that are greater than 670.

To Do: Use Comparison Operators for Criteria

1. Select any cell in your database. This step selects a cell within the list you want to search.
2. Choose Data, Form. Click the Criteria button. The criteria form appears.
3. In the EmpID box, type **>670** (see Figure 21.8). Entering the greater than symbol and 670 tells Excel to find any entry whose employee ID number is greater than 670.

FIGURE 21.8

Entering a comparison operator in the criteria form.

21

▼ 4. To use the criteria record, click the Find Next button. The fourth record displays in the data form, showing the employee ID number 680.

5. Click the Find Next button again. The next record matching the criteria, record 5, displays. You should see the employee ID number 672.

 Notice that Excel finds the matching records in the order in which they appear in the rows in the worksheet, even though the number 672 comes before 680. If you sort the data according to employee ID number, Excel would find the ID numbers greater than 670 in numeric order. Hour 22, "Working with Your Database," teaches you how to sort data in a database.

6. Click the Find Next button again. You hear a beep because no more records match the criteria. You are done searching for data.

7. Click the Clear button to clear the criteria in the form.

▲ 8. Click the Close button to close the criteria form.

Using AutoFilter

Another way to search for data in a database is to use AutoFilter. This feature displays a subset of data without moving or sorting the data. Filtering data inserts drop-down arrows next to column headings in an Excel database. Selecting an item from a drop-down list hides all rows except rows that contain the selected value. You can edit and format the cells that are visible.

At certain times, you might want to work with a subset of data. For example, you might want to extract a partial list of data to give to someone who doesn't need the entire database list. Or maybe you want to use a filtered view of the data to create a report uncluttered by extraneous information. You can filter your data and move it somewhere else, such as to another worksheet, workbook, or application. At some point, you might want to delete unwanted records from the data. You can do so by filtering or extracting data from your list.

Filters enable you to display six types of criteria:

- All—Displays all records in the field.
- Top Ten—Shows up to 10 records from the top or bottom of the list in the field.

- Custom—Opens the Custom AutoFilter dialog box so that you can create AND or OR criteria.

- Exact Values—Shows only records with this exact value in the field.

- Blanks—Shows all records with blanks in the field only when a column contains blank fields.

- Nonblanks—Displays all records with values that are not blanks in the field only when a column contains blank fields.

Perform the steps in the next To Do exercise to filter data and display specific data in your My Database file. First, you add a field name and field to the database, adding a column for the number of years an employee is with the company.

> Data stored to the left or right of the Excel database can be hidden when you filter the database. If other data shares the worksheet with the list, store the data in rows above or below the database area or on another sheet in the workbook.

To Do: Filter Data

1. Click cell F4 and type **EmpPeriod**. This entry is a field name for an employee's employment period with the company.

2. Select cells F5:F10 and type **20**, **12**, **5**, **8**, **10**, **15**. Remember to use the Enter key to move to the next cell. Now, in column F, you have the length of employment for each employee.

3. Click the Save button on the Standard toolbar to save the new data in your file.

4. Select any cell in the list. This step selects a cell within the list you want to filter.
   Remember, you can only filter one list at a time on a worksheet.

5. Choose Data, Filter, AutoFilter. Excel displays drop-down arrow buttons next to each column heading in the database, as shown in Figure 21.9.

6. Click the drop-down arrow for the Dept column. The drop-down list shows the unique values for the column.

> You can click the column heading and press Alt+Down Arrow to see a drop-down list of data you want to display.

21

FIGURE 21.9

AutoFilter arrow buttons next to the column headings.

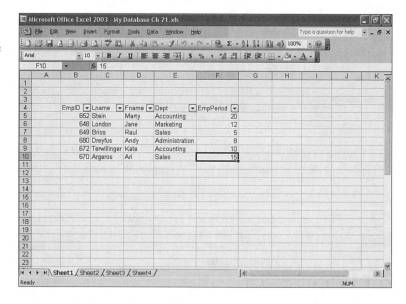

7. Select Sales. You should see two records, and the rest of the records are hidden. The blue arrow on the filter button indicates the filtered data is based on criteria you selected in the Dept column. The row header numbers for the filtered records also appear in blue.

8. To show all the records again, choose Data, Filter, Show All. Now you should see all six records, so that Excel can filter records based on all the records in the entire database.

9. Now that you're finished filtering, shut off AutoFilter. Choose Data, Filter, AutoFilter. This step removes the drop-down arrow buttons from the column headings in the database, redisplays the hidden rows, and turns off the AutoFilter feature for this database.

When you choose Data, Filter and a check mark appears next to AutoFilter, select AutoFilter to turn it off before selecting another Excel database.

Saving the Database

You save a database the same way you save a worksheet. Just click the Save button on the Standard toolbar. Excel saves your database that contains all the field names and records you entered on the worksheet.

Summary

During this hour, you learned database terminology, how to build a database, search for data in the database, and filter records. Now you should have a basic understanding of how databases can be created in Excel.

In the upcoming hour, you put the database you created to good use by subtotaling numbers, using advanced AutoFiltering techniques, as well as sorting and querying data.

Q&A

Q My field names take up two rows in my database. Why couldn't I successfully search for data?

A The field names must be placed in the first row of the database. Also, they should be placed in one row only. These field names must contain text. You cannot use values as field names.

Q I used spaces to align my data in the fields. Why doesn't Excel find any records I search for?

A You can't use spaces or extra spaces within a field entry. Also, don't align your data left, right, or center. Use the alignment default Excel uses for text (left) and numbers (right). Otherwise, if you align numbers center or left and use comparison operators in your search, Excel doesn't recognize the numbers and treats them as text.

Q After I filtered a database on my worksheet, why wouldn't Excel let me filter another database on the same sheet?

A You need to turn off the AutoFilter feature that you used on the first database. When you choose Data, Filter, a check mark appears next to the AutoFilter option. Select AutoFilter to turn it off before selecting another Excel database.

21

Q I have two databases on one worksheet. Can I filter records in both at one time?

A You can filter only one list at a time on a worksheet.

Q Is it okay to have other data on my worksheet next to my database when I filter records?

A Data stored to the left or right of the Excel database should be hidden when you filter the database. If other data shares the worksheet with the list, store the data in rows above or below the database area or on another sheet in the workbook.

Hour **22**

Working with Your Database

This hour explains how to work with your database and perform all kinds of operations on it to display the information you need. You'll be subtotaling your data with statistical functions, using advanced AutoFilter functions, and setting up a criteria range to retrieve data.

When you're through with the exercises in this hour, you'll be quite comfortable with retrieving data in your database. Then you can use your own databases and practice retrieving data in various and sundry ways.

The highlights of this hour include the following:

- How to work with subtotals
- How to use advanced AutoFilter functions
- How to set a criteria range

Working with Subtotals

Now that you have a database to work with, you might want to evaluate your database with the Data, Subtotals option. Excel has several database statistical functions that are similar in design and use Excel's standard statistical functions. Hour 5, "Letting Excel Do the Math," discusses the standard statistical function in more detail. Some of the common functions are SUM, AVERAGE, MIN, and MAX.

An example of using the SUM function is to find the total amount the company spends on salaries. You would choose the SUM function for the Salary field in the Subtotal dialog box. Excel would display each salary subtotal in the Salary column with the grand total for salaries at the bottom of the Salary column.

In the next To Do exercise, you use the SUM function to find the grand total for salaries at the company. Before you create any subtotals, you need to change some of the data and enter data in column G for the salary amounts. Be sure to open the My Database workbook you used in Hour 21, "Building an Excel Database."

To Do: Use Subtotals in a Database

▲ To Do

1. In Sheet1, click cell E5, point to the fill handle and slowly drag to cell E7. Now there are three employees in the Accounting department. Click cell E8, point to the fill handle, and slowly drag to cell E10. Now there are three employees in the Administration department.

2. Click cell G4, type **Salary**, and press Enter. Starting in cell G5, type **35000** and press Enter. Type the rest of the data in cells G6 through G10: **40000**, **50000**, **45000**, **32000**, and **51000**. Format the numbers with commas and zero decimal places. Now you have data that you can subtotal and total, as shown in Figure 22.1.

FIGURE 22.1

Data you can subtotal and total.

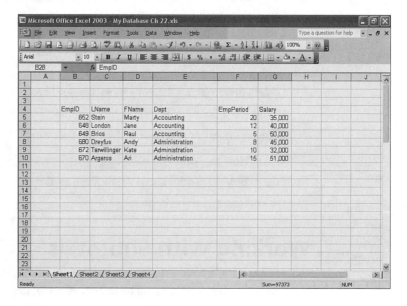

▼

22

▼ 3. Select any cell in the list. This step selects a cell within the list you want to subtotal.

4. Choose Data, Subtotals. Excel shows you the Subtotal dialog box. Notice the entire database is selected automatically. From here, you choose the column you want to subtotal and the function you want to use.

5. In the At Each Change In box, choose Dept. This selection tells Excel that you want to subtotal the data for the Dept column.

6. In the Use Function box, choose Sum if necessary. Now Excel will know that you want to find the subtotals and total for the data in the Dept column. In the Add Subtotal To list, notice that Salary is chosen. That option tells Excel to add the subtotals and grand total to the Salary column.

   Figure 22.2 shows you the Subtotal dialog box with the options you have selected so far and the other options you can choose from at the bottom of the dialog box. You can replace the current subtotals, insert a page break between subtotal groups, and place a summary below the data in the database. The Remove All button allows you to remove the subtotals.

FIGURE 22.2

The Subtotal dialog box.

7. Click OK. Excel places the SUM function results in cell G13. You want to widen column E to accommodate the long entries. Just double-click the column border between columns E and F. Figure 22.3 shows the subtotals in column E and the grand total in cell G13. The result should be 253,000. Notice the buttons with a minus sign (–) to the left of the row header numbers on the worksheet. You can use ▲ these buttons to hide and show any one or all the subtotals in your database.

FIGURE 22.3

The subtotals and grand total in the database.

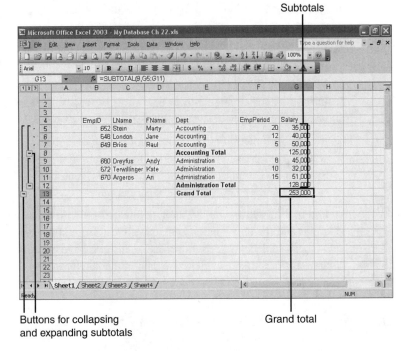

Buttons for collapsing
and expanding subtotals

Grand total

Different Subtotaling Functions

The following list shows the database statistical functions available in the Subtotal dialog box. You can use these functions to subtotal and evaluate the database:

- Sum
- Count
- Average
- Max
- Min
- Product
- Count Nums
- StdDev
- StdDevp
- Var
- Varp

22

The Use Function list box in the Subtotal dialog box gives you a list of all the functions. Choose one, and Excel subtotals your data in the column you specify in the Subtotal dialog box.

Collapsing and Expanding a Subtotaled Database

You might want to hide some of the subtotal information in your database. You can do so by collapsing the subtotals. To collapse a subtotaled database, click the minus sign (–) button on the left side of the worksheet. Figure 22.4 shows two collapsed subtotals in the database. A plus sign (+) button appears in each subtotal row you collapsed.

FIGURE 22.4

Collapsed subtotals in the database.

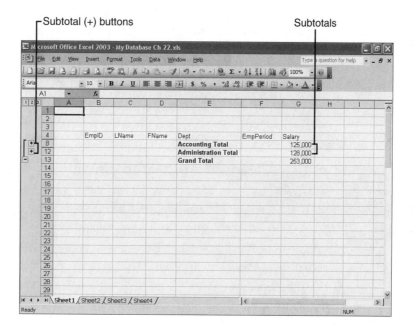

To display the hidden subtotals in your database, you can expand the subtotals by clicking each plus sign button on the left side of your worksheet. Excel displays the subtotals you expanded. Excel displays a minus sign button in each subtotal row you expanded.

Removing Subtotals

What if you no longer want the subtotals in your database? You can easily dispose of them by removing them from the worksheet. To do so, click any cell in the database, and choose Data, Subtotal. In the Subtotal dialog box, click the Remove All button. The dialog box closes and Excel removes the subtotals from your database. Go ahead and remove the subtotals from your database.

Using Advanced AutoFilter Functions

In Hour 21, you learn about filtering data with Excel's nifty AutoFilter feature. This session takes that discussion one step further and talks about using advanced AutoFilter functions, such as extracting filtered data, and using the Top 10 AutoFilter and Custom AutoFilter options.

After you filter your records to display specific data in your database, you can extract that data by copying it to another worksheet or workbook. It's simple to do—just use the Copy and Paste tools to place the filtered data somewhere else.

As for fancy AutoFilter functions, you have Custom AutoFilter that lets you set up comparison criteria, as well as create AND or OR criteria. For example, you can search for all the employee ID numbers less than 650. An AND criteria could be filtering all employee ID numbers less than 650, and they must be in the Accounting department. An OR criteria could be filtering all employee ID numbers greater than 660 or employees who have worked more than 10 years for the company.

Perform the steps in the To Do exercise using the Top 10 and Custom AutoFilter features to display specific data in the My Database file.

To Do: Use Advanced AutoFilter Functions

1. Widen column F to accommodate the long column heading. Simply double-click the column border between columns F and G. Select any cell in the list. Now you've selected a cell within the list you want to filter.

2. Choose Data, Filter, AutoFilter. Excel displays drop-down arrow buttons next to each column heading in the database, as shown in Figure 22.5.

3. Click the drop-down arrow for the EmpPeriod column. The drop-down list shows the unique values for the column. Select Top 10. The Top 10 AutoFilter dialog box opens, as shown in Figure 22.6.

> You can click the column heading and press Alt+Down Arrow to see a drop-down list of data you want to display.

4. Change the number 10 to 4 and click OK to show the top four items. You should see four records, and the rest of the records are hidden. The blue arrow on the filter button indicates the filtered data is based on criteria you selected in the EmpPeriod column. The row header numbers for the filtered records also appear in blue.

▼

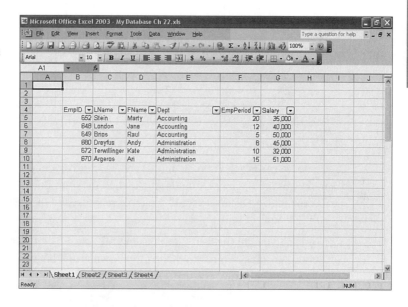

FIGURE 22.5
AutoFilter arrow buttons next to the column headings.

FIGURE 22.6
The Top 10 AutoFilter dialog box.

5. To show all the records again, choose Data, Filter, Show All. Now you should see all six records so that Excel can filter records based on all the records in the entire database. Now you want to enter a custom filter to show all records with a salary greater than $40,000.

> When you choose Data, Filter, if a check mark appears next to the AutoFilter option, select AutoFilter to turn it off before selecting another Excel database.

6. Click the drop-down arrow for the Salary column. Choose Custom to open the Custom AutoFilter dialog box (see Figure 22.7).

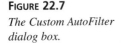

FIGURE 22.7

The Custom AutoFilter dialog box.

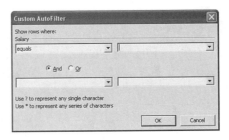

7. In the first Salary box on the left (it shows equals), choose is greater than. In the second Salary box on the right, click the drop-down arrow and choose 40,000. Click OK. You should see three records, and the rest of the records should be hidden.

8. Now that you are finished filtering, shut off AutoFilter. Choose Data, Filter, AutoFilter. This step removes the drop-down arrow buttons from the column headings in the database, redisplays the hidden rows, and turns off the AutoFilter feature for this database.

Setting a Criteria Range

The data form that you worked with in Hour 21 can be an easy way to enter, view, and delete records. As your database grows, however, you might need a more efficient way of maintaining it.

Excel provides an alternative method for finding, viewing, and deleting records. You can set up a criteria range, a range of information separate from the data form criteria. This criteria range allows you to easily inspect data from a large database.

The criteria range you use to view the database can contain comparison criteria, such as the type you use in the data form, or computed criteria. A computed criterion finds the result of computing several values in the database, such as EmpPeriod*2.

The criteria range is a special section of your worksheet that contains a row of criteria names, with at least one additional row below those names where you enter values you want to use as your criteria. You define the criteria range by selecting the field names and at least one additional row below the criteria names, and then you select Data, Filter, Advanced Filter.

The next To Do exercise sets up a criteria range and uses Data, Filter, Advanced Filter to display all employees who work in the Administration department and receive a salary of more than $40,000.

To Do: Set a Criteria Range

To Do ▼

1. Select cells B4:G4. This step selects the field names in the database that you want to copy to the criteria range.

2. Click the Copy button on the Standard toolbar.

3. Click cell B13 and then click the Paste button on the Standard toolbar. Excel copies the field names to row 13. Press Esc to remove the copy marquee.

4. Click cell E14. This cell will contain the first criterion. In cell E14, type **Administration** and press Enter. This criteria tells Excel to filter data in the Dept field that is equal to Administration.

5. Click cell G14. This cell will contain the second criterion. In cell G14, type **>40000** and press Enter. This criteria tells Excel to filter data in the Salary field that is greater than 40000.

6. Click any cell in the database and then select Data, Filter, Advanced Filter. The Advanced Filter dialog box appears, as shown in Figure 22.8.

FIGURE 22.8

The Advanced Filter dialog box.

7. In the Action section, choose Copy to Another Location.

8. In the List Range box, you should see the range $B$4:g10, which is the range for the database. If it's different, change it to the correct range.

9. Click in the Criteria Range box and drag the Advanced Filter dialog box so that it doesn't cover the criteria range on the worksheet. Select cells B13 to G14. This step specifies the criteria range.

10. Click in the Copy To box and then click cell B18. This step specifies where you want to copy the filtered data on the worksheet.

11. Click OK. Excel copies the field names and records starting in row 18. You should see two records.

▲

Retrieving Data with the Query Wizard

Querying data is the process of retrieving specific information from a database to create a list in an Excel worksheet. The Query Wizard lets you create a simple query to retrieve data in an external database and places that data in an Excel worksheet. You can also filter and sort data in the external database and place the imported data in an Excel worksheet.

The Query Wizard lets you use data from various external databases in your Excel worksheets. The wizard can establish links to various databases and use data query features to locate specific information. After this data is inside the Query Wizard, Excel can access the data for you whenever you need it.

Querying data in a database can be a complex process, but the Query Wizard helps you set up queries that perform exactly as intended. The wizard walks you through the process of querying data, making it as quick and painless as possible.

Installing Microsoft Query

You might find that Microsoft Query is not installed on your computer when you choose New Database Query in Excel's Import External Data menu on the Data menu. In this case, Excel asks whether you want to install the feature. Click Yes, insert your Microsoft Office or Microsoft Excel CD-ROM, and click OK. Excel does the rest. After Microsoft Query is installed, it is ready for you to use.

Choosing a Data Source

To use Microsoft Query, choose Data, Import External Data, New Database Query. The Choose Data Source dialog box appears, as shown in Figure 22.9.

FIGURE 22.9

The Choose Data Source dialog box.

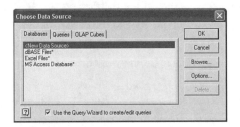

The first step involved in using the Query Wizard is choosing a data source on the Databases tab. This item is the database driver that Excel uses to access the data. The database driver can be any of the following:

- dBASE Files (*.dbf)
- Excel files (*.xls)
- MS Access Database (*.mdb)

After you select a database driver, click OK. The Select Database dialog box opens. Navigate to the folder that contains the database, select the database file, and click OK.

The Query Wizard—Choose Columns dialog box opens, as shown in Figure 22.10. You should see two lists: Available Tables and Columns and Columns in Your Query. Now you need to further define the data source. There are two things you must do to accomplish this task. First you select the database file, and then you choose the tables and columns you want to use for the query.

Available Tables
and Columns   Columns in Your Query

FIGURE 22.10

Query Wizard—Choose Columns dialog box.

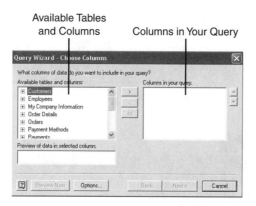

To choose a table, click the plus (+) sign next to the name of the table in the Available Tables and Columns list. The column names appear beneath the table name. Click a column name and click the right arrow button to move the column name into the Columns in Your Query list (see Figure 22.11).

Repeat the previous step for each column you want to include in the query. When you're finished selecting columns, click the Next button.

Filtering Data

Earlier in this hour and in Hour 21, you learned how to filter records in various ways. Well, Excel offers yet another filter feature. After you choose the data source and define it, you can use the Query Wizard to filter data.

Right arrow button

FIGURE 22.11

Selecting columns for the query.

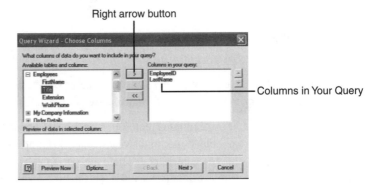

Columns in Your Query

When filtering data with the Query Wizard, you choose the column you want to filter and specify how you want to filter the data in the Query Wizard—Filter Data dialog box (see Figure 22.12). For example, you select the EmpID column and choose Is Greater Than. The next step is to choose the specific item in the column you want to filter the records with. For example, an item can be a specific employee ID number such as 652. In this case, you choose Equals and type **652** in the text box. When you're done, click the Next button.

Employee ID   Equals   652

FIGURE 22.12

Query Wizard—Filter Data dialog box.

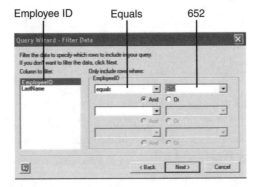

Sorting Data

You can sort the data and arrange the rows of a database in a particular order, based on the contents of the fields or columns. You can use the Query Wizard to sort your data.

When you sort your data, you can specify how Excel should reorder the data rows. If you specify an ascending sort order, the lowest number, the beginning of the alphabet, or the earliest data appears first in the list. Excel uses the following order for an ascending sort:

22

- Numbers
- Text and text that includes numbers
- Logical values
- Error values
- Blanks

Descending order starts with the highest number, the end of the alphabet, or the latest data. Sorting in descending order reverses the order mentioned in the preceding list, except for blanks, which are always sorted last.

Figure 22.13 shows an example of sorting the Employee ID column in ascending order. When you finish selecting the sort order, click the Next button.

FIGURE 22.13

Query Wizard—Sort Order dialog box.

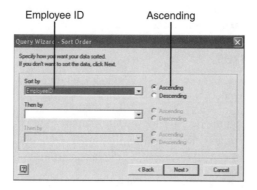

Saving Data Queries

The Query Wizard lets you save your query in a file with the file type DQY. Click the Save Query button in the Query Wizard—Finish dialog box (see Figure 22.14) and Excel stores all your queries in the Queries subfolder. To view your query files, open Windows Explorer. In the All Folders pane on the left, open the Documents and Settings folder, Administrator, Application Data, Microsoft, and then you should see the Queries subfolder. When you click Queries, Windows displays your queries in the pane on the right. From here, you can rename or delete query files.

If you want to delete a query that you no longer use, go to Windows Explorer. In the All Folders pane on the left, display the following folders: Documents and Settings, Administrator, Application Data, Microsoft, Queries. A query file has the file type DQY. Select the queries you want to delete and click the Delete button on the Explorer toolbar.

Return Data to Microsoft Excel

FIGURE 22.14

*Query Wizard—Finish
dialog box.*

Save Query

After you save your query, select Return Data to Microsoft Excel, if necessary, in the Query Wizard—Finish dialog box. Then click the Finish button. You should see the data you queried from the external database in your worksheet.

Reusing Queries

After you create a query and save it with the Query Wizard, you can run it again and again to retrieve the data you need.

When you want to rerun the query, choose Data, Import External Data, Import Data. Select a query in the list and click Open. In the Import Data dialog box, click a cell in the worksheet and click OK. Excel displays the data starting in the cell you selected.

Another way to rerun the query is to double-click its icon in the folder where you saved it. This method runs the query, starts Excel, and displays the data in a new workbook.

Summary

This hour gave you enough information about retrieving data in a database so that you can get started on your work. If you need some help on any of the features covered in this hour, you can always step yourself through a To Do exercise to refresh and reinforce how you retrieve data.

The next hour explains how to share work with your colleagues by sharing templates and workbooks, tracking the changes in them, and accepting and rejecting changes you and others make to the templates and workbooks.

Q&A

Q I used the SUM function to subtotal a column of data in my database, and I don't want others to see some of the subtotals. What can I do?

A You can hide each subtotal by collapsing it. Just click the minus sign (–) button for the subtotal on the far left side of the worksheet.

Q Is there an easy way to delete the subtotals in my database?

A Sure. Choose Data, Subtotal and click the Remove All button.

Q I filtered my records with the Top 10 AutoFilter, and I didn't get the results I expected. What should I do?

A You can either click the Undo button on the Standard toolbar or choose Data, Filter, Show All. This step displays all the records again. Then start over to choose the Top 10 AutoFilter options you want.

Q How do I delete a query I no longer use?

A That's a good question. Go to Windows Explorer and display the Queries subfolder in the All Folders pane on the left. Then you can delete your query that has the file type DQY. You can find the Queries subfolder under the following folders: Documents and Settings, Administrator, Application Data, Microsoft.

PART VI

At the Office and on the Internet/Intranet

Hour

HOUR 23

Sharing Your Work with Your Colleagues

This hour brings you all the information you need to share workbooks with others on a network. You look at how to share Excel workbooks, track and display changes in workbooks, and protect your workbooks from changes.

When you finish this session, you'll know how to share your workbooks with others. Before long, you'll be sharing, reviewing, and protecting your workbooks like a pro.

The topics in this hour include the following:

- Defining a network
- Sharing workbooks
- Tracking changes in your worksheet
- Protecting your worksheet from changes

What Is a Network?

 Network—The connection of computers and printers that provides workgroup services, such as information sharing and messaging.

Sharing Workbooks

Excel's shared-workbooks feature allows multiple users to modify a single workbook simultaneously. The shared workbook resides on a network so that several users can make changes at the same time. Then the shared workbook is updated to incorporate the changes. Each user can format the workbooks and make other choices, such as viewing and printing choices, that are used for their own filtered version of the workbook.

Setting Up a Shared Workbook

The Tools, Shared Workbook selection lets you set up options for sharing workbooks on a network. The shared workbook options include the following:

- Allow Simultaneous Access to a Workbook
- Control How to Track Changes
- Control How Changes Get Updated
- Control How Conflicting Changes Are Resolved

The first option in the preceding list is found on the Editing tab in the Share Workbook dialog box.

The other options in the list are on the Advanced tab in the Share Workbook dialog box.

The steps in the following To Do exercise show you how to set up shared workbooks. If you're not working on a network, you should be able to set up most of the options successfully and still be able to share workbooks and track changes. You use the My Database workbook for sharing purposes in the exercise. Open the workbook before you begin with step 1.

To Do: Set Up Shared Workbooks

1. Save the My Database workbook to a network drive.
2. Click the Sheet1 tab if it's not already in front. Next, choose Tools, Share Workbook. Excel brings up the Share Workbook dialog box, as shown in Figure 23.1. The Editing tab should be in front.
3. Choose Allow Changes by More Than One User at the Same Time option. A check mark in the check box means the option is turned on. Now you want to specify keeping a history of the changes for 45 days.

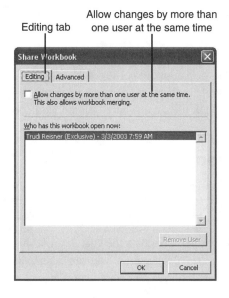

FIGURE 23.1
The Share Workbook dialog box.

23

4. Click the Advanced tab. Figure 23.2 shows the options on the Advanced tab. The options are available in the following sections: Track Changes, Update Changes, and Conflicting Changes Between Users.

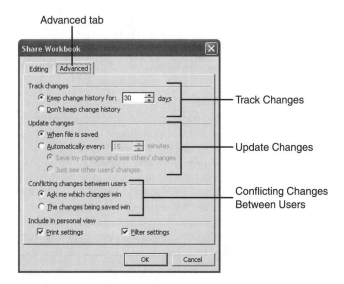

FIGURE 23.2
The Advanced tab in the Share Workbook dialog box.

▼ 5. Change the number of days to 45. This setting keeps the changes history for 45 days.

6. Click OK. Excel prompts you to save the workbook.

7. Click OK to save the workbook. Excel saves the workbook on the network drive if you saved it there, so that others can gain access to the shared workbook. You should see the workbook filename [Shared] in the workbook's title bar at the top of

▲ the Excel window.

Defining Workbook Options

In the Track Changes section on the Advanced tab in the Share Workbook dialog box, you can control how long to track workbook changes. For example, you might want to track workbook changes for 30 days.

You can also tell Excel how often to update the changes in a shared workbook. In the Update Changes section on the Advanced tab, you can control how changes made by multiple users are consolidated in the main document. You can choose to save the changes whenever the file is saved or in minute-based intervals.

In the Conflicting Changes Between Users section, you can control how conflicting changes are resolved—for instance, when two users change the same cell to different values. Usually, this item should be set to the Ask Me Which Changes Win option.

Opening a Shared Workbook

You open a shared workbook just as you would any workbook in Excel. Click the Open button on the Standard toolbar. Excel opens the shared workbook.

To remove a workbook from shared use, choose Tools, Share Workbook. Click the Allow Changes by More Than One User at a Time check box. This setting should clear the Allow Changes by More Than One User at a Time check box. Click OK. Excel prompts you to confirm removing the workbook from shared use. Click Yes. After you remove the file from the shared list, Excel removes the History sheet from the workbook. The History sheet contains a history of the changes made for the number of days you specify. When you set up the shared workbook, you specify the number of days to keep the changes.

Tracking Changes in Your Worksheet

When a workbook is set up to be shared, you and the others involved in sharing the workbook can make as many changes to it as you want. Then you can use the Accept or Reject Changes feature to accept or reject the various changes.

Excel lets you review shared workbooks by tracking the changes you and others make to a shared workbook. There are two ways to track changes:

- Onscreen
- On a printed copy

23

Accepting or Rejecting Changes

The To Do steps demonstrate how to accept or reject changes in a shared workbook. You start by making a change to a value in a cell so that you can accept or reject it.

To Do: Accept or Reject Changes in a Shared Workbook

To Do

1. Click cell G5, type **37000**, and press Enter. This entry makes a change to the value in cell G5.

2. Choose Tools, Track Changes, Accept or Reject Changes. Excel prompts you to save the workbook.

3. Choose OK to save the workbook. Excel opens the Select Changes to Accept or Reject dialog box, as you see in Figure 23.3. Notice that the When box is selected and shows that the workbook is not yet reviewed.

Specify the time you want to review changes

FIGURE 23.3

The Select Changes to Accept or Reject dialog box.

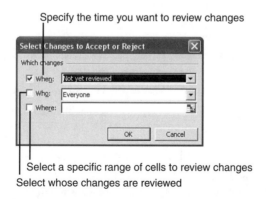

Select a specific range of cells to review changes
Select whose changes are reviewed

4. Select the Who check box. In the Who box, you should see Everyone. The other options are Everyone but Me and a list of users who are sharing the workbook with you. For this exercise, leave the Everyone option selected and the default option (Not Yet Reviewed) in the When box.

| If you want to review changes by all the users, clear the Who check box. |

5. Select the Where check box. In the Where text box, the current cell G6 is highlighted. Click cell G5 on the worksheet. This step enters the cell reference in the Where box and indicates where you made a change to a value in a specific area on the worksheet. You should see $G$5 in the Where text box.

| If you want to review changes made to the entire workbook, clear the Where check box. |

6. Click OK. In the Accept or Reject Changes dialog box, read the information about the first change (see Figure 23.4). The information also contains any dependent changes that are affected by the action you take for this change. If necessary, use the scroll arrows to see all the information.

Change made in the worksheet

FIGURE 23.4

The Accept or Reject Changes dialog box.

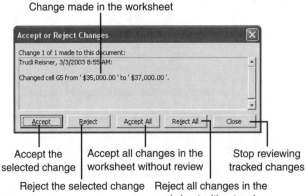

Accept the selected change

Reject the selected change

Accept all changes in the worksheet without review

Reject all changes in the worksheet without review

Stop reviewing tracked changes

To accept the change and clear its marquee, click the Accept button. To undo the change, click the Reject button. If Excel prompts you to select a value for a cell, click the value you want and then click the Accept button.

For each change, click the Accept or Reject button; alternatively, click the Accept All or the Reject All button to accept or reject the rest of the changes.

▼   7. Click the Accept button. The Accept or Reject Changes dialog box disappears
        because there are no more changes to review.

> You must accept or reject a change before you can advance to the next
> change.

▲

When two people work on a shared workbook, if person 1 makes a change to a cell and
saves the workbook and then person 2 also saves a copy of the workbook, person 2 sees
any changes that person 1 made. The changes are highlighted with a comment indicator
in the workbook that shows person 2 the changes that person 1 made, and the changes
are accepted as a matter of course.

Tracking Changes Onscreen

When you share workbooks, you can track changes made by users over a number of
days. Excel uses the History sheet to show a complete list of changes to the workbook.
The History sheet includes the names of the users who made the changes, data that was
deleted or replaced, and information about conflicting changes.

To track changes onscreen, you need to ensure that the options in the Track Changes section on the Advanced tab in the Share Workbook dialog box meet your needs.

> To prevent change tracking from being removed in a shared workbook,
> choose Tools, Protect, Protect and Share Workbook. In the Protect Shared
> Workbook dialog box, click the Sharing with track changes check box to put
> a check mark in the box. Then click OK.

The next To Do exercise helps you track changes onscreen in the My Database workbook.

To Do: Track Changes Onscreen

    1. Choose Tools, Track Changes, Highlight Changes. The Highlight Changes dialog
       box appears (see Figure 23.5). Note the check box is selected for Track changes
       while editing. This also shares your workbook. When you turned on workbook
       sharing, Excel turns on the Track Changes feature.

23

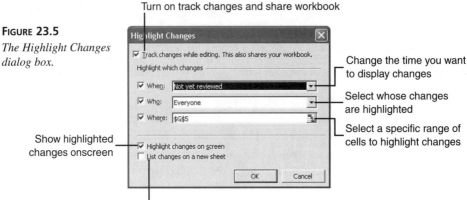

Turn on track changes and share workbook

FIGURE **23.5**

The Highlight Changes dialog box.

Change the time you want to display changes

Select whose changes are highlighted

Select a specific range of cells to highlight changes

Show highlighted changes onscreen

Display changes in a history worksheet

2. In the When drop-down list, you can choose

    - Since I Last Saved

    - All

    - Not Yet Reviewed

    - Since Date

    To show a history of all the changes, click the When check box to clear it. Notice that the All option appears, indicating that all changes will be tracked.

3. In the Who drop-down list, you can choose

    - Everyone

    - Everyone but Me

    - Each User's Name Individually

    Click the Who check box to clear it.

4. In the Where drop-down list, select the cells that will be shown. If you leave this item blank, all cells are included. You want to leave it blank for now to show a history of the changes. Click in the Where check box to clear it. This step also clears the Where text box.

5. Choose List Changes on a New Sheet. This option controls where changes are displayed—in this case, onscreen. The option Highlight Changes on Screen is also selected, which tells Excel to display the changes directly on the worksheet.

6. Click OK. Excel inserts a History sheet in the workbook to show a history of the changes, as shown in Figure 23.6. Also, Excel highlights the changes on the screen and shows comments where changes were made.

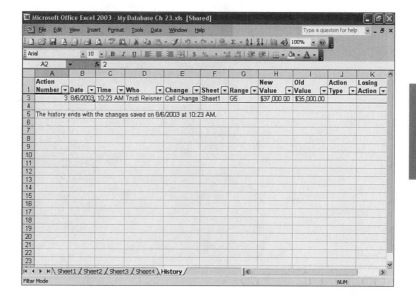

FIGURE 23.6
The History sheet.

The History sheet shows you a detailed record of changes made to a sheet, based on the changes that fit the criteria you selected in the Highlight Changes dialog box (When, Who, and Where).

7. Click the Sheet1 tab. Take a look at cell G5. A dark blue border surrounds the cell, and a blue triangle appears in the upper-left corner of the cell. The border and triangle indicate the cell has been changed.

8. Point to cell G5. A comment explaining the change that was made pops up next to cell G5 (see Figure 23.7).

Tracking Changes in the Printed Copy

You have seen how Excel indicates the changes onscreen and in the History sheet. But those aren't the only places you can track and monitor your changes. Why not print a hard copy of the History sheet? Printing a History sheet is handled just like any other print job.

To print this special sheet, click the History sheet and then click the Print button on the Standard toolbar. Excel prints the History sheet for you. Now you can track changes on a printout. You could punch holes in the printed History sheets and store them in a binder to help everyone keep track of the changes.

FIGURE 23.7

*Changes shown on the
worksheet.*

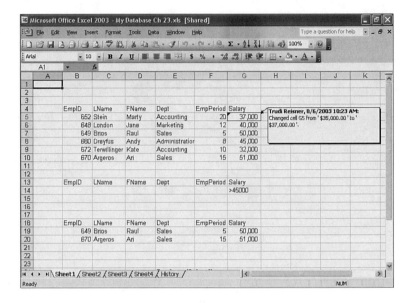

Summary

Hour 23 provided the tools you need to share your workbooks with others on a network. With practice, you should be able to set up shared workbooks, accept or reject changes, and track the changes.

In Hour 24, "Worksheets and the Web," you learn to work with Excel and the Internet, making your own Web pages, creating hyperlinks from your Excel workbooks to the Internet, and browsing the Web right from Excel.

Q&A

Q I set up a workbook for shared use, and it doesn't appear in the shared list. Why not?

A Did you click the Allow Changes by More Than One User at a Time check box in the Editing tab in the Share Workbook dialog box? If the check box is empty, you haven't set up your workbook for shared use.

Q How do I tell Excel to review changes by all the users?

A First, you have to choose Tools, Track Changes, Accept or Reject Changes. Then, in the Select Changes to Accept or Reject dialog box, clear the check mark from the Who check box.

Q **How do I specify that I want to review changes made to the entire workbook, not to just a portion of it?**

A To review changes to the entire workbook, choose Tools, Track Changes, Accept or Reject Changes. In the Select Changes to Accept or Reject dialog box, clear the Where check box.

Q **Can I skip over a change instead of accepting or rejecting it?**

A No. You must accept or reject a change before you can advance to the next change.

23

Hour **24**

Worksheets and the Web

By the end of this hour, you'll be creating Web pages from your Excel worksheets, spending time on the Web, and getting there directly from Excel.

The subjects discussed in this hour are as follows:

- What the Internet is
- How to use Internet Explorer 6.0
- How to search on the Web
- How to add a hyperlink to a worksheet
- How to save an Excel document to the Web
- How to post your worksheet to the Web

What Is the Internet?

The Internet is a worldwide networked computing community with millions of users that links together government, business, research, education, industry, and individuals. The World Wide Web is one portion of the Internet.

NEW TERM *Internet*—The global network of networks that enables some or all of the following: exchange of email messages, instant messages, files, newsgroups, and World Wide Web pages.

New Term *ISP*—An acronym for *Internet service provider*; users access the Internet by dialing into their ISP's computer across a phone line and then connecting to the Internet via the ISP's server. ISP also indicates a local service provider and mail delivery service.

New Term *DSL*—An acronym for *Digital Subscriber Line*; a service that offers a faster Internet connection than a standard dial-up connection. DSL uses the existing phone line, and in most cases does not require an additional phone line.

New Term *Cable modem*—Devices that allow high-speed access to the Internet via a cable television network. More powerful, and capable of delivering data at a much faster rate, than a traditional modem.

The World Wide Web puts pages of information at your disposal. Web sites are your destinations when you surf the World Wide Web. A Web site is either a Web page, or all the documents that together make up the destination to which you surf. A typical Web page contains several files, including the main HTML file and associated graphic, sound, animation, and other files. That HTML file usually contains hypertext links to other HTML documents at the same Web site.

New Term *World Wide Web*—A portion of the Internet that contains Web pages. These Web pages are made up of text, graphics, sound, animation, and hyperlinks to other Web pages, thereby creating a spiderweb effect.

Intranet Versus Internet

An intranet is an internal network within a company that is based around the same services as the Internet; an intranet may or may not be accessible to or through the Internet. Intranets are growing in popularity very quickly.

New Term *Intranet*—The network of networks at your company that enables some or all of the following: exchange of email messages, files, and World Wide Web pages.

With access to an intranet, you have a mail service, can share files, and have a gateway to the Internet. You can publish your Excel worksheets as Web pages on your Web site by using the company intranet. To do so, you publish the worksheet Web page internally to a folder on your hard drive. Before you publish your Web pages on the Web, make sure other users on the network can access that folder. If other users do not have access to the folder that will contain your Web pages, you can ask your network administrator about creating shared folders.

Using Internet Explorer 6.0

Microsoft Internet Explorer (IE) 6.0 is a browser program with the latest and greatest browser technology. IE 6.0 provides a gateway to the Internet, the capability to browse through Web pages, as well as the capability to send and receive email. Figure 24.1 shows you the IE 6.0 window with its menu bar and toolbar for browsing Web pages.

FIGURE 24.1

The Microsoft Internet Explorer 6.0 window.

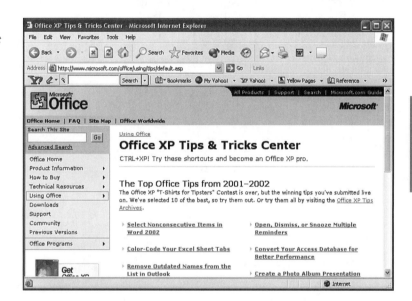

24

Searching on the Web

You can browse the Web to your heart's content by using Excel to start Microsoft Internet Explorer. You don't have to leave the program and start Internet Explorer or any other browser you might normally use. First, you need to connect to go online, and then just use the Web toolbar in Excel. You can enter a uniform resource locator (URL) and search for a specific Web page or browse around the Web at any time.

 URL—Stands for *Uniform Resource Locator*; similar to a filename or address. The Web uses it to locate the Web page.

Using the Web Toolbar

To display the Web toolbar in Excel, right-click any toolbar and choose Web from the shortcut menu. Excel docks the Web toolbar above the Formula bar.

Figure 24.2 shows the tools on the Web toolbar that are for browsing pages backward and forward, refreshing the current page, searching the Web, storing Web pages in the Favorites folder, and entering a URL.

Table 24.1 lists the Web tools on the Web toolbar and what they do.

FIGURE 24.2

The Web toolbar.

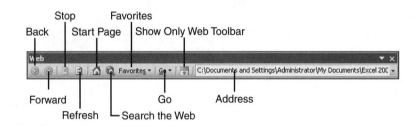

TABLE 24.1   Web Toolbar Tools

Tool	What It Does
Back	Displays the previous Web page
Forward	Displays the next Web page
Stop	Stops the browser from searching for a Web page
Refresh	Reloads the current Web page and updates it with the latest information
Start Page	Displays the home page for a Web site
Search the Web	Displays the Web site you requested in the Address box
Favorites	Stores your favorite Web site addresses
Go	Displays the Go menu that contains commands for navigating through Web pages
Show Only Web Toolbar	Hides all other Excel toolbars and displays only the Web toolbar
Address	Lets you enter a Web address

Opening a Web Page in Excel

When you find the Web page you want to read, you can open that page directly in Excel. To do so, make sure you are connected and online. With the Web toolbar displayed in Excel, type the URL into the Address box on the Web toolbar. When the browser finds the Web site you requested, the Web page displays in your Excel window.

Adding a Hyperlink to a Worksheet

In Hour 19, "Integrating Excel with Other Office Applications," you learned how to create a hyperlink that links to other Office documents. In this hour, you'll add a hyperlink to a worksheet that links to Web pages on the Internet.

When you point to a hyperlink, Excel displays the document path (for example, `http://www.samspublishing.com`) to which the link points. When you click a hyperlink, Excel moves to the location to which the link points. A hyperlink appears in blue (default color) text in the worksheet.

Hyperlinks are useful when you want to browse through files on the Internet. The Web toolbar displays a list of the last 10 documents you jumped to by using the Web toolbar or a hyperlink. This feature makes it easy for you to return to these documents.

The Insert, Hyperlink option lets you create a hyperlink so that you can move to a Web page from a worksheet. In the next To Do exercise, you create a hyperlink to move from an Excel worksheet to a Web document. Once again, you should be using the Sales 1st Qtr workbook.

24

To Do: Create a Hyperlink to a Web Document

▲ To Do

1. Click cell D16 on the Detail sheet. This cell will contain the hyperlink that brings you to the Web document.

2. Choose Insert, Hyperlink. Excel opens the Insert Hyperlink dialog box, as shown in Figure 24.3.

A quick way to create a hyperlink is to press Ctrl+K or click the Insert Hyperlink button on the Standard toolbar. Excel displays the Insert Hyperlink dialog box.

Browsed Page

FIGURE 24.3
The Insert Hyperlink dialog box.

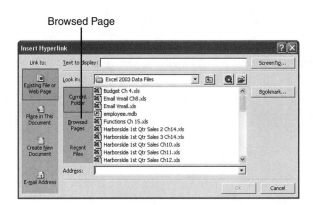

▼

▼   3. Click the Browsed Pages button on the Places bar to the left of the file list. A list of recently browsed Web pages appears.

> If you know the Web page's name, you can enter it in the Type the File or Web Page Name box. For example, `http://www.samspublishing.com`.

4. Click the URL to the page that you browsed to in the hyperlink list. Click OK. The Web page name is now a hyperlink and appears as underlined blue text in cell D16.

5. Point to the hyperlink. Notice how the mouse pointer becomes a hand. A ScreenTip containing the Web page address appears above the hyperlink (see Figure 24.4).

FIGURE 24.4

The hyperlink and ScreenTip with the Web page address.

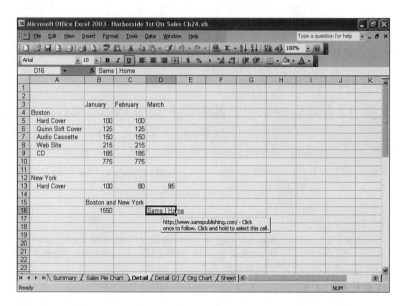

6. Click the hyperlink. Internet Explorer opens, and you see the Sams Publishing home page.

7. Click the Close (×) button in the upper-right corner of Internet Explorer. This step closes the Internet Explorer document and then returns you to the Excel worksheet. Notice the hyperlink text appears in purple, indicating that you have visited that site. Close the sales workbook.

▲

Saving Excel Documents to the Web

You can publish an Excel document to the World Wide Web so that other people on the Web can see your work. To place Web pages on the Web, you need to have an ISP that provides you with space for Web pages, or you need access to a Web service established at your company. You can ask the Webmaster (or whoever manages the Web servers) at your company where to place your Web pages.

You can use an existing Excel document for a Web page by saving it as a Web page. Excel closes the document and reopens it in Hypertext Markup Language (HTML) format. The alternative is to create your own Web page in Excel from scratch and then format it the way you want. No matter which method you use, you can publish many types of Excel documents on the Internet—for example, an annual report or a database.

You can even add audio and video to your Web page in Excel. That way, the reader of your Web page can play a sound file or view a video while visiting the Web site. You can use the Insert, Object command to insert sound and video clips into your Web page.

Understanding HTML Formatting

Every Web page is basically a plain text file with additional formatting instructions for the text, graphics, and links. This file is called the *HTML source* because the instructions are written in HTML format. The way a Web page looks on the Web is similar to the way it looks in Excel's Web Page Preview.

When you save a document in HTML format, Excel saves any graphics and other objects in separate files.

Saving as a Web Document

You can convert an Excel document into a Web page by selecting File, Save as Web Page. Excel saves your workbook with the file type MHT, the Web Archive format. For example, My Web Database.mht. The MHT file type saves text and images in a single file that you can send as an attachment in an email message.

In the following To Do exercise, you convert the My Database workbook into a Web page. Be sure to open the My Database workbook before you start the exercise.

To Do: Save as a Web Document

1. Choose File, Save as Web Page. The Save as Web Page dialog box pops up (see Figure 24.5). It looks the same as a Save As dialog box except for the HTML document choice in the Save as Type list.

2. Type **My Web Database** in the File Name text box.

▼ 3. Click the Save button. If you are advised that the Custom Views feature will not be saved in the HTML file, click Yes to continue saving. Excel converts the document to HTML format so it can be published on the Web. The document appears with

▲   the name My Web Database.mht in the title bar.

FIGURE 24.5

The Save As dialog box for saving an Excel document as a Web document.

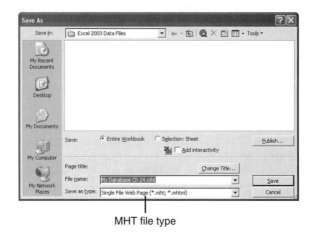

MHT file type

Previewing Your Document in Web Page Preview

The Web Page Preview in Excel enables you to see your document as it will look in a Web browser. A browser is a program with which you can read information on the Internet. This preview makes the data (text and numbers) easy to read because it wraps to fit the window. You cannot edit and format data in Web Page Preview.

Your Web page might look different in a browser such as Internet Explorer than it does in Excel, depending on how your browser interprets HTML codes.

To look at your document in Web Page Preview, choose File, Web Page Preview. Excel shows the document in the Web Page Preview window (see Figure 24.6). By default, Excel shows you the Web page the way it would look in the Microsoft Internet Explorer window even if you use a different browser.

You can use the scroll bar to see the rest of the document. To close Web Page Preview, click the Close (×) button in the upper-right corner of the Microsoft Internet Explorer window.

FIGURE 24.6

The Web Page Preview window.

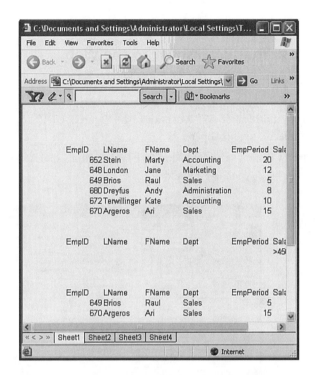

Posting Your Worksheet to the Web

After you convert an Excel document to a Web page, you can post your worksheet to the Web on the Internet by sending the page to a file transfer protocol (FTP) site on the Internet. FTP is a protocol that the Internet uses to send files between your computer and other computers on the Internet. Computers that offer files for download are called FTP sites. Using FTP is a fast and reliable way to download files from other Internet computers and to upload your own files.

FTP addresses begin with FTP://. For example, FTP://FTP.SAMSPUBLISHING.COM is the FTP site for Sams Publishing. If you don't know the correct FTP site name, ask the site's system administrator.

If you have a personal account at the FTP site, choose the User option in the Log On As area. Then enter your username and password. Otherwise, leave the default option, Anonymous, selected. Anonymous users are given access only to certain public area of a site. In most cases, you connect as an anonymous user if you want to download files. An anonymous user might not be able to upload files.

After you post the worksheet to the Web, you see the document as it would appear in a Web browser. Then you can get on the Internet while you're in Excel and view your own Web page. Other users will also be able to view your Web page.

This To Do exercise walks you through posting a Web page to an FTP site.

To Do: Post Your Worksheet to the Web

1. Choose File, Save As. The Save As dialog box opens.

2. Click the Save In drop-down arrow.

3. Choose Add/Modify FTP Locations (see Figure 24.7). The Add/Modify FTP Locations dialog box opens.

4. Figure 24.8 shows the Add/Modify FTP Locations dialog box. In the Name of FTP Site text box, type the FTP address.

FIGURE 24.7

Choosing Add/Modify FTP Locations in the Save As dialog box.

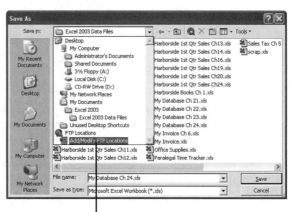

Add/Modify FTP Locations

FIGURE 24.8

Add/Modify FTP Locations dialog box.

5. Click the Add button to add the FTP site. The FTP site should appear in the FTP sites box at the bottom of the Add/Modify FTP Locations dialog box.

▼   6. Click OK. Notice the name of the new FTP site in the Save In box. Next, you want
       to send the Web page from Excel to the FTP site.

   7. Connect to the Internet using any ISP you have.

   8. Make sure the filename My Web Document.HTM is in the File Name text box. In
      Excel's Save As dialog box, choose the FTP location.

> You can also type the URL for the file in the File Name text box, as in
> `ftp://ftp.mcp.com/my web document.htm`.

   9. Click the Open button to upload the file to the FTP site. You are now connected to
      the top level of the FTP site.

  10. Move through the folders to find the one you want to use and then select the folder.

  11. Click the Save button. Your HTM document is saved in the selected folder.

24

> Any associated GIF, sound, or video files are not saved with the HTM docu-
> ment in the FTP site. You need to transfer them separately with an FTP pro-
> gram. Or better yet, you can use the Publish to the Web Wizard that comes
> with Microsoft Office 2000 to transfer all files types to a server.

▲

Summary

This hour presented a brief overview of the features built into Excel for creating and
working with Web pages. Now you have an idea of how to use Excel to create a Web
page. After you're comfortable with the tools and features you practiced in this hour,
you'll be able to experiment with Excel and learn the advanced concepts.

Q&A

Q When I try to open my Web page files, I can't find them. What do I do?

A Web page files that were converted to HTML format have the file extension HTM
or HTML. In the Open dialog box, choose Web Pages (*.htm;*html) in the Files of
Type box.

Q When I try to use my Web browser, I can't access the Internet. What next?

A You are probably experiencing either modem or network connection problems.
Check your modem connection. Log on to your Internet service provider again.
Consult your network administrator.

Q **I attempted to add an FTP site, and Excel displays an error message informing me that the FTP site doesn't exist. What should I do?**

A All FTP address begin with FTP://. Be sure that you typed the FTP address correctly. Otherwise, ask the FTP site's system administrator for the correct FTP site name.

Q **I logged on as an anonymous user to an FTP site. I can access only certain areas of the site, and I can't upload my Web pages from Excel. What is wrong?**

A Anonymous users are given access to only certain public areas of a site. You might find that you can download files from the FTP site, but you might not be able to upload files. Ask the FTP site's system administrator if you can have a user ID and a password that gives you access to more FTP site areas and lets you upload files.

Index

Symbols

+ (addition operator), 87, 316
* (asterisks), 403
#DIV/0! error, 101, 325
$ (dollar signs), 74
/ (division operator), 87
= (equal signs), 86
= (equal to operator), 87, 405
^ exponentiation operator, 87
> (greater than operator), 87, 405
>= (greater than or equal to operator), 87, 405
< (less than operator), 87, 405
<= (less than or equal to operator), 87, 405
* (multiplication operator), 87
#N/A error, 325
#NAME? error, 101, 325
< > not equal to operator, 405
#NULL! error, 325
#NUM! error, 325
% (percentage operator), 87
? (question marks), 403
#REF! error, 101, 325

signs, decimals, 175
- (subtraction operator), 87
#VALUE! error, 102, 325
3-D pie charts, 237
3-D Style tool, 196
3D charts, 231
3D references, 265-266

A

absolute cell references, 96-97
access (workbooks), 62
Accounting number format, 163
Add Scenario dialog box, 336
add-ins, 289
    Analysis ToolPak, 289
    Analysis ToolPak VBA, 289
    Conditional Sum Wizard, 289
    Euro Currency Tools, 289
    installation, checking, 289
    Internet Assistant VBA, 289
    Lookup Wizard, 289
    Solver, 289

How can we make this index more useful? Email us at indexes@samspublishing.com

Number format, 162

number of pay periods for investments function (NPER), 298-299

Number tab (Format Cells dialog box), 165

numbers, 138

date & time, 172-174

decimal places, 166-167, 175

formats, 162-163

Accounting, 163

conditional formatting, 169-170

currency, 162

custom, 167-169

customizing, 175

Euro, 166

Format Cells dialog box, 164-166

Formatting toolbar, 163-164

Fraction, 163

General, 162

Number, 162

Percentage, 163

Scientific, 163

shortcuts, 175

Text, 163

rounding, 167

zeros, 170-172

O

Object command (Insert menu), 367

Object dialog box, 367

Object Linking and Embedding. *See* OLE

objects

embedding, 364-366

graphics. *See* graphics objects

inserting, 367-369

linking, 362-364

Office documents

embedding, 364-366

linking, 363-364

OLE (Object Linking and Embedding), 362

hyperlinks, 369-371

objects

embedding, 364-366

inserting, 367-369

linking, 362-364

opening

shared workbooks, 432

templates, 104-105

Web pages, 444

workbooks, 65-66

options, 66-67

troubleshooting, 66, 83

operators

comparison, 405-406

mathematical, 86-90

precedence, 88

OR function, 310

order of operations, 88-90

Organization Chart Style Gallery dialog box, 244

Organization Chart toolbar, 243

Organization charts

creating, 242-243

editing, 243-244

formatting, 244-245

organization diagrams, 247

organization tools, 61-62

orientation

page, 133

worksheets, 118-119

Other Task Panes button (task pane), 19

outline borders, 190

Oval tool, 195

workbooks, 281-282

worksheets, 281

files, 285-288

scenarios, 339

Protection tab (Format Cells dialog box), 280

Protection toolbar, 270

Protection, Protect Sheet command (Tools menu), 281

Protection, Protect Workbook command (Tools menu), 282

Protection, Unprotect Sheet command (Tools menu), 281

Protection, Unprotect Workbook command (Tools menu), 282

pyramid diagrams, 247

Q

queries, 420, 423-424

Query Wizard

data filters, 421

data sorting, 422-423

data source selection, 420-421

databases, 420

queries, saving, 423-424

Query Wizard—Choose Columns dialog box, 421

Query Wizard—Filter Data dialog box, 422

question marks (?), 403

R

radial diagrams, 247

range names, 94

ranges, 71

borders, 180

adding, 181

deleting, 182, 185, 190

Draw Border tools, 184-185

Format Cells dialog box, 181-182

Formatting toolbar, 183

line style, 184

outline, 190

names, 71-74

printing, 131

RATE function, 304

read-only files, 287-288

Record Macro dialog box, 379

recording macros, 377-381

records, 397

adding, 402

data forms, 400-402

recovering deleted files, 62

Rectangle tool, 195

rectangles, 197

references (cells), 91-92, 262-263

absolute, 96-97

relative, 95

Refresh External Data tool, 355

rejecting changes, 433-435

relative cell references, 95

Remove All Arrows tool, 319

Remove Dependent Arrows tool, 319

Remove Precedent Arrows tool, 319

renaming workbooks, 56-57

Replace command (Edit menu), 155

replacing data, 155-156

reports

pivot tables, 356, 360

Scenario Summary, 340

T

Your Guide to Computer Technology

www.informit.com